James Foxall

D0573290

Sams **Teach Yourself**

Visual
Basic 2012

in **24**
Hours

SAMS 800 East 96th Street, Indianapolis, Indiana, 46240 USA

Sams Teach Yourself Visual Basic 2012 in 24 Hours, Complete Starter Kit: Barnes & Noble Special Edition

ISBN-13: 978-0-672-33685-0
ISBN-10: 0-672-33685-5

Library of Congress Cataloging-in-Publication Data is on file.

Printed in the United States of America

First Printing October 2012

Trademarks

All terms mentioned in this book that are known to be trademarks or service marks have been appropriately capitalized. Sams Publishing cannot attest to the accuracy of this information. Use of a term in this book should not be regarded as affecting the validity of any trademark or service mark.

Warning and Disclaimer

Every effort has been made to make this book as complete and as accurate as possible, but no warranty or fitness is implied. The information provided is on an "as is" basis. The author and the publisher shall have neither liability nor responsibility to any person or entity with respect to any loss or damages arising from the information contained in this book or from the use of the DVD or programs accompanying it.

Bulk Sales

Sams Publishing offers excellent discounts on this book when ordered in quantity for bulk purchases or special sales. For more information, please contact

U.S. Corporate and Government Sales
1-800-382-3419
corpsales@pearsontechgroup.com

For sales outside of the U.S., please contact

International Sales
international@pearsoned.com

Editor-in-Chief
Greg Wiegand

Executive Editor
Neil Rowe

Development Editor
Mark Renfrow

Managing Editor
Sandra Schroeder

Project Editor
Mandie Frank

Copy Editor
Margo Catts

Indexer
Cheryl Lenser

Proofreader
Sarah Kearns

Technical Editor
J. Boyd Nolan

Publishing Coordinator
Cindy Teeters

Multimedia Developer
Tim Warner

Designer
Gary Adair

Composition
TnT Design, Inc.

Contents at a Glance

Table of Contents

About the Author

James Foxall is president of Tigerpaw Software, Inc. (www.tigerpawsoftware.com), a Bellevue, Nebraska, Microsoft Certified Partner specializing in software solutions for technology providers. Tigerpaw's award-winning business automation solution is designed to automate contact management, marketing, service and repair, proposal generation, inventory control, and purchasing. At the start of 2012, the current release of Tigerpaw had more than 35,000 licensed users. Foxall's experience in creating certified Office-compatible software has made him an authority on application interface and behavior standards of applications for the Microsoft Windows and Microsoft Office environments.

Foxall has been writing commercial production Visual Basic code for more than 14 years. He's the author of numerous books, including *Practical Standards for Microsoft Visual Basic* and *MCSD in a Nutshell: The Visual Basic Exams*. He also has written articles for *Access-Office-VBA Advisor* and *Visual Basic Programmer's Journal*. Foxall has a bachelor's degree in management of information systems (MIS) and a master's degree in Business Administration (MBA). He is a Microsoft Certified Solution Developer and an international speaker on programming technologies as well as business process improvements. James enjoys spending time with his family, playing guitar, listening to amazing bands, and playing computer games. You can reach him at www.jamesfoxall.com.

Dedication

This book is dedicated to all of my great co-workers at Tigerpaw;
thank you for your dedication and your passion!

Acknowledgments

I would like to thank all the great people at Sams for their input and hard work; this book would not be possible without them!

We Want to Hear from You!

As the reader of this book, *you* are our most important critic and commentator. We value your opinion and want to know what we're doing right, what we could do better, what areas you'd like to see us publish in, and any other words of wisdom you're willing to pass our way.

You can email or write me directly to let me know what you did or didn't like about this book—as well as what we can do to make our books stronger.

Please note that I cannot help you with technical problems related to the topic of this book, and that due to the high volume of mail I receive, I might not be able to reply to every message.

When you write, please be sure to include this book's title and author as well as your name and phone or email address. I will carefully review your comments and share them with the author and editors who worked on the book.

Email: consumer@samspublishing.com

Mail: Neil Rowe
            Executive Editor
            Sams Publishing
            800 East 96th Street
            Indianapolis, IN 46240 USA

Reader Services

Visit our website and register this book at www.samspublishing.com/register for convenient access to any updates, downloads, or errata that might be available for this book.

Introduction

Visual Basic 2012 is Microsoft's latest incarnation of the enormously popular Visual Basic language, and it's fundamentally different from the versions that came before it. Visual Basic is more powerful and more capable than ever before, and its features and functionality are on par with "higher-level" languages such as C++. One consequence of this newfound power is added complexity. Gone are the days when you could sit down with Visual Basic and the online Help and teach yourself what you needed to know to create a functional program.

Audience and Organization

This book is targeted toward those who have little or no programming experience or who might be picking up Visual Basic as a second language. The book has been structured and written with a purpose: to get you productive as quickly as possible. I've used my experiences in writing large commercial applications with Visual Basic and teaching Visual Basic to create a book that I hope cuts through the fluff and teaches you what you need to know. All too often, authors fall into the trap of focusing on the technology rather than on the practical application of the technology. I've worked hard to keep this book focused on teaching you practical skills that you can apply immediately to a development project. Feel free to post your suggestions or success stories at www.jamesfoxall.com/forums.

This book is divided into five parts, each of which focuses on a different aspect of developing applications with Visual Basic. These parts generally follow the flow of tasks you'll perform as you begin creating your own programs with Visual Basic. I recommend that you read them in the order in which they appear:

▶ Part I, "The Visual Basic 2012 Environment," teaches you about the Visual Basic environment, including how to navigate and access Visual Basic's numerous tools. In addition, you'll learn about some key development concepts such as objects, collections, and events.

▶ Part II, "Building a User Interface," shows you how to build attractive and functional user interfaces. In this part, you'll learn about forms and controls—the user interface elements such as text boxes and list boxes.

▶ Part III, "Making Things Happen—Programming," teaches you the nuts and bolts of Visual Basic 2012 programming—and there's a lot to learn. You'll discover how to create modules and procedures, as well as how to store data, perform loops, and make decisions in code. After you've learned the core programming skills, you'll move into object-oriented programming and debugging applications.

▶ Part IV, "Working with Data," introduces you to working with graphics, text files, and programming databases and shows you how to automate external applications such as Word and Excel. In addition, this part teaches you how to manipulate a user's file system and the Windows Registry.

▶ Part V, "Deploying Solutions and Beyond," shows you how to distribute an application that you've created to an end user's computer. In Hour 24, "The 10,000-Foot View," you'll learn about Microsoft's .NET initiative from a higher, less-technical level.

Many readers of previous editions have taken the time to give me input on how to make this book better. Overwhelmingly, I was asked to have examples that build on the examples in the previous chapters. In this book, I have done that as much as possible. Instead of learning concepts in isolated bits, you'll be building a feature-rich Picture Viewer program throughout the course of this book. You'll begin by building the basic application. As you progress through the chapters, you'll add menus and toolbars to the program, build an Options dialog box, modify the program to use the Windows Registry and a text file, and even build a setup program to distribute the application to other users. I hope you find this approach beneficial in that it enables you to learn the material in the context of building a real program.

Conventions Used in This Book

This book uses several design elements and conventions to help you prioritize and reference the information it contains:

By the Way

By the Way boxes provide useful sidebar information that you can read immediately or circle back to without losing the flow of the topic at hand.

Did you Know?

Did You Know? boxes highlight information that can make your Visual Basic programming more effective.

Watch Out!

Watch Out! boxes focus your attention on problems or side effects that can occur in specific situations.

New terms appear in an *italic* typeface for emphasis.

In addition, this book uses various typefaces to help you distinguish code from regular English. Code is presented in a `monospace` font. Placeholders—words or characters that represent the real words or characters you would type in code—appear in *`italic monospace`*. When you are asked to type or enter text, that text appears in **bold**.

Menu options are separated by a comma. For example, when you should open the File menu and choose the New Project menu option, the text says "Select File, New Project."

Some code statements presented in this book are too long to appear on a single line. In these cases, a line-continuation character (an underscore) is used to indicate that the following line is a continuation of the current statement.

Onward and Upward!

This is an exciting time to be learning how to program. It's my sincerest wish that when you finish this book, you feel capable of using many of Visual Basic's tools to create, debug, and deploy modest Visual Basic programs. Although you won't be an expert, you'll be surprised at how much you've learned. And I hope this book will help you determine your future direction as you proceed down the road to Visual Basic mastery.

I love programming with Visual Basic, and sometimes I find it hard to believe I get paid to do so. I hope you find Visual Basic as enjoyable as I do!

Jumping in with Both Feet: A Visual Basic 2012 Programming Tour

What You'll Learn in This Hour:

▶ Building a simple (yet functional) Visual Basic application

▶ Letting a user browse a hard drive

▶ Displaying a picture from a file on disk

▶ Getting familiar with some programming lingo

▶ Learning about the Visual Studio 2012 IDE

Learning a new programming language can be intimidating. If you've never programmed before, the act of typing seemingly cryptic text to produce sleek and powerful applications probably seems like a black art, and you might wonder how you'll ever learn everything you need to know. The answer, of course, is one step at a time. I believe the first step to mastering a programming language is *building confidence*. Programming is part art and part science. Although it might seem like magic, it's more akin to illusion. After you know how things work, a lot of the mysticism goes away, and you are free to focus on the mechanics necessary to produce the desired result.

Producing large, commercial solutions is accomplished by way of a series of small steps. After you've finished this hour, you'll have a feel for the overall development process and will have taken the first step toward becoming an accomplished programmer. In fact, you will build on the examples in this hour in subsequent hours. By the time you complete this book, you will have built a robust application, complete with resizable screens, an intuitive interface including menus and toolbars, manipulation of the Windows Registry, and robust code with professional error handling. But I'm getting ahead of myself.

In this hour, you'll complete a quick tour of Visual Basic that takes you step by step through creating a complete, albeit small, Visual Basic program. Most introductory programming books start by having the reader create a simple Hello World program. I've yet to see a Hello World program that's the least bit helpful. (They usually do nothing more than print hello world to the screen—what fun!) So, instead, you'll create a Picture Viewer application that lets you view Windows bitmaps and icons on your computer. You'll learn how to let a user browse for a file and how to display a selected picture file on the screen. The techniques you learn in this hour will come in handy in many real-world applications that you'll create, but the goal of this hour is for you to realize just how much fun it is to program using Visual Basic 2012.

Starting Visual Basic 2012

Before you begin creating programs in Visual Basic 2012, you should be familiar with the following terms:

▶ **Distributable component:** The final, compiled version of a project. Components can be distributed to other people and other computers, and they don't require the Visual Basic 2012 development environment (the tools you use to create a .NET program) to run (although they do require the .NET runtime, which I'll discuss in Hour 23, "Deploying Applications"). Distributable components are often called *programs*. In Hour 23, you'll learn how to distribute the Picture Viewer program that you're about to build to other computers.

▶ **Project:** A collection of files that can be compiled to create a distributable component (program). There are many types of projects, and complex applications might consist of multiple projects, such as Windows application projects, and support dynamic link library (DLL) projects.

▶ **Solution:** A collection of projects and files that make up an application or component.

By the Way

In the past, Visual Basic was an autonomous language. This has changed. Now, Visual Basic is part of a larger entity known as the *.NET Framework*. The .NET Framework encompasses all the .NET technology, including Visual Studio .NET (the suite of development tools) and the common language runtime (CLR), which is the set of files that make up the core of all .NET applications. You'll learn about these items in more detail as you progress through this book. For now, realize that Visual Basic is one of many languages that exist within the Visual Studio family. Many other languages, such as C#, are also .NET languages, make use of the CLR, and are developed within Visual Studio.

Visual Studio 2012 is a complete development environment, and it's called the *IDE* (short for *integrated development environment*). The IDE is the design framework in which you build applications; every tool you'll need to create your Visual Basic projects is accessed from within the Visual Basic IDE. Again, Visual Studio 2012 supports development using many different languages, Visual Basic being the most popular. The environment itself is not Visual Basic, but the language you'll be using within Visual Studio 2012 *is* Visual Basic. To work with Visual Basic projects, you first start the Visual Studio 2012 IDE.

Start Visual Studio 2012 now by choosing Microsoft Visual Basic 2012 Express Edition from the Start/Programs menu. If you are running the full retail version of Visual Studio, your shortcut may have a different name. In this case, locate the shortcut on the Start menu and click it once to start the Visual Studio 2012 IDE.

Creating a New Project

When you first start Visual Studio 2012, you see the Start Page tab within the IDE, as shown in Figure 1.1. You can open projects created previously or create new projects from this Start page. For this quick tour, you'll create a new Windows application, so select File, New Project to display the New Project dialog box shown in Figure 1.2.

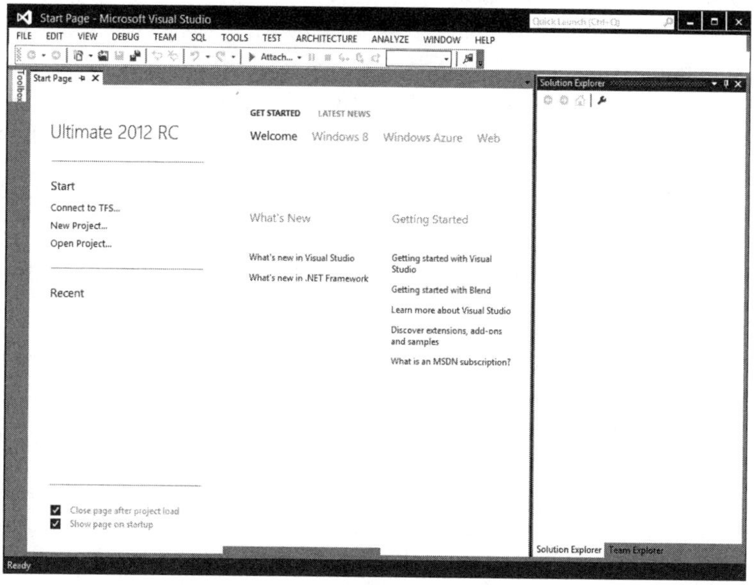

FIGURE 1.1
You can open existing projects or create new projects from the Visual Studio Start page.

By the Way

Your Start page might look a little different than the one shown in Figure 1.1—depending on what version of Visual Studio you are using.

The New Project dialog box is used to specify the type of Visual Basic project to create. (You can create many types of projects with Visual Basic, as well as with the other supported languages of the .NET Framework.) The options shown in Figure 1.2 are limited because I am running the Express edition of Visual Basic for all examples in this book. If you are running the full version of Visual Studio, you will have many more options available.

Create a new Windows Forms Application now by following these steps:

1. Make sure that the Windows Forms Application item is selected. (If it's not, click it once to select it.)

2. At the bottom of the New Project dialog box is a Name text box. This is where, oddly enough, you specify the name of the project you're creating. Enter **Picture Viewer** in the Name text box.

3. Click OK to create the project.

Did you Know?

Always set the Name text box to something meaningful before creating a project, or you'll have more work to do later if you want to move or rename the project.

When Visual Basic creates a new Windows Forms Application project, it adds one form (the empty gray window) for you to begin building the *interface* for your application, as shown in Figure 1.3.

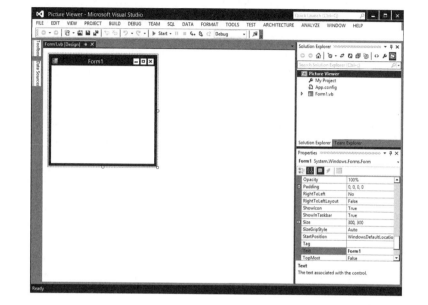

FIGURE 1.3
New Windows
Forms Applica-
tions start with a
blank form; the
fun is just begin-
ning!

Within Visual Studio 2012, *form* is the term given to the design-time view of a window that can be displayed to a user.

By the Way

Your Visual Studio 2012 environment might look different from that shown in the figures in this hour, depending on the edition of Visual Studio 2012 you're using, whether you've already played with Visual Studio 2012, and other factors, such as your monitor's resolution. All the elements discussed in this hour exist in all editions of Visual Studio 2012, however. (If a window shown in a figure doesn't appear in your IDE, use the View menu to display it.)

To create a program that can be run on another computer, you start by creating a project and then compiling the project into a component such as an *executable* (a program a user can run) or a *DLL* (a component that can be used by other programs and components). The compilation process is discussed in detail in Hour 24. The important thing to note at this time is that when you hear someone refer to *creating or writing a program*, just as you're creating the Picture Viewer program now, that person is referring to the completion of all steps up to and including compiling the project to a distributable file.

By the Way

Understanding the Visual Studio 2012 Environment

The first time you run Visual Studio 2012, you'll notice that the IDE contains a number of windows, such as the Properties window on the lower-right, which is used to view and set properties of objects. In addition to these windows, the IDE contains a number of tabs, such as the vertical Toolbox tab on the left edge of the IDE (refer to Figure 1.3). Try this now: Click the Toolbox tab to display the Toolbox window (clicking a tab displays an associated window). You can hover the mouse over a tab for a few seconds to display the window as well. To hide the window, simply move the mouse off the window (if you hovered over the tab to display it) or click another window. To close the window, click the Close (X) button in the window's title bar.

By the Way

> If you opened the toolbox by clicking its tab rather than hovering over the tab, the toolbox does not close automatically. Instead, it stays open until you click another window.

You can adjust the size and position of any of these windows, and you can even hide and show them as needed. You'll learn how to customize your design environment in Hour 2.

Watch Out!

> Unless specifically instructed to do so, don't double-click anything in the Visual Studio 2012 design environment. Double-clicking most objects produces an entirely different result than single-clicking does. If you mistakenly double-click an object on a form (discussed shortly), a code window appears. At the top of the code window is a set of tabs: one for the form design and one for the code. Click the tab for the form design to hide the code window and return to the form.

The Properties window on the right side of the design environment is perhaps the most important window in the IDE, and it's the one you'll use most often. If your computer display resolution is set to 800×600, you can probably see only a few properties at this time. This makes it difficult to view and set properties as you create projects. All the screen shots in this book were captured on Windows 8 running at 1024×768 because of publishing constraints, but you should run at a higher resolution if you can. I highly recommend that you develop applications with Visual Basic at a screen resolution of 1280×768 or higher to have plenty of work space. To change your display settings, right-click the desktop and select Screen Resolution. Keep in mind, however, that end users might be running at a lower resolution than you are using for development.

Changing the Characteristics of Objects

Almost everything you work with in Visual Basic is an object. Forms, for instance, are objects, as are all the items you can put on a form to build an interface, such as list boxes and buttons. There are many types of objects, and objects are classified by type. For example, a form is a `Form` object, whereas items you can place on a form are called `Control` objects, or controls. (Hour 3, "Understanding Objects and Collections," discusses objects in detail.) Some objects don't have a physical appearance but exist only in code. You'll learn about these kinds of objects in later hours.

You'll find that I often mention material coming up in future hours. In the publishing field, we call these *forward references*. For some reason, these tend to unnerve some people. I do this only so that you realize you don't have to fully grasp a subject when it's first presented; the material will be covered in more detail later. I try to keep forward references to a minimum, but unfortunately, teaching programming is not a perfectly linear process. There will be times I'll have to touch on a subject that I feel you're not ready to dive into fully yet. When this happens, I give you a forward reference to let you know that the subject will be covered in greater detail later.

Watch Out!

Every object has a distinct set of attributes known as *properties* (regardless of whether the object has a physical appearance). Properties define an object's characteristics. You have certain properties as a person, such as your height and hair color. Visual Basic objects have properties as well, such as `Height` and `BackColor`. When you create a new object, the first thing you need to do is set its properties so that the object appears and behaves the way you want it to. To display an object's properties, click the object in its designer (the main work area in the IDE).

Click anywhere in the default form now (it's the window with the title Form1), and check to see that its properties are displayed in the Properties window. You'll know because the drop-down list box at the top of the Properties window contains the form's name: `Form1 System.Windows.Forms.Form`. Form1 is the object's name, and `System.Windows.Forms.Form` is the object's type.

Naming Objects

The property you should always set first when creating any new object is the `Name` property. Press F4 to display the Properties window (if it's not already visible), and scroll toward the top of the properties list until you see the (`Name`) property, as shown in Figure 1.4. If the `Name` property isn't one of the first properties listed, the Properties window is set to show properties categorically instead of alphabetically. You can show the list alphabetically by clicking the Alphabetical button that appears just above the properties grid.

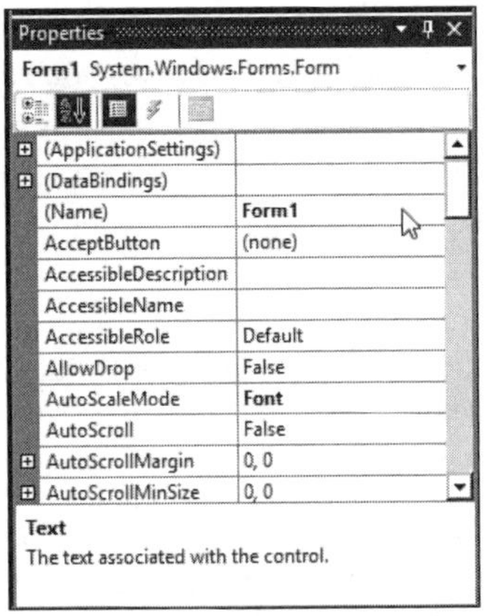

FIGURE 1.4
The Name property is the first property you should change when you add a new object to your project.

> I recommend that you keep the Properties window set to show properties in alphabetical order; doing so makes it easier to find properties that I refer to in the text. Note that the Name property always stays toward the top of the list and is called (Name). If you're wondering why it has parentheses around it, it's because symbols come before letters in an alphabetical sort, and this keeps the Name property at the top of the list.

When saving a project, you also choose a name and a location for the project and its files. When you first create an object within the project, Visual Basic gives the object a unique, generic name based on the object's type. Although these names are functional, they simply aren't descriptive enough for practical use. For instance, Visual Basic named your form Form1, but it's common to have dozens (or even hundreds) of forms in a project. It would be extremely difficult to manage such a project if all forms were distinguishable only by a number (Form2, Form3, and so forth).

> What you're actually working with is a *form class*, or *template*, that will be used to create and show forms at runtime. For the purposes of this quick tour, I simply call it a form. See Hour 5, "Building Forms: The Basics," for more information.

To better manage your forms, give each one a descriptive name. Visual Basic gives you the chance to name new forms as they're created in a project. Visual Basic created this default form for you, so you didn't get a chance to name it. It's important not only to change the form's name but also to change its filename. Change the programmable name and the filename by following these steps:

1. Click the Name property and change the text from Form1 to ViewerForm. Notice that this does not change the form's filename as it's displayed in the Solution Explorer window, located above the Properties window.

2. Right-click Form1.vb in the Solution Explorer window (the window above the Properties window).

3. Choose Rename from the context menu that appears.

4. Change the text from Form1.vb to ViewerForm.vb.

The form's Name property is actually changed for you automatically when you rename the file. In future examples, I will have you rename the form file so that the Name property is changed automatically. I had you set it in the Properties window here so that you could see how the Properties window works.

Setting the Form's Text Property

Notice that the text that appears in the form's title bar says Form1. Visual Basic sets the form's title bar to the name of the form *when it's first created*, but doesn't change it when you change the name of the form. The text in the title bar is determined by the value of the form's Text property. Change the text now by following these steps:

1. Click the form once more so that its properties appear in the Properties window.

2. Use the scrollbar in the Properties window to locate the Text property.

3. Change the text to Picture Viewer. Press the Enter key or Tab key, or click a different property to commit your edit. You'll see the text in the form's title bar change.

Saving a Project

The changes you've made so far exist only in memory. If you were to turn off your computer at this time, you would lose all your work up to this point. Get into the habit of frequently saving your work, which commits your changes to disk.

Click the Save All button on the toolbar (the picture of two floppy disks) now to save your work. Visual Basic displays the Save Project dialog box, shown in Figure 1.5.

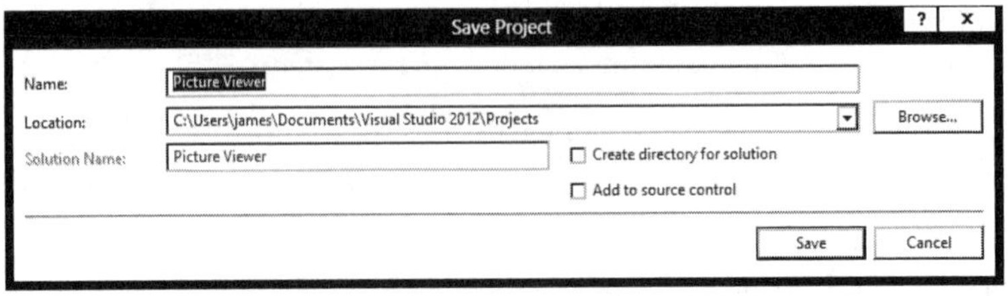

FIGURE 1.5
When saving a
project, choose
a name and
location for the
project and its
files.

Notice that the Name property is already filled in because you named the project when you created it. The Location text box is where you specify the location in which the project is to be saved. Visual Basic creates a subfolder in this location, using the value in the Name text box (in this case, Picture Viewer). You can use the default location or change it to suit your purposes. You can have Visual Basic create a solution folder, and if you do Visual Basic creates the solution file in the folder, and it creates a sub-folder for the project and the actual files. On large projects, this is a handy feature. For now, it's an unnecessary step, so uncheck the Create Directory for Solution box if it's checked, and then click Save to save the project.

Giving the Form an Icon

Everyone who's used Windows is familiar with icons—the little pictures that represent programs. Icons most commonly appear on the Start menu next to the name of their respective programs. In Visual Basic, you not only have control over the icon of your program file, you can also give every form in your program a unique icon if you want to.

By the Way

> The following instructions assume that you have access to the source files for the examples in this book. They are available at http://www.samspublishing.com. You can also get these files in the Downloads section of my website at http://www.jamesfoxall.com. When you unzip the samples, a folder is created for each hour, and within each hour's folder are subfolders for the sample projects. You'll find the icon for this example in the folder Hour 01\Samples.
>
> You don't have to use the icon I've provided for this example; you can use any icon. If you don't have an icon available (or you want to be a rebel), you can skip this section without affecting the outcome of the example.

To give the form an icon, follow these steps:

1. In the Properties window, click the Icon property to select it.

2. When you click the Icon property, a small button with three dots appears to the right of the property. Click this button.

3. Use the Open dialog box that appears to locate the Picture Viewer.ico file or another icon file of your choice. When you've found the icon, double-click it, or click it once to select it and then choose Open.

After you've selected the icon, it appears in the Icon property along with the word Icon. A small version of the icon appears in the upper-left corner of the form as well. Whenever this form is minimized, this is the icon displayed on the Windows taskbar.

Changing the Form's Size

Next, you'll change the form's Width and Height properties. The Width and Height values are shown collectively under the Size property; Width appears to the left of the comma, and Height to the right. You can change the Width or Height property by changing the corresponding number in the Size property. Both values are represented in pixels. (That is, a form that has a Size property of 200, 350 is 200 pixels wide and 350 pixels tall.) To display and adjust the Width and Height properties separately, click the small plus sign next to the Size property. (After you click it, it changes to a minus sign, as shown in Figure 1.6.)

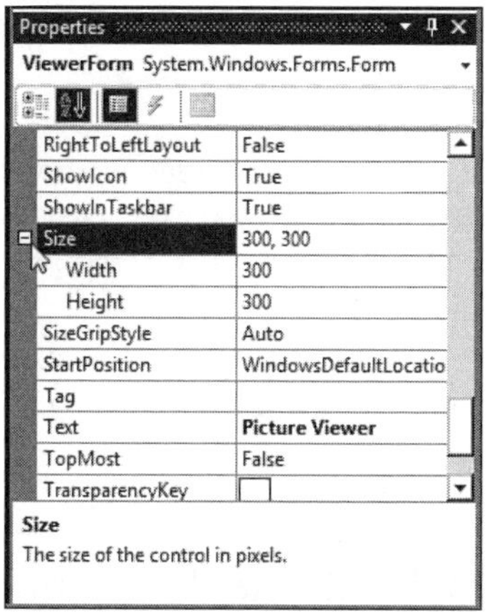

FIGURE 1.6
Some properties can be expanded to show more specific properties.

> A pixel is a unit of measurement for computer displays; it's the smallest visible "dot" on the screen. The resolution of a display is always given in pixels, such as 800×600 or 1024×768. When you increase or decrease a property by one pixel, you're making the smallest possible visible change to the property.

By the Way

Change the Width property to 400 and the Height to 325 by typing in the corresponding box next to a property name. To commit a property change, press Tab or Enter, or click a different property or window. Your screen should now look like the one shown in Figure 1.7.

FIGURE 1.7
Changes made
in the Properties
window are
reflected as
soon as they're
committed.

 You can also resize a form by dragging its border, which you'll learn about in Hour 2, or by using code to change its properties, which you'll learn how to do in Hour 5.

Save the project now by choosing File, Save All from the menu or by clicking the Save All button on the toolbar—it has a picture of two floppy disks.

Adding Controls to a Form

Now that you've set the initial properties of your form, it's time to create a user interface by adding objects to the form. Objects that can be placed on a form are called *controls*. Some controls have a visible interface with which a user can interact, whereas others are always invisible to the user. You'll use controls of both types in this example. On the left side of the screen is a vertical tab titled Toolbox. Click the Toolbox tab to display the Toolbox window to see the most commonly used controls, expanding the Common Controls section if necessary (see Figure 1.8). The toolbox contains all the controls available in the project, such as labels and text boxes.

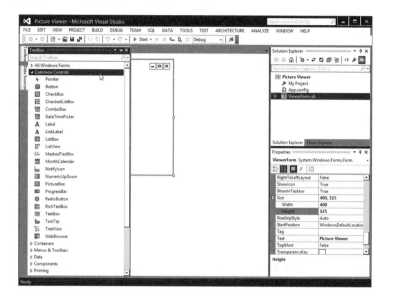

FIGURE 1.8
The toolbox is used to select controls to build a user interface.

The toolbox used to close after you added a control to a form and then moved the pointer away from the toolbox. This behavior has changed, and now you have to click off the toolbox to make it disappear. To make the toolbox stay visible, even when you click something else, click the little picture of a pushpin located in the toolbox's title bar.

I don't want you to add them yet (I'll walk you through the process), but your Picture Viewer interface will consist of the following controls:

- **Two Button controls:** The standard buttons that you're used to clicking in pretty much every Windows program you've ever run.

- **A PictureBox control:** A control used to display images.

- **An OpenFileDialog control:** A hidden control that exposes the Windows Open File dialog box functionality.

Designing an Interface

It's generally best to design a form's user interface and then add the code behind the interface to make the form functional. You'll build your interface in the following sections.

Adding a Visible Control to a Form

Start by adding a Button control to the form. Do this by double-clicking the Button item in the toolbox. Visual Basic creates a new button and places it in the upper-left corner of the form, as shown in Figure 1.9. Click off the toolbox to make it go away so that you can see the new button control.

FIGURE 1.9
When you double-
click a control in
the toolbox, the
control is added
to the upper-left
corner of the
form.

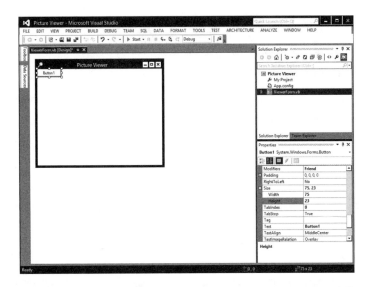

Using the Properties window, set the button's properties as shown in the following list.
Remember, when you view the properties alphabetically, the Name property is listed
first, so don't go looking for it down in the list or you'll be looking a while.

Property	Value
Name	btnSelectPicture
Location	295,10 (295 is the x coordinate; 10 is the y coordinate.)
Size	85,23
Text	Select Picture

By the Way

If you see the word "Select" on your button, chances are you've set your Windows
fonts to a size larger than standard. Right-click the desktop and choose Personalize from the shortcut menu that appears. Next, click Display in the lower-right corner and change the font size on the Display dialog box that appears.

Now you'll create a button that the user can click to close the Picture Viewer program.
Although you could add another new button to the form by double-clicking the
Button control on the toolbox again, this time you'll add a button to the form by
creating a copy of the button you've already defined. This enables you to easily create
a button that maintains the size and other style attributes of the original button
when the copy was made.

To do this, right-click the Select Picture button, and choose Copy from its context
menu. Next, right-click anywhere on the form, and choose Paste from the form's

shortcut menu. (You can also use the keyboard shortcuts Ctrl+C to copy and Ctrl+V to paste.) The new button appears centered on the form, and it's selected by default. Notice that it retains almost all the properties of the original button, but the name has been reset. Change the properties of the new button as follows:

Property	Value
Name	btnQuit
Location	295,40
Text	Quit

The last visible control you need to add to the form is a PictureBox control. A PictureBox has many capabilities, but its primary purpose is to show pictures, which is precisely what you'll use it for in this example. Add a new PictureBox control to the form by double-clicking the PictureBox item in the toolbox, and set its properties as follows:

Property	Value
Name	picShowPicture
BorderStyle	FixedSingle
Location	8,8
Size	282,275

After you've made these property changes, your form will look like the one shown in Figure 1.10. Click the Save All button on the toolbar to save your work.

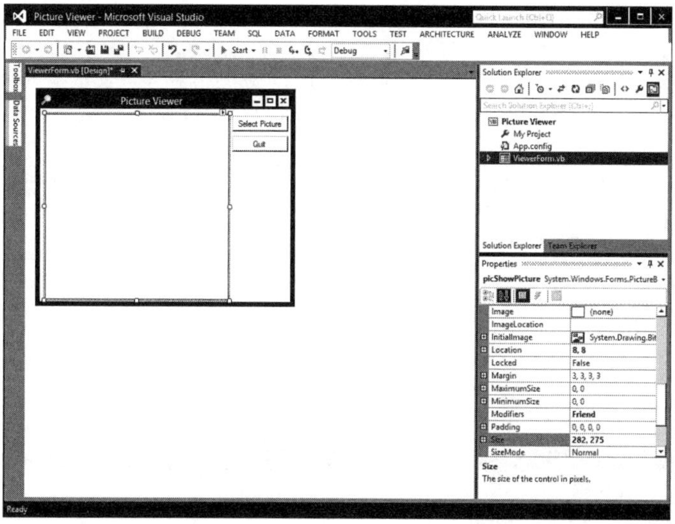

FIGURE 1.10
An application's interface doesn't have to be complex to be useful.

Adding an Invisible Control to a Form

All the controls you've used so far sit on a form and have a physical appearance when a user runs the application. Not all controls have a physical appearance, however. Such controls, called *nonvisual controls* (or *invisible-at-runtime controls*), aren't designed for direct user interactivity. Instead, they're designed to give you, the programmer, functionality beyond the standard features of Visual Basic.

To enable users to select a picture to display, for example, you need to give them the ability to locate a file on their hard drives. You might have noticed that whenever you choose to open a file from within any Windows application, the dialog box displayed is almost always the same. It doesn't make sense to force every developer to write the code necessary to perform standard file operations, so Microsoft has exposed the functionality via a control that you can use in your projects. This control is called OpenFileDialog, and it will save you dozens of hours that would otherwise be necessary to duplicate this common functionality.

By the Way

> Other controls in addition to the OpenFileDialog control give you file functionality. For example, the SaveFileDialog control provides features for allowing the user to specify a filename and path for saving a file.

Display the toolbox and scroll down until you can see the Dialogs category. Expand the Dialogs category and then double-click the OpenFileDialog to add it to your form. Note that the control isn't placed on the form; rather, it appears in a special area below the form (see Figure 1.11).

FIGURE 1.11
Controls that have no interface appear below the form designer.

vopenfiledialog1

This happens because the OpenFileDialog control has no form interface to display to the user. It does have an interface (a dialog box) that you can display as necessary, but it has nothing to display directly on a form.

Select the OpenFileDialog control and change its properties as follows:

Property	Value
Name	ofdSelectPicture
Filename	<make empty>
Filter	Windows Bitmaps|*.bmp|JPEG Files|*.jpg|PNG Files|*.png
Title	Select Picture

Don't actually enter the text <make empty> for the filename; I really mean delete the default value and make this property value empty.

By the Way

The Filter property is used to limit the types of files that will be displayed in the Open File dialog box. The format for a filter is description|filter. The text that appears before the first pipe symbol is the descriptive text of the file type, whereas the text after the pipe symbol is the pattern to use to filter files. You can specify more than one filter type by separating each description|filter value with another pipe symbol. Text entered into the Title property appears in the title bar of the Open File dialog box.

The graphical interface for your Picture Viewer program is now finished. If you pinned the toolbox open, click the pushpin in the title bar of the toolbox now to close it. Click Save All on the toolbar now to save your work.

Writing the Code Behind an Interface

You have to write code for the program to be capable of performing tasks and responding to user interaction. Visual Basic is an *event-driven* language, which means that code is executed in response to events. These events might come from users, such as a user clicking a button and triggering its Click event, or from Windows itself (see Hour 4, "Understanding Events," for a complete explanation of events). Currently, your application looks nice, but it won't do anything. Users can click the Select Picture button until they can file for disability with carpel tunnel syndrome, but nothing will happen, because you haven't told the program what to do when the user clicks the button. You can see this for yourself now by pressing F5 to run the project. Feel free to click the buttons, but they don't do anything. When you're finished, close the window you created to return to Design mode.

You'll write code to accomplish two tasks. First, you'll write code that lets users browse their hard drives to locate and select a picture file and then display it in the picture box (this sounds a lot harder than it is). Second, you'll add code to the Quit button that shuts down the program when the user clicks the button.

Letting a User Browse for a File

The first bit of code you'll write enables users to browse their hard drives, select a picture file, and then see the selected picture in the `PictureBox` control. This code executes when the user clicks the Select Picture button; therefore, it's added to the `Click` event of that button.

When you double-click a control on a form in Design view, the default event for that control is displayed in a code window. The default event for a `Button` control is its `Click` event, which makes sense, because clicking is the most common action a user performs with a button. Double-click the Select Picture button now to access its `Click` event in the code window (see Figure 1.12).

FIGURE 1.12
You'll write all your code in a window such as this.

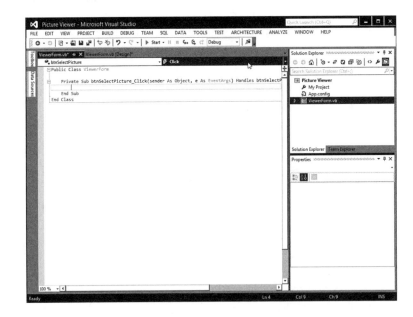

When you access an event, Visual Basic builds an *event handler*, which is essentially a template procedure in which you add the code that executes when the event occurs.

The cursor is already placed within the code procedure, so all you have to do is add code. Although this may seem daunting, by the time you're finished with this book, you'll be madly clicking and clacking away as you write your own code to make your applications do exactly what you want them to do—well, most of the time. For now, just enter the code as I present it here.

It's important that you get in the habit of commenting your code, so the first statement you'll enter is a comment. Beginning a statement with an apostrophe (') designates that statement as a comment. The compiler won't do anything with the statement, so you can enter whatever text you want after the apostrophe. Type the following statement exactly as it appears, and press the Enter key at the end of the line:

```
' Show the open file dialog box.
```

The next statement you'll enter triggers a method of the OpenFileDialog control that you added to the form. Think of a method as a mechanism to make a control do something. The ShowDialog() method tells the control to show its Open dialog box and let the user select a file. The ShowDialog() method returns a value that indicates its success or failure, which you'll then compare to a predefined result (DialogResult.OK). Don't worry too much about what's happening here; you'll be learning the details of all this in later hours. The sole purpose of this hour is to get your feet wet. In a nutshell, the ShowDialog() method is invoked to let a user browse for a file. If the user selects a file, more code is executed. Of course, there's a lot more to using the OpenFileDialog control than I present in this basic example, but this simple statement gets the job done. Enter the following statement and press Enter to commit the code (don't worry about capitalization; Visual Basic will fix the case for you):

```
If ofdSelectpicture.ShowDialog = DialogResult.OK Then
```

By the Way

After you insert the statement that begins with If and press Enter, Visual Basic automatically creates the End If statement for you. If you type in End If, you'll wind up with two End If statements, and your code won't run. If this happens, delete one of the statements. Hour 13, "Making Decisions in Visual Basic Code," has all the details on the If statement.

It's time for another comment. The cursor is currently between the statement that starts with If and the End If statement. Leave the cursor there and type the following statement, remembering to press Enter at the end of the line:

```
' Load the picture into the picture box.
```

Did you Know?

Don't worry about indenting the code by pressing the Tab key or using spaces. Visual Basic automatically indents code for you.

This next statement, which appears within the `If` construct (between the `If` and `End If` statements), is the line of code that actually displays the picture in the picture box.

Enter the following statement and press Enter:

```
picShowPicture.Image = Image.FromFile(ofdSelectPicture.Filename)
```

In addition to displaying the selected picture, your program will also display the path and filename of the picture in the title bar. When you first created the form, you changed its `Text` property in the Properties window. To create dynamic applications, properties need to be constantly adjusted at runtime, and you do this using code. Insert the following two statements, pressing Enter at the end of each line:

```
' Show the name of the file in the form's caption.
Me.Text = "Picture Viewer(" & ofdselectpicture.FileName & ")"
```

After you've entered all the code, your editor should look like that shown in Figure 1.13.

FIGURE 1.13
Make sure that your code exactly matches the code shown here.

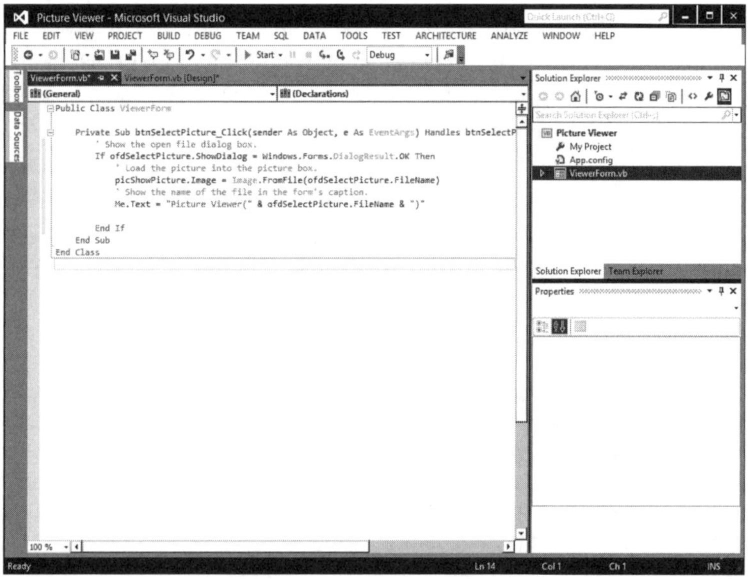

Terminating a Program Using Code

The last bit of code you'll write terminates the application when the user clicks the Quit button. To do this, you need to access the `Click` event handler of the `btnQuit` button. At the top of the code window are two tabs. The current tab says ViewerForm.vb*. This tab contains the code window for the form that has the filename ViewerForm.vb. Next to this is a tab that says ViewerForm.vb [Design]*. Click this tab to switch from Code view to the form designer. If you receive an error when you click the tab, the code you entered contains an error, and you need to edit it to make it the same, as shown in Figure 1.13. After the form designer appears, double-click the Quit button to access its `Click` event.

Enter the following code in the Quit button's `Click` event handler; press Enter at the end of each statement:

```
' Close the window and exit the application
Me.Close()
```

The `Me.Close()` statement closes the current form. When the last loaded form in a program is closed, the application shuts itself down—completely. As you build more robust applications, you'll probably want to execute all kinds of cleanup routines before terminating an application, but for this example, closing the form is all you need to do.

Running a Project

Your application is now complete. Click the Save All button on the toolbar (the button with two floppy disks), and then run your program by pressing F5. You can also run the program by clicking the button on the toolbar that looks like a right-facing triangle and resembles the Play button on a DVD player. (This button is called Start, and it can also be found on the Debug menu.) Learning the keyboard shortcuts will make your development process move along faster, so I recommend that you use them whenever possible.

When you run the program, the Visual Basic interface changes, and the form you've designed appears, floating over the design environment (see Figure 1.14).

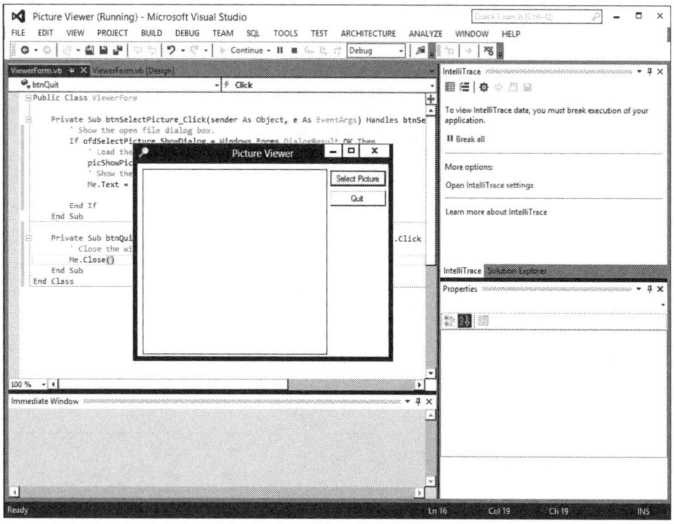

FIGURE 1.14
When in Run mode, your program executes just as it would for an end user.

You are now running your program as though it were a stand-alone application running on another user's machine; what you see is exactly what users would see if they ran the program (without the Visual Studio 2012 design environment in the background, of course). Click the Select Picture button to display the Select Picture dialog box, shown in Figure 1.15. Use this dialog box to locate a picture file. When you've found a file, double-click it, or click once to select it and then click Open. The selected picture is then displayed in the picture box, as shown in Figure 1.16.

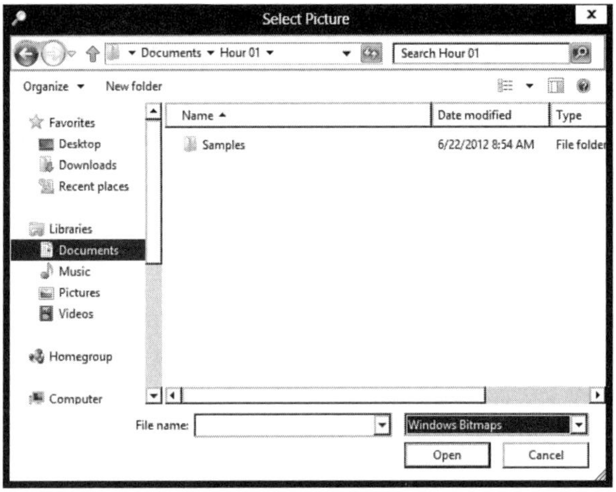

FIGURE 1.15
The `OpenFileDialog` control handles all the details of browsing for files. Cool, huh?

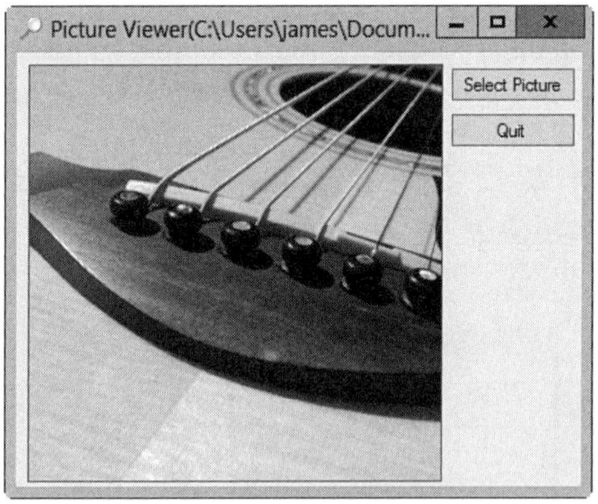

FIGURE 1.16
Displaying pictures is easy if you know just a few techniques.

By the Way

When you click the Select Picture button, the default path shown depends on the last active path in Windows, so it might be different for you than shown in Figure 1.15.

If you want to select and display a picture from your digital camera, chances are the format is JPEG, so you'll need to select this from the Files of Type drop-down. Also, if your image is very large, you'll see only the upper-left corner of the image (what fits in the picture box). In later hours, I'll show you how you can scale the image to fit the picture box, and even resize the form to show a larger picture in its entirety.

When you're finished playing with the program, click the Quit button to return to Design view.

Summary

That's it! You've just created a bona fide Visual Basic program. You've used the tool-box to build an interface with which users can interact with your program, and you've written code in strategic event handlers to empower your program to do things. These are the basics of application development in Visual Basic. Even the most complicated programs are built using this fundamental approach: You build the interface and add code to make the application do things. Of course, writing code to do things *exactly* the way you want things done is where the process can get complicated, but you're on your way.

If you take a close look at the organization of the hours in this book, you'll see that I start out by teaching you the Visual Basic (Visual Studio .NET) environment. I then move on to building an interface, and later I teach you about writing code. This organization is deliberate. You might be eager to jump in and start writing serious code, but writing code is only part of the equation—don't forget the word *Visual* in Visual Basic. As you progress through the hours, you'll build a solid foundation of development skills.

Soon, you'll pay no attention to the man behind the curtain—*you'll* be that man (or woman)!

Q&A

Q. *Can I show bitmaps of file types other than BMP, JPG, and PNG?*

A. Yes. `PictureBox` supports the display of images with the extensions BMP, JPG, ICO, EMF, WMF, PNG, and GIF. `PictureBox` can even save images to a file using any of the supported file types.

Q. *Is it possible to show pictures in other controls?*

A. PictureBox is the control to use when you are just displaying images. However, many other controls allow you to display pictures as part of the control. For instance, you can display an image on a button control by setting the button's Image property to a valid picture.

Workshop

Quiz

1. What type of Visual Basic project creates a standard Windows program?

2. What window is used to change the attributes (location, size, and so on) of a form or control in the IDE?

3. How do you access the default event (code) of a control?

4. What property of a picture box do you set to display an image?

5. What is the default event for a button control?

Answers

1. Windows Forms Application

2. The Properties window

3. Double-click the control in the designer

4. The Image property

5. The Click event

Exercises

1. Change your Picture Viewer program so that the user can also locate and select GIF files. (Hint: Change the Filter property of the OpenFileDialog control.)

2. Create a new project with a new form. Create two buttons on the form, one above the other. Next, change their position so that they appear next to each other.

Navigating Visual Basic 2012

What You'll Learn in This Hour:

▶ Navigating Visual Basic

▶ Using the Visual Studio 2012 Start Page to open and create projects

▶ Showing, hiding, docking, and floating design windows

▶ Customizing menus and toolbars

▶ Adding controls to a form using the toolbox

▶ Viewing and changing object attributes using the Properties window

▶ Working with the many files that make up a project

▶ How to get help

The key to expanding your knowledge of Visual Basic is to become as comfortable as possible—as quickly as possible—with the Visual Basic design environment. Just as a carpenter doesn't think much about hammering a nail into a piece of wood, performing actions such as saving projects, creating new forms, and setting object properties should become second nature to you. The more comfortable you are with Visual Basic's tools, the more you can focus your energies on what you're creating with the tools.

In this hour, you'll learn how to customize your design environment by moving, docking, floating, hiding, and showing design windows, as well as how to customize menus and toolbars. After you've gotten acquainted with the environment, I'll teach you about projects and the files they're made of (taking you beyond what was briefly discussed in Hour 1, "Jumping in with Both Feet: A Visual Basic 2012 Programming Tour"). I'll also introduce you to the design windows with which you'll work most frequently. Finally, I'll show you how to get help when you're stuck.

Using the Visual Basic 2012 Start Page

By default, the Visual Basic 2012 Start Page, shown in Figure 2.1, is the first thing you see when you start Visual Basic. (If Visual Basic isn't running, start it now.) The Visual Basic 2012 Start Page is a gateway for performing tasks with Visual Basic. From this page, you can open previously edited projects, create new projects, and get help.

FIGURE 2.1
The Start Page is the default entry point for all .NET languages.

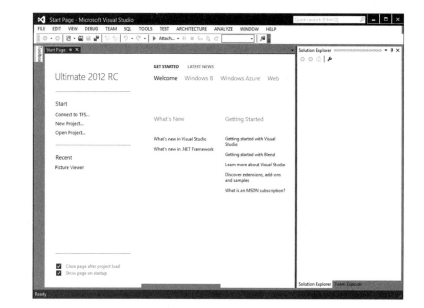

Creating New Projects

The Start Page consists of three category boxes. The Start category in the upper-left corner is used to create new projects or open projects already created. To create new projects, click the New Project link. This opens the New Project dialog box, shown in Figure 2.2. The Templates list varies from machine to machine, depending on which products of the Visual Studio .NET family are installed. Of course, we're interested in only the Visual Basic Project types in this book.

By the Way

You can create many types of projects with Visual Basic. However, this book focuses mostly on creating Windows Forms applications, the most common of the project types and the primary application type of the Express edition of Visual Basic 2012. You will learn about some of the other project types as well, but when you're told to create a new project and unless you are told otherwise, make sure that the Windows Forms Application icon is selected.

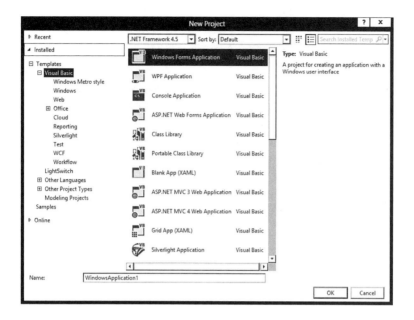

FIGURE 2.2
Use the New Project dialog box to create Visual Basic projects from scratch.

When you create a new project, be sure to enter a name for it in the Name text box before clicking OK or double-clicking a Templates icon. This ensures that the project is created with the proper path and filenames, eliminating work you would otherwise have to do to change these values later. After you specify a name, you can create the new project. Either double-click the type that represents the Template type of project you want to create (that is, Windows Forms Application), or click the template icon to select it and then click OK. After you've performed either of these actions, the New Project dialog box closes, and a new project of the selected type is created.

When you first create a project, the project files are virtual—they haven't been saved to the hard drive. When you click Save or Save All for the first time, you are prompted to specify a path in which to save the project. The name you give your project is used as its folder name by default, but the path chosen depends on the last project you created. If you're on a team of developers, you might choose to locate your projects on a shared drive so that others can access the source files.

> You can create a new project at any time (not just when starting Visual Basic) by choosing File, New Project. When you create or open a new project, the current project is closed. Visual Basic will ask you whether you want to save any changes to the current project before it closes it.

By the Way

Opening an Existing Project

Over time, you'll open existing projects more often than you create new ones. There are essentially two ways to open projects from the Visual Studio Start Page:

▶ If it's a project you've recently opened, the project name appears in the Recent category toward the upper-left corner of the Start Page (as Picture Viewer does in Figure 2.1, shown earlier). The project will also appear in File | Receipt Project and Solutions. Because the name displayed for the project is the one given when it was created, it's important to give your projects descriptive names. Clicking a project name opens the project. I'd venture to guess that you'll use this technique 95% of the time.

▶ To open a project for the first time (such as when opening sample projects), click the Open Project link on the Visual Basic 2012 Start Page. This displays a standard dialog box that you can use to locate and select a project file.

By the Way

> As with creating new projects, you can open an existing project at any time, not just when starting Visual Basic, by selecting File, Open Project. Remember that opening a project causes the current project to be closed. Again, if you've made changes to the current project, you'll get a chance to save them before the project is closed.

Navigating and Customizing the Visual Basic Environment

Visual Basic lets you customize many of its interface elements such as windows and toolbars, enabling you to be more efficient in the work you do. Create a new Windows application now by opening the File menu and choosing New Project. This project illustrates manipulating the design environment, so name this project **Environment Tutorial** and click OK to create the project. (This exercise won't create anything reusable, but it will help you learn how to navigate the design environment.) Your screen should look like the one shown in Figure 2.3.

By the Way

> Your screen might not look exactly like that shown in Figure 2.3, but it'll be close. By the time you've finished this hour, you'll be able to change the appearance of the design environment to match this figure—or to any configuration you prefer.

Working with Design Windows

Design windows, such as the Properties window and Solution Explorer shown in Figure 2.3, provide functionality for building complex applications. Just as your desk isn't organized exactly like that of your coworkers, your design environment doesn't have to be the same as anyone else's.

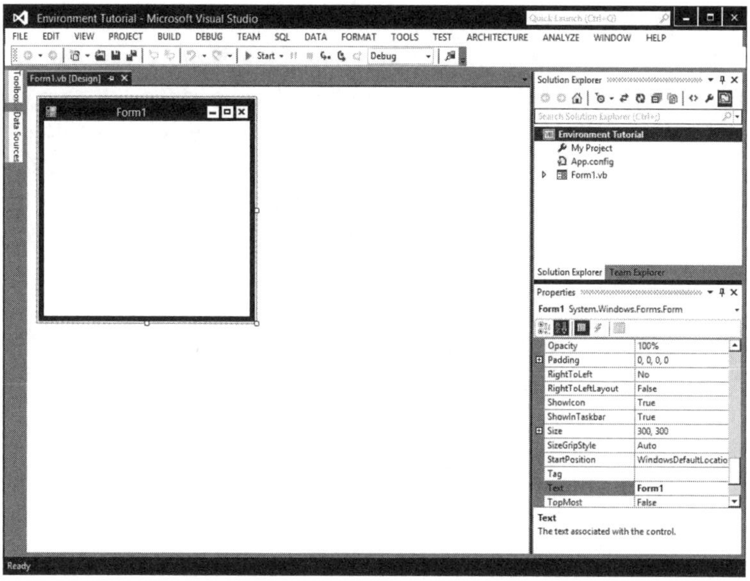

FIGURE 2.3
This is pretty
much how the
integrated devel-
opment environ-
ment (IDE)
appears when
you first install
Visual Basic.

A design window can be placed in one of four primary states:

▶ **Closed:** The window is not visible.

▶ **Floating:** The window floats over the IDE.

▶ **Docked:** The window is attached to an edge of the IDE. The Solution Explorer and Properties window in Figure 2.3 are docked.

▶ **Automatically hidden:** The window is docked, but it hides itself when not in use (like the Toolbox).

Showing and Hiding Design Windows

When a design window is closed, it doesn't appear anywhere. There is a difference between being closed and being automatically hidden, as you'll learn shortly. To display a closed or hidden window, choose the corresponding menu item from the View menu. For example, if the Properties window isn't displayed in your design environment, you can display it by choosing View, Properties Window (or by pressing its keyboard shortcut—F4). Whenever you need a design window and can't find it, use the View menu to display it. To close a design window, click its Close button (the button on the right side of the title bar with an X), just as you would close an ordinary window.

Floating Design Windows

Floating design windows are visible windows that float over the workspace, as shown in Figure 2.4. Floating windows are like typical application windows in that you can drag them around and place them anywhere you please, even on other monitors when you're using a multiple-display setup. In addition to moving a floating window, you can change its size by dragging a border. To make a window float, click the title bar of the docked window and drag it away from the edge that is currently docked.

FIGURE 2.4
Floating windows appear over the top of the design environment.

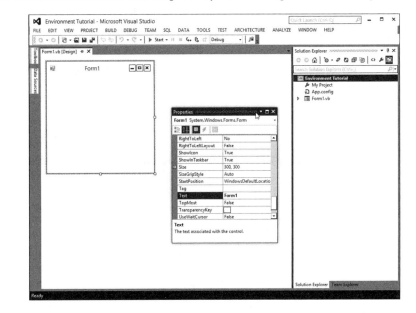

Docking Design Windows

Visible windows appear docked by default. A *docked* window appears attached to the side, top, or bottom of the work area or to some other window. The Properties window shown in Figure 2.3, for example, is docked to the right side of the design environment (contrast this to where it's floating in Figure 2.4). To make a floating window become a docked window, drag the title bar of the window toward the edge of the design environment to which you want to dock the window. As you drag the window, guides appear on the screen, as shown in Figure 2.5. If you move the mouse over one of the icons that appear as part of the guides, Visual Basic shows a blue rectangle where the window will appear if you release the mouse button. This is a quick and easy way to dock a window. You can also drag the window to an edge and get the same blue rectangle. This rectangle will "stick" in a docked position. If you release the mouse while the rectangle appears this way, the window is docked. Although it's difficult to explain, this is very easy to do.

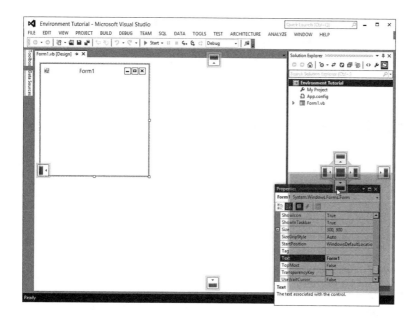

FIGURE 2.5
The guide icons
make it easy to
dock a window.

You can size a docked window by dragging its edge opposite the side that's docked. If two windows are docked to the same edge, dragging the border between them enlarges one while shrinking the other.

By the Way

To try this, you'll need to float a window that's already docked. To float a window, you "tear" the window away from the docked edge by dragging the title bar of the docked window away from the edge to which it's docked. Note that this technique doesn't work if a window is set to Auto Hide (which is explained next). Try docking and floating windows now by following these steps:

1. Ensure that the Properties window is currently displayed (if it's not, show it by pressing F4). Make sure that the Properties window isn't set to Auto Hide by right-clicking its title bar and deselecting Auto Hide from the shortcut menu (if it's selected).

2. Drag the title bar of the Properties window away from the docked edge (drag it to the left). When the window is away from the docked edge, release the mouse button. The Properties window should now float.

3. Dock the window once more by dragging the window's title bar toward the right edge of the design environment. When the guide diamond appears, mouse over the bottom icon (see Figure 2.5). You see a blue rectangle appear where the Properties window will be docked. Release the mouse button to dock the window.

Auto Hiding Design Windows

Visual Basic windows can auto hide themselves when you're not using them. Although you might find this a bit disconcerting at first, after you get the hang of things, this is a productive way to work. Your workspace is freed up, yet design windows are available whenever you move the mouse over them. Windows that are set to Auto Hide are always docked; you can't set a floating window to Auto Hide. When a window auto hides, it appears as a vertical tab on the edge to which it's docked—much as minimized applications are placed in the Windows taskbar.

Look at the left edge of the design environment. Notice the vertical tab titled Toolbox. This tab represents an auto-hidden window. To display an auto-hidden window, click the tab representing the window. When you click the tab, Visual Basic displays the design window so that you can use its features. When you click off of the window, the window automatically hides itself—hence the name. To make any window hide itself automatically, right-click its title bar and select Auto Hide from its shortcut menu. You can also click the little picture of a pushpin appearing in the title bar next to the Close button to toggle the window's Auto Hide state.

Using the techniques discussed so far, you can tailor the appearance of your design environment in all sorts of ways. There is no one best configuration. You'll find that different configurations work better for different projects and in different stages of development. Sometimes when I'm designing the interface of a form, for example, I want the toolbox to stay visible but out of my way, so I tend to make it float, or I turn off its Auto Hide property and leave it docked to the left edge of the design environment. However, after the majority of the interface elements have been added to a form, I want to focus on code. Then I dock the toolbox and make it auto hide itself; it's there when I need it, but it's out of the way when I don't. Don't be afraid to experiment with your design windows, and don't hesitate to modify them to suit your changing needs.

Working with Toolbars

Toolbars are the mainstay for performing functions quickly in almost every Windows program. (You'll probably want to add them to your own programs at some point, and in Hour 9, "Adding Menus and Toolbars to Forms," I'll show you how.) Every toolbar has a corresponding menu item, and buttons on toolbars are essentially shortcuts to their corresponding menu items. To maximize your efficiency when developing with Visual Basic 2012, you should become familiar with the available toolbars. As your skills improve, you can customize existing toolbars and even create your own toolbars to more closely fit the way you work.

Showing and Hiding Toolbars

Visual Basic includes a number of built-in toolbars you can use when creating projects. There is one toolbar that is visible in most of the figures shown so far in this hour: the Standard toolbar. You'll probably want this toolbar displayed all the time.

The toolbars you'll use most often as a new Visual Basic developer are the Standard, Text Editor, and Debug toolbars; each of these is discussed in this hour. You can also create your own custom toolbars to contain any functions you think necessary.

To show or hide a toolbar, open the View menu and choose Toolbars to display a list of available toolbars. Toolbars that are currently visible are checked, as shown in Figure 2.6. Click a toolbar name to toggle its visible state.

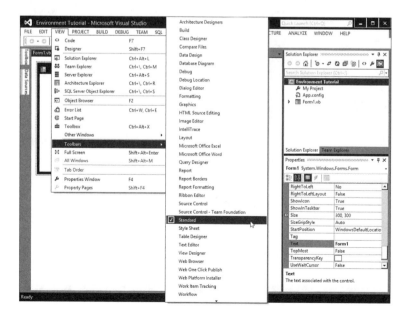

FIGURE 2.6
Hide or show toolbars to make your workspace more efficient.

> You can also right-click any visible toolbar to quickly access the list of available toolbars.

Adding Controls to a Form Using the Toolbox

The IDE offers some fantastic tools for building a graphical user interface (GUI) for your applications. Most GUIs consist of one or more forms (Windows) with various elements on the forms, such as text boxes, list boxes, and buttons. The toolbox is used to place controls on a form. Figure 2.7 shows the default toolbox you see when you first open or create a Visual Basic project. These controls are discussed in detail in Hour 7, "Working with Traditional Controls," and Hour 8, "Using Advanced Controls."

You can add a control to a form in one of four ways:

▶ In the toolbox, click the tool representing the control that you want to place on a form, and then click and drag on the form where you want the control placed. You're essentially drawing the border of the control. The location at which you start dragging is used for one corner of the control, and the point at which you release the mouse button and stop dragging becomes the lower-right corner. You'll probably need to pin the toolbox open so that it doesn't overlap the form in order to use this technique.

FIGURE 2.7
The standard toolbox contains many useful controls you can use to build robust interfaces.

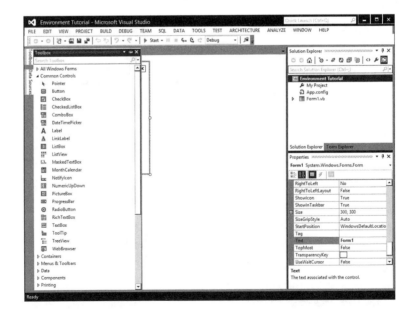

▶ Double-click the desired control type in the toolbox. A new control of the selected type is placed in the upper-left corner of the form. If a control is selected when you do this (rather that the form being selected), the new control appears slightly to the right and down from the selected control. The control's height and width are set to the default height and width of the selected control type. If the control is a runtime-only control, such as the OpenFileDialog control you used in Hour 1, it appears below the form.

▶ Drag a control from the toolbox and drop it on a form. If you hover the mouse pointer over the form for a second, the toolbox disappears, and you can drop the control on the form anywhere you want.

▶ Right-click an existing control and choose Copy; then right-click the form and choose Paste to create a duplicate of the control.

If you prefer to draw controls on your forms by clicking and dragging, I strongly suggest that you dock the toolbox to the right or bottom edge of the design environment or float it. The toolbar tends to interfere with drawing controls when it's docked to the left edge because it covers part of the form.

Did you Know?

The first item in each category in the toolbox, titled Pointer, isn't actually a control. When the pointer item is selected, the design environment is placed in a select mode rather than in a mode to create a new control. With the pointer item selected, you can click a control on the form to display all its properties in the Properties window.

Setting Object Properties Using the Properties Window

When developing a project's interface, you'll spend a lot of time viewing and setting object properties in the Properties window, shown in Figure 2.8. The Properties window contains four items:

▶ An object drop-down list

▶ A list of properties

▶ A set of tool buttons used to change the appearance of the properties grid

▶ A section showing a description of the selected property

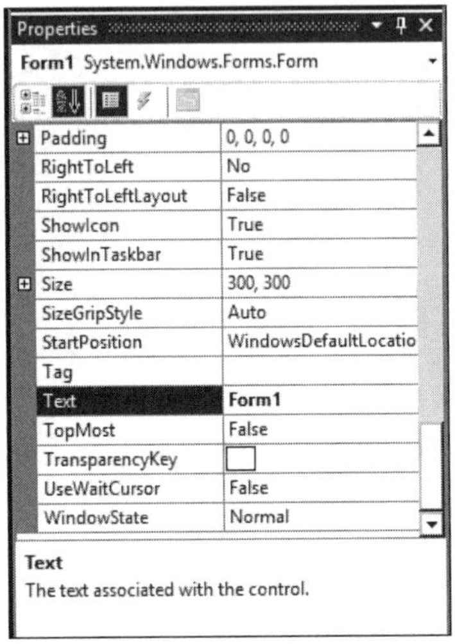

FIGURE 2.8
Use the Proper-
ties window to
view and change
properties of
forms and
controls.

Selecting an Object and Viewing Its Properties

The drop-down list at the top of the Properties window contains the name of the form with which you're currently working and all the objects on the form (the form's controls). To view a control's properties, select it from the drop-down list, or find it on the form and click it. Remember that you must have the pointer item selected in the toolbox to click an object to select it.

Viewing and Changing Properties

The first two buttons in the Properties window (Categorized and Alphabetical) enable you to select the format in which you view properties. When you select the Alphabetical button, the selected object's properties appear in the Properties window in alphabetical order. When you click the Categorized button, all the selected object's properties are listed by category. The Appearance category, for example, contains properties such as BackColor and BorderStyle. When working with properties, select the view with which you're most comfortable and feel free to switch back and forth between the views.

The Properties pane of the Properties window is used to view and set the properties of a selected object. You can set a property in one of the following ways:

▶ Type in a value.

▶ Select a value from a drop-down list.

▶ Click a Build button for property-specific options.

By the
Way

You can use more than one of these methods to change many properties. For example, color properties supply a drop-down list of colors, but you can enter a numeric color value as well.

To better understand how changing properties works, follow these steps:

1. Add a new text box to the form by double-clicking the TextBox tool in the toolbox. Next you'll change a few properties of the new text box.

2. Select the Name property in the Properties window by clicking it. (If your properties are alphabetical, it will be at the top of the list, not with the N's.) Type in a name for the text box—call it **txtComments**.

3. Click the BorderStyle property and try to type in the word **Big**. You can't; the BorderStyle property supports only the selection of values from a list, although you can type a value that exists in the list. When you select the BorderStyle property, a drop-down arrow appears in the Value column. Click this arrow to display a list of the values that the BorderStyle property accepts. Select FixedSingle and notice how the appearance of the text box changes. To make the text box appear three-dimensional again, open the drop-down list and select Fixed3D.

4. Select the BackColor property, type the word **guitar**, and press the Tab key to commit your entry. Visual Basic displays a message telling you the property value isn't valid. This happens because although you can type in text, you're restricted to entering specific values. In the case of BackColor, the value must be a named color or a number that falls within a specific range. Clear out the text, click the drop-down arrow of the BackColor property, and select a color from the drop-down list.

5. Select the Font property. Notice that a Build button appears (a small button with three dots). When you click the Build button, a dialog box specific to the property you've selected appears. In this instance, a dialog box that lets you manipulate the font of the text box appears, as shown in Figure 2.9. Different properties display different dialog boxes when you click their Build buttons. Feel free to change the font, and then close the window.

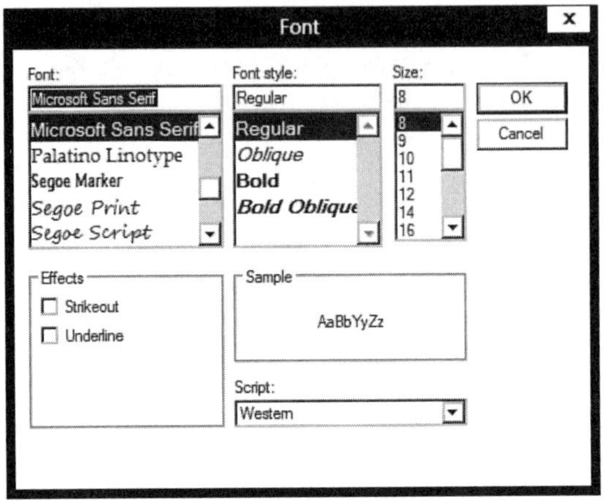

FIGURE 2.9
The Font dialog
box allows you
to change the
appearance of
text in a control.

6. Scroll down to the Size property and notice that it has a small button with a plus sign next to it. This indicates that the property has one or more subproperties. Click the triangle to expand the property, and you'll see that Size is composed of Width and Height.

By simply clicking a property in the Properties window, you can easily tell the type of input the property requires.

Working with Color Properties

Properties that deal with colors are unique in how they accept values, yet all color-related properties behave the same way. In Visual Basic, colors are expressed as a set of three numbers, each having a value from 0 to 255. A given set of numbers represents the red, green, and blue (RGB) components of a color, respectively. The value 0,255,0, for example, represents pure green, whereas the value 0,0,0 represents black and 255,255,255 represents white. In some cases, colors have also been given specific names that you can use.

A colored square is displayed for each color property in the Properties window; this color is the selected color for the property. Text is displayed next to the colored rectangle. This text is either the name of a color or a set of RGB values that define the color. Clicking a color property causes a drop-down arrow to appear, but the drop-down you get by clicking the arrow isn't a typical drop-down list. Figure 2.10 shows what the drop-down list for a color property looks like when the System tab is selected.

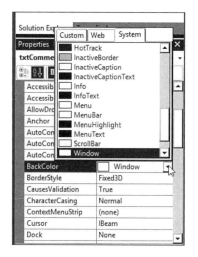

FIGURE 2.10
The color drop-down list enables you to select from three sets of colors: Custom, Web, and System.

The color drop-down list is composed of three tabs: Custom, Web, and System. Most color properties use a system color by default. Hour 5, "Building Forms: The Basics," goes into great detail on system colors. I only want to mention here that system colors vary from computer to computer. They're determined by users when they right-click the desktop and choose to personalize their colors. Use a system color when you want a color to be one of the user's selected system colors. When a color property is set to a system color, the name of the system color appears in the property sheet.

The Custom tab, shown in Figure 2.11, is used to specify a color regardless of the user's system color settings; changes to system colors have no effect on the property. The most common colors appear on the palette of the Custom tab, but you can specify any color you want.

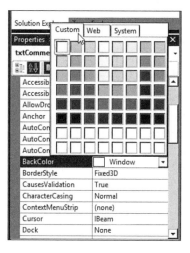

FIGURE 2.11
The Custom tab of the color drop-down list lets you specify any color imaginable.

The bottom two rows in the Custom color palette are used to mix your own colors. To assign a color to an empty color slot, right-click a slot in one of the two rows to access the Define Color dialog box, shown in Figure 2.12. Use the controls in the Define Color dialog box to create the color you want, and then click Add Color to add the color to the color palette in the slot you selected. In addition, the custom color is automatically assigned to the current property.

FIGURE 2.12
The Define Color
dialog box
enables you to
create your own
colors.

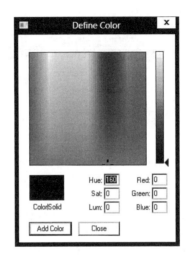

The Web tab is used in web applications to pick from a list of browser-safe colors. However, you can use these colors even if you're not creating a web application.

Viewing Property Descriptions

It's not always immediately apparent just exactly what a property is or does—especially for new users of Visual Basic. The Description section at the bottom of the Properties window shows a simple description of the selected property. To view a description, click a property or value area of a property. For a more complete description of a property, click it to select it and then press F1 to display Help about the property.

You can hide or show the Description section of the Properties window at any time. Right-click anywhere within the Properties window (other than in the value column or on the title bar) to display the Properties window shortcut menu and then choose Description. Each time you do this, you toggle the Description section between visible and hidden. To change the size of the Description box, click and drag the border between it and the Properties pane.

Managing Projects

Before you can effectively create an interface and write code, you need to understand what makes up a Visual Basic 2012 project and how to add and remove various components within your own projects. In this section, you'll learn about the Solution Explorer window and how it's used to manage project files. You'll also learn specifics about projects and project files, including how to change a project's properties.

Managing Project Files with the Solution Explorer

As you develop projects, they'll become more and more complex, often containing many objects such as forms and modules (grouped sets of code). Each object is defined by one or more files on your hard drive. In addition, you can build complex solutions composed of more than one project. The Solution Explorer window, shown in Figure 2.13, is *the* tool for managing all the files in a simple or complex solution. Using the Solution Explorer, you can add, rename, and remove project files, as well as select objects to view their properties. If the Solution Explorer window isn't visible on your screen, show it now by choosing View, Other Windows, Solution Explorer.

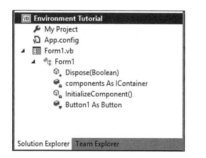

FIGURE 2.13
Use the Solution Explorer window to manage all the files that make up a project.

To better understand the Solution Explorer window, follow these steps:

1. Locate the Picture Viewer program you created in Hour 1 by choosing File, Open Project. If prompted, do not save your current project.

2. Open the Picture Viewer project. The file you need to select is located in the Picture Viewer folder that Visual Basic created when the project was constructed. The file has the extension .vbproj (for Visual Basic Project). If you're asked whether you want to save the current project, choose No.

3. Select the Picture Viewer project item in the Solution Explorer. When you do, a button becomes visible toward the top of the window. This button has a picture of pieces of paper and has the ToolTip Show All Files, as shown in Figure 2.14. Click this button, and the Solution Explorer displays all files in the project.

FIGURE 2.14
Click Show All
Files to view
secondary file
information.

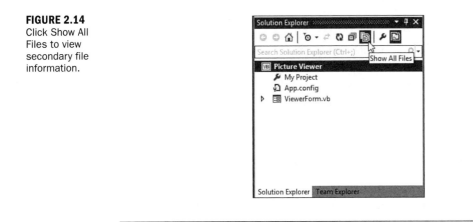

By the
Way

Some forms and other objects might be composed of more than one file. By default, Visual Basic hides project files that you don't directly manipulate. Click the right-facing triangle next to the `ViewerForm.vb` form item, and you'll see a subitem titled ViewerForm. This also has a triangle you can click to display more subitems. You'll learn about some of these additional files in Hour 5. For now, click the Show All Files button again to hide these related files.

You can view any object listed within the Solution Explorer with the object's default viewer by double-clicking the object. Each object has a default viewer but might actually have more than one viewer. For instance, a form has a Form Design view as well as a Code view. By default, double-clicking a form in the Solution Explorer displays the form in Form Design view, where you can manipulate the form's interface. Double-click ViewerForm.vb in the Solutions Explorer window now to display the form in the Form Designer.

You've already learned one way to access the code behind a form: Double-click an object to access its default event handler. You'll frequently need to get to a form's code without adding a new event handler. One way to do this is to use the Solution Explorer. When a form is selected in the Solution Explorer, buttons are visible at the top of the Solution Explorer window that can be used to display the code editor or the form designer.

You'll use the Solution Explorer window so often that you'll probably want to dock it to an edge and set it to Auto Hide, or perhaps keep it visible all the time. The Solution Explorer window is one of the easiest to get the hang of in Visual Basic. Navigating the Solution Explorer window will be second nature to you before you know it.

Working with Solutions

A project is what you create with Visual Basic. Often, the words *project* and *program* are used interchangeably, but this isn't much of a problem if you understand the important distinctions. A *project* is the set of source files that make up a program or component. A *program* is the binary file that you build by compiling source files into something such as a Windows executable file (`.exe`). Projects always consist of a main project file and can be made up of any number of other files, such as form files or class module files. The main project file stores information about the project—all the files that make up the project, for example—as well as properties that define aspects of a project, such as the parameters to use when the project is compiled into a program.

What, then, is a *solution*? As your abilities grow and your applications increase in complexity, you'll find that you have to build multiple projects that work harmoniously to accomplish your goals. For instance, you might build a custom user control such as a custom data grid that you use within other projects you design. Or you might isolate the business rules of a complex application into separate components to run on isolated servers. All the projects used to accomplish those goals are collectively called a solution. Therefore, a solution (at its most basic level) is really nothing more than a grouping of projects.

Did you Know?

You should group projects into a single solution only when the projects relate to one another. If you're working on a number of projects, but each of them is autonomous, work with each project in a separate solution.

Visual Basic creates a solution file for you when you save a project. The solution file is saved with the extension `.sln`, and you can open this file just as you would a project file. If a solution contains a single project, it really doesn't matter which you open— the solution or the project file. However, when you need to work with multiple projects together, you should open the solution file.

Understanding Project Components

As I stated earlier, a project always consists of a main project file, and it might consist of one or more secondary files, such as files that make up forms or code modules. As you create and save objects within your project, one or more corresponding files are created and saved on your hard drive. Each file that's created for a Visual Basic 2012 source object has the extension `.vb`, denoting that it defines a Visual Basic object. Be sure that you save your objects with understandable names, or things will get confusing as your project grows in size.

By the Way

With previous editions of Visual Basic (version 6 and earlier), you could easily tell the type of object defined by project files by looking at the file extension. For example, form files had the extension `.frm`. Unfortunately, this is no longer the case, so you need to be diligent about giving your files unique names.

All files that make up a project are stored as text files on your hard drive. Some objects need to store binary information, such as a picture for a form's `BackgroundImage` property. Binary data is stored in an XML file (which is still a text file). Suppose that you had a form with an icon on it. You'd have a text file defining the form—its size, the controls on it, and the code behind it. You also would have an associated resource file with the same name as the form file, but with the extension `.resx`. This secondary file would be in XML format and would contain all the binary data needed to create the form.

By the
~~Way~~

If you want to see what the source file of a form file looks like, use Notepad to open one on your computer. Don't save any changes to the file, however, or it might never work again (insert evil laugh here).

The following is a list of some of the components you might use in your projects:

- ▶ Modules enable you to store code procedures without needing a specific form to attach them to.

- ▶ A class modules is a special type of module that enables you to create object-oriented applications. Throughout the course of this book, you'll learn how to program using an object-oriented language, but mostly you'll learn how to use objects supplied by Visual Basic. In Hour 16, "Designing Objects Using Classes," you'll learn how to use class modules to create your own objects.

- ▶ Forms are the visual windows that make up your application's interface. A special type of class module is used to define forms.

- ▶ User controls (formerly ActiveX controls, which themselves are formerly OLE controls) are controls that can be used on the forms of other projects. For example, you could create a user control with a calendar interface for a contact manager. Creating user controls requires much programming experience, so I won't cover them in this book.

Setting Project Properties

Visual Basic projects have properties, just as other objects such as controls do. Projects have many properties, many of them related to advanced functionality not covered in this book. You need to be aware of how to access project properties, however, and how to change some of the more commonly used properties.

To access the properties for a project, right-click the project name (Picture Viewer) in the Solution Explorer window and choose Properties from the shortcut menu. You could also double-click the My Project item in the Solutions Explorer to accomplish the same goal. Perform one of these actions now.

The properties for a project are presented as a set of vertical tabs, as shown in Figure 2.15.

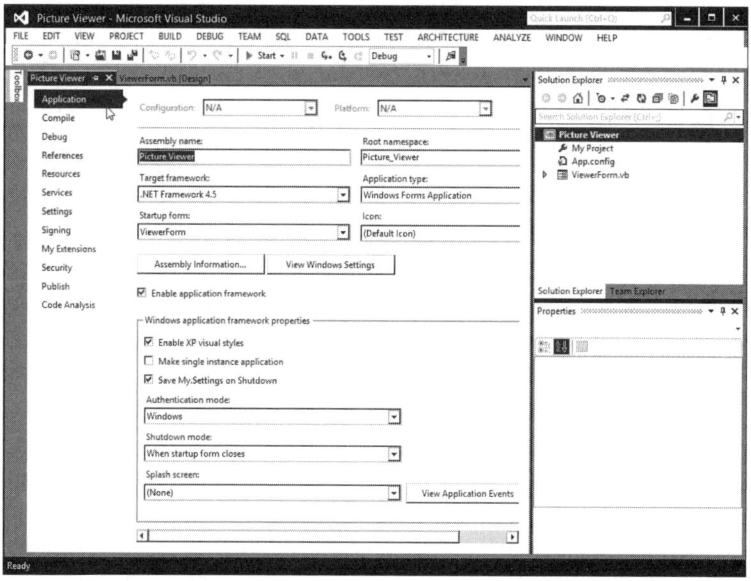

FIGURE 2.15
The project properties are used to tailor the project as a whole.

As you work through the hours in this book, I'll refer to the Project Properties dialog box as necessary, explaining pages and items in context with other material. Feel free to take a look at your Picture Viewer properties, but don't change any at this time. You can close the project properties by clicking the small X in the upper-right corner of the tab section in the IDE. You can also just click a different tab.

Adding and Removing Project Files

When you first start Visual Basic 2012 and create a new Windows Forms Application project, Visual Basic creates the project with a single form. You're not limited to having one form in a project, however; you can create new forms or add existing forms to your project at will (feeling powerful yet?). You can also create and add code modules and classes as well as other types of objects.

You can add a new or existing object to your project in one of two ways:

▶ Choose the appropriate item from the Project menu.

▶ Right-click the project name in the Solution Explorer window, and then choose Add from the shortcut menu to access a submenu from which you can select object types (see Figure 2.16).

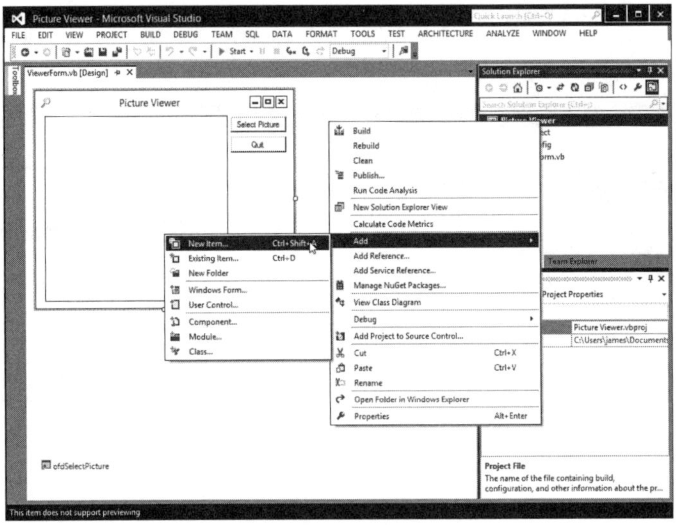

FIGURE 2.16
This menu is
one of two ways
to add objects to
a project.

When you select Add ObjectType from any of these menus, a dialog box appears,
showing you the objects that can be added to the project. Your chosen item type is
selected by default, as shown in Figure 2.17. Simply name the object and click Open
to create a new object of the selected type. To create an object of a different type, click
the type to select it, name it, and then click Open.

Adding new forms and modules to your project is easy, and you can add as many as
you want. You'll come to rely on the Solution Explorer more and more to manage all
the objects in the project as the project becomes more complex.

FIGURE 2.17
Regardless of
the menu option
you select, you
can add any type
of object you
want by using
this dialog box.

Although it won't happen as often as adding project files, you might sometimes need to remove an object from a project. Removing objects from your project is even easier than adding them. To remove an object, right-click the object in the Solution Explorer window and select Delete. This not only removes the object from the project, it also deletes the source file from the disk!

A Quick-and-Dirty Programming Primer

Programming is complicated. Everything is so interrelated that it's difficult, if not impossible, to isolate each programming concept and then present the material in a linear fashion. Instead, while learning one subject, you often have to touch on elements of another subject before you've had a chance to learn about the secondary topic. As I mentioned in Hour 1, I've made every effort to avoid such forward references, but there are some concepts you'll need to be at least slightly familiar with before proceeding. You'll learn the basics of each of these topics in their respective hours, but you'll need to have at least heard of them before digging any deeper into this book.

Storing Values in Variables

A *variable* is an element in code that holds a value. You might create a variable that holds the name of a user or perhaps the user's age, for example. Each variable (storage entity) must be created before it can be used. The process of creating a variable is known as *declaring a variable*. In addition, each variable is declared to hold data of a specific type, such as text (called a *string*) for a person's name or a number for a person's age. An example of a variable declaration is

```
Dim strFirstName As String
```

This statement creates a variable called strFirstName. This variable is of type String, which means that it can hold any text you choose to put into it. The contents of a variable can be changed as often as you like.

The key primer point to remember is that variables are storage locations that must be declared before use and that hold a specific type of data.

Using Procedures to Write Functional Units of Code

When you write Visual Basic code, you place the code in a *procedure*. A procedure is a group of code statements that perform a specific function. You can call a procedure from code in another procedure. For example, you might create one procedure that totals the items on an order and another procedure that calculates the tax on the entire sale. There are two types of procedures: procedures that don't return values and procedures that do return values. In addition, some procedures allow data to be passed to them. For example, the tax calculation procedure mentioned previously might allow a calling statement to pass a monetary total into the procedure and then use that total to calculate tax. When a procedure accepts data from the calling code, the data is called a *parameter*. Procedures don't have to accept parameters.

The keyword Sub is used to declare a procedure that doesn't return a value. It looks like this:

```
Public Sub MyProcedure()
    ' The procedure's code goes here.
End Sub
```

The keyword Function is used to delare a procedure that returns a value. In addition, it has a data type specified at the end of the procedure, which denotes the type of data returned by the procedure:

```
Public Function MyProcedure() As String
    ' The procedure's code goes here.
End Function
```

Notice the words As String. The keyword As is used to specify a data type. In this example, the function returns a string, which is text.

If a procedure accepts a parameter, it is enclosed in the parentheses. Again, notice how the word As is used to denote the type of data being accepted:

```
Public Function CalculateTax(dblItemTotal As Double) As String
    ' The procedure's code goes here.
End Function
```

MessageBox.Show()

You're almost certainly familiar with the Windows message box. It's the little dialog box used to display text to a user, as shown in Figure 2.18. Visual Basic 2012 provides an easy way to display such messages: the MessageBox.Show() statement. The following is a MessageBox.Show() statement in its most basic form:

```
MessageBox.Show("This is a simple message box")
```

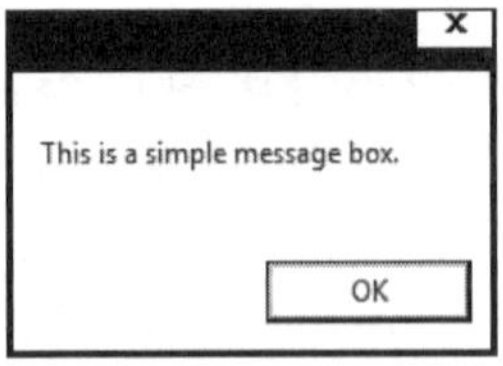

FIGURE 2.18
Visual Basic makes it easy to display simple message boxes like this.

You'll use message boxes throughout this book, and you'll learn about them in detail in Hour 17, "Interacting with Users."

Getting Help

Although Visual Basic was designed to be as intuitive as possible, you'll find that you occasionally need help performing a task. In all honesty, Visual Basic isn't as intuitive as its predecessors. With all its additional power and flexibility comes complexity. It doesn't matter how much you know; Visual Basic is so complex and contains so many features that you'll have to use Help at times. This is particularly true when writing Visual Basic code; you won't always remember the command you need or a command's syntax. Fortunately, Visual Basic includes a comprehensive Help feature.

To access Help from within the design environment, press F1. Generally, when you press F1, Visual Basic shows you a Help topic directly related to what you're doing. This is known as *context-sensitive help*. For example, you can display help for any Visual Basic syntax or keyword (functions, objects, methods, properties, and so on) when writing Visual Basic code. Type the word into the code editor, position the cursor anywhere within the word (including before the first letter or after the last), and press F1. You can also get to Help by using the Help menu.

> If your project is in Run mode, Visual Basic's Help doesn't appear when you press F1. Instead, the Help for your application appears—if you've created Help.

By the Way

Summary

In this hour, you learned how to use the Visual Basic Start Page—your gateway to Visual Basic 2012. You learned how to create new projects and how to open existing projects. The Visual Basic environment is your workspace, toolbox, and much more. You learned how to navigate this environment, including how to work with design windows (hide, show, dock, and float).

Visual Basic has many different design windows, and in this hour, you began learning about some of them in detail. You learned how to get and set properties using the Properties window, how to manage projects using the Solution Explorer, and how to add controls to a form using the toolbox. You'll use these skills often, so it's important to get familiar with them right away. Finally, you learned how to access Visual Basic's Help feature, which I guarantee you'll find important as you learn to use Visual Basic.

Visual Basic 2012 is a vast and powerful development tool—far more powerful than any version that's come before it. Don't expect to become an expert overnight; that's simply not possible. However, by learning the tools and techniques presented in this hour, you've begun your journey. Remember, you'll use most of what you learned in this hour each time you use Visual Basic. Get proficient with these basics, and you'll be building useful programs in no time!

Q&A

Q. *How can I easily get more information about a property when the Description section of the Properties window just doesn't cut it?*

A. Click the property in question to select it, and then press F1. Context-sensitive Help applies to properties in the Properties window as well.

Q. *I find that I need to see a lot of design windows at one time, but I can't find that "magic" layout. Any suggestions?*

A. Run at a higher resolution. Personally, I won't develop in less than 1024×768. As a matter of fact, all my development machines have two displays, both running at 1680×1050 or higher. You'll find that any investment you make in having more screen real estate will pay big dividends.

Workshop

Quiz

1. Unless instructed otherwise, you're to create what type of project when building examples in this book?

2. To make a docked design window appear when you click its tab and disappear when you click off of it, you change what setting of the window?

3. What design window do you use to add controls to a form?

4. What design window is used to change an object's attributes?

5. To modify a project's properties, you must select the project in what design window?

Answers

1. Windows Forms Application

2. Its Auto Hide settings

3. The toolbox window

4. The Properties window

5. The Solutions Explorer window

Exercises

1. Use the Custom Color dialog box to create a color of your choice, and then assign the color to the BackColor property of a form.

2. Move the toolbox to the right side of the IDE and dock it there. Make it Auto Hide. When you're finished, move it back.

Understanding Objects and Collections

What You'll Learn in This Hour:

▶ Understanding objects

▶ Getting and setting properties

▶ Triggering methods

▶ Understanding method dynamism

▶ Writing object-based code

▶ Understanding collections

▶ Using the Object Browser

In Hour 1, "Jumping in with Both Feet: A Visual Basic 2012 Programming Tour," you were introduced to programming in Visual Basic by building a Picture Viewer project. You then spent Hour 2, "Navigating Visual Basic 2012," digging into the integrated development environment (IDE) and learning skills critical to your success with Visual Basic. In this hour, you begin learning about an important programming concept: *objects*.

The term *object* as it relates to programming might have been new to you prior to this book. The more you work with Visual Basic, the more you'll hear about objects. Visual Basic 2012, unlike its early predecessors, is a true object-oriented language. This hour doesn't discuss object-oriented programming in any detail; object-oriented programming is a complex subject and well beyond the scope of this book. Instead, you'll learn about objects in a more general sense.

Everything you use in Visual Basic is an object, so understanding this material is critical to your success with Visual Basic. For example, forms are objects, as are the controls you place on a form. Pretty much every element of a Visual Basic project is an object and belongs to a collection of objects. All objects have attributes (called *properties*), most have methods, and many have events. Whether creating simple applications or building large-scale enterprise solutions, you must understand what an object is and how it works. In this hour, you'll learn what makes an object an object, and you'll also learn about collections.

If you've listened to the programming press at all, you've probably heard the term *object-oriented*, and perhaps words such as *polymorphism*, *encapsulation*, and *inheritance*. In truth, these object-oriented features of Visual Basic are exciting, but they're far beyond this hour (or the last hour, for that matter). You'll learn a little about object-oriented programming in this book, but if you're really interested in taking your programming skills to the next level, you should buy a book dedicated to the subject after you've completed this book.

Understanding Objects

Object-oriented programming has been a technical buzzword for quite some time, but as far as Visual Basic programmers are concerned, it became a reality only with Visual Basic .NET. (No previous version of Visual Basic was a true object-oriented language.) Almost everywhere you look—the Web, publications, books—you read about objects. What exactly is an object? Strictly speaking, an *object* is a programming structure that encapsulates data and functionality as a single unit and for which the only public access is through the programming structure's interfaces (properties, methods, and events). In reality, the answer to this question can be somewhat ambiguous, because there are so many types of objects—and the number grows almost daily. All objects share specific characteristics, however, such as properties and methods.

The most commonly used objects in Visual Basic are the form object and the control object. Earlier hours introduced you to working with forms and controls and even showed you how to set form and control properties. In your Picture Viewer project from Hour 1, for example, you added a picture box and two buttons to a form. Both the PictureBox and the Button controls are *control objects*, but each is a specific type of control object. Another, less-technical example uses pets. Dogs and cats are definitely different entities (objects), but they both fit into the category of pet objects. Similarly, a text box and a button is each a unique type of object, but they're both considered control objects. This small distinction is important.

Understanding Properties

All objects have attributes that are used to specify and return the state of the object. These attributes are properties, and you've already used some of them in previous hours in the Properties window. Indeed, every object exposes a specific set of properties, but not every object exposes the same set of properties. To illustrate this point, I'll continue with the hypothetical pet object. Suppose that you have an object, and the object is a dog. This Dog object has certain properties common to all dogs. These properties include attributes such as the dog's name, the color of its hair, and even the number of legs it has. All dogs have these same properties; however, different dogs have different values for these properties. Figure 3.1 illustrates such a Dog object and its properties.

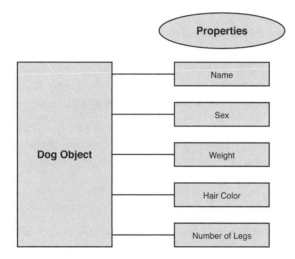

FIGURE 3.1
Properties are the attributes that describe an object.

Getting and Setting Properties

You've already seen how to read and change properties using the Properties window. The Properties window is available only at design time, however, and is used only to manipulate the properties of forms and controls. Most getting and setting of properties you'll perform will be done with Visual Basic code, not in the Properties window. When referencing properties in code, you specify the object's name first, followed by a period (.), and then the property name, as in the following syntax:

```
ObjectName.Property
```

If you had a Button object named btnClickMe, for example, you would reference the button's Text property this way:

```
btnClickMe.Text
```

This line of code would return whatever value was contained in the Text property of the Button object btnClickMe. To set a property to some value, you use an equals sign (=). To change the Button object's Left property, for example, you'd use a line of code such as the following:

```
btnClickMe.Left = 90
```

When you reference a property on the left side of an equals sign, you're setting the value. When you reference a property on the right side of the equals sign, you're getting (reading) the value. In the early days of BASIC, you actually used the word `Let` when setting values. This made the code easier to read for novices, but it was unnecessarily tedious. Nevertheless, using `Let` makes the statement clearer for this example, so I'll show the same code statement as before with the word `Let`:

```
Let btnClickMe.Left = 90
```

It's easier to see here that referencing the property on the left side of the equals sign indicates that you're setting the property to some value. The keyword `Let` is no longer a valid way to make variable assignments. If you enter a code statement that uses `Let`, you won't receive an error, but the code editor (also known as *the gremlins*) automatically removes the word `Let` from the statement for you.

The following line of code places the value of the `Left` property of the `Button` object called `btnClickMe` into a temporary variable. This statement retrieves the value of the `Left` property because the `Left` property is referenced on the right side of the equals sign:

```
intLeftVariable = btnClickMe.Left
```

Variables are discussed in detail in Hour 11, "Using Constants, Data Types, Variables, and Arrays." For now, think of a variable as a storage location. When the processor executes this statement, it retrieves the value in the `Left` property of the `Button` object `btnClickMe` and places it in the variable (storage location) titled `intLeftVariable`. Assuming that `btnClickMe`'s `Left` property value is 90, as set in the previous example, the computer would process the code statement like this:

```
intLeftVariable = 90
```

Just as in real life, some properties can be read but not changed. Think back to the hypothetical pet object, and suppose that you have a `Gender` property to designate the gender of a `Dog` object. It's impossible for you to change a dog from a male to a female or vice versa (at least, I think it is). Because the `Gender` property can be retrieved but not changed, it's known as a *read-only* property. You'll often encounter properties that can be set in Design view but become read-only when the program is running.

One example of a read-only property is the `Height` property of the Combo Box control. Although you can view the value of the `Height` property in the Properties window, you can't change the value—no matter how hard you try. If you attempt to change the `Height` property using Visual Basic code, Visual Basic simply changes the value back to the default—eerie gremlins.

The best way to determine which properties of an object are read-only is to consult the online help for the object in question.

Working with an Object and Its Properties

Now that you know what properties are and how they can be viewed and changed, you'll experiment with properties by modifying the Picture Viewer project you built in Hour 1. Recall from Hour 1 how you learned to set the `Height` and `Width` properties of a form in the Properties window. Here, you'll change the same properties, now using Visual Basic code.

You'll add two buttons to your Picture Viewer. One button will enlarge the form when clicked, and the other will shrink the form. This is a simple example, but it illustrates well how to change object properties in Visual Basic code.

Start by opening your Picture Viewer project from Hour 1. If you download the code samples from my site, I provide a Picture Viewer project for you to start with. Double-click `ViewerForm.vb` in the Solution Explorer window to show the form designer.

When the project first runs, the form has the `Height` and `Width` you specified in the Properties window. You'll add buttons to the form that a user can click to enlarge or shrink the form at runtime by following these steps:

1. Add a new button to the form by double-clicking the Button tool in the toolbox. Set the new button's properties as follows:

Property	Value
Name	btnEnlarge
Location	338,261
Size	21,23
Text	^ (Note: This is Shift+6.)

2. Now for the Shrink button. Again, double-click the Button tool in the toolbox to create a new button on the form. Set this new button's properties as follows:

Property	Value
Name	btnShrink
Location	359,261
Size	21,23
Text	v

Your form should now look like the one in shown in Figure 3.2.

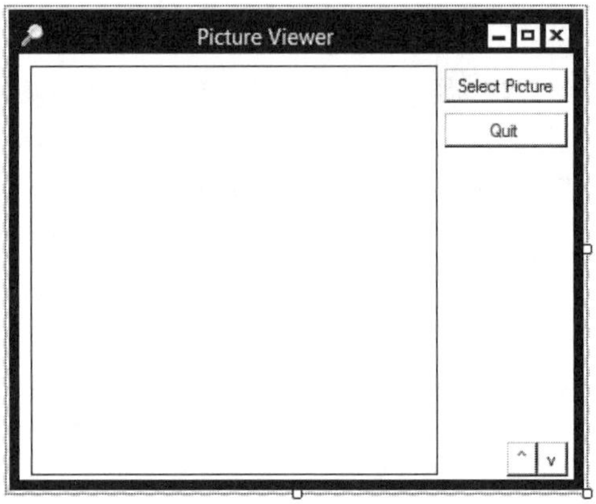

FIGURE 3.2
Each button is
an object, as is
the form on
which the but-
tons sit.

To complete the project, you need to add the small amount of Visual Basic code necessary to modify the form's `Height` and `Width` properties when the user clicks a button.

3. Access the code for the Enlarge button by double-clicking the ^ button. Type the following statement exactly as you see it here. Do not press the Enter key or add a space after you've entered this text:

```
Me.Width
```

When you type the period, or *dot*, as it's called, a small drop-down list like the one shown in Figure 3.3 appears. Visual Basic is smart enough to realize that Me represents the current form (more on this in a moment). To help you write code for the object, it gives you a drop-down list containing all the properties and methods of the form. This feature is called *IntelliSense*. When an Intelli-Sense drop-down box appears, you can use the up and down arrow keys to navigate the list and press Tab to select the highlighted list item. This prevents you from misspelling a member name, thereby reducing compile errors. Because Visual Basic is fully object-oriented, you'll come to rely on IntelliSense drop-down lists in a big way; I think I'd rather dig ditches than program without them.

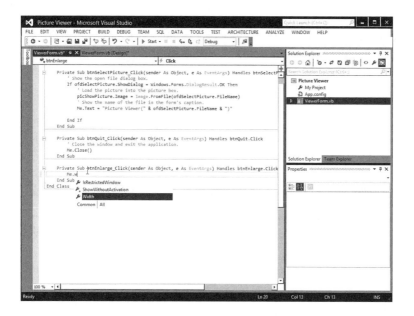

FIGURE 3.3
IntelliSense
drop-down lists
(also called auto-
completion drop-
down lists) make
coding dramati-
cally easier.

4. Use the Backspace key to erase the code you just entered, and enter the following code in its place (press Enter at the end of each line):

```
Me.Width = Me.Width + 20
Me.Height = Me.Height + 20
```

Remember from before that the word Me doesn't refer to a person; it refers to the
object to which the code belongs (in this case, the form). Me is a *reserved* word;
it's a word that you can't use to name objects or variables because Visual Basic
has a specific meaning for it. When writing code within a form module, as
you're doing here, always use the reserved word Me rather than the name of the
form. Me is much shorter than using the full name of the current form, and it
makes the code more portable. (You can copy and paste the code into another
form module and not have to change the form name to make the code work.)
Also, should you change the name of the form at any time in the future, you
won't have to change references to the old name.

The code you just entered does nothing more than set the form's Width and
Height properties to their current value plus 20 pixels.

5. Redisplay the form designer by selecting the tab named ViewerForm.vb [Design] at the top of the designer window. Then double-click the button with the v to access its Click event, and add the following code:

```
Me.Width = Me.Width - 20
Me.Height = Me.Height - 20
```

This code is similar to the code in the btnEnlarge_Click event, except that it reduces the form's Width and Height properties by 20 pixels. Your screen should now look like Figure 3.4.

FIGURE 3.4
The code you've entered should look exactly like this.

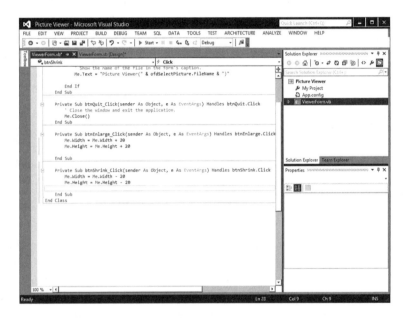

 As you create projects, it's a good idea to save frequently. When an asterisk appears to the right of a tab's title (as you can see in Figure 3.4), you know that the file edited within that tab has been changed but not saved. Save your project now by clicking the Save All button on the toolbar.

Again, display the form designer by clicking the tab ViewerForm.vb [Design]. Your Properties Example project is now ready to be run! Follow these steps to test your changes:

1. Press F5 to put the project in Run mode.

2. Click the Select Picture button, and choose a picture from your hard drive.

3. Click the ^ button a few times and notice how the form gets bigger (see Figure 3.5).

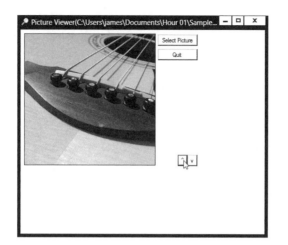

FIGURE 3.5
The form gets bigger, but it still looks just as you designed it.

4. Next, click the v button to make the form smaller. When you've clicked enough to satisfy your curiosity (or until you get bored), end the running program, and return to Design mode by clicking the Stop Debugging button on the toolbar.

Did you notice how the buttons and the image on the form didn't resize as the form's size changed? In Hour 6, "Building Forms: Advanced Techniques," you'll learn how to make your forms resize their contents.

Understanding Methods

In addition to properties, most objects have *methods*. Methods are actions the object can perform, in contrast to attributes, which describe the object. To understand this distinction, think about the pet object example one more time. A Dog object has a certain set of actions it can perform. These actions, called methods in Visual Basic, include barking, tail wagging, and chewing carpet (don't ask). Figure 3.6 illustrates the Dog object and its methods.

FIGURE 3.6
Invoking a
method causes
the object to per-
form an action.

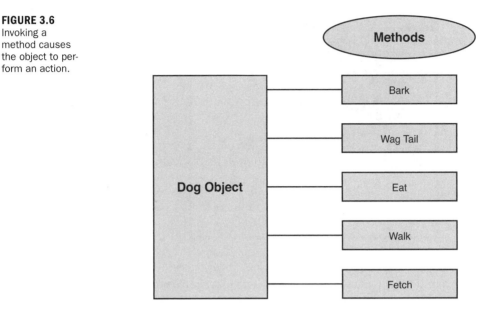

Triggering Methods

Think of methods as functions—which is exactly what they are. When you invoke a
method, code is executed. You can pass data to a method, and methods can return
values. However, a method is not required to accept parameters (data passed to it by
the calling code) or return a value; many methods simply perform an action in code.
Invoking (triggering) a method is similar to referencing the value of a property. First
you reference the object's name, and then provide a dot, and then the method name:

```
ObjectName.Method
```

For example, to make the hypothetical Dog object Bruno bark using Visual Basic code,
you would use this line of code:

```
Bruno.Bark()
```

By the Way

> Methods generally are used to have an object perform an action, such as saving
> or deleting a record in a database. Properties, on the other hand, are used to get
> and set the object's attributes. One way to tell in code whether a statement is a
> property reference or method call is that a method call has a set of parentheses
> after it, like this:
> ```
> AlbumForm.ShowDialog()
> ```

Invoking methods is simple; the real skill lies in knowing what methods an object
supports and when to use a particular method.

Understanding Method Dynamism

Properties and methods go hand in hand, and at times a particular method might become unavailable because of one or more property values. For example, if you were to set the NumberofLegs property on the Dog object Bruno equal to 0, the Walk() and Fetch() methods obviously would be inapplicable. If you were to set the NumberofLegs property back to 4, you could then trigger the Walk() or Fetch() methods again.

Building a Simple Object Example Project

The only way to really grasp what objects are and how they work is to use them. I've said this before, but I can't say it enough: Everything in Visual Basic 2012 is an object. This fact has its good points and bad points. One of the bad points is that in some instances, it takes more code to accomplish a task than it did in the past—sometimes more characters, sometimes more statements. If you're moving from Visual Basic 6, you have some learning and adjusting ahead of you, but it's worth the effort!

Every project you've built so far uses objects, but now you'll create a sample project that specifically illustrates using objects. If you're new to programming with objects, you'll probably find this a bit confusing. However, I'll walk you through step by step, explaining each section in detail.

You'll modify your Picture Viewer project to include a button that, when clicked, draws a colored border around the picture. You'll get a taste of some drawing functions in this example. Don't worry; you're not expected to understand all the intricacies of the drawing code. Your sole responsibility is grasping how objects work.

Creating the Interface for the Drawing Project

Continuing with the Picture Viewer project you've been using in this hour, add a new button to the form, and set its properties as follows:

Property	Value
Name	btnDrawBorder
Location	295,70
Size	85,23
Text	Draw Border

Writing the Object-Based Code

Now you'll add code to the button's `Click` event. I'll explain each statement, and at the end of the steps, I'll show the complete code listing. Follow these steps to create the code that draws the border:

1. Double-click the Draw Border button to access its `Click` event.

2. Enter the first line of code as follows (remember to press Enter at the end of each statement):

```
Dim objGraphics As Graphics
```

Here you've just created a variable that will hold an instance of an object. Objects don't materialize out of thin air; they have to be created. When a form is loaded into memory, it loads all its controls (that is, it creates the control objects), but not all objects are created automatically as they are in this situation. The process of creating an instance of an object is called *instantiation*. When you load a form, you instantiate the form object, which in turn instantiates its control objects. You could load a second instance of the form, which in turn would instantiate a new instance of the form and new instances of all controls. You would then have two forms in memory, and two of each used control.

To instantiate an object in code, you create a variable that holds a reference to an instantiated object. The `Dim` statement you wrote in step 2 creates a new variable called `objGraphics`, which holds a reference to an object of type `Graphics`. You'll learn more about variables in Hour 11.

Next, enter the second line of code exactly as shown here:

```
objGraphics = Me.CreateGraphics
```

`CreateGraphics` is a method of the form. (Remember, the keyword `Me` is shorthand for referencing the current form.) Under the hood, the `CreateGraphics` method is pretty complicated. For now, understand that the method `CreateGraphics` instantiates a new object that represents the client area of the current form. The client area is the gray area within a form's borders and title bar. Anything drawn on the `objGraphics` object appears on the form. What you've done is set the variable `objGraphics` to point to an object that was returned by the `CreateGraphics` method. Notice how values returned by a property or method don't have to be traditional values such as numbers or text; they could also be objects.

Enter the third line of code:

```
objGraphics.Clear(SystemColors.Control)
```

This statement clears the form's background using whatever color the user has selected as the Windows Control color, which Windows uses to paint forms.

How does this happen? After declaring the objGraphics object, you used the CreateGraphics method of the form to instantiate a new graphics object in the variable objGraphics. With the code statement you just entered, you're calling the Clear() method of the objGraphics object. The Clear() method is a method of all Graphics objects used to clear the graphic surface. The Clear() method accepts a single parameter: the color you want used to clear the surface.

The value you're passing to the parameter might seem a bit odd. Remember that "dots" are a way of separating objects from their properties and methods. (Properties, methods, and events are often called object *members*.) Knowing this, you can discern that SystemColors is an object because it appears before any of the dots. Object references can and do go pretty deep, and you'll use many dots throughout your code. The key points to remember are

- ▶ Text that appears to the left of a dot is always an object (or namespace).

- ▶ Text that appears only to the right of a dot is a property reference or method call. If the text is followed by parentheses, it's a method call. If not, it's most likely a property.

- ▶ Methods can return objects, just as properties can. The only surefire ways to know whether the text between two dots is a property or method are to look at the icon of the member in the IntelliSense drop-down or to consult the object's documentation.

The final text in this statement is the word Control. Because Control isn't followed by a dot, you know that it's not an object; therefore, it must be a property or method. You expect this string of object references to return a color value to be used to clear the graphic object. Therefore, you know that Control in this instance must be a property or method that returns a value (because you need the return value to set the Clear() method). A quick check of the documentation would tell you that Control is indeed a property. The value of Control always equates to the color designated on the user's computer for the face of forms and buttons. By default, this is a light gray (often fondly referred to as *battleship gray*), but users can change this value on their computers. By using this property to specify a color rather than supplying the actual value for gray, you're assured that no matter the color scheme used on a computer, the code will clear the form to the proper system color.

Enter the following statement. (Note: Do not press Enter until you're finished entering *all* the code shown here. The code appears on two lines only because of the size restriction of this page.)

```
objGraphics.DrawRectangle(Pens.Blue, picShowPicture.Left - 1,
picShowPicture.Top - 1, picShowPicture.Width + 1, picShowPicture.Height + 1)
```

This statement draws a blue rectangle around the picture on the form. Within this statement is a single method call and five property references. Can you tell what's what? Immediately following objGraphics (and a dot) is DrawRectangle. Because no equals sign is present but there is an open parenthesis, you can deduce that this is a method call. As with the Clear() method, the parentheses after DrawRectangle are used to enclose values passed to the method.

The DrawRectangle() method accepts the following parameters in the order in which they appear here:

- ▶ A pen
- ▶ X value of the upper-left corner
- ▶ Y value of the upper-left corner
- ▶ Width of the rectangle
- ▶ Height of the rectangle

The DrawRectangle() method draws a prefect rectangle using the X, Y, Width, and Height values passed to it. The attributes of the line (color, width, and so on) are determined by the pen specified in the Pen parameter. (I won't go into detail on pens here; check the online help if pens interest you.) Looking at the dots once more, notice that you're passing the Blue property of the Pens object. Blue is an object property that returns a predefined Pen object that has a width of 1 pixel and the color blue.

For the next two parameters, you pass property values. Specifically, you pass the top and left values for the picture, less 1. If you passed the exact left and top values, the rectangle would be drawn on the form at exactly the top and left properties of the PictureBox. You wouldn't see them because controls by default overlap any drawing performed on the form.

The last two property references are for the height and width of the PictureBox. Again, we adjust the values by 1 to ensure that the rectangle is drawn outside the borders of the PictureBox.

Finally, you have to clean up after yourself by entering the following code statement:

```
objGraphics.Dispose()
```

Objects often use other objects and resources. The underlying mechanics of an object can be mind-boggling and are almost impossible to discuss in an entry-level programming book. The net effect, however, is that you must explicitly destroy most objects when you're finished with them. If you don't destroy an object, it might persist in memory, and it might hold references to other objects or resources that exist in memory. This means that you can create a *memory leak* within your application that slowly (or rather quickly) munches system memory and resources. This is one of the cardinal no-no's of Windows programming. However, the nature of using resources and the fact that you're responsible for telling your objects to clean up after themselves make this easy to do. If your application causes memory leaks, your users won't call for a plumber, but they might reach for a monkey wrench—in an effort to smack you upside the head!

Objects that must explicitly be told to clean up after themselves usually provide a `Dispose()` method. When you're finished with such an object, call `Dispose()` on the object to make sure that it frees any resources it might be holding.

For your convenience, here are all the lines of code:

```
Dim objGraphics As Graphics
objGraphics = Me.CreateGraphics
objGraphics.Clear(System.Drawing.SystemColors.Control)

objGraphics.DrawRectangle(System.Drawing.Pens.Blue, _
   picShowPicture.Left - 1, picShowPicture.Top - 1, _
   picShowPicture.Width + 1, picShowPicture.Height + 1)

objGraphics.Dispose()
```

> **By the Way**
>
> The statement calling `DrawRectangle()` is shown here as three lines of code. At the end of the first and second lines is an underscore character (_), also known as a *line continuation character*. It tells the Visual Basic compiler that the statement immediately following the character is a continuation of the current statement. You can, and should, use this character to break up long statements in your code.

Click Save All on the toolbar to save your work before continuing.

Testing Your Object Example Project

Now the easy part: Run the project by pressing F5 or by clicking the Start button on the toolbar. Your form looks pretty much as it did at design time. Clicking the button causes a blue rectangle to be drawn around the `PictureBox`, as shown in Figure 3.7.

FIGURE 3.7
You can create
simple lines and
complex draw-
ings by using
objects.

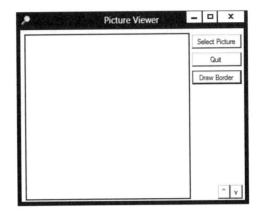

By the Way

> If you receive any errors when you attempt to run the project, go back and make
> sure that the code you entered exactly matches the code I've provided.
>
> If you use Alt+Tab to switch to another application after drawing the rectangle, the rectan-
> gle will be gone when you come back to your form. In fact, this occurs any time you over-
> lay the graphics with another form. In Hour 18, "Working with Graphics," you will learn
> how to persist images so that they don't disappear when the form becomes obscured.

Stop the project now by clicking Stop Debugging on the Visual Basic toolbar. What I
hope you've gained from building this example is not necessarily that you can now
draw a rectangle (which is cool), but rather an understanding of how objects are used
in programming. As with learning almost anything, repetition aids understanding.
That said, you'll be working with objects *a lot* throughout this book.

Understanding Collections

A *collection* is just what its name implies: a collection of objects. Collections make it
easy to work with large numbers of similar objects by enabling you to create code
that performs iterative processing on items within the collection. *Iterative processing* is
an operation that uses a loop to perform actions on multiple objects, rather than
requiring you to write the operative code for each object. In addition to containing an
indexed set of objects, collections have properties and might have methods. Figure 3.8
illustrates the structure of a collection.

Continuing with the Dog/Pet object metaphor, think about what an Animals collection might look like. The Animals collection might contain one or more pet objects,
or it might be empty (contain no objects). All collections have a Count property that
returns the total count of objects contained in the collection. Collections might also
have methods, such as a Delete() method used to remove objects from the collection, and an Add() method used to add a new object to the collection.

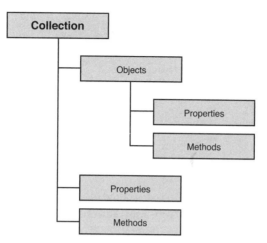

FIGURE 3.8
Collections contain sets of like objects, and they have their own properties and methods.

To better understand collections, you'll create a small Visual Basic project that cycles through the Controls collection of a form and tells you the value of the Name property of every control on the form. To create your sample project, follow these steps:

1. Start Visual Basic (if it's not already loaded), and create a new Windows Application project titled **Collections Example**.

2. Change the form's filename to CollectionsExampleForm.vb using the Solution Explorer (right-click Form1.vb in the Solution Explorer and choose Rename), and set the form's Text property to **Collections Example** in the Properties window (you need to click the form first to view its properties).

3. Add a new button to the form by double-clicking the Button tool in the toolbox. Set the button's properties as follows:

Property	Value
Name	btnShowNames
Location	88, 112
Size	120, 23
Text	Show Control Names

4. Next, add some Text Box and Label controls to the form. As you add the controls to the form, be sure to give each control a unique name. Feel free to use any name you want, but you can't use spaces in a control name. You might want to drag the controls to different locations on the form so that they don't overlap.

5. When you're finished adding controls to your form, double-click the Show Control Names button to add code to its `Click` event. Enter the following code:

```
Dim intIndex As Integer
For intIndex = 0 To Me.Controls.Count - 1
    MessageBox.Show("Control #" & intIndex & " has the name " & _
        Me.Controls(intIndex).Name)
Next intIndex
```

By the Way

> Every form has a `Controls` collection, which might not contain any controls; even if no controls are on the form, the form still has a `Controls` collection.

The first statement of the preceding code should look familiar to you by now. As with the `Object` example you created earlier, this statement creates a variable to hold a value. Rather than create a variable that can hold an object, as you did in the earlier example, this statement creates a variable that can hold only a number.

The next statement (the one that begins with `For`) accomplishes a few tasks. First, it initializes the variable `intIndex` to 0, and then it starts a loop (loops are discussed in Hour 14, "Looping for Efficiency"). It increments `intIndex` by 1 until `intIndex` equals the number of controls on the form, less 1. The reason you subtract 1 from the `Count` property is that collections are 0-based—the first item is always item 0. Thus, the first item is in index 0, the second item is in location 1, and so forth. If you tried to reference an item of a collection in the location of the value of the `Count` property, an error would occur. You would be referencing an index that's 1 higher than the actual locations within the collection.

The `MessageBox.Show()` method (mentioned in Hour 2 and discussed in detail in Hour 17, "Interacting with Users") is a class of the .NET Framework that's used to display simple dialog boxes with text. The text that you're providing, which the `Show()` method displays, is a concatenation of multiple strings of text. (*Concatenation* is the process of adding strings together; it's discussed in Hour 12, "Performing Arithmetic, String Manipulation, and Date/Time Adjustments.")

Run the project by pressing F5 or by clicking Start on the toolbar. Ignore the additional controls that you placed on the form, and click the Show Control Names button. Your program then displays a message box similar to the one shown in Figure 3.9 for each control on your form (because of the loop). When the program is finished displaying the names of the controls, choose Debug, Stop Debugging to stop the program, and then save the project.

Because everything in Visual Basic 2012 is an object, you can expect to use numerous collections as you create your programs. Collections are powerful, and the quicker you become comfortable using them, the more productive you'll be.

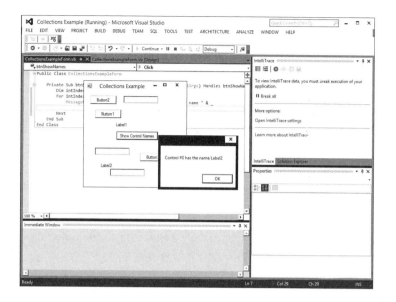

FIGURE 3.9
The Controls collection enables you to get to every control on a form.

Using the Object Browser

Visual Basic 2012 includes a useful tool that enables you to easily view members (properties, methods, and events) of all the objects in a project: the Object Browser (see Figure 3.10). This is useful when you're dealing with objects that aren't well documented because it enables you to see all the members an object supports. To view the Object Browser, press F2 or select it in the View menu.

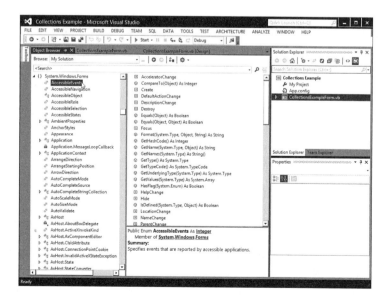

FIGURE 3.10
The Object Browser enables you to view all properties and methods of an object.

The Browse drop-down list in the upper-left corner of the Object Browser is used to determine the *browsing scope*. You can choose My Solution to view only the objects referenced in the active solution, or you can choose All Components to view all possible objects. You can customize the object set by clicking the drop-down arrow next to the Object Browser Settings button to the far right of the Browse drop-down list. I don't recommend changing the custom object setting until you have some experience using Visual Basic .NET objects, as well as experience using the Object Browser.

The top-level nodes (each item in the tree is called a *node*) in the Objects tree are libraries. *Libraries* are usually DLL or EXE files on your computer that contain one or more objects. To view the objects in a library, simply expand the library node. As you select objects within a library, the list to the right of the Objects tree shows information about the members of the selected object (refer to Figure 3.10). For even more detailed information, click a member in the list on the right. The Object Browser shows information about the member in the area below the member list.

Summary

In this hour, you learned a lot about objects. You learned how objects have properties, which are attributes that describe the object. Some properties can be set at design time in the Properties window, and most can also be set at runtime in Visual Basic code. You learned that referencing a property on the left side of the equals sign has the effect of changing the property, whereas referencing a property on the right side of the equals sign retrieves the property's value.

In addition to properties, you learned that objects have executable functions, called methods. Like properties, methods are referenced by using a dot at the end of an object reference. An object might contain many methods and properties, and some properties can even be objects themselves. You learned how to "follow the dots" to interpret a lengthy object reference.

Objects are often used as a group, called a collection. You learned that a collection often contains properties and methods, and that collections let you easily iterate through a set of like objects. Finally, you learned that the Object Browser can be used to explore all the members of an object in a project.

The knowledge you've gained in this hour is fundamental to understanding programming with Visual Basic, because objects and collections are the basis on which applications are built. After you have a strong grasp of objects and collections—and you will have by the time you've completed all the hours in this book—you'll be well on your way to fully understanding the complexities of creating robust applications with Visual Basic 2012.

Q&A

Q. *Is there an easy way to get help about an object's member?*

A. Absolutely. Visual Basic's context-sensitive Help extends to code as well as visual objects. To get help on a member, write a code statement that includes the member (it doesn't have to be a complete statement), position the cursor within the member text, and press F1. For instance, to get help on the `Integer` data type, you could type `Integer`, position the cursor within the word `Integer`, and press F1.

Q. *Are there any other types of object members besides properties and methods?*

A. Yes. An event is actually a member of an object, although it's not always thought of that way. Although not all objects support events, most objects do support properties and methods.

Workshop

Quiz

1. True or false: Visual Basic 2012 is a true object-oriented language.

2. An attribute that defines the state of an object is called a _____.

3. For you to change the value of a property, the property must be referenced on which side of the equals sign?

4. What is the term for when a new object is created from a template class?

5. An external function of an object (one that is available to code manipulating an object) is called a _____.

6. True or false: A property of an object can be another object.

7. A group of like objects is called a _____.

8. What tool is used to explore the members of an object?

Answers

1. True

2. Property

3. The left side

4. Instantiation

5. Method

6. True

7. Collection

8. The Object Browser

Exercises

1. Create a new project, and add two text boxes and a button to the form. Write code that, when a button is clicked, places the text in the first text box into the second text box. Hint: Use the `Text` property of the `TextBox` controls.

2. Modify the collections example in this hour to print the height of all controls, rather than the name.

HOUR 4

Understanding Events

What You'll Learn in This Hour:

▶ Understanding event-driven programming

▶ Triggering events

▶ Avoiding recursive events

▶ Accessing an object's events

▶ Working with event parameters

▶ Creating event handlers

▶ Keeping event names current

It's easy to produce an attractive interface for an application with Visual Basic 2012's integrated design tools. You can create beautiful forms that have buttons to click, text boxes in which to type information, picture boxes that display pictures, and many other creative and attractive elements with which users can interact. However, that's just the start of producing a Visual Basic program. In addition to designing an interface, you have to empower your program to perform actions in response to both how a user interacts with the program and how Windows interacts with the program. This is accomplished through the use of *events*. In Hour 3, "Understanding Objects and Collections," you learned about objects and their members—notably, properties and methods. In this hour, you'll learn about object events and event-driven programming, and you'll learn how to use events to make your applications responsive.

Understanding Event-Driven Programming

With traditional programming languages (often called *procedural languages*), the program itself fully dictates what code is executed, as well as *when* it's executed. When you start such a program, the first line of code in the program executes, and the code continues to execute in a completely predetermined path. The execution of code might branch and loop on occasion, but the execution path is wholly determined by the program. This often means that such a program is restricted in how it can respond to the user. For example, the program might expect text to be entered into controls on the screen in a predetermined order. This is unlike a Windows application, in which a user can interact with different parts of the interface—often in any order he or she chooses.

Visual Basic 2012 incorporates an event-driven programming model. Event-driven applications aren't bound by the constraints of procedural programs. Instead of the top-down approach of procedural languages, event-driven programs have logical sections of code placed within events. Events don't occur in a predetermined order; the user often has complete control over what code is executed in an event-driven program by interactively triggering specific events, such as by clicking a button.

Triggering Events

In Hour 3, you learned that a method is simply a function of an object. An event, in a sense, is really a special kind of method used by an object to signal state changes that might be useful to clients (code using the object). In fact, the Visual Basic 2012 documentation often calls events *methods* (something that no doubt confuses new programmers). Events are methods that can be called in special ways—usually by the user interacting with something on a form or by Windows itself—rather than being called from a statement in your code.

There are many types of events and many ways to trigger them. You've already seen how a user can trigger the event of a button by clicking it. User interaction isn't the only thing that can trigger an event; an event can be triggered in one of the following four ways:

▶ Users can trigger events by interacting with your program. Clicking a button, for example, triggers the button's `Click` event.

▶ Objects can trigger their own events as needed. The `Timer` control, for example, can trigger its `Timer` event at regular intervals.

▶ The operating system (whichever version of Windows the user is running) can trigger events.

▶ You can trigger events by calling them much as you would invoke a method when using Visual Basic code.

Events Triggered Through User Interaction

The most common way an event is triggered is when a user interacts with a program. Every form, and almost every control you can place on a form, has a set of events specific to its object type. The Button control, for example, has a number of events, including the Click event you've already used in previous hours. When the user clicks a button, the button's Click event is triggered, and then the code within the Click event executes.

The Textbox control enables users to enter information with the keyboard, and it also has a set of events. The Textbox control has some of the same types of events as the Button control, such as a Click event, but the Textbox control also has events not supported by the Button control, such as the MultilineChanged event. The MultilineChanged event occurs when the Multiline property of the text box changes. Because you can't enter text into a Button control, it doesn't have a Multiline property and therefore no MultilineChanged event. Every object that supports events supports a unique set of events.

Each type of event has its own behavior, and it's important to understand the events you work with. The TextChanged event, for example, exhibits a behavior that might not be intuitive to a new developer because the event fires each time the contents of the text box change. Consider what would happen if you were to type the following sentence into an empty text box in a project you created:

www.TigerpawSoftware.com

Although it's easy to think that the TextChanged event fires only when you commit your entry, such as by leaving the text box or pressing Enter, this isn't how it works. Instead, the TextChanged event would be triggered 24 times—once for each character typed—because each time you enter a new character, the contents of the text box change. Again, it's important to learn the nuances and the exact behavior of the events you're using. If you use events without fully understanding how they work, your program might exhibit unusual (which usually means undesirable) results.

Events Triggered by an Object

Sometimes an object triggers its own events. The most common example of this is the Timer control's Tick event. The Timer control is a nonvisual control like the common dialog control. It doesn't appear on a form when the program is running; it appears at design time in the space reserved for nonvisual controls. The Timer control's sole purpose is to trigger its Tick event at an interval specified in its Interval property.

By setting the `Timer` control's `Interval` property, you control the interval (in milliseconds) at which the `Timer` event executes. After firing its `Timer` event, a `Timer` control resets itself and fires its `Timer` event again when the interval has passed. This occurs until the interval is changed, the `Timer` control is disabled, or the `Timer` control's form is unloaded. A common use of timers is to create a clock on a form. You can display the time in a label and update it at regular intervals by placing the code to display the current time in the `Timer` event. You'll create a project with a `Timer` control in Hour 8, "Using Advanced Controls."

Events Triggered by the Operating System

The third way an event can be triggered is by Windows itself. Often, you might not even realize these events exist. For example, when a form is fully or partially obstructed by another window, the program needs to know when the offending window is resized or moved so that it can repaint the area of the window that's hidden. Windows and Visual Basic work together in this respect. When the obstructing window is moved or resized, Windows tells Visual Basic to repaint the form, which Visual Basic does. This also causes Visual Basic to raise the form's `Paint` event. You can place code into the `Paint` event to create a custom display for the form, such as drawing shapes on the form with a `Graphics` object. When you do so, your custom drawing code executes every time the form repaints itself.

Avoiding Recursive Events

You must ensure that you never create code where an event can endlessly trigger itself. This is called a *recursive* event. To illustrate a situation that causes a recursive event, think of the `Textbox` control's `TextChanged` event, discussed earlier. The `TextChanged` event fires every time the text in the text box changes. Placing code in the `TextChanged` event that alters the text in the text box causes the `Change` event to be fired again, which could result in an endless loop. Recursive events terminate when Windows returns a `StackOverflow` exception (see Figure 4.1), indicating that Windows no longer has the resources to follow the recursion.

Recursive behavior can occur with more than one event in the loop. For example, if Event A triggers Event B, which in turn triggers Event A, you can have infinite looping of the two events. Recursive behavior can take place among a sequence of many events, not just one or two.

By the Way

Uses for recursive procedures actually exist, such as when writing complex math functions or for getting all of the directories and files on a hard drive. For instance, recursive events are often used to compute factorials. However, when you purposely create a recursive event, you still have to make sure that the recursion isn't infinite.

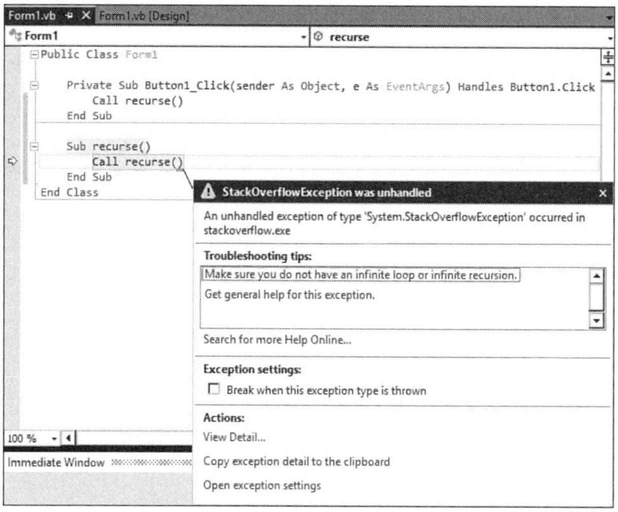

FIGURE 4.1
When you receive a Stack-Overflow exception, you should look for a recursive event as the culprit.

Accessing an Object's Events

Accessing an object's events is simple. If you've been following the examples in this book, you've already accessed a number of objects' default events. To access an object's events, you double-click the object in Form Design view.

You'll now create a project to get a feel for working with events. Start Visual Basic 2012, create a new Windows Application project named View Events, and then follow these steps:

1. Right-click Form1.vb in the Solutions Explorer and choose Rename. Change the filename to **ViewEventsForm.vb**. Next, change the Text property of the form to **View Events Example**. Remember, you will have to click the form once to select it in order to see its properties.

2. Use the toolbox to add a picture box to the form.

3. Change the name of the picture box to **picText**, and then double-click the picture box to access its event procedures.

Your screen should look like the one shown in Figure 4.2. Notice the two combo boxes at the top of the code window. One contains the word picText, and the other reads Click. The combo box on the left contains a list of all the objects of the current form (including the form itself and all its controls). The combo box on the right contains all the events for the object selected in the first drop-down list.

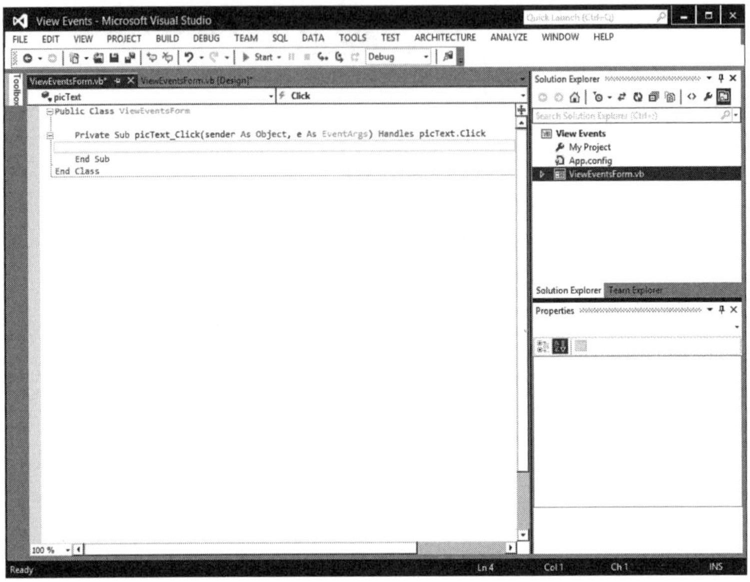

FIGURE 4.2
Use the events
drop-down list in
the code editor
to create event
procedures.

Currently, you're viewing the `Click` event for the `picText` object. The cursor is placed within the `Click` event procedure, ready for you to enter code. The code statement above the cursor is the *event declaration*—a statement that defines the structure of an event. Notice that this event declaration contains the name of the object, an underscore character (_), and then the event name. Following the event name is a set of parentheses. The items within the parentheses are called *parameters*, which are the topic of the next section. This is the standard declaration structure for an event procedure.

Click the events drop-down list (the list on the right), and take a look at all the events that the picture box supports. Select `MouseDown` from the list (see Figure 4.3), and notice how your code window changes.

When you select an event from the list, Visual Basic creates a new event procedure for that event. The full event declaration is shown here:

```
Private Sub picText_MouseDown(ByVal sender As Object, _
                ByVal e As MouseEventArgs) _
                Handles picText.MouseDown
```

Notice that the new event declaration is similar to the first one in the window in that it's titled with the object's name followed by an underscore. However, the remainder of the event procedure declaration is different. It's the name of the event—in this case, `MouseDown`.

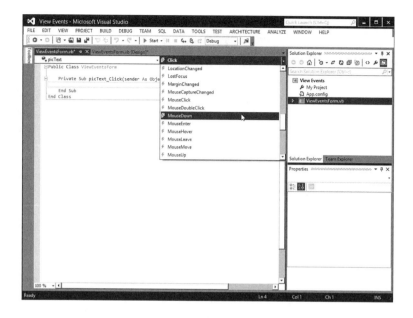

FIGURE 4.3
Visual Basic creates an empty event procedure the first time you select an object's event.

> The words *Private* and *Sub* are Visual Basic reserved words that indicate the scope and type of the procedure. Scope and type are discussed in Hour 10, "Creating and Calling Code Procedures."

By the Way

Working with Event Parameters

As mentioned previously, the items within the parentheses of an event declaration are called *parameters*. An event parameter is a variable that's created and assigned a value by Visual Basic. These parameter variables are used to get, and sometimes set, relevant information within the event. This data may be text, a number, an object—almost anything. Multiple parameters within an event procedure are always separated by commas. As you can see, the MouseDown event has two parameters. When the event procedure is triggered, Visual Basic automatically creates the parameter variables and assigns them values for use in this single execution of the event procedure. The next time the event procedure occurs, the values in the parameters are reset. You use the values in the parameters to make decisions or perform operations in your code.

The MouseDown event of a form has the following parameters:

```
ByVal sender As Object
```

and

```
ByVal e As MouseEventArgs
```

For now, ignore the ByVal keywords. These are discussed in Hour 11, "Using Constants, Data Types, Variables, and Arrays."

The text following ByVal is the name of the parameter, and the string after the word As indicates the type of data the parameter contains. The first parameter, sender, holds a generic object. Object parameters can be any type of object supported by Visual Basic. Some contain text, others contain numbers, and still others (many others) contain objects. In the case of the sender parameter, it always holds a reference to the control causing the event.

The e parameter of the MouseDown event, on the other hand, is where the real action is. The e parameter also holds an object, and in this case the object is of type MouseEventArgs. This object has properties that relate to the MouseDown event. To see them, type in the following code, but don't press anything after entering the dot (period):

```
e.
```

When you enter the period, you get a drop-down list showing you the members (properties and methods) of the e object, as shown in Figure 4.4. Using the e object, you can determine a number of things about the occurrence of the MouseDown event. Table 4.1 lists some of the more interesting items.

FIGURE 4.4
IntelliSense drop-down lists alleviate the need to memorize the makeup of hundreds of objects.

TABLE 4.1 Commonly Used Members of MouseEventArgs

Property	Description
Clicks	Returns the number of times the user clicked the mouse button.
Button	Returns the button that was clicked (left, middle, right).
Delta	Returns a positive or negative number indicating the number of clicks performed (forward or backward) with the mouse wheel.
X	Returns the horizontal coordinate at which the pointer was located when the user clicked.
Y	Returns the vertical coordinate at which the pointer was located when the user clicked.
Location	Returns a Point object that contains the X and Y coordinates at which the pointer was located when the user clicked.

Each time the event occurs, Visual Basic initializes the parameters so that they always reflect the current occurrence of the event.

By the Way

Each event has parameters specific to it. For instance, the TextChanged event returns parameters that are different from the MouseDown event. As you work with events—and you'll work with a *lot* of events—you'll quickly become familiar with the parameters of each event type. You'll learn how to create parameters for your own functions and procedures in Hour 10.

Building an Event Example Project

You'll now learn how to use the MouseMove event by modifying the Picture Viewer project of Hour 3. You'll make it so that as a user moves the mouse over a picture, the cursor's x- and y-coordinates are displayed on the form. You'll use the e parameter to get the coordinates of the mouse pointer.

Go ahead and open the Picture Viewer project you completed in Hour 3 now. If prompted to save your changes, answer No. If you don't have this project, you can download it from my website.

Creating the User Interface

You'll need two Label controls on the form—one for the X value and one for the Y value. Label controls are used to display static text; users can't type text into a label.

Start by double-clicking ViewerForm.vb in the Solutions Explorer window to display the form, and then add a Label control to the form by double-clicking the Label tool in the toolbox. Set its properties as follows:

Property	Value
Name	lblX
Location	300, 110
Text	X:

Use the toolbox to add one more Label control to the form. Set its properties as follows:

Property	Value
Name	lblY
Location	300, 125
Text	Y:

Your form should now look like the one shown in Figure 4.5. It's a good idea to save frequently, so save your project now by clicking the Save All button on the toolbar.

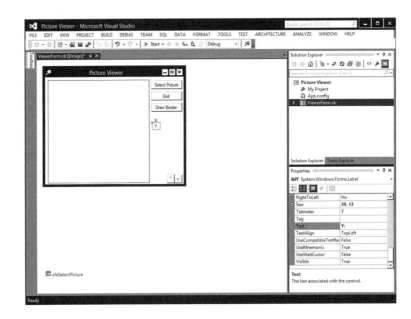

Creating Event Handlers

The interface for this example is complete—now on to the fun part. You're going to create an event procedure that empowers the program to do something. The first event that we're interested in is the MouseMove event. Double-click the picture box on the form to access its event procedures. When you double-click a control, the event procedure that's created is always for the default event for the type of control. For picture boxes, this is the Click event. We're not interested in the Click event at this time, however. Open the event list (the drop-down list in the upper right), and then select MouseMove in the list. Visual Basic creates a new MouseMove procedure for the text box.

Notice that Visual Basic left the default event procedure it created for you. It's best not to leave dead code (code that isn't used), so delete the Click event procedure now.

To fully delete the event procedure, you must delete *all* the following code:

```
Private Sub picShowPicture_Click(ByVal sender As Object, _
    ByVal e As EventArgs) _
    Handles picShowPicture.Click

End Sub
```

After you've deleted the procedure, your code should look like Figure 4.6.

FIGURE 4.6
Each time you select a new event, Visual Basic creates an empty event procedure—if one wasn't created previously for the control.

Now, place the cursor on the line between the Private Sub and End Sub statements of the picShowPicture_MouseMove procedure.

Enter the following code into the `MouseMove` event procedure:

```
lblX.Text = "X: " & e.X
lblY.Text = "Y: " & e.Y
```

This code is simple, and it may already make sense to you. If it's still not clear, it will be soon. Consider the first line of code (called a *statement*). `lblX.Text` is on the left of the equals sign, so `Text` is a property of the label, and you'll set it to some value. The text `"X: "` is a literal value that we're placing in the `Text` property of the `Label` control. The reason you include this literal is that when you set the `Text` property, you overwrite the property's current value. So, even though you entered X: as the property in the properties window, you need to include it when setting the property as well. To make this useful, we also have to include the actual value for X, which is stored in the X property of the e object. Again, we're *concatenating* the literal value of `"X: "` with the value stored in `e.X`. The second statement does the same thing, only with the Y value.

The nice thing about objects is that you don't have to commit every detail about them to memory. For example, you don't need to memorize the return values for each type of button. (Who wants to remember `e.X`, `e.Y`, or `e.Button`, anyway?) Just remember that the e parameter contains information about the event. When you type e and press the period, the IntelliSense drop-down list appears and shows you the members of e. Don't feel overwhelmed by all the object references you'll encounter throughout this book. Simply accept that you can't memorize them all, nor do you need to; you'll learn the ones that are important, and you'll use Help when you're stuck. Also, after you know the parent object in a situation (such as the e object in this example), it's easy for you to determine the objects and members that belong to it by using the IntelliSense drop-down lists.

Click the Save All button in the toolbar to save your work. (You wouldn't want to lose it!) Next, press F5 to run the project, and move the mouse pointer over the picture box. You'll see the coordinates of the pointer (as it relates to the picture box) displayed in the two `Label` controls you created, as shown in Figure 4.7.

Now, move the mouse pointer off the picture box. Notice that the labels display the last coordinate that the pointer moved over on the picture box. The `MouseMove` event fires *only* when the mouse pointer is moved *over* the control to which the event is attached: the picture box in this example. We can't just leave those numbers dangling there, can we?

The `PictureBox` just so happens to have another event you can use to fix this: the `MouseLeave` event. Oddly enough, the `MouseLeave` event fires when the mouse pointer leaves the control's space. (Woot—something that's actually intuitive!) Follow these steps to clear the coordinates when the pointer leaves the picture box:

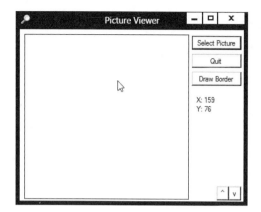

FIGURE 4.7
The MouseMove
event makes it
easy to track the
pointer over a
control.

1. Stop the project if it's still running by closing the Picture Viewer form.

2. Open the Events drop-down list for the `picShowPicture` control, and
   choose `MouseLeave`. If you don't see this event, you will need to reselect
   `picShowPicture` in the left combo box.

3. Enter the following code into the `MouseLeave` event:

```
lblX.Text = ""
lblY.Text = ""
```

Press F5 to run the project again. Move the mouse pointer over the picture box and
then off it. Notice that the coordinates go away. Move the pointer over the picture
box again, and they reappear—perfect! Go ahead and stop the running project now.

There's only one thing left to do. Did you notice that when you first start the project,
the labels have "X:" and "Y:" in them? Wouldn't it be better to not display this text
until the user mouses over the picture box? You could set the Text properties of these
labels to empty by using the Properties window. However, if you do this, you won't see
the labels on the form in the designer and may place other controls over the top of
them. A better solution is to initialize their values when the form first loads. You'll do
just that by following these steps:

1. Open the object drop-down list in the upper left and select (ViewerForm Events).
   This is the object reference to your form (see Figure 4.8).

FIGURE 4.8
The form itself
always appears
at the top of the
object list.

2. Open the event drop-down list in the upper-right corner and choose Load. The Load event executes automatically when the form first loads—the perfect place to initialize the Label controls.

3. Enter the following two code statements:

```
lblX.Text = ""
lblY.Text = ""
```

That's it—you're finished! Go ahead and press F5 to run the project and give it a test drive. When the form first loads, the coordinate labels should be empty (this makes them appear invisible). When you mouse over the picture box, the coordinates are displayed, and when you leave the confines of the picture box, the coordinates are hidden again. A little bit of code and the right event selection can go a long way.

Keeping Event Names Current

As you know, the name of an event procedure is defined by the control's name, followed by an underscore and then the event name (such as txtAddress_TextChanged). When you change the name of a control, Visual Basic doesn't change the control's event declarations to reflect the new name, but it does keep the event attached to the control. The way this works is that at the end of each event declaration is the keyword Handles, followed by an object name. The Handles keyword effectively "hooks up" an event handler to the event of a control. When you change the name of a control, Visual Basic changes the Handles reference, but it doesn't change the event name itself. Although your code will work, you should manually change the name of the corresponding procedures so that they match the new name of the control. This will help a lot when you debug complicated code.

Although Visual Basic doesn't update the name of event procedures when you change the name of a control, it updates any references to the control you have in other procedures. This is a great time-saving feature that is relatively new to Visual Basic.

Did you Know?

Summary

In this hour, you learned about event-driven programming, including what events are, how to trigger them, and how to avoid recursive events. In addition, you learned how to access an object's events and how to work with parameters. Much of the code you write will execute in response to an event of some kind, and you'll often write code for multiple events of one control. By understanding how events work, including being aware of the available events and their parameters, you'll be able to create complex Visual Basic programs that react to a multitude of user and system input.

Q&A

Q. *Is it possible to create custom events for an object?*

A. Yes, you can create custom events for your own objects (you'll learn about such objects in Hour 16, "Designing Objects Using Classes"), and you can also create them for existing objects. Creating custom events for existing Visual Basic objects, however, is beyond the scope of this book.

Q. *Is it possible for objects that don't have an interface to support events?*

A. Yes. To use the events of such an object, however, the object variable must be dimensioned a special way, or the events aren't available. This gets a little tricky and is beyond the scope of this book. If you have an object in code that supports events, look in Help for the keyword WithEvents for information on how to use such events.

Workshop

Quiz

1. Name three things that can cause events to occur.

2. True or false: All objects support the same set of events.

3. What is the default event type for a button?

4. What is it called when you write code in an event that causes that same event to be triggered, setting off a chain reaction of the event triggered repeatedly?

5. What is the easiest way to access a control's default event handler?

6. All control events pass a reference to the control causing the event. What is the name of the parameter that holds this reference?

7. What should you do when you change a control's name?

Answers

1. User input, system input, and other code

2. False

3. `Click`

4. Recursion

5. Double-click the control in the form designer

6. `sender`

7. Change the name of its defined events accordingly

Exercises

1. Use the knowledge you've gained so far to create a new project with a form that is gray at design time but that appears blue when it is displayed.

2. Create a project with a form and a text box. Add code to the `TextChange` event to cause a recursion when the user types in text. Hint: Concatenate a character to the end of the user's text, using a statement such as

   ```
   TextBox1.Text = TextBox1.Text & "a"
   ```

   The ampersand tells Visual Basic to add the letter a to the end of the existing text box contents. Notice how you eventually get a Stack Over-Flow error—not a good thing!

HOUR 5

Building Forms: The Basics

With few exceptions, forms are the cornerstone of every Windows application interface. Forms are essentially windows, and the two terms are often used interchangeably. More accurately, *window* refers to what the user sees and interacts with, whereas *form* refers to what you see when you design. Forms enable users to view and enter information in a program (such as the form you built in your Picture Viewer program in Hour 1, "Jumping in with Both Feet: A Visual Basic 2012 Programming Tour"). Such information may be text, pictures, graphs—almost anything that can be seen on the screen. Understanding how to design forms correctly enables you to begin creating solid interface foundations for your programs.

Think of a form as a canvas on which you build your program's interface. On this canvas, you can print text, draw shapes, and place controls with which users can interact. The wonderful thing about Visual Basic forms is that they behave like a dynamic canvas. Not only can you adjust a form's appearance by manipulating what's on it, you also can manipulate specific properties of the form itself.

In previous hours, you manipulated the following form appearance properties:

▶ `Text`

▶ `Height`

▶ `Left`

▶ `Top`

▶ `Width`

The ability to tailor your forms goes far beyond these basic property manipulations, as you'll see.

There's so much to cover about Windows forms that I've broken the material into two hours. In this hour, you'll learn the basics of forms—adding them to a project, manipulating their properties, and showing and hiding them using Visual Basic code. Although you've done some of these things in previous hours, here you'll learn the nuts and bolts of the tasks you've performed. In the next hour, you'll learn more advanced form techniques.

Changing a Form's Name

The first thing you should do when you create a new object is give it a descriptive name, so that's the first thing I'll talk about in this hour. Start by opening the Picture Viewer project you completed in Hour 4, "Understanding Events." If you don't have this project, you can download it from my website.

Your Picture Viewer currently has some useful functionality, but it's not very flexible. In this hour, you'll start building an Options dialog box for the program. Add a new form for the dialog box by following these steps:

1. Choose Project, Add Windows Form to display the Add New Item dialog box.

2. In the Name text box, enter **OptionsForm.vb**. This will be the name of your form as well as the name of the file that defines the form on the hard drive.

3. Click the Add button (or double-click the Windows Form icon) to close the Add New Item dialog box and add the form to your project (see Figure 5.1).

You can use the Properties window to change the name of a form at any time. Doing so changes the form's `Name` property (but not the name of the file on the hard disk). Whenever possible, give your forms solid names when creating them.

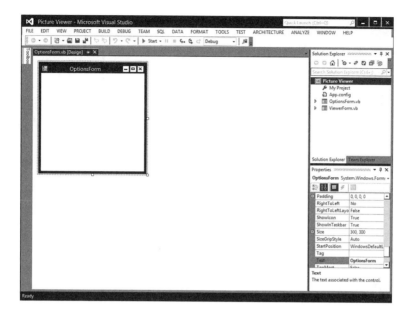

FIGURE 5.1
Each new form starts off as a blank canvas.

Changing a Form's Appearance

The Properties window can actually show two different sets of properties for a form. Clicking the form in the designer shows the form's development properties, which should be visible now, whereas clicking the form's name in the Solution Explorer shows you the form's physical file properties (see Figure 5.2). This is why I usually tell you to click the form before setting its properties.

Take a moment to browse the form's properties in the Properties window. In this hour, I'll show you how to use the form's more common properties to tailor its appearance.

Displaying Text on a Form's Title Bar

You should always set the text in a form's title bar to something meaningful. (Not all forms have title bars, as you'll see later in this hour.) The text displayed in the title bar is the value placed in the form's Text property. Generally, the text should be one of the following:

▶ **The name of the program:** This is most appropriate when the form is the program's main or only form. You used the name of the program for your main form when you defined it in Hour 1.

▶ **The purpose of the form:** This is perhaps the most common type of text displayed in a title bar. For example, if a form is used to select a printer, consider setting the Text property to **Select Printer**. When you take this approach, use active voice (for instance, don't use **Printer Select**).

FIGURE 5.2
File properties
can be useful,
but they don't
allow you to do
much with the
form.

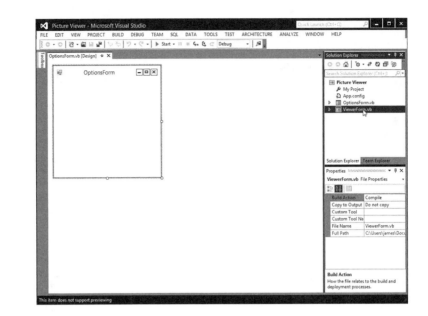

▶ **The name of the form:** If you choose to place the form's name in the form's title bar, use the English name, not the actual form name. For instance, if you've used a naming convention and you named a form LoginForm, use the text **Login** or **User Login**.

Change the Text property of your form to **Picture Viewer Options**. Remember, you may have to click the form to select it and see its properties. Your form should now look like the one shown in Figure 5.3.

As with most other form properties, you can change the Text property at any time using Visual Basic code.

Changing a Form's Background Color

Although most forms appear with a gray background (this is part of the standard 3D color scheme in Windows), you can change a form's background to any color you want. To change a form's background color, you change its BackColor property. The BackColor property is a unique property in that you can specify a named color or an RGB value in the format red, green, blue.

By default, the BackColor property is set to the color named Control. This color is a system color and might not be gray. When Windows is installed, it's configured to a default color scheme. In the default scheme for all Windows versions earlier than XP, the color for forms and other objects is the familiar "battleship gray." For XP, Vista, and Windows 7 installations, this color is a light tan (although it still looks gray on most monitors). As a Windows user, you're free to change any system color you want. For instance, some people with color blindness prefer to change their system colors to colors that have more contrast than the defaults so that objects are more clearly distinguishable. When you assign a system color to a form or control, the object's appearance adjusts itself to the current user's system color scheme. This doesn't just occur when a form is first displayed; changes to the system color scheme are immediately propagated to all objects that use the affected colors.

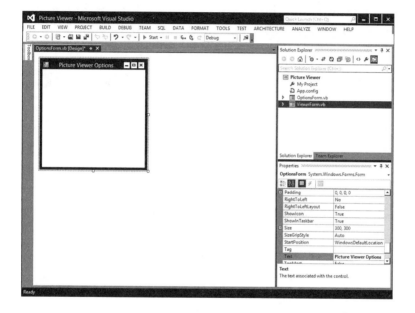

FIGURE 5.3
Use common sense when setting title bar text.

> Try to use system colors whenever possible. This will make your application behave as closely as possible to what the user expects and will avoid problems such as using colors that are indistinguishable from one another to someone who is color-blind.

By the Way

Change your form's background color by deleting the word Control in the BackColor property in the Properties window. In its place, enter **0,0,255** and press Enter or Tab to commit your entry. When you commit the entry, the RGB value changes to the word Blue. If Visual Basic has a named color that matches your RGB values, it automatically switches to the name for you.

Your form should now be blue, because you entered an RGB value in which you specified no red, no green, and maximum blue (color values range from 0 to 255). In reality, you'll probably rarely enter RGB values. Instead, you'll select colors from color palettes. To view color palettes from which you can select a color for the BackColor property, click the drop-down arrow in the BackColor property in the Properties window, as shown in Figure 5.4.

FIGURE 5.4
All color properties have palettes from which you can choose a color.

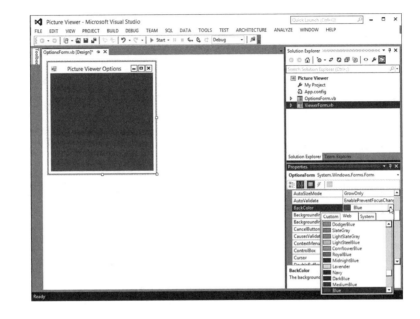

System colors are discussed in detail in Hour 18, "Working with Graphics."

When the drop-down list appears, the color blue is selected on the Web tab. Again, this happens because when you enter the RGB value 0,0,255, Visual Basic looks for a named color composed of the same values and finds blue. The color palettes were explained in Hour 2, "Navigating Visual Basic 2012," so I won't go into detail about them here. For now, select the System tab to see a list of the available system colors. Choose Control from the list to change your form's BackColor property back to the default Windows color.

Adding an Image to a Form's Background

In addition to changing the color of a form's background, you can place a picture on it. To add a picture to a form, set the form's BackgroundImage property. When you add an image to a form, the image is painted on the form's background. All the controls that you place on the form appear on top of the picture.

Add an image to your form by following these steps:

1. Click the form to select it.

2. Change the form's Size property to **400, 300**.

3. Click the BackgroundImage property in the Properties window.

4. Click the Build button that appears next to the property (the small button with three dots).

5. The Select Resource dialog box appears, as shown in Figure 5.5. Click the Local Resource option button.

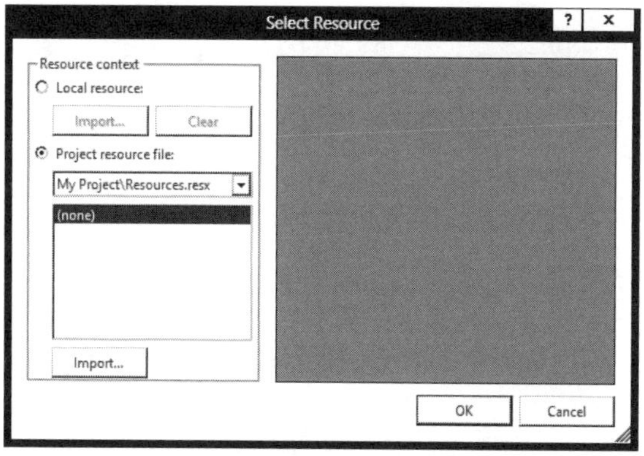

FIGURE 5.5
Images on your hard drive are considered local resources.

6. Click Import and locate the file Options.bmp, which you can get from downloading the example files from my website.

7. You are returned to the Select Resource dialog box. Click OK to load the picture. The selected image is displayed on the form's background, as shown in Figure 5.6.

If the image you select is smaller than the form, Visual Basic displays additional copies of the picture, creating a tiled effect. The image you just selected was specifically made to be the same size as the form, so you don't have to worry about this.

Notice that to the left of the BackgroundImage property in the Properties window is a small box containing a plus sign. This indicates that the BackgroundImage property has related properties, or *subproperties*. Click the plus sign to expand the list of subproperties, as shown in Figure 5.7. In the case of the BackgroundImage property, Visual Basic shows you a number of properties related to the image assigned to the property, such as its dimensions and image format. Note that these subproperties are read-only (with the exception of the Tag property); not all subproperties are read-only.

Adding a background image to a form can add pizzazz to a program, but it can also confuse users by making the form unnecessarily busy. Try to avoid adding images just because you can. Use discretion, and add an image to a form only when the image adds value to the interface.

Did you Know?

FIGURE 5.6
A form can display a picture, just as a picture box does.

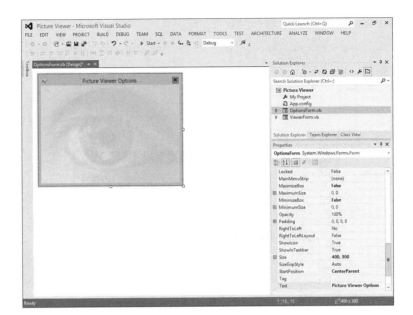

FIGURE 5.7
The subproperties show you details about the image.

Removing an image from a form is just as easy as adding the image in the first place. To remove the picture you just added to your form, right-click the BackgroundImage property name and choose Reset from the shortcut menu that appears. You must right-click the Name column of the property or right-click the Build button in the Value column, but don't right-click the Value column itself. If you right-click the property's value, you get a different shortcut menu that doesn't have a Reset option. Feel free to try this, but load the image again before continuing.

Giving a Form an Icon

The icon assigned to a form appears on the left side of the form's title bar, in the taskbar when the form is minimized, and in the iconic list of tasks when you press Alt+Tab to switch to another application, as well as in other places. The icon often represents the application; therefore, you should assign an icon to any form that a user can minimize. If you don't assign an icon to a form, Visual Basic supplies a default icon to represent the form when it's minimized. This default icon is generic and unattractive and doesn't really represent anything; you should avoid it.

In the past, it was recommended that every form have a unique icon that represented the form's purpose. This proved difficult to accomplish in large applications containing dozens or even hundreds of forms. Instead, it's usually just best to set the Icon property of all your forms to the icon that best represents your application. Because you used the Properties window to set the icon of the main form in Hour 1, you'll use that icon again, but you'll do it with Visual Basic code. To assign the main icon to your form, follow these steps:

1. Double-click the form in the Form Designer to access its default event: the Load event.

2. Enter the following code statement into the Load event:

   ```
   Me.Icon = ViewerForm.Icon
   ```

Recall from earlier that Me represents the form in which the code resides—your Options form. This code sets the Options form icon to the icon of the Picture Viewer form (your main form). Now, if you change the icon of the main form in design view, you can be certain that the Options form will always appear with the proper icon. If you were to use the Properties window to set an icon for the Options form, you would lose this flexibility.

Adding Minimize, Maximize, and Control Box Buttons to a Form

Click the OptionsForm.vb [Design]* tab at the top of the work area to switch to the Form Designer. Take a look at the title bar of the Picture Viewer Options form that you've created, and notice that it has three buttons on it, as shown in Figure 5.8.

The three buttons in the form's title bar are

▶ Minimize

▶ Maximize

▶ Close

FIGURE 5.8
You control
which, if any, of
these buttons
are displayed.

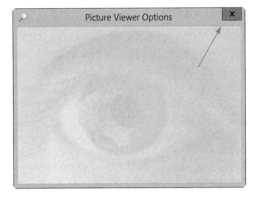

Also note that the form's icon acts as a button as well, but only while the application is running, not while it is in design mode. If the user clicks the icon, a drop-down menu appears with some basic options, as shown in Figure 5.9.

FIGURE 5.9
A form's icon
acts like a
button.

The Minimize and Maximize buttons make it easy for a user to quickly hide a form or make it fill the entire display, respectively. You've probably used these buttons on applications you work with. You'll be happy to know that you don't have to write code to implement this—Windows handles it automatically. All you have to do is decide whether you want a Maximize or Minimize button on a form. In the case of this Options form, the contents won't be resizable, so there's no need for a Maximize button. Also, you'll want the user to close the form when she's finished with it, so there's no need for a Minimize button either. To remove these buttons, set the following properties of the form:

Property	Value
MaximizeBox	False
MinimizeBox	False

If you don't want the user to be able to close the form with the Close button (the button with the X in the upper-right corner of the form), you would set the `ControlBox` property to `False`. Be aware, however, that the Minimize and Maximize buttons are hidden automatically when `ControlBox` is set to `False`. If you want a Minimize or Maximize button, you have to set `ControlBox = True`.

Changing the Appearance and Behavior of a Form's Border

You might have noticed while working with other Windows programs that the borders of forms can vary. Some forms have borders that you can click and drag to change the size of the form, some have fixed borders that can't be changed, and still others have no borders at all. The appearance and behavior of a form's border are controlled by its `FormBorderStyle` property.

The `FormBorderStyle` property can be set to one of the following values:

- ▶ `None`
- ▶ `FixedSingle`
- ▶ `Fixed3D`
- ▶ `FixedDialog`
- ▶ `Sizable`
- ▶ `FixedToolWindow`
- ▶ `SizableToolWindow`

Run your project now by pressing F5, and move the mouse pointer over one of the borders of your main Picture Viewer form. This form has a sizable border, which means that you can resize the form by dragging the border. Move the pointer over an edge of the form. Notice how the pointer changes from a large arrow to a line with arrows pointing to either side, indicating the direction in which you can stretch the border. When you move the pointer over a corner, you get a diagonal cursor that indicates that you can stretch both of the sides that meet at the corner. Clicking and dragging the border changes the size of the form.

Stop the project now by choosing Debug, Stop Debugging (or click the Close button on the form), and change the OptionsForm form's `FormBorderStyle` property to None. Notice that the title bar disappears as well, as shown in Figure 5.10. Of course, when the title bar is gone, there's no visible title bar text, no control box, and no Minimize or Maximize buttons. In addition, there's no way to move or resize the form. It's rarely appropriate to specify None for a form's `BorderStyle`, but if you need to do so (making a splash screen comes to mind), Visual Basic 2012 makes it possible.

FIGURE 5.10
A form with no
border also has
no title bar.

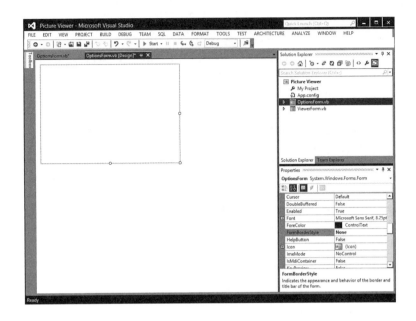

Next, change the OptionsForm form's `FormBorderStyle` property to `FixedToolWindow`.
This setting causes the form's title bar to appear smaller than normal and the text to be
displayed in a smaller font, as shown in Figure 5.11. In addition, the only thing displayed on the title bar besides the text is a Close button. Visual Basic's various design
windows, such as the Properties window and the toolbox, are good examples of tool
windows.

FIGURE 5.11
A tool window is
a special window
whose title bar
takes up the
minimum space
possible.

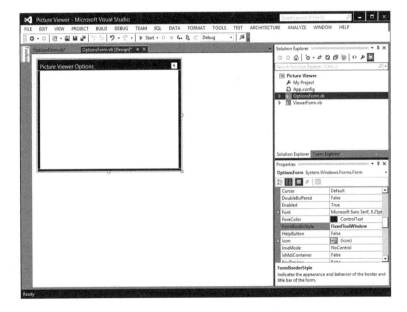

The FormBorderStyle offers a good example of how changing a single property can greatly affect an object's appearance and behavior. Set the form's FormBorderStyle back to FixedSingle before continuing.

Controlling a Form's Minimum and Maximum Size

Ordinarily, if a form can be resized, it can be maximized to fill the user's entire display. The form can be minimized right down to the taskbar as well. If you want to restrict a form's minimum or maximum size, set the MinimumSize or MaximumSize properties, respectively. In general, you should avoid doing this, but it can be useful. Be aware that setting a specific MinimumSize doesn't stop the user from minimizing the form if it has a minimize button.

Showing and Hiding Forms

Part III, "Making Things Happen—Programming," is devoted to programming in Visual Basic 2012. I've avoided going into much programming detail in this hour so that you can focus on the concepts at hand. However, knowing how to create forms does nothing for you if you don't have a way to show and hide them. Visual Basic 2012 can display a single form automatically only when a program starts. To display other forms, you have to write code.

Showing Forms

There are a couple of ways to show a form, and you'll learn about the most common methods in this section.

Now you'll make it so that the user of your Picture Viewer program can display the Options form you've built. Follow these steps to add this functionality to your program:

1. Double-click ViewerForm.vb in the Solution Explorer to display the main form in the designer.

2. Right-click the Draw Border button, and choose Copy from the shortcut menu.

3. Right-click the form (somewhere below the X and Y labels) and choose Paste.

4. Set the properties of your new button as follows:

Property	Value
Name	btnOptions
Location	295, 155
Text	Options

5. Double-click the Options button to access its `Click` event.

6. Enter the following code:

```
OptionsForm.Show()
```

Press F5 to run the project, and click the Options button. The Options form appears on top of the main Picture Viewer form. Click the title bar of the Picture Viewer form (the form in the background). Notice how this brings the Picture Viewer form to the front and obscures the Options form. There will be times when you want this behavior. However, many times you won't. For most forms, it's desirable to force the focus to the form with which the user is working and make the user dismiss the form before working with another. In the next section, you'll learn how to change this behavior. Stop the running project before continuing.

Understanding Form Modality

You can present two types of forms to the user: modal and nonmodal. A *nonmodal window* is one that doesn't cause other windows to be disabled. (When you used `Show()` to display the Options form, you displayed it as a nonmodal form. This is why you could click over to the main Picture Viewer form while the Options form remained displayed.) Another example of a nonmodal window is the Find and Replace window in Word (and in Visual Basic 2012, as well). When the Find and Replace window is visible, the user can still access other windows.

On the other hand, when a form is displayed as a *modal* form, all other forms in the same application become disabled until the modal form is closed; the other forms won't accept any keyboard or mouse input. The user is forced to deal with only the modal form. After the modal form is closed, the user is free to work with other visible forms within the program. If the form was displayed by another modal form, that form retains the focus until closed, and so on. Modal forms are most often used to create dialog boxes in which the user works with a specific set of data and controls before moving on. The Print dialog box of Microsoft Word, for example, is a modal dialog box. When the Print dialog box is displayed, you can't work with the document on the main Word window until the Print dialog box is closed. Most secondary windows in any given program are modal windows.

By the Way

You can display one modal form from another modal form, but you cannot display a nonmodal form from a modal form.

A form's modality is determined by how you *show* the form rather than by how you *create* it. (Both modal and nonmodal forms are created the same way.) You already learned that to show a form as a nonmodal window, you use the form's Show() method. To show a form as a modal form, you call the form's ShowDialog() method instead. Change the code in your button's Click event to read as follows:

```
OptionsForm.ShowDialog()
```

When your code looks like this, press F5 to run the project. Click the Options button to display your Options form. Drag the form away from the main form just a bit, and then try to click the main Picture Viewer form or some control on it; you can't. Close the modal form now by clicking the Close button in the title bar. Now the main Picture Viewer form is enabled again, and you can click the Options button once more (or any other button of your choosing). When you're finished testing this, stop the running project.

Did you Know?

You can test to see whether a form has been shown modally by testing the form's Modal property in code.

Displaying a Form in a Normal, Maximized, or Minimized State

Using a form's Size and Location properties in conjunction with the StartPosition property enables you to display forms at any location and at any size. You can also force a form to appear minimized or maximized. Whether a form is maximized, minimized, or shown normally is known as the form's *state*, and it's determined by the form's WindowState property.

Click the OptionsForm.vb [Design] tab to view the form designer. Look at your form's WindowState property now in the Properties window. New forms have their WindowState property set to Normal by default. When you run the project, as you have several times, the form displays in the same size as that in which it appears in the form designer and at the location specified by the form's Location property. Now change the WindowState property to Minimized. Nothing happens in the Form Design view, but run your project by pressing F5, and then click the Options button. At first, you might think the form didn't get displayed, but it did. It just appeared minimized to the taskbar.

Stop the project and change the WindowState property to Maximized. Again, nothing happens in the Form Design view. Press F5 to run the project, and then click the Options button. This time, the Options form fills the screen. Notice too how the image is tiled to fill the form (see Figure 5.12), as explained when you added the image to the form.

FIGURE 5.12
Images placed on a form are tiled if the form's Background ImageLayout property is set to Tiled.

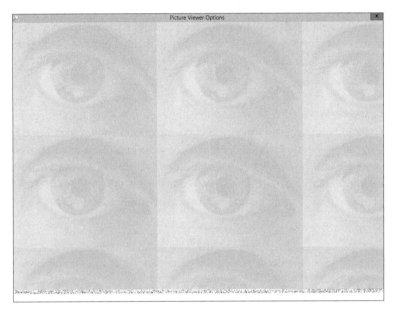

When a form is maximized, it fills the entire screen, regardless of the current screen resolution being used in Windows.

Stop the project, and change the WindowState property back to Normal. You'll rarely set a form's WindowState property to Minimize at design time (although you might specify Maximize), but you'll probably encounter situations in which you need to change (or determine) the WindowState at runtime. As with most properties, you can accomplish this using code. For example, the following statement would minimize the Options form:

```
OptionsForm.WindowState = FormWindowState.Minimized
```

You don't have to remember the names of the values when entering code; you'll get an IntelliSense drop-down list when you type the equals sign.

Specifying a Form's Initial Display Position

The location on the display (monitor) where a form first appears isn't random; it is controlled by the form's StartPosition property. The StartPosition property can be set to one of the values described in Table 5.1.

TABLE 5.1 Values for the StartPosition Property

Value	Description
Manual	The value of the Location property at design time determines where the form first appears.
CenterScreen	The form appears centered in the display.
WindowsDefaultLocation	The form appears in the Windows default location, which is toward the upper left of the display.
WindowsDefaultBounds	The form appears in the Windows default location with its bounds (size) set to the Windows default bounds.
CenterParent	The form is centered within the bounds of its parent form (the initial form that displayed the form in question).

It's generally best to set the StartPosition property of all your forms to CenterParent unless you have a specific reason to do otherwise. For the first form that appears in your project, you might consider using the WindowsDefaultLocation (but I generally prefer CenterScreen).

To see how this property affects a form, try this:

1. Press F5 to run the project.

2. Move the Picture Viewer form, and click the Options button. Notice where the Options form appears.

3. Close the Options form.

4. Move the Picture Viewer form to the upper-right corner, and click the Options button again.

Did you notice that the Options form always appears in the same location, regardless of where the Picture Viewer form is placed when the Options button is clicked? I'm not fond of this behavior. Stop the running project, and change the StartPosition of the Options form to `CenterParent`. Next, repeat the previous steps. You'll see that the Options form always appears centered over the Picture Viewer form, regardless of where that form is positioned.

Stop the project now, and save your work.

Preventing a Form from Appearing in the Taskbar

Being able to display an icon for a minimized form is nice, but sometimes it's necessary to prevent a form from even appearing in the taskbar. If your application has a number of tool windows that float over a main window, such as the Solutions Explorer and toolbox in Visual Basic 2012, for example, it's unlikely that you'd want any but your main form to appear in the taskbar. To prevent a form from appearing in the taskbar, set the form's `ShowInTaskbar` property to `False`. If the user minimizes a form with its `ShowInTaskbar` property set to `False`, he can still get to the application by pressing Alt+Tab even though the program can't be accessed via the taskbar; Visual Basic doesn't allow the application to become inaccessible to the user.

Unloading Forms

After a form has served its purpose, you'll want it to go away. However, *go away* can mean one of two things. First, you can make a form disappear without closing it or freeing its resources (this is called *hiding*). To do so, you set its `Visible` property to `False`. This hides the visual part of the form, but the form still resides in memory and can still be manipulated by code. In addition, all the form's variables and controls retain their values when a form is hidden, so if the form is displayed again, it looks the same as it did when its `Visible` property was set to `False`.

The second method closes a form and releases the resources it consumes. You should close a form when it's no longer needed so that Windows can reclaim all resources used by the form. To do so, you invoke the `Close()` method of the form like this:

```
Me.Close()
```

In Hour 3, "Understanding Objects and Collections," you learned how `Me` is used to reference the current `Form` object. Because `Me` represents the current `Form` object, you can manipulate properties and call methods of the current form using `Me`. (`Me.Visible = False`, and so forth).

The `Close()` method tells Visual Basic not to simply hide the form but to destroy it—*completely*.

Follow these steps to create a button to close the Options form:

1. Select the OptionsForm.vb [Design] tab to display the form designer for the Options form (if it isn't displayed already).

2. Add a new button to the form, and set its properties as follows:

Property	Value
Name	btnOK
Location	305, 12
Size	75, 23
Text	OK

3. Double-click the OK button in the designer to access its Click event, and then enter the following statement:

```
Me.Close()
```

4. Run the project by pressing F5. Click the Options button to display the Options form, and then click OK to close the Options form. Again, the form isn't just hidden; it is completely unloaded from memory and no longer exists.

If you simply wanted to hide a form, but not unload it from memory, you would call the Hide() method of the form or set the form's Visible property to False. This would preserve the state of the form for the time you choose to show it again.

By the Way

Stop the running project and save your work now.

Summary

In this hour, you learned the basics of creating forms. You learned how to add them to your project, set basic appearance properties, and show and hide them using Visual Basic code. In the next hour, you'll learn more advanced functionality for working with forms. After you've mastered the material in this hour and the next, you'll be ready to dig into Visual Basic's controls. That's where the fun of building an interface *really* begins!

Q&A

Q. *How many form properties should I define at design time as opposed to runtime?*

A. You should set all the properties that you can at design time. First, it will be easier to work with the form, because you can see exactly what the user will see. Also, debugging is easier, because there's less code.

Q. *Should I let the user minimize and maximize all forms?*

A. Probably not. There's no point in letting a form be maximized if it isn't set up to adjust its controls accordingly. About dialog boxes, print dialog boxes, and spell-check windows are examples of forms that should not be resizable.

Workshop

Quiz

1. True or false: The text displayed in the form's title bar is determined by the value in the `TitleBarText` property.

2. The named color Control is what kind of color?

3. Name three places where a form's icon is displayed.

4. What is a window with a smaller-than-normal title bar called?

5. For a Minimize or Maximize button to be visible on a form, what other element must be visible?

6. In general, what is the best value to use for a form's `StartPosition` property?

7. To maximize, minimize, or restore a form in code, you set what property?

8. What property do you set to make a hidden form appear?

Answers

1. False. The text displayed in the form's title bar is determined by the value in the form's `Text` property.

2. A system color

3. In the title bar, on the task bar, and when the user presses Alt+Tab

4. The Tool window

5. The form's `ControlBox` property must be set to `True`.

6. `CenterScreen` for the main form and `CenterParent` for all other forms

7. The form's `WindowState` property

8. Set the form's `Visible` property to `True`.

Exercises

1. Create a Windows Application project with a single form that has two buttons. One button, when clicked, should move the form to the left by two pixels. The other should move the form to the right by two pixels. Hint: Use the form's `Left` property.

2. Create a Windows Application with three forms. Give the startup form two buttons. Make the other two forms tool windows, and make one button display the first tool window and the other button display the second tool window.

HOUR 6

Building Forms: Advanced Techniques

What You'll Learn in This Hour:

▶ Adding controls to a form

▶ Positioning, aligning, sizing, spacing, and anchoring controls

▶ Creating intelligent tab orders

▶ Adjusting the z-order of controls

▶ Creating forms that always float over other forms

▶ Creating transparent forms

▶ Creating multiple-document interfaces

A form is just a canvas, and although you can tailor a form by setting its properties, you need to add controls to make it functional. In the previous hour, you learned how to add forms to a project, set basic form properties, and show and hide forms. In this hour, you'll learn about adding controls to a form, including arranging and aligning controls to create an attractive and functional interface. You'll also learn how to create advanced multiple-document interfaces (MDIs), as used in applications such as Photoshop. After you complete the material in this hour, you'll be ready to learn the specifics about the various controls available in Visual Basic.

Working with Controls

Controls are the objects that you place on a form for users to interact with. If you've followed the examples in the previous hours, you've already added controls to a form. However, you'll be adding a lot of controls to forms, and it's important for you to understand all aspects of the process.

Adding Controls to a Form

All the controls that you can add to a form can be found in the toolbox. The toolbox appears as a docked window on the left side of the design environment by default. This location is useful when you only occasionally add controls to forms. However, when doing serious form-design work, I find it best to dock the toolbox to the right edge of the design environment, or to pin it open when docked on the left, to prevent obscuring the form I'm working on.

> Remember that before you can undock a toolbar to move it to a new location, you must make sure that it isn't set to Auto Hide.

The toolbox has category headings that you can expand and collapse. For most of your design, you'll use the controls in the Common Controls category. As your skills progress, however, you might find yourself using more complex and highly specialized controls found in the other categories.

You can add a control to a form in four ways, and you've already been exposed to a few of these methods. Open the Picture Viewer project you created in the previous hour (or open the starting project provided at my website), and double-click Options-Form.vb in the Solution Explorer window to view the Options form in the designer.

Adding a Control by Double-Clicking It in the Toolbox

The easiest way to add a control to a form is to double-click the control in the toolbox. Try this now: Display the toolbox and double-click the TextBox tool. Visual Basic creates a new text box in the upper-left corner of the form (you have to move the mouse away from the toolbox to close the toolbox and see the new control). When you double-click a control in the toolbox (excluding controls that are invisible at run-time), Visual Basic creates the new control on top of the control that currently has the focus. It has the default size for the type of control you're adding. If no other controls are on the form, the new control is placed in the upper-left corner, as you've seen here. After the control is added to the form, you're free to move and size the control as you please.

Adding a Control by Dragging from the Toolbox

If you want a little more authority over where a new control is placed, you can drag a control to the form. Try this now: Display the toolbox, click the Button control, and drag it to the form. When the cursor is roughly where you want the button created, release the mouse button.

Adding a Control by Drawing It

The last and most precise method of placing a control on a form is to draw the control on a form. Follow these steps:

1. Display the toolbox and click the ListBox tool to select it.

2. Move the pointer to where you want the upper-left corner of the list box to appear, and then click and hold the mouse button.

3. Drag the pointer to where you want the bottom-right corner of the list box to be and release the button.

The list box is created, with its dimensions set to the rectangle you drew on the form. This is by far the most precise method of adding controls to a form.

> If you prefer to draw controls on your forms by clicking and dragging, I strongly suggest that you float the toolbox or pin it open. The toolbox interferes with drawing controls when it's docked but set to Auto Hide, because it obscures a good bit of the underlying form.

It's important to note that the first item in each tool category is titled Pointer. Pointer isn't actually a control. When the Pointer item is selected, the design environment is placed in Select mode rather than in a mode to create a new control. With the pointer chosen, you can select a control and view its properties simply by clicking it in the designer. This is the default behavior of the development environment.

Manipulating Controls

Getting controls on a form is the easy part. Arranging them so that they create an intuitive and attractive interface is the challenge. Interface possibilities are nearly endless, so I can't tell you how to design any given interface here (but I strongly suggest that you create forms that closely match the appearance and behavior of similar commercial applications). I can, however, show you the techniques to move, size, and arrange controls so that they appear the way *you* want them to. By mastering these techniques, you'll be much more efficient at building interfaces, freeing your time for writing the code that makes things happen.

Using the Grid (Size and Snap)

You may have noticed as you've worked with controls in this book that controls seem to "snap" to an invisible grid. You're not crazy—they actually do. When you draw or move a control on a form in a project with grids enabled, the coordinates of the control automatically snap to the nearest grid coordinates. This offers some precision when adjusting the size and location of controls. In practical use, I often find the grid to be only slightly helpful, because the size or location I want often doesn't fit neatly with the grid locations. However, you can control the grid's granularity and even visibility, and I suggest you do both.

Grid settings are global to Visual Basic—you don't set them for each individual project or form. To display the grid settings on your computer, choose Tools, Options to display the Options form. Next, click Windows Forms Designer in the tree on the left to view the designer settings, as shown in Figure 6.1.

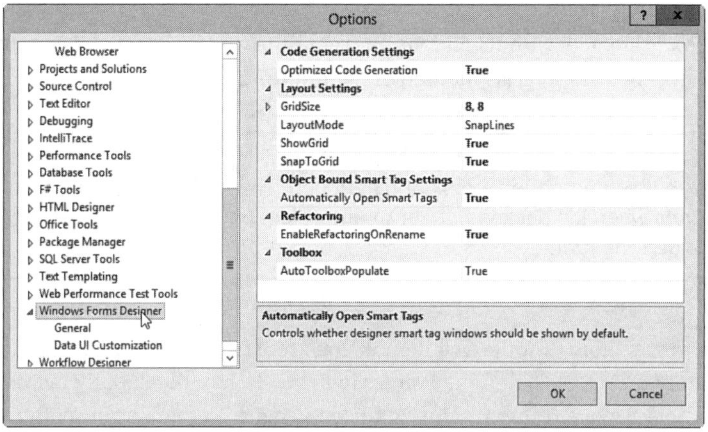

FIGURE 6.1
Grid settings are global to Visual Basic 2012.

The settings we're interested in here are as follows:

▶ GridSize determines the granularity of the grid in pixels both horizontally and vertically. A smaller grid size means that you have finer control over control size and placement.

▶ LayoutMode determines whether the designer snaps a control you are moving to the grid or aligns it with other controls.

▶ ShowGrid determines whether grid dots are displayed on forms in the designer.

▶ SnapToGrid determines whether the grid is used. If this setting is False, the grid size setting is ignored, and nothing is snapped to the grid.

Right now, you're not using the grid for drawing controls, but you are using snap lines when moving controls because your LayoutMode is set to SnapLines. I'll talk about this in more detail later in this section. Right now, I want to show you how grids work, so change your LayoutMode setting to SnapToGrid.

Now you'll assign a higher level of granularity to the grid (the space between the grid points will be smaller). I find that this helps with design because edges aren't so easily snapped to unwanted places.

To adjust the grid's granularity, you change the GridSize setting. Setting the grid's Width or Height to a smaller number creates a more precise grid, which gives you finer control over sizing and placement. Using larger values creates a much coarser grid and offers less control. With a larger grid, you'll find that edges snap to grid points much more easily and at larger increments, making it impossible to fine-tune the size or position of a control. Follow these steps:

1. Change the GridSize property to **6, 6**.

2. Change the ShowGrid property to True if it's not already set to True.

3. Click OK to save your changes and return to the Forms Designer. Notice that grid dots now appear, as shown in Figure 6.2. If the dots don't appear, you need to close the tab in the designer and then double-click the OptionsForm.vb item in the Solutions Explorer to force a refresh.

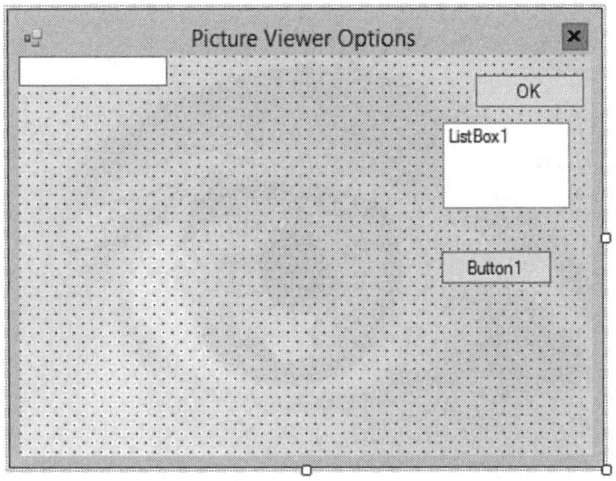

FIGURE 6.2
Grids don't have to be visible to be active.

Try dragging the controls on your form or dragging their edges to size them. Notice that you have more control over the placement with the finer grid. Try changing the GridSize to a set of higher numbers, such as **25, 25**, and see what happens.

An unfortunate side effect of a smaller grid is that the grid can become distracting. Again, you'll decide what you like best, but I generally turn off the grids on my forms. In fact, I prefer the new Snap to Lines feature, discussed next.

The ShowGrid property determines only whether the grid is drawn, not whether it's active; whether a grid is active is determined by the form's SnapToGrid property.

By the Way

Using Snap Lines

A relatively new and useful feature is the Snap to Lines layout feature. Tell Visual Basic 2012 to use Snap to Lines now by following these steps:

1. Choose Tools, Options to display the Options dialog box.

2. Click Windows Forms Designer to display the layout settings.

3. Change the LayoutMode property to SnapLines.

4. Turn off the grid by setting the ShowGrid property to False.

5. Click OK to save your settings.

Again, you might have to close the form and redisplay it for your changes to take effect.

Snap lines is a feature designed to help you create better interfaces faster by "snapping" control edges to imaginary lines along the edges of other controls. The easiest way to understand this is to try it. Follow these steps:

1. Drag your controls so that they are roughly in the position of Figure 6.3.

FIGURE 6.3
Start from this layout.

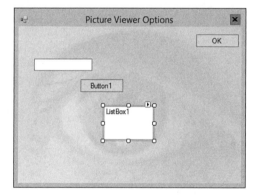

2. Click the ListBox to select it.

3. Click the white square that appears on the left edge of the control and drag it to the left. As the edge nears vertical alignment with the button above it, a snap line appears and the edge "snaps" to the line, as shown in Figure 6.4.

You're free to continue dragging the edge, and as you do so, Visual Basic creates more snap lines as you near vertical alignment with other controls. Controls also support horizontal snap lines, and all snap lines also work when you drag a control. This may seem like a small feature, but trust me when I say this is a great feature of Visual Basic that will save you many tedious hours over time.

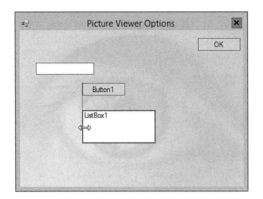

FIGURE 6.4
Snap lines make
it easy to align
the edges of
controls.

Selecting a Group of Controls

As your skills increase, you'll find your forms becoming increasingly complex. Some forms might contain dozens, or even hundreds, of controls. Visual Basic has a set of features that makes it easy to align groups of controls.

By default, clicking a control on a form selects it while *simultaneously* deselecting any controls that were previously selected. To perform actions on more than one control, you need to select a group of controls. You can do this in one of two ways, the first of which is to *lasso* the controls. To lasso a group of controls, you first click and drag the mouse pointer anywhere on the form. As you drag, a rectangle is drawn on the form. When you release the mouse button, all controls intersected by the rectangle become selected. Note that you don't have to completely surround a control with the lasso (also called a *marquee*); you have to intersect only part of the control to select it. Try this now: Click somewhere in the lower-left corner of the form, and drag the pointer toward the upper-right of the form without releasing the mouse button. Intersect or surround all controls *except* the OK button, as shown in Figure 6.5. When the rectangle has surrounded or intersected all the controls, release the button, and the controls are selected, as shown in Figure 6.6.

When a control is selected, it has a dotted border and a number of sizing handles (squares located in the dotted border at the corners and midpoints of the control). Pay careful attention to the sizing handles. The control with the white sizing handles is the active control in the selected group. When you use Visual Basic's tools to work on a group of selected controls (such as the alignment and formatting tools), the values of the active control are used. For example, if you were to align the left side of the selected controls shown in Figure 6.6, each of the controls would have its Left property value set to that of the active control (the control with the white handles—the listbox). When you use the lasso technique to select a group of controls, you really don't have much influence over which control Visual Basic makes the active control. In this example, you want to align all controls to the button, so you have to use a different technique to select the controls. Deselect all the controls now by clicking anywhere on the form (just don't click a control).

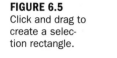

FIGURE 6.5
Click and drag to create a selection rectangle.

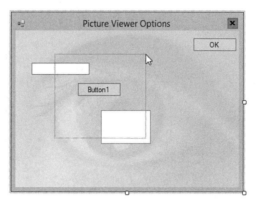

FIGURE 6.6
All selected controls appear with a dotted border and sizing handles (rectangles).

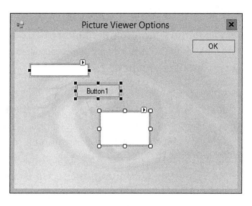

By the Way

Not all sizing handles can be moved at all times. Before you set the Multiline property of a text box to True, for example, Visual Basic doesn't let you change the height of the text box. Therefore, only the sizing handles at the left and right edges can be moved, so they are white when the control is selected.

The second technique for selecting multiple controls is to use the Shift or Ctrl key while clicking controls (either key can be used to the same effect). This method is much like that used for selecting multiple files in Explorer. Follow these steps:

1. Click the bottom control (the list box) to select it. (When only one control is selected, it's considered the active control.)

2. Hold down the Shift key and click the text box in the upper-left corner; the list box and text box are now selected. The list box is the active control because it is the first control you clicked when selecting this group. Again, when more than one control is selected, the active control has its sizing handles set to white so that you can identify it.

3. With the Shift key still pressed, click the button control (not the OK button) to add it to the group of selected controls. All the controls should now be selected, and the list box should be the active control. Let go of the Shift key now.

Clicking a selected control while holding down the Shift key deselects the control.

You can combine the two selection techniques when needed. For instance, you could first lasso all the controls to select them. If you happen to select a control that you don't want in the group, simply hold down the Shift key and click that control to deselect it.

If you must click the same control twice, such as to deselect and then reselect it, do so s-l-o-w-l-y. If you click too fast, Visual Basic interprets your actions as a double-click and creates a new event handler for the control.

Aligning Controls

Visual Basic includes a number of formatting tools you can use to design attractive interfaces. You use the Layout toolbar, shown in Figure 6.7, to access most of these. Display the Layout toolbar now by right-clicking a toolbar at the top of Visual Basic and choosing Layout from the shortcut menu that appears. The Layout toolbar includes options for aligning controls horizontally and vertically to the controls' edges or centers.

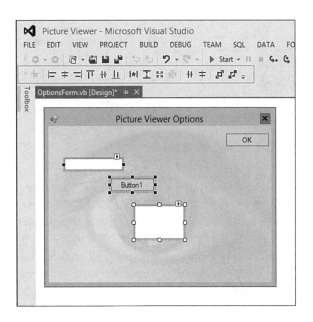

FIGURE 6.7
The Layout toolbar makes it quick and easy to align controls.

Slowly move the mouse pointer from left to right over the buttons on this toolbar to read their ToolTips. Notice that with this toolbar, you can

▶ Align the controls to the grid if it's enabled.

▶ Align the left edge, middle, or right edge of selected controls.

▶ Align the top edge, middle, or bottom edge of selected controls.

▶ Make the selected controls the same width, height, or both.

▶ Make horizontal or vertical spacing between the selected controls nice and even.

▶ Move layering of the selected controls backward or forward.

The first item simply aligns the selected controls to the grid—not much fun there. However, the remainder of the buttons are very useful. Remember that Visual Basic uses the active control as its baseline when performing alignment. This is important. Click the Align Tops button, and notice that the selected controls are now aligned with the active control, as shown in Figure 6.8.

FIGURE 6.8
The selected control is used as the baseline when you align groups of selected controls.

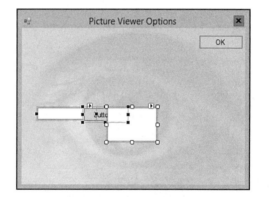

Making Controls the Same Size

In addition to aligning controls, you can make all selected controls the same size—height, width, or both. To do this, use the Make Same Size button on the toolbar. (The size of the first control is applied to all selected controls.) Make all your controls the same size now by clicking the Make the Same Size button. This makes the selected controls the same size as the list box (rather large). Now try this: In the Properties window, enter **75, 25** in the Size property, and press Tab to commit the entry. Notice that your change affects all the selected controls. Having the Properties window affect all selected controls like this makes it easy to quickly modify a number of controls that need to share property values. I'll talk about this in a little more detail shortly.

Evenly Spacing a Group of Controls

As many a salesman has said, "...and that's not all," you can also make the spacing between controls uniform, using the Layout toolbar. Try this now: Click the Make Horizontal Spacing Equal button on the toolbar. All the controls are now evenly spaced. In previous versions of Visual Basic, additional buttons were available on the toolbar to increase and decrease horizontal spacing. For some reason, those have been removed, but you can still access them through the Format menu by choosing Format > Horizontal Spacing. You can also increase the horizontal or vertical spacing or remove the spacing between the controls, using items in the Format menu. Save your project now by clicking the Save All button on the toolbar.

Setting Property Values for a Group of Controls

The following is a technique that many experienced Visual Basic developers seem to overlook: You can change a property value in the Properties window when multiple controls are selected. This causes the corresponding property to change for all selected controls.

Make sure that all three controls are still selected, and then display the Properties window (if it's not already displayed). When a group of controls is selected, the Properties window appears with some modifications, as shown in Figure 6.9:

▶ No Name property is shown. This occurs because you're not allowed to have two controls with the same name, so Visual Basic doesn't let you even try.

▶ Only properties shared by all controls are displayed. Because you have selected controls of different types, only a small subset of common properties are available. If you selected controls all of the same type, you'd see more properties available.

▶ For properties where the values of the selected controls differ (such as the Location property in this example), the value is left empty in the Properties window.

Entering a value in a property changes the corresponding property for *all* selected controls. To see how this works, change the BackColor property to a shade of yellow, and you'll see that all controls have their BackColor set to yellow.

You won't actually use the three controls you've been experimenting with so far in this hour, so click the white area outside of the form to remove focus from the Properties window and press the Delete key to delete all the selected controls.

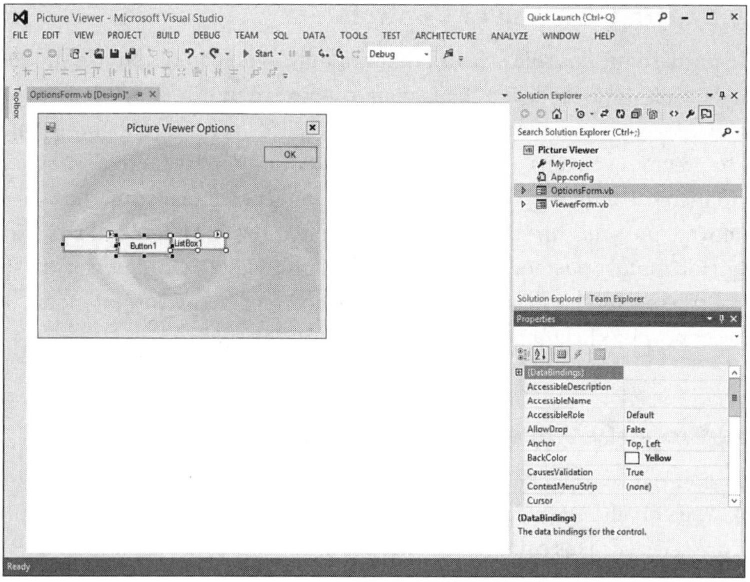

FIGURE 6.9
You can view the
property values
of many controls
at once, with
some caveats.

Anchoring and Autosizing Controls

Some of my favorite evolutions to the forms engine in Visual Basic are the capability
to anchor controls to one or more edges of a form and the capability for controls to
size themselves appropriately when the user sizes a form. In the past, you had to use
a (usually cumbersome) third-party component or resort to writing code in the form
Resize event to get this behavior, but it's an intrinsic capability of Visual Basic 2012's
form engine.

The default behavior of all new controls is that controls are docked to the top and left
edges of their containers. What if you want a control to always appear in the upper-
right or lower-left corner of a form? Now you'll learn how to anchor controls so that
they adapt accordingly when the form is resized.

Follow these steps:

1. Double-click the form ViewerForm.vb in the Solutions Explorer window. This is
   the form you'll modify.

2. Press F5 to run the project.

3. Drag the lower-right corner of the form to make it bigger. Notice that the controls don't follow the edge of the form (see Figure 6.10).

4. Stop the running project by choosing Stop Debugging on the toolbar.

5. Click the Select Picture button to select it and, more importantly, deselect the form.

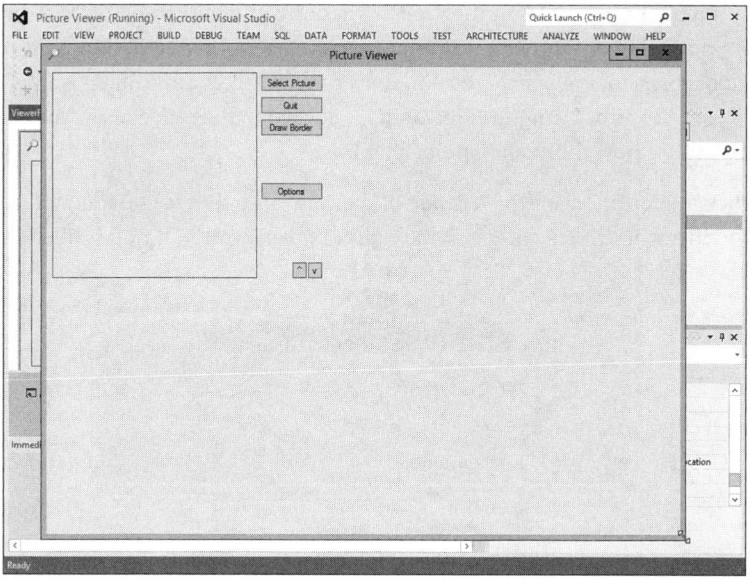

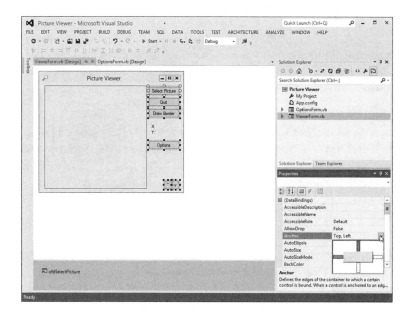

FIGURE 6.10
By default, controls are anchored to the top-left corner of the form.

6. Hold down the Shift key and click the following additional buttons: Quit, Draw Border, Options, ^, and v.

7. Click the Anchor property in the Properties window, and then click the drop-down arrow that appears. You'll see a drop-down box that's unique to the Anchor property, as shown in Figure 6.11.

FIGURE 6.11
You use this unique drop-down box to set a control's Anchor property.

The gray square in the center of the drop-down box represents the control(s) whose property you're setting. The thin rectangles on the top, bottom, left, and right represent the possible edges to which you can dock the control. If a rectangle is filled in, the edge of the control facing that rectangle is docked to that edge of the form. Follow these steps to see how the Anchor property works:

1. Click the rectangle on the left side of the control so that it's no longer filled in, and then click the rectangle to the right of the control so that it *is* filled in (see Figure 6.12).

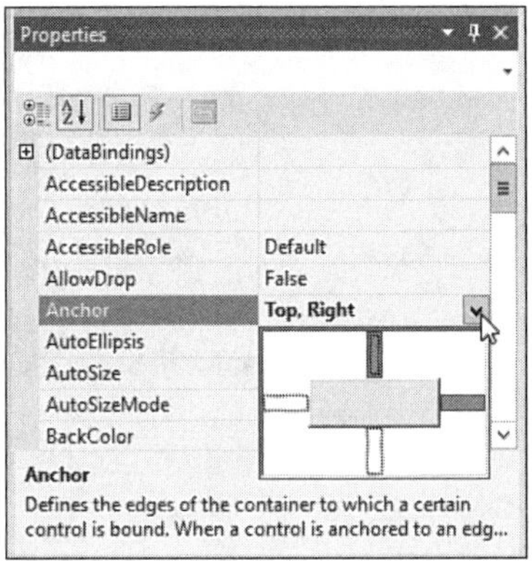

FIGURE 6.12
This setting anchors the controls to the top and right edges of the form.

2. Click any other property to close the drop-down box. The Anchor property should now read Top, Right.

3. Press F5 to run the project, and then drag an edge of the form to make it larger.

Pretty interesting, huh? What Visual Basic has done is anchored the right edge of the buttons to the right edge of the form, as shown in Figure 6.13. Really, anchoring means keeping an edge of the control a constant, relative distance from an edge of the form. It's an *unbelievably powerful* tool for building interfaces.

Notice that the picture box and the coordinate labels still retain their original locations when the form is resized. No problem—you can address that with the Anchor property as well. Start by changing the anchoring of the X and Y labels by following these steps (stop the running project if you haven't already):

1. Click the X label to select it.

2. Hold down the Shift key, and click the Y label to select it.

3. Set the Anchor property the same as you did for the buttons—deselect the left side and select the right side (refer to Figure 6.12).

4. Click any other property to close the Anchor drop-down box.

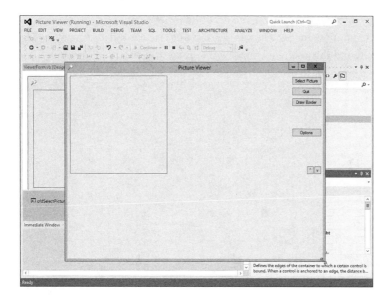

FIGURE 6.13
Anchoring is a
powerful feature
for creating
adaptable
forms.

Now the picture box is a bit of a different beast from the other controls. You want the top and left anchored the way they are now, but you want the right and bottom edge to grow and shrink with the form. This is actually easy to accomplish. Follow these steps:

1. Click the picture box to select it.

2. Open the Anchor property and select all four anchor points. (All four rectangles should be filled with solid gray, as shown in Figure 6.14.)

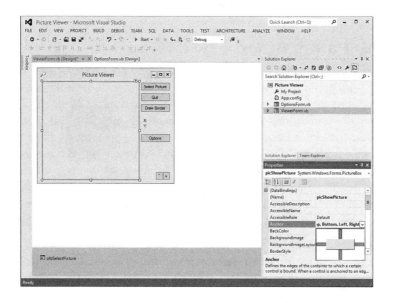

FIGURE 6.14
This setting
anchors the con-
trol relative to all
four sides of the
form.

Now press F5 to run the project, and drag the lower right of the form to make it bigger. Notice that now the picture box sizes itself to match the form size (see Figure 6.15). You'll find this useful when viewing larger images.

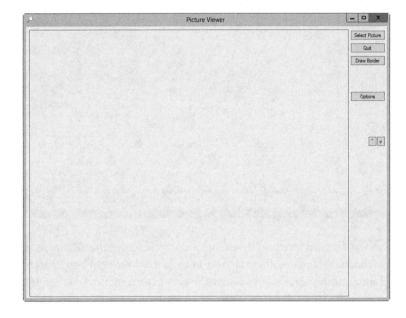

Now that you know how to use the Anchor property, you can make forms that users can resize without having to write any code. One caveat: Depending on its Anchor setting, a control might disappear if the form is shrunk quite small.

Creating a Tab Order

Tab order is something that is often (emphasis on *often*) overlooked by even seasoned Visual Basic programmers. You're probably familiar with tab order as a user, although you might not realize it. When you press Tab while on a form, the focus moves from the current control to the next control in the tab order. This enables easy keyboard navigation on forms. The tab order for controls on a form is determined by the TabIndex properties of the controls. The control with the TabIndex value of 0 is the first control that receives the focus when the form is first displayed. When you press Tab, the control with a TabIndex of 1 receives the focus, and so on. When you add a control to a form, Visual Basic assigns the next available TabIndex value to the new control (it will be last in the tab order). Each control has a unique TabIndex value, and TabIndex values are always traversed in ascending order.

If the tab order isn't set correctly for a form, pressing Tab causes the focus to jump from control to control in no apparent order. This is a great way to frustrate a user. In the past, the only way to change the tab order for controls on a form was to manu-ally change the TabIndex values in the Properties window. For instance, to make a control the first control in the tab order, you would change its TabIndex property to 0; Visual Basic would then bump the values of all other controls accordingly. This was a painful process—believe me. Although it can be handy to set a TabIndex property manually, such as when you want to insert a control into an existing tab sequence, there is a much better way to set the tab order of forms.

Press F5 to run the project, and notice that the Select Picture button has the focus (it's highlighted by a blue rectangle). If you pressed Enter now, the button would be "clicked" because it has the focus. Now press Tab, and the Quit button has the focus because you added the Quit button to the form right after you added the Select Pic-ture button. Press Tab once more. Did you expect the Draw Border button to get the focus? So would a user. Instead, the ^ button receives the focus because it was the next control you added to the form. You're about to fix that, so stop the project by clicking Stop Debugging on the toolbar or close the running window.

Follow these steps to set the tab order of the form via the visual method of Visual Basic:

1. Click the form to give it focus, and then select Tab Order from the View menu. Notice how Visual Basic superimposes a set of numbers over the controls, as shown in Figure 6.16. The number on a control indicates its TabIndex property value. Now it's easy to see that the tab order is incorrect.

2. Click the Select Picture button. The background of the number changes from blue to white to show that you selected the control. Had this control had a TabIndex value other than 0, it would have been changed to 0 when you clicked it.

3. Click the Quit button to designate it as the next button in the tab order.

4. Currently, the Draw Border button is fifth in the tab order. Click it, and the number changes to 2.

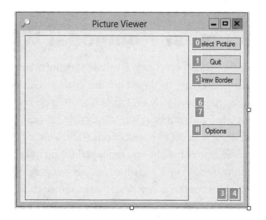

FIGURE 6.16
The numbers over each con-trol indicate the control's TabIndex.

5. Click the remaining controls in the following order: X label, Y label, Options button, ^ button, and v button.

6. When you click the last button, all the numbers change back to a blue background; the tab order is now set. Click Tab Order on the View menu once more to take the designer out of Tab Order mode.

7. Press F5 to run the project again, and you'll see that pressing Tab now moves the focus logically.

> You can programmatically move the focus via the tab order by calling the SelectNextControl() method of a control or form.

To remove a control from the tab sequence, set its TabStop property to False. When a control's TabStop property is set to False, users can still select the control with the mouse, but they can't enter the control by using the Tab key. You should still set the TabIndex property to a logical value so that if the control receives the focus (such as by being clicked), pressing Tab moves the focus to the next logical control.

Layering Controls

Tab order and visual alignment are key elements for effectively placing controls on forms. However, these two elements address control placement in only two dimensions—the x,y axis. Although it's rare that you'll need to do so, at times you might need to have controls overlap. Whenever two controls overlap, whichever control was added to the form most recently appears on top of the other. You can control the ordering of controls by using the Bring to Front or Send to Back buttons found on the right side of the Layout toolbar.

Did you Know?

> You can use code to move a control forward or backward by invoking the control's BringToFront() or SendToBack() methods.

Creating Topmost Nonmodal Windows

As you're probably aware, when you click a window, it usually comes to the foreground, and all other windows are displayed behind it (unless it's a modal window). At times, you might want a window to stay on top of other windows, regardless of whether it's the current window (that is, it has the focus). An example of this is the Find window in Visual Basic and other applications such as Word. Regardless of which window has the focus, the Find form always appears floating over all other windows. You create such a window by setting the form's TopMost property to True. It's not exactly rocket science, but that's the point: A simple property change or method call is often all it takes to accomplish what might otherwise seem to be a difficult task.

Creating Transparent Forms

A relatively new property of forms that I think is very cool is the Opacity property. This property controls the form's opaqueness as well as all controls on the form. The default Opacity value of 100% means that the form and its controls are completely opaque (solid), whereas a value of 0% creates a completely transparent form (no real point in that). A value of 50%, then, creates a form that's between solid and invisible, as shown in Figure 6.17. Microsoft Outlook 2003 and newer make good use of opacity in their alerts that pop up to tell you when you've received an email. The Opacity of these alerts is cycled from 0 to 100, is left at 100 for a short time, and then cycles back down to 0 as it disappears. You can do this in your program using a simple loop, as discussed in Hour 14, "Looping for Efficiency."

Creating Scrollable Forms

A scrollable form is one that can display scrollbars when its contents are larger than the form's physical size. Not only is this a great feature, but it's also easy to implement in your own applications.

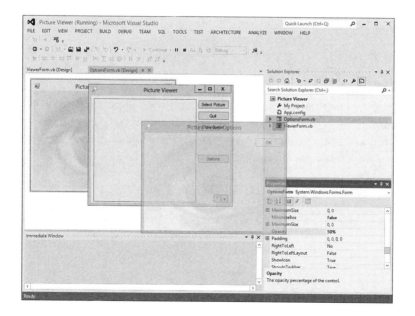

FIGURE 6.17
Ghost forms!

A form's scrolling behavior is determined by the following three properties:

Property	Description
AutoScroll	Determines whether scrollbars will ever appear on a form.
AutoScrollMinSize	The minimum size of the scroll region (area). If the size of the form is adjusted so that the client area of the form (the area of the form not counting borders and title bar) is smaller than the AutoScrollMinSize, scrollbars appear.
AutoScrollMargin	Determines the margin given around controls during scrolling. This essentially determines how far past the edge of the outermost controls you can scroll.

Press F5 to run your project, and size the form smaller than it is by dragging the lower-right corner toward the upper left. Notice that, although the controls adjust themselves the best they can, some controls disappear from view as the form gets smaller. The only way you can access these controls is to make the form bigger again—unless you make this form a scrollable form.

Follow these steps:

1. If the project is still running, stop it.

2. Set the AutoScroll property of the ViewerForm.vb form to True.

3. Press F5 to run the project.

4. Drag the lower-right corner of the form toward the upper left to make the form smaller. Notice that as you do so, a scrollbar appears on the right side of the form, as shown in Figure 6.18. You can use the scrollbar to scroll the contents of the form and access controls that would otherwise be unavailable.

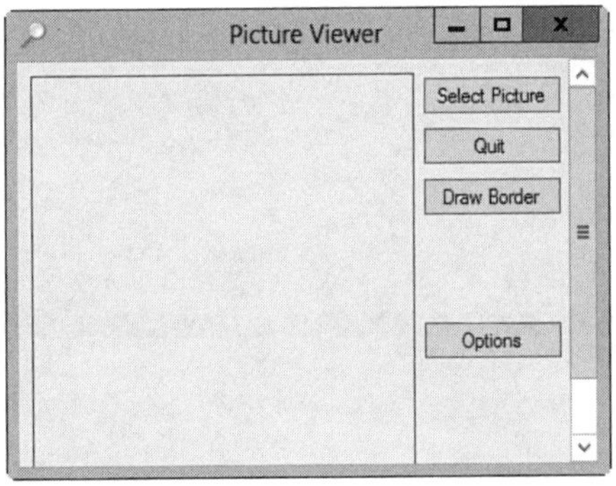

FIGURE 6.18
Without scroll-bars, it's possible to have controls that can't be seen.

Stop the project now, and save your work.

Creating MDI Forms

All the projects you've created so far have been single-document interface (SDI) projects. In SDI programs, every form in the application is a peer of all other forms; no
intrinsic hierarchy exists between forms. Visual Basic also lets you create multiple-document interface (MDI) programs. An MDI program contains one parent window (also
called a *container*) and one or more child windows. A classic example of an MDI program is Adobe Photoshop. When you run Photoshop, a single parent window appears.
Within this parent window, you can open any number of documents, each appearing
in its own child window. In an MDI program, all child windows share the same toolbar
and menu bar, which appear on the parent window. One restriction of child windows
is that they can exist only within the confines of the parent window. Figure 6.19 shows
an example of Photoshop running with a number of child document windows open.

FIGURE 6.19
Le Collage! MDI
applications con-
sist of a single
parent window
and one or more
child windows.

MDI applications can have any number of normal windows (dialog boxes, for
example) in addition to child windows.

By the Way

Now you'll create a simple MDI project. Follow these steps:

1. Choose File, New Project to display the New Project dialog box (note how this is
   a modal form). If asked, save your changes to the Picture Viewer project.

2. Enter the name **MDI Example** and click OK to create the project.

3. Right-click Form1.vb in the Solutions Explorer window and choose Rename from the shortcut menu. Change the name of the form to **MDIParentForm.vb**. Next, change the form's Text property to **MDI Parent**, and change its IsMdiContainer property to True. (If you don't set the IsMdiContainer property to True, this example won't work.)

The first thing you'll notice is that Visual Basic changed the client area to a dark gray and gave it a sunken appearance. This is the standard appearance for MDI parent windows; all visible child windows appear in this area.

4. Create a new form by choosing Project, Add Windows Form. Name the form **Child1Form**, and change its Text property to Child 1.

5. Add a third form to the project in the same way. Name it **Child2Form**, and set its Text property to Child 2.

6. Click Save All on the toolbar, and name the project **MDI Example**.

7. Double-click MDIParentForm.vb in the Solution Explorer to show the parent window in the designer.

8. Double-click the form to access its default event—the Load event. Enter the following code:

```
Child1Form.MdiParent = Me
Child1Form.Show()
```

By now, you should know what the last statement does: It shows the form non-modally. What we're interested in here is the first statement. It sets the form's MdiParent property to the current form, which is an MDI parent form because its IsMdiContainer property is set to True. When the new form is displayed, it's shown as an MDI child.

Press F5 to run the project, and notice how the child form appears on the client area of the parent form. If you size the parent form so that one or more child windows can't be displayed fully, a scrollbar appears (see Figure 6.20). If you were to remove the statement that set the MdiParent property, the form would simply appear floating over the parent form (because it wouldn't be a child) and therefore wouldn't be bound by the confines of the parent.

FIGURE 6.20
Child forms appear only within the confines of the parent form.

Stop the project by clicking Stop Debugging on the toolbar, and follow these steps:

1. In the Solution Explorer, double-click the Child1Form.vb form to display it in the designer.

2. Add a button to the form, and set the button's properties as follows:

Property	Value
Name	btnShowChild2
Location	105, 100
Size	85, 23
Text	Show Child 2

3. Double-click the button to access its Click event, and then add the following code:

```
Child2Form.MdiParent = Me.MdiParent
Child2Form.Show()
```

This code shows the second child form. Note that differences exist between this code and the code you entered earlier. You can't set the second child's MdiParent property to Me because Me refers to the current form (Child1Form, which is not an MDI container). However, you know that Me.MdiParent references a child's parent form because this is precisely the property you set to make the form a child in the first place. Therefore, you can simply pass the parent of the first child to the second child, and they'll both be children of the same form.

Any form can be a child form (except, of course, an MDI parent form). To make a form a child form, set its MdiParent property to a form that's defined as an MDI container.

By the Way

4. Press F5 to run the project. Feel free to resize the parent form so that it's bigger. You'll see the button on the child form, so go ahead and click it. (If you don't see the button, you might have mistakenly added it to the second child form.) When you click the button, the second child form appears, as shown in Figure 6.21. Notice how the new child form is also bound by the constraints of the parent form.

Did you Know?

> The MDI parent form has an ActiveMdiChild property, which you can use to get a reference to the currently active child window.

FIGURE 6.21
Child forms are peers with one another.

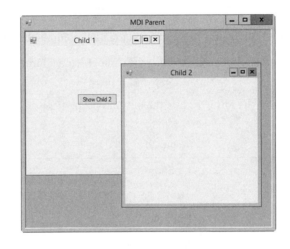

By the Way

> To make the parent form larger when the project is first run, you would set the form's Size.Height and Size.Width properties either at design time or at run-time in the form's Load event.

One thing to keep in mind about forms is that you can create as many instances of a form as you want. Managing multiple instances of the same form gets tricky, however, and is beyond the scope of this book.

Setting the Startup Form

The Startup object in a Windows Application project is, by default, the first form added to the project. This also happens to be the form that Visual Basic creates automatically when you create a new Windows Application project.

Every Windows Forms project must have a Startup form as the entry point to the program. You change the Startup form by right-clicking the project name in the Solution Explorer and choosing Properties. The Startup form property appears on the first property page that appears, as shown in Figure 6.22.

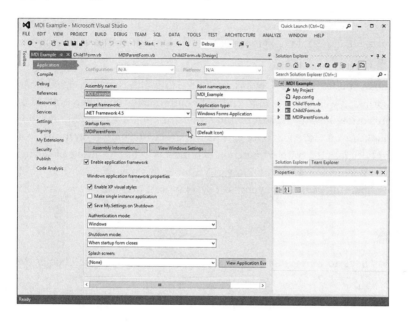

FIGURE 6.22
The application's entry point is determined by the Startup form property.

If the Startup object property is set to show a child window, you might not get the behavior you expect when the project starts. The designated form would appear, but it wouldn't be a child, because no code would execute to set the form's MdiParent property to a valid MDI parent form.

If MDI forms still confuse you, don't worry. Most of the applications you'll write as a new Visual Basic programmer will be SDI programs. As you become more familiar with creating Visual Basic projects in general, start experimenting with MDI projects. Remember, you don't have to make a program an MDI program simply because you can; make an MDI program if the requirements of the project dictate that you do so.

Summary

Understanding forms is critical because forms are the dynamic canvases on which you build your user interface. If you don't know how to work with forms, your entire application will suffer. Many things about working with forms go beyond simply setting properties, especially as you begin to think about the end user. As your experience grows, you'll get into the groove of form design, and things will become second nature to you.

In this hour, you learned how to do some interesting things, such as creating transparent forms, as well as some high-end techniques, such as building an MDI application. You learned how to create scrolling forms—an interface element that shouldn't be overlooked. You also spent a lot of time working with controls on forms, which is important because the primary function of a form is to host controls. In the next two hours, you'll learn the details of many of Visual Basic's powerful controls that will become important weapons in your vast development arsenal.

Q&A

Q. *Do I need to worry about the anchoring and scrolling capabilities of every form I create?*

A. Absolutely not. The majority of forms in most applications are dialog boxes. A dialog box is a modal form used to gather data from the user. A dialog box is usually of a fixed size, which means that its border style is set to a style that can't be sized. With a fixed-size form, you don't need to worry about anchoring or scrolling.

Q. *How do I know whether a project is a candidate for an MDI interface?*

A. If the program will open many instances of the same type of form, that project is a candidate for an MDI interface. For example, if you're creating an image-editing program and the intent is to enable the user to open many images at once, MDI makes sense. Also, if you'll have many forms that will share a common toolbar and menu, you might want to consider MDI.

Workshop

Quiz

1. True or false: The first control selected in a series is always made the active control.

2. How many ways are there to add a control to a form from the toolbox?

3. If you double-click a tool in the toolbox, where on the form is it placed?

4. Which property fixes an edge of a control to an edge of a form?

5. What do you change to hide the grid on a form?

6. Which toolbar contains the functions for spacing and aligning controls?

7. Which property do you set to make a form an MDI parent?

Answers

1. True

2. There are three primary methods: Double-click a tool in the toolbox, drag a tool from the toolbox, and click a tool in the toolbox and then draw it on a form.

3. The control is placed over the currently selected control, or in the upper-left corner if no control is selected.

4. The Anchor property

5. The ShowGrid property, found in the Options dialog box

6. The Layout toolbar

7. You set the IsMdiContainer property to True to make a form an MDI parent.

Exercises

1. Create a new Windows Application, and add a button to the middle of the form. Experiment with different values for the button's Anchor property, running the project in between property changes.

2. Modify the MDI Example project in this hour so that the first child that appears is Child2Form, which in turn shows Child1Form.

HOUR 7

Working with Traditional Controls

What You'll Learn in This Hour:

▶ Displaying static text with the Label control

▶ Allowing users to enter text using a text box

▶ Creating password fields

▶ Working with buttons

▶ Using panels, group boxes, check boxes, and option buttons

▶ Displaying lists with list boxes and combo boxes

The preceding two hours described in considerable detail how to work with forms. Forms are the foundation of a user interface but are pretty much useless by themselves. To create a functional interface, you need to use *controls*. Controls are the various widgets and doodads on a form with which users interact. Dozens of different types of controls exist, from the simple Label control, used to display static text, to the more complicated Tree View control, used to present trees of data like those found in Explorer. In this hour, I'll introduce you to the most common (and simple) controls, which I call *traditional* controls. In Hour 8, "Using Advanced Controls," you'll learn about the more advanced controls that you can use to create professional-level interfaces.

Displaying Static Text with the Label Control

Label controls are used to display static text to the user. By *static*, I mean that the user can't change the text directly (but you can change the text with code). Label controls are among the most commonly used controls, and, fortunately, they're also among the easiest. Labels are most often used to provide descriptive text for other

controls such as text boxes. Labels are also great for providing status-type information to a user, as well as for providing general instructions on a form.

You'll build on the Picture Viewer project from Hour 6, "Building Forms: Advanced
Techniques," for most of this hour. Although you'll add the controls to the interface,
you won't make them functional until you progress to Part III, "Making Things Happen—Programming."

Start by following these steps:

1. Open the Picture Viewer you worked on in Hour 6.

2. Double-click OptionsForm.vb in the Solution Explorer window to display the
   Options form in the designer.

3. Add a new Label control to the form by double-clicking the Label item in the
   toolbox. The primary property of the Label control is the Text property, which
   determines the text displayed to the user. When a Label control is first added
   to a form, the Text property is set to the control's name. This isn't very useful.
   Set the properties of the new Label control as follows:

Property	Value
Name	lblUserName
Location	40, 41
Text	User Name:

Notice how the label resizes automatically to fit your text. To create a multiline label,
you would click in the Text property to display a drop-down arrow and then click the
arrow to access a text editor, as shown in Figure 7.1. You could then enter text and
separate the lines by pressing Enter. In most cases, it's best to place label text on a
single line, but it's nice to have the option.

Allowing Users to Enter Text Using a Text Box

A Label control is usually the best control for displaying text that a user can't
change. However, when you need to allow users to enter or edit text, the text box is
the tool for the job. If you've ever typed information on a form, you've almost

FIGURE 7.1
Multiline labels
are created with
this text editor.

certainly used a text box. Add a new text box to your form now by double-clicking
the TextBox item in the toolbox. Set the text box's properties as follows:

Property	Value
Name	txtUserName
Location	105, 38
Size	139, 20

Your form should now look like Figure 7.2.

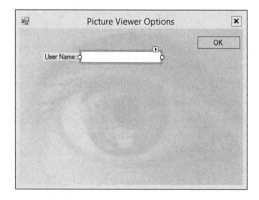

FIGURE 7.2
Labels and text
boxes work well
together.

Although you'll leave the Text property of a text box empty 99% of the time, certain
aspects of the text box are easier to understand when it contains text. For now, set
the text box's Text property to This is sample text. Remember to press Enter or
Tab to commit your property change.

Specifying Text Alignment

Both the Text Box and Label controls have a TextAlign property (as do many other controls). The TextAlign property determines the alignment of the text within the control, much like the justification setting in a word processor. You can select from Left, Center, and Right.

Follow these steps to see how the TextAlign property works:

1. Change the TextAlign property of the text box to Right, and see how the text becomes right-aligned within the text box.

2. Change TextAlign to Center to see what center alignment looks like. As you can see, this property is pretty straightforward.

3. Change the TextAlign property back to Left before continuing.

Creating a Multiline Text Box

In Hour 6, I talked about the sizing handles of a selected control. I mentioned how handles that can be sized are filled with white. Notice how only the left and right edges of the text box have white sizing handles. This means that you can adjust only the left and right edges of the control (you can alter only the width, not the height). This text box is defined as a single-line text box, meaning that it displays only one line of text. What would be the point of a really tall text box that showed only a single line of text?

To allow a text box to display multiple lines of text, set its Multiline property to True. Set the Multiline property of your text box to True now, and notice how all the sizing handles become white. Although you could set this using the Properties window, there is a nifty shortcut for setting the MultiLine property of a text box. Select the text box, and then click the little square with the arrow that appears above the text box (refer to Figure 7.2). This displays a simple shortcut menu showing the MultiLine property value. Click the check box next to the value, and then click off the menu to close it. Most controls have such a shortcut menu, but the contents depend on the type of control selected. Get used to opening these shortcut menus when you see the little box with the arrow so that you can become familiar with the properties each control makes available in its shortcuts.

Change the Text property of the text box to **This is sample text**. A multiline text box will wrap its contents as necessary. Press Enter or Tab to commit the property change. Figure 7.3 shows how the text box displays only part of what you entered because the control simply isn't big enough to show all the text. Change the Size property to **139, 52**, and you'll then see the entire contents of the text box, as shown in Figure 7.4.

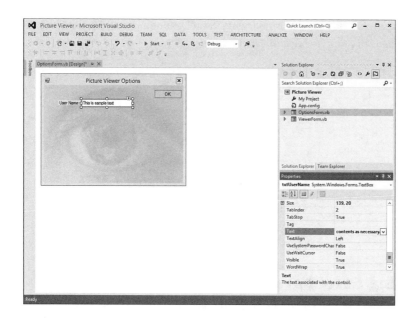

FIGURE 7.3
A text box might contain more text than it can display.

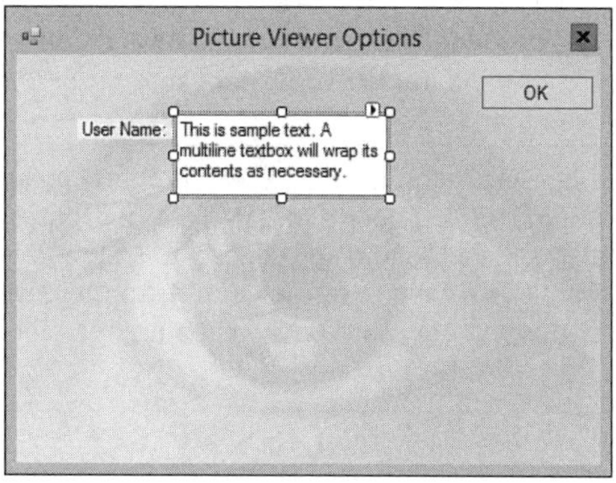

FIGURE 7.4
A multiline text box can be sized as large as necessary.

There will be times when you won't want a user to be able to interact with a control. For example, you might implement a security model in an application, and if the user doesn't have the necessary privileges, you might prevent him or her from altering data. The Enabled property, which almost every control has, determines whether the user can interact with the control. Change the Enabled property of the text box to False, press F5 to run the project, and click Options to show the Options form. Although no noticeable change occurs in the control in Design view, there's a big change to the control at runtime: The text appears in gray rather than black, and the text box doesn't accept the focus or allow you to change the text (see Figure 7.5).

Stop the project now by choosing Debug, Stop Debugging, and then change the control's Enabled property back to True.

Adding Scrollbars

Even though you can size a multiline text box, there will still be times when the contents of the control are more than can be displayed. If you believe this is a possibility for a text box you're adding to a form, give the text box scrollbars by changing the ScrollBars property from None to Vertical, Horizontal, or Both.

> **By the Way**
>
> For a text box to display scrollbars, its Multiline property *must* be set to True. Also, if you set the ScrollBars property to Both, the horizontal scrollbar won't appear unless you also set the WordWrap property to False. If you set WordWrap equal to True, text will always wrap to fit the control, so there will never be any text off to the right of the text box, and there will be no need for a horizontal scrollbar.

Change the ScrollBars property of your text box to Vertical, and notice how a scrollbar appears in the text box (see Figure 7.6).

> **By the Way**
>
> If you set a text box's AcceptsReturn property to True, the user can press Enter to create a new line in the text box. When the AcceptsTabs property is set to True, the user can press Tab within the control to create columns (rather than moving the focus to the next control).

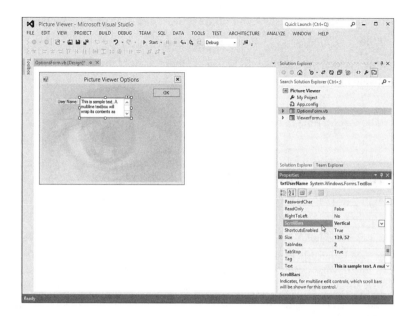

FIGURE 7.6
If a text box
might contain a
lot of text, give it
a scrollbar.

Limiting the Number of Characters a User Can Enter

You can limit how many characters a user can type into a text box by using the
MaxLength property. All new text boxes are given the default value of 32767 for
MaxLength, but you can change this as needed. To see how this works, follow these steps:

1. Change the text box's properties as follows:

Property	Value
Text	Make empty (*This means that you should clear out the value.*)
MaxLength	10
Multiline	False
ScrollBars	None

2. Press F5 to run the project.

3. Click the Options button to display the Options form.

4. Enter the following text into the new text box: **So you run and you run**. Notice
   that you can't enter more than 10 characters of text; all you're allowed to enter
   is **So you run**. The text box allows only 10 characters, whether you use the
   keyboard or a Paste operation. The MaxLength property is most often used
   when the text box's content is to be written to a database, in which field sizes

are usually restricted. (Using a database is discussed in Hour 21, "Working with a Database.")

5. Stop the project, and change the MaxLength property of the text box to 0, which effectively means that no maximum is defined.

Now would be a good time to save your work.

Creating Password Fields

You've probably used a password field: a text box that displays an asterisk for each character entered. You can make any text box a password field by assigning a character to its PasswordChar field. Select the PasswordChar property of the text box and enter an asterisk (*) for the property value. Run the project once more, and display the Options form. Next, enter text into the text box. An asterisk is displayed for each character you enter, as shown in Figure 7.7. Although the user doesn't see the actual text contained in the text box, referencing the Text property in code always returns the true text.

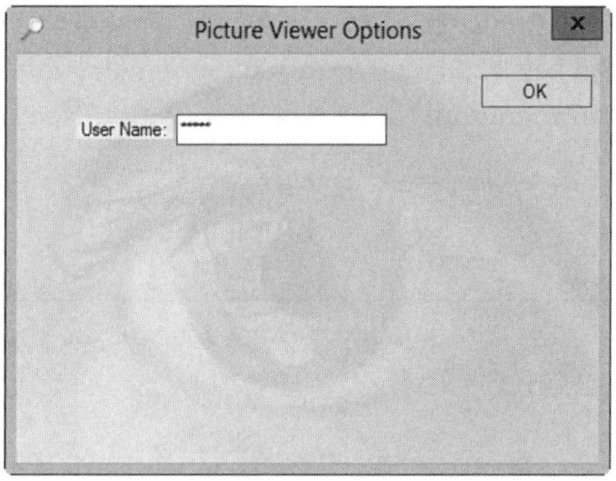

FIGURE 7.7
A password field displays its password character for all entered text.

By the Way

A text box displays password characters only if its Multiline property is set to False.

Stop the project by choosing Stop Debugging on the toolbar. Delete the asterisk from the PasswordChar field, and then save the project by clicking Save All on the toolbar.

Understanding the Text Box's Common Events

You'll rarely use a label's events, but you'll probably use text box events quite a bit. The text box supports many different events; Table 7.1 lists the ones you're most likely to use regularly.

TABLE 7.1   Commonly Used Events of the Text Box Control

Event	Description
TextChanged	Occurs every time the user presses a key or pastes text into the text box. Use this event to deal with specific keypresses (such as to capture specific keys) or when you need to perform an action whenever the contents change.
Click	Occurs when the user clicks the text box. Use this event to capture clicks when you don't care about the coordinates of the mouse pointer.
MouseDown	Occurs when the user first presses a mouse button over the text box. This event is often used in conjunction with the MouseUp event.
MouseUp	Occurs when the user releases a mouse button over the text box. Use MouseDown and MouseUp when you need more functionality than provided by the Click event.
MouseMove	Occurs when the user moves the mouse pointer over the text box. Use this event to perform actions based on the cursor's movement.

Creating Buttons

Every dialog box that Windows displays has at least one button. Buttons enable a user to invoke a function with a click of the mouse.

The options form already has an OK button. Typically, an OK button accepts the user's values and closes the form. Later in this book, you'll make your OK button do just that. When you have an OK button, it's also a good idea to create a Cancel button, which unloads the form but doesn't save the user's values.

Add a new button to the form by double-clicking the Button item in the toolbox. Set the button's properties as follows:

Property	Value
Name	btnCancel
Location	305, 38
Text	Cancel

There's no point in having a button that doesn't do anything, so double-click the button now to access its Click event, and then add the following statement:

```
Me.Close()
```

Recall from Hour 5, "Building Forms: The Basics," that this statement closes the current form. Right now, the Cancel button does the same thing as the OK button, but you'll change that soon.

> You can programmatically trigger a button's Click event, just as though a user clicked it, by calling the button's PerformClick method.

Accept and Cancel Buttons

When creating dialog boxes, it's common to assign one button as the default button (called the Accept button). If a form has an Accept button, that button's Click event is fired when the user presses Enter, regardless of which control has the focus. This is great for dialog boxes in which the user enters some text and presses Enter to commit the data and close the form.

Follow these steps to designate the OK button as the Accept button:

1. Double-click OptionsForm.vb in the Solution Explorer window to show the form in the designer once more.

2. Click the form to display its properties in the Properties window.

3. Click the form's AcceptButton property in the Properties window; a drop-down arrow appears. Click the arrow, and choose the button btnOK from the list. Notice that the button now has a blue border on the form, indicating that it is the default button for the form (see Figure 7.8).

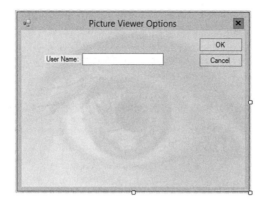

FIGURE 7.8
The Accept button appears blue.

4. Press F5 to run the project, and then click Options to display the Options form.

5. Click in the text box to make sure that it has the focus, and then press Enter; the form closes. Again, pressing Enter on a form that has a designated Accept button causes that button's Click event to fire the same as if the user clicked it with the mouse, regardless of which control has the focus. Actually, there is one exception. If the control with the focus is a multiline text box, pressing Enter creates a new line in the text box and doesn't cause the Accept button's Click event to fire.

Generally, when you create an Accept button for a form, you should also create a Cancel button. A Cancel button fires its Click event when the user presses the Esc key (as opposed to the Enter key), regardless of which control has the focus. Generally, you place code in a Cancel button to shut down the form without committing any changes the user made. Make your Cancel button an official Cancel button by following these steps:

1. Stop the running project.

2. Change the form's CancelButton property to btnCancel.

Use the following hints when deciding what buttons to assign as a form's Accept and Cancel buttons:

▶ If a form has an OK or Close button, that button probably should be assigned as the AcceptButton.

▶ If a form has both an OK and Cancel button, assign the OK button as the AcceptButton and the Cancel button as the CancelButton (yeah, this is pretty obvious, but it's often overlooked).

▶ If a form has a single Close or OK button, assign it to both the form's `AcceptButton` and `CancelButton` properties.

▶ If the form has a Cancel button, assign it to the form's `CancelButton` property.

Presenting Yes/No Options Using Check Boxes

A check box is used to display true/false and yes/no values on a form. You've probably run into many check boxes as you've worked with different Windows applications. Clicking the check box control toggles it between checked and unchecked (true/false, yes/no, and so on).

Add a new check box to the Options form now, and set its properties as follows:

Property	Value
Name	chkPromptOnExit
Location	105, 79
Text	Prompt to confirm on exit

The `CheckState` property of the check box determines whether the check box is checked. Try changing the value of this property, and watch the effect on the form. Notice that you can set the check box's `CheckState` to `Indeterminate`, which shows a big square in the control. You won't often need to use this, but it's good to know the feature is available. Be sure to set the `CheckState` to `Unchecked` before continuing.

Your form should now look like Figure 7.9.

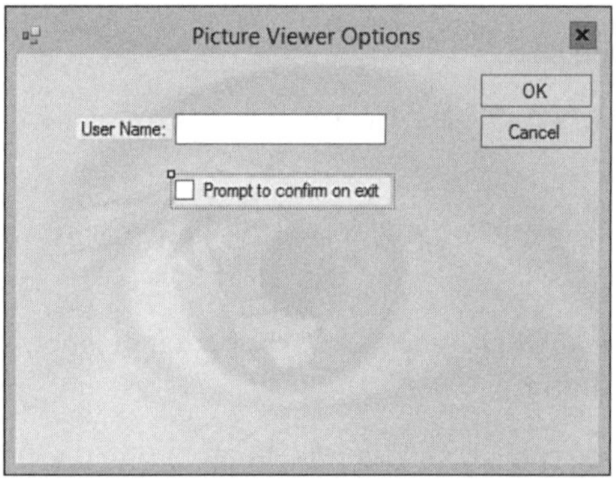

FIGURE 7.9
Use the check box to indicate a true/false or yes/no state.

Creating Containers and Groups of Option Buttons

In this section, you'll learn how to create containers for groups of controls, using panels and group boxes. You'll also learn how to use the Option Button control in conjunction with these container controls to present multiple choices to a user.

Using Panels and Group Boxes

Controls can be placed on a form because the form is a *container* object—an object that can host controls. A form isn't the only type of container, however. Some controls act as containers as well, and a container can host one or more other containers. The Panel and Group Box controls are both container controls that serve a similar purpose, yet each is more suited to a particular application.

The Group Box is a container control with properties that let you create a border (*frame*), and a caption. Add a new group box to your form now by double-clicking the GroupBox item in the toolbox (you'll find it in the Containers control category). When you create a new group box, it has a border by default, and its caption is set to the name of the control.

Try clicking in the center of the group box and dragging it around as you would another type of control. You can't. Think of the group box as a mini form—you can't click and drag a form to move it around. Clicking and dragging a group box lassos any controls placed on the group box—the same behavior you experience on a form. To drag a group box, click and drag the little image with the four arrows on it, as shown in Figure 7.10.

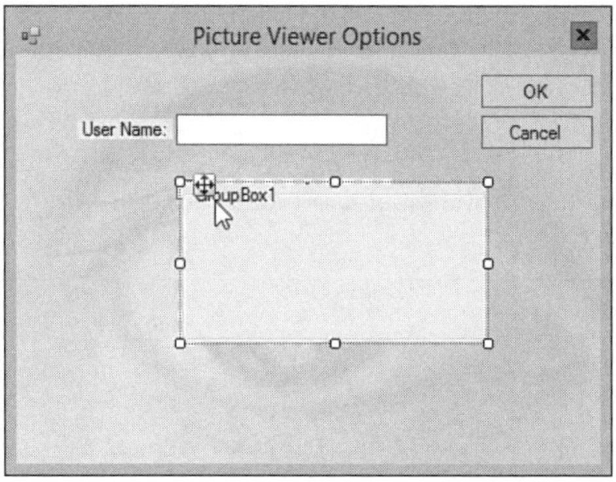

FIGURE 7.10
Click and drag this box to move a group box.

Set the properties of the group box as follows:

Property	Value
Name	grpDefaultBackcolor
Location	105, 112
Size	200, 72
Text	Default Picture Background Color

Your group box should now look like the one shown in Figure 7.11.

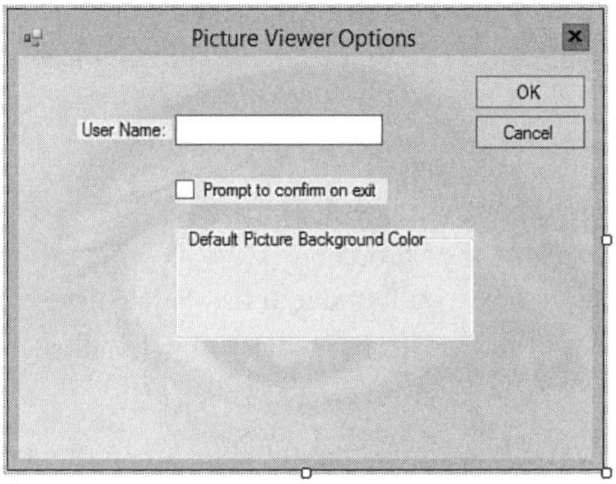

FIGURE 7.11
A group box acts
like a form within
a form.

The Group Box is a fairly straightforward control. Other than defining a border and displaying a caption, the purpose of a group box is to provide a container for other controls. The next section demonstrates the benefits of using a group box as a container.

By the Way

For the most part, the Panel control is a slimmed-down version of the Group Box control, so I won't discuss it in depth. If you need a basic container control without the additional features offered by the Group Box control (such as a border and caption), use the Panel control. The primary exception to this is that the panel offers scrolling capabilities just like those found on forms, which group boxes do not support.

Working with Radio Buttons

Check boxes are excellent controls for displaying true/false and yes/no values. However, check boxes work independently of one another. If you have five check boxes on a form, each one can be checked or unchecked—in any combination. Radio buttons, on the other hand, are mutually exclusive to the container on which they're placed. This means that only one radio button per container can be selected at a time. Selecting one radio button automatically deselects any other radio buttons on the same container. Radio buttons are used to offer a selection of items when the user is allowed to select only one item at a time. To better see how mutual exclusivity works, you'll create a small group of radio buttons for your Options form.

You can perform any of the following actions to place a control on a group box:

▶ Draw the control directly on the group box.

▶ Drop the control on the group box.

▶ Add the control to the form, cut the control from the form, select the group box, and paste the control on the group box.

You'll use the second method: dropping a new control directly on the group box. Follow these steps:

1. Click the RadioButton item in the toolbox, and drag it to the group box.

2. Release the mouse button when you're over the group box.

3. Move the radio button around by clicking and dragging it. Don't drag the radio button off the container, or it will be moved to the new container or form over which it is placed when you release the mouse button.

Set the properties of the radio button as follows:

Property	Value
Name	optBackgroundDefault
Location	14, 19
Text	Default Gray

Note that the Location property always refers to the container form's upper-left corner. If the control is on a group box, the location is relative to the upper-left corner of the group box. Now you'll copy this radio button and paste a copy of the control on the group box:

1. Right-click the radio button, and choose Copy from its context menu.

2. Click the group box to select it.

3. Right-click the group box, and choose Paste from its context menu to create a new radio button. Set the properties of the radio button as follows:

Property	Value
Name	optBackgroundWhite
Checked	True
Location	14, 42
Text	White

Now that you have your two radio buttons, as shown in Figure 7.12, run the project by pressing F5.

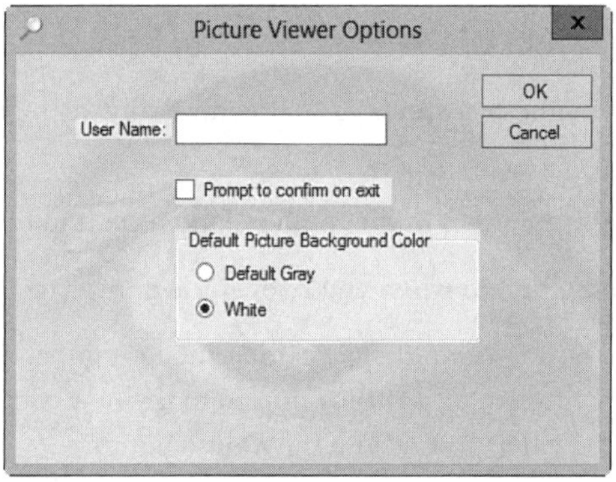

FIGURE 7.12
Radio buttons
restrict a user to
selecting a sin-
gle item.

Click the Options button to display your Options form, and take a look at the radio buttons. The second radio button is selected, so click the first radio button (Default Gray). Notice how the second radio button becomes deselected automatically (its Checked property is set to False). Two radio buttons are sufficient to demonstrate mutual exclusivity, but be aware that you could add as many radio buttons to the group box as you want to and the behavior would be the same.

The important thing to remember is that mutual exclusivity is shared only by radio buttons *placed on the same container*. To create radio buttons that behave independently of one another, you would need to create a second set on another container. You could easily create a new group box (or panel, for that matter) and place the second set of radio buttons on the new container. The two sets of radio buttons would behave independently of one another, but mutual exclusivity would still exist among the buttons within each set.

Stop the running project, change the Checked property of the optBackgroundDefault radio button to True, and save your work.

Displaying a List with the List Box

A list box is used to present a list of items to a user. You can add items to, and remove items from, the list at any time with very little Visual Basic code. In addition, you can set up a list box so that a user can select only a single item or multiple items. When a list box contains more items than it can show because of the control's size, a scrollbar appears automatically.

> The cousin of the list box is the combo box, which looks like a text box with a down-arrow button on its right side. Clicking a combo box's button causes the control to display a drop-down list box. Working with the list of a combo box is pretty much identical to working with a list box. Therefore, I'll discuss the details of list manipulation in this section and then discuss the features specific to the combo box in the next section.

By the Way

You won't add a list box or combo box to your Picture Viewer project at this time, so follow these steps to create a new project:

1. Create a new Windows Forms Application project titled **Lists**.

2. Rename the default form ListsForm.vb, and set its Text property to Lists Example.

3. Add a new List Box control to the form by double-clicking the ListBox item in the toolbox, and then set the list box's properties as follows:

Property	Value
Name	lstChemicalEchoSongs
Location	64, 32
Size	160, 121

Every item in a list box is a member of the list box's Items collection. You work with items, including adding and removing items, using the Items collection. You'll most often manipulate the Items collection using code (as I'll show you a little later in this hour), but you can also work with the collection at design time by using the Properties window.

Manipulating Items at Design Time

The Items collection is available as a property of the list box. Locate the Items property in the Properties window and click it to select it. The familiar button with three dots appears, indicating that you can do advanced things with this property. Click the button now to show the String Collection Editor. To add items to the collection, simply enter the items into the text box—one item to a line.

Enter the following items:

▶ Persian Wind

▶ Portal

▶ Dark and Stormy Night

▶ Cadence of Madness

▶ Lift Off

▶ Reentry

When you're finished, your screen should look like that shown in Figure 7.13. Click OK to commit your entries and close the window. Notice that the list box contains the items you entered.

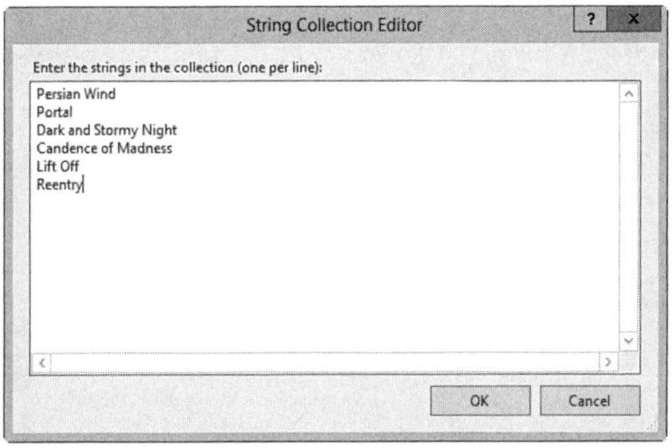

FIGURE 7.13
Use this dialog box to manipulate an Items collection at design time.

Manipulating Items at Runtime

In Hour 3, "Understanding Objects and Collections," you learned about objects, properties, methods, and collections. All this knowledge comes into play when you manipulate lists at runtime. The Items property of a list box (and a combo box, for that matter) is an object property that returns a collection. Collections in many ways are like objects—they have properties and methods. To manipulate list items, you manipulate the Items collection.

A list can contain duplicate values, as you'll see in this example. Visual Basic therefore needs a mechanism other than an item's text to treat each item in a list as unique. You do this by assigning each item in an Items collection a unique index. The first item in the list has an index of 0, the second an index of 1, and so on. The index is the ordinal position of an item relative to the first item in the Items collection—*not* the first item visible in the list.

Adding Items to a List

You add new items to the Items collection by using the Add() method of the Items collection. Now you'll create a button that adds a song to the list. Add a new button to the form, and set its properties as follows:

Property	Value
Name	btnAddSong
Location	96, 159
Size	100, 23
Text	Add a Song

Double-click the button to access its Click event, and add the following code:

```
lstChemicalEchoSongs.Items.Add("Orbit")
```

Notice that the Add() method accepts a string argument—the text to add to the list.

> Unlike items added at design time, items added through code aren't preserved when the program ends.

By the Way

Press F5 to run the project, and click the button. When you do, the new song is added to the bottom of the list. Clicking the button a second time adds another item to the list with the same album name. The list box doesn't care whether the item already exists in the list; each call to the Add() method of the Items collection adds a new item to the list.

The Add() method of the Items collection can be called as a function. In that case, it returns the index (the ordinal position of the newly added item in the underlying collection), as in the following:

```
Dim intIndex As Integer
intIndex = lstChemicalEchoSongs.Items.Add("Orbit")
```

Knowing the index of an item can be useful, as you will see.

Stop the running project, and save your work before continuing.

Did you Know?

> To add an item to an Items collection at a specific location in the list, use the Insert() method. The Insert() method accepts an index in addition to text. Remember, the first item in the list has an index of 0, so to add an item at the top of the list, you could use a statement such as lstChemicalEchoSongs. Items.Insert(0,"Orbit").

Removing Items from a List

Removing an individual item from a list is as easy as adding an item. It requires only a single method call: a call to the Remove() method of the Items collection. The Remove() method accepts a string, which is the text of the item to remove. Now you'll create a button that removes an item from the list.

Display the form designer, and create a new button on the form. Set the button's properties as follows:

Property	Value
Name	btnRemoveSong
Location	96, 188
Size	100, 23
Text	Remove Song

Double-click the new button to access its Click event, and enter the following statement:

```
lstChemicalEchoSongs.Items.Remove("Orbit")
```

The Remove() method tells Visual Basic to search the Items collection, starting at the first item (index = 0), and to remove the first item found that matches the specified text. Remember, you can have multiple items with the same text. The `Remove()` method removes only the first occurrence. After the text is found and removed, Visual Basic stops looking.

Press F5 to run the project again. Click the Add a Song button a few times to add Orbit to the list, as shown in Figure 7.14. Next, click the Remove a Song button, and notice how Visual Basic finds and removes one instance of the specified song.

FIGURE 7.14
The list box can contain duplicate entries, but each entry is a unique item in the `Items` collection.

To remove an item at a specific index, use the `RemoveAt()` method. For example, to remove the first item in the list, you would use the following statement: `lstChemicalEchoSongs.Items.RemoveAt(0)`. Be aware that this code will throw an exception (an error) if there are no items in the list when it is called.

Stop the running project, and save your work.

Clearing a List

To clear the contents of a list box, use the `Clear()` method. You'll add a button to the form that, when clicked, clears the list. Add a new button to the form, and set the button's properties as follows:

Property	Value
Name	btnClearList
Location	96, 217
Size	100, 23
Text	Clear List

Double-click the new button to access its `Click` event, and enter the following statement:

```
lstChemicalEchoSongs.Items.Clear()
```

Press F5 to run the project, and then click the Clear List button. The `Clear()` method doesn't care whether an item was added at design time or runtime; `Clear()` always removes all items from the list. Stop the project, and again save your work.

Remember that the `Add()`, `Insert()`, `Remove()`, `RemoveAt()`, and `Clear()` methods are all methods of the `Items` collection, not of the list box itself. If you forget that these are members of the `Items` collection, you might be confused when you don't find them when you enter a period after typing a list box's name in code.

Retrieving Information About the Selected Item in a List

Two properties provide information about the selected item: `SelectedItem` and `SelectedIndex`. It's important to note that these are properties of the list box itself, not of the `Items` collection of a list box. The `SelectedItem` property returns the text of the currently selected item. If no item is selected, the property returns an empty string. It is sometimes desirable to know the index of the selected item, and you can obtain this by using the `SelectedIndex` property of the list box. As you know, the first item in a list has an index of 0. If no item is selected, `SelectedIndex` returns –1, which is never a valid index for an item.

Now you'll add a button to the form that, when clicked, displays the selected item's text and index in a message box. First, stop the running project, and change the form's `Size.Height` property to 320 to accommodate one more button. As you build your interfaces, you'll often have to make small tweaks like this because it's nearly impossible to anticipate everything ahead of time.

Add a new button to the form, and set its properties as follows:

Property	Value
Name	btnShowItem
Location	96, 246
Size	100, 23
Text	Show Selected

Double-click the new button to access its `Click` event, and enter the following statement (be sure to press Enter at the end of the first line):

```
MessageBox.Show("You selected " & lstChemicalEchoSongs.SelectedItem & _
    ", which has an index of " & lstChemicalEchoSongs.SelectedIndex)
```

`MessageBox.Show()` is a Visual Basic function used to show a message to the user. You'll learn about `MessageBox.Show()` in detail in Hour 17, "Interacting with Users."

Press F5 to run the project, and click the Show Selected button. Notice that because nothing is selected, the message box doesn't read quite right, and it says that the selected index is –1 (which indicates that nothing is selected). Click an item in the list to select it, and then click Show Selected again. This time, you see the text of the selected item and its index in the message box, as shown in Figure 7.15. Stop the running project, and save your work.

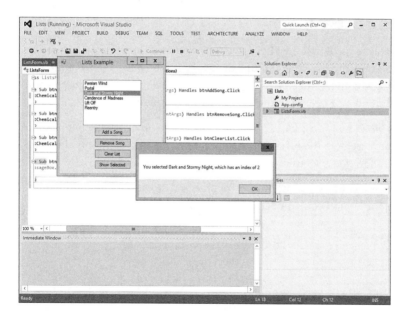

FIGURE 7.15
The `SelectedItem` and `SelectedIndex` properties make it easy to determine which item in a list is selected.

> You can set up a list box to allow multiple items to be selected at once. To do this, you change the `SelectionMode` property of the list box to `MultiSimple` (clicking an item toggles its selected state) or `MultiExtended` (you have to hold down Ctrl or Shift to select multiple items). To determine which items are selected in a multiselection list box, use the list box's `SelectedItems` collection.

By the Way

Sorting a List

List boxes and combo boxes have a `Sorted` property. This property is set to `False` when a control is first created. Changing this property value to `True` causes Visual

Basic to sort the contents of the list alphabetically. When the contents of a list are sorted, the index of each item in the Items collection is changed; therefore, you can't use an index value obtained prior to setting Sorted to True.

Sorted is a property, not a method. Realize that you don't have to call Sorted to sort the contents of a list; Visual Basic enforces a sort order as long as the Sorted property is set to True. This means that all items added via the Add() method or the Insert() method are automatically inserted into the proper sorted location, in contrast to being inserted at the end of the list or in a specific location.

Stop the running project, and save your work.

Creating Drop-Down Lists Using the Combo Box

List boxes are great, but they have two shortcomings. First, they take up quite a bit of space. Second, users can't enter their own values; they have to select from the items in the list. If you need to conserve space, or if you want to enable a user to enter a value that might not exist in the list, use the Combo Box control.

Combo boxes have an Items collection that behaves exactly like that of the List Box control (refer to the preceding section for information on manipulating lists). Here I'll show you the basics of how a combo box works.

Add a new combo box to the form by double-clicking the ComboBox item in the toolbox. Set the combo box's properties as follows:

Property	Value
Name	cboColors
Location	64, 5
Size	160, 21
Text	*Leave blank*

The first thing you should note is that the combo box has a Text property, whereas the list box doesn't. This works the same as the Text property of a text box. When the user selects an item from the drop-down list, the value of the selected item is placed in the Text property of the text box. The default behavior of a combo box is to allow the user to enter any text in the text box portion of the control—even if the text doesn't exist in the list. I'll show you how to change this behavior shortly.

Select the Items property of the combo box in the Properties window, and click the button that appears. Add the following items to the String Collection Editor, and click OK to commit your entries:

- ▶ Black

- ▶ Blue

- ▶ Gold

- ▶ Green

- ▶ Red

- ▶ Yellow

Press F5 to run the project. Click the arrow at the right side of the combo box, and a drop-down list appears, as shown in Figure 7.16.

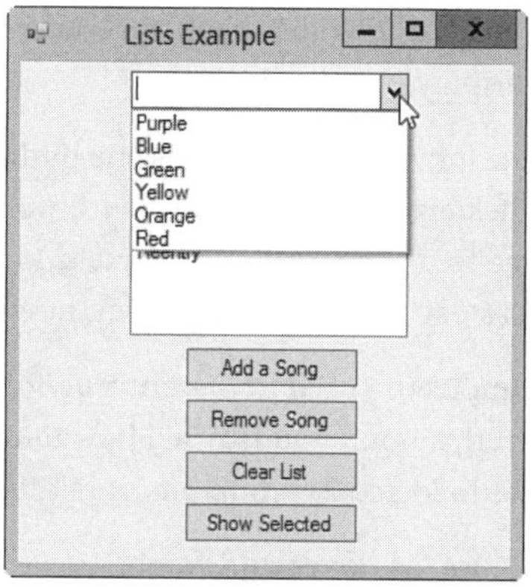

FIGURE 7.16
Combo boxes conserve space.

Try typing in the text **Magenta**. Visual Basic lets you do this. Indeed, you can type any text that you want. This may be the behavior you want, but more often you'll want to restrict a user to entering only values that appear in the list. To do this, you change the DropDownStyle property of the combo box. Close the form to stop the running project, and change the DropDownStyle property of the combo box to DropDownList. Press F5 to run the project again, and try to type text into the combo box. You can't. The combo box doesn't allow any text entry, so the user is limited to selecting items from the list. As a matter of fact, clicking in the "text box" portion of the combo box opens the list the same as though you clicked the drop-down arrow. Stop the running project, and change the DropDownStyle back to DropDown. Next, change the AutoCompleteSource property to ListItems and the AutoCompleteMode property to Suggest. Run the project again, and type **B** in the combo box. The combo box opens and suggests items starting with B. Try changing `AutoCompleteMode` to Append, and run the project again. This time, it fills the combo box with the closest match as you type! This is a very handy interface to give users.

As you can see, the combo box and list box offer similar functionality; in fact, the coding of their lists is identical. Each one of these controls serves a slightly different purpose, however. Which one is better? That depends entirely on the situation. As you use professional applications, pay attention to their interfaces; you'll start to get a feel for which control is appropriate in a given situation.

Summary

In this hour, you learned how to present text to a user. You learned that the `Label` control is perfect for displaying static text (text the user can't enter) and that the text box is the control to use for displaying edited text. You can now create text boxes that contain many lines of text, and you know how to add scrollbars when the text is greater than what can be displayed in the control.

I don't think I've ever seen a form without at least one button. You've learned how to add and work with their Click events. For the most part, working with buttons is a simple matter of adding one to a form, setting its `Name` and `Text` properties, and adding some code to its `Click` event—all of which you now know how to do.

Check boxes and option buttons are used to present true/false and mutually exclusive options, respectively. In this hour, you learned how to use each of these controls and how to use group boxes to logically group sets of related controls.

Finally, you learned how to use list boxes and combo boxes to present lists of items to a user. You now know how to add items to a list at design time as well as runtime, and you know how to sort items. The `List Box` and `Combo Box` are powerful controls, and I encourage you to dig deeper into their functionality.

Without controls, users would have nothing to interact with on your forms. In this hour, you learned how to use the standard controls to begin building functional interfaces. The controls discussed in this hour have been around since the early days of Visual Basic. In fact, they still behave much as they did years ago. Keep in mind that I only scratched the surface of each of these controls; most do far more than I've hinted at here. Mastering these controls will be easy, because you'll be using them a lot. Also, as you progress through this book, you will add code that saves the values the user enters into these controls, and shows the values again when the form is displayed.

Q&A

Q. *Can I place radio buttons directly on a form?*

A. Yes. The form is a container, so all radio buttons placed on a form are mutually exclusive to one another. If you wanted to add a second set of mutually exclusive buttons, they'd have to be placed on a container control. In general, I think it's best to place radio buttons in a group box rather than on a form. The group box provides a border and a caption for the radio buttons. It's also much easier to move around the set of radio buttons when you're designing the form. (You simply move the group box.)

Q. *I've seen what appear to be list boxes that have a check box next to each item in the list. Is this possible?*

A. Yes. In earlier versions of Visual Basic, this functionality was inherent in the standard list box control. In Visual Basic 2012, this is accomplished using an entirely different control: the checked list box.

Workshop

Quiz

1. Which control would you use to display text that the user can't edit?

2. What common property is shared by the Label control and text box and whose value determines what the user sees in the control?

3. What property must be set to True before you can adjust the height of a text box control?

4. What is the default event of a Button control?

5. What do you call a button whose Click event is triggered when the user presses Enter while another control has the focus?

6. Which control would you use to display a yes/no value to a user?

7. How would you create two distinct sets of mutually exclusive option buttons?

8. To manipulate items in a list, you use what collection?

9. What method adds an item to a list in a specific location?

Answers

1. The Label control

2. The Text property

3. The MultiLine property

4. The Click event

5. An Accept button

6. A check box

7. Place the radio buttons on two different container controls.

8. The Items collection

9. The Insert() method

Exercises

1. Use the skills you learned in the previous hours to set the tab order for your Options form. Make the user name text box the first in the tab order.

2. Create a form with two list boxes. Add a number of items to one list box at design time using the Properties window. Create a button that, when clicked, removes the selected item in the first list and adds it to the second list. Be sure to select an item before clicking your button!

Using Advanced Controls

What You'll Learn in This Hour:

▶ Creating timers

▶ Creating tabbed dialog boxes

▶ Storing pictures in an Image List control

▶ Building enhanced lists using the List View control

▶ Creating hierarchical lists using the Tree View control

The standard controls presented in Hour 7, "Working with Traditional Controls," enable you to build many types of functional forms. However, to create truly robust and interactive applications, you must use the more advanced controls. As a Windows user, you've encountered many of these controls, such as the Tab control, which presents data on tabs, and the Tree View control, which displays hierarchical lists such as the one in Explorer. In this hour, you'll learn about these advanced controls and how to use them to make professional interfaces like those you're accustomed to seeing in commercial products.

Many of the examples in this hour show you how to add items to collections at design time. Keep in mind that everything you can do at design time you can also accomplish using Visual Basic code.

By the Way

Creating Timers

All the controls you used in Hour 7 had in common the fact that the user can interact with them. Not all controls have this capability—or restriction, depending on how you look at it. Some controls are designed to be used only by the developer. One such control is the `Open File Dialog` control you used in your Picture Viewer application in Hour 1, "Jumping in with Both Feet: A Visual Basic 2012 Programming Tour." Another control that's invisible at runtime is the `Timer` control. The `Timer` control's sole purpose is to trigger an event at a specified time interval.

Follow these steps to build a timer sample project:

1. Create a new Windows Application titled Timer Example.

2. Right-click Form1.vb in the Solution Explorer, choose Rename, and change the name of the form to **TimerExampleForm.vb**.

3. Set the form's `Text` property to `Timer Example`. (Remember to click the form itself to view its properties.)

4. Add a new `Timer` control to your form by double-clicking the Timer item in the toolbox (it's located in the Components toolbox category).

The `Timer` control is invisible at runtime, so it's added to the gray area at the bottom of the screen rather than placed on the form, as shown in Figure 8.1.

Set the properties of the `Timer` control as follows:

Property	Value
Name	tmrClock
Enabled	True
Interval	1000

You probably noticed that the `Timer` control has very few properties compared to the other controls you've worked with; it doesn't need many. The most important property of the `Timer` control is the `Interval` property. It determines how often the `Timer` control fires its `Tick` event (where you'll place code to do something when the designated time elapses). The `Interval` property is specified in milliseconds, so a setting of 1,000 is equal to 1 second, which is exactly what you set the `Interval` to for this example. As with many controls, the best way to understand how the `Timer` control works is to use it. Now you will create a simple clock using the `Timer` and a `Label` control. The way the clock works is that the `Timer` control fires its `Tick` event once every second (because you've set the Interval property to 1,000 milliseconds). Within the Tick event, you update the label's Text property to the current system time.

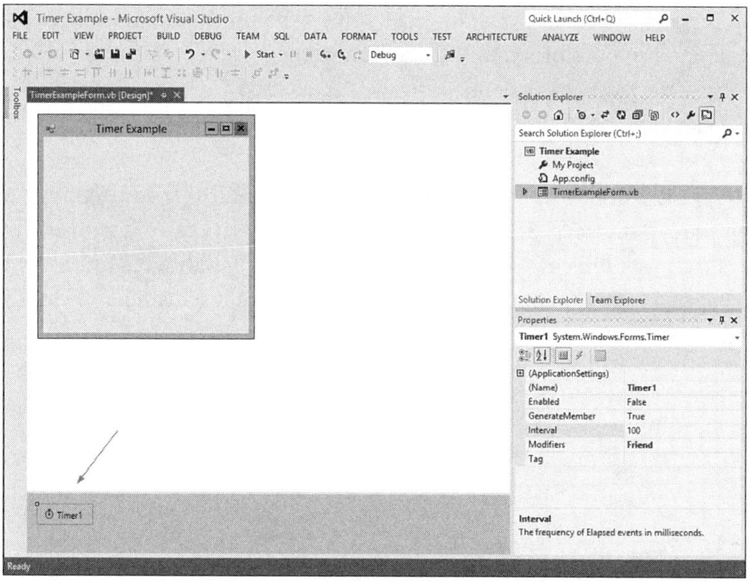

FIGURE 8.1
Invisible-at-runtime controls are shown at the bottom of the designer, not on a form.

Add a new label to the form, and set its properties as follows:

Property	Value
Name	lblClock
AutoSize	False
BorderStyle	FixedSingle
Location	95, 120
Size	100, 23
Text	Make blank (*literally make this property empty*)
TextAlign	MiddleCenter

The label's AutoSize property determines whether the label automatically adjusts its size when its Text property changes. Because we're aligning the text to the middle of the control, we don't want it to autosize.

Next, double-click the `Timer` control to access its `Tick` event. When a timer is first enabled, it starts counting from 0 in milliseconds. When the number of milliseconds specified in the `Interval` property passes, the `Tick` event fires, and the timer starts counting from 0 once again. This cycle continues until and if the timer is disabled (its `Enabled` property is set to `False`). Because you set the timer's `Enabled` property to `True` at design time, it starts counting as soon as the form on which it's placed is loaded. Enter the following statement in the `Tick` event:

```
lblClock.Text = TimeOfDay
```

`TimeOfDay()` is a handy function of Visual Basic that returns the current time of day based on the system clock. So, all this statement does is set the `Text` property of the label to the current time of day. It's important to remember that it does this once per second. Press F5 to run the project. You see the `Label` control acting as a clock, updating the time once every second, as shown in Figure 8.2.

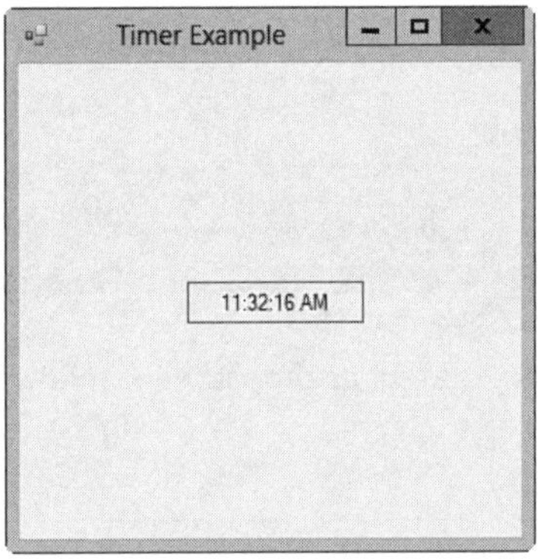

FIGURE 8.2
Timers make it easy to execute code at specified intervals.

Stop the running project, and save your work.

Timers are powerful, but you must take care not to overuse them. For a timer to work, Windows must be aware of the timer and must constantly compare the current internal clock to the timer's interval. It does all this so that it can notify the timer at the appropriate time to execute its `Tick` event. In other words, timers take system resources. This isn't a problem for an application that uses a few timers, but I wouldn't overload an application with a dozen timers unless I had no other choice (and there's almost always another choice).

Creating Tabbed Dialog Boxes

Windows 95 was the first version of Windows to introduce a tabbed interface. Since then, tabs have been widely adopted as a primary interface element. Tabs provide two major benefits: a logical grouping of controls and a reduction of required screen space. Although tabs might look complicated, they are actually easy to build and use.

You'll add a set of tabs to your Options dialog box in your Picture Viewer program. In this case, the tabs will be overkill, because you won't have much on them, but the point is to learn how they work, so follow these steps:

1. Start by opening the Picture Viewer project you completed in Hour 7.

2. Double-click OptionsForm.vb in the Solution Explorer to display it in the designer.

3. Add a new Tab control to your form by double-clicking the TabControl item in the toolbox (it's located in the Containers toolbox category). The Tab control defaults to having two tabs, which happens to be what you need for this example. Set the Tab control's properties as follows:

Property	Value
Name	tabOptions
Location	2, 2
Size	202, 94

4. The tabs that appear on a Tab control are determined by the control's TabPages collection. Click the TabPages property of the Tab control in the Properties window, and then click the small button that appears. Visual Basic shows the Tab-Page Collection Editor. Your Tab control has two tabs by default, as shown in Figure 8.3.

5. Each tab in the collection is called a page. Visual Basic names each new page TabPage$X$, where X is a unique number. Although you technically don't have to change the name of a page, it's easier to work with a Tab control if you give each tab a meaningful name, such as pgeGeneralPage, pgePreferencesPage, and so forth. The page TabPage1 is selected for you by default, and its properties appear to the right. Change the tab's name to pgeGeneral and set its Text property (which is what actually appears on the tab) to General (you might want to view the properties alphabetically to make this easier).

6. Click TabPage2 in the list on the left to select it. Change its Name property to pgeAppearance and set its Text property to Appearance.

7. Click OK to save your changes.

FIGURE 8.3
Use the TabPage
Collection Editor
to define tabs.

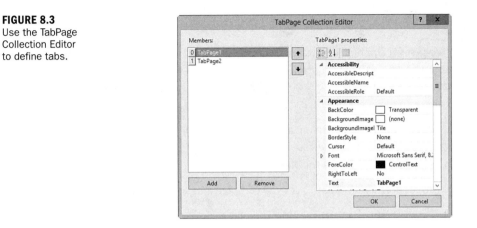

Your Tab control now has two properly defined tabs (pages), as shown in Figure 8.4.

FIGURE 8.4
Each tab should
have meaningful
text.

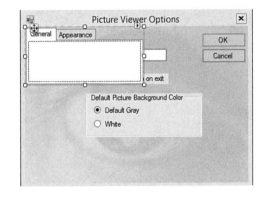

A quick way to add or remove a tab is to use the shortcuts provided in the description pane at the bottom of the Properties window.

Each page on a Tab control acts as a container, much like a Panel or Group Box control. This is why you can't drag the Tab control by clicking in the middle of it. To drag a container control, you have to click and drag the small image with the four arrows that appears over the General tab (refer to Figure 8.4). Follow these steps to move the options controls you created in Hour 7 to your new tabs:

1. Click the group box to select it (be sure not to click one of the radio buttons); then right-click it and choose Cut.

2. Click the Tab control to select it.

3. Now that the Tab control is selected, click the Appearance page to switch to the second page of the Tab control. Then click the center of the Appearance page.

4. Right-click in the center of the Appearance page and choose Paste.

5. Click the General tab to return to the first page of the Tab control. You might have to click it twice—do so slowly.

6. Get the Tab control out of the way by dragging the Move image (the little square with the directional arrows). Drag the tabs to the bottom of the form.

7. Click the User Name Label control to select it. Hold down the Shift key and click the User Name text box, and then click the check box.

8. Press Ctrl+X to cut the selected controls from the form.

9. Click the Tab control to select it.

10. Right-click in the center of the General tab and choose Paste.

11. Set the Tab control's Location property to 12, 12 and its Size property to 287, 145.

12. Click and drag the controls on the General tab so that they appear roughly centered on the tab, as shown in Figure 8.5.

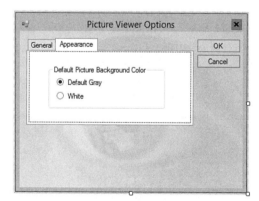

FIGURE 8.5
Tabs make it easy to group related controls.

To wrap up the Tab control, click the Appearance tab to switch to the Appearance page, and then move the group box to the middle of the page (by dragging and dropping it). When you're satisfied with its location, click the General tab again to switch to the first page.

By understanding two simple programming elements, you'll be able to do 99% of what you need to with the Tab control. The first element is that you'll need to know which tab is selected at runtime. The control's SelectedIndex property (not the TabIndex property) sets and returns the index of the currently selected tab: 0 for the first tab, 1 for the second, and so forth. The second thing to know is how to tell when the user switches tabs. The Tab control has a SelectedIndexChanged event, which fires whenever the selected tab is changed. In this event, you can check the value of SelectedIndex to determine which tab the user selected.

Perhaps the trickiest issue with the Tab control is that each tab page has its own set of events. If you double-click the tabs themselves, you get a set of global events for the Tab control (this is where you'll find the SelectedIndexChanged event). If you double-click a page on the tabs, you get a unique set of events for that page; each page has its own set of events.

Feel free to run your project now and check out how your tabs work. When you're finished, be sure to save your project.

Storing Pictures in an Image List Control

Many of the controls I discuss in this hour can attach pictures to different types of items. The Tree View control, which is used in Explorer to navigate folders, for example, displays images next to each folder node. Not all these pictures are the same; the control uses specific pictures to denote information about each node. It would have been possible for Microsoft to make each control store its images internally, but that would be highly inefficient because it wouldn't allow controls to share the same pictures. This would also cause a maintenance headache. For example, say that you have 10 Tree View controls, and each displays a folder image for folder nodes. Now it's time to update your application, and you want to update the folder image to something a bit nicer. If the image were stored in each Tree View control, you'd have to update all 10 of them (and risk missing one). Instead, Microsoft created a control dedicated to storing pictures and serving them to other controls: the Image List. When you put images in an Image List control, it's easy to share them among other types of controls.

You won't use the Picture Viewer for this section, so follow these steps to create a new project:

1. Create a new Windows Application named Lists and Trees.

2. Right-click Form1.vb in the Solution Explorer and rename it **ListsAndTrees Form.vb**. Also, set its Text property to Lists and Trees.

3. Add a new Image List control by double-clicking the ImageList item in the toolbox (it's located in the Components toolbox category). As with the Timer control, the Image List is an invisible-at-runtime control, so it appears below the form, not on it. Change the name of the Image List to imgMyImages.

4. The sole purpose of an Image List control is to store pictures and make them available to other controls. The pictures are stored in the control's Images collection. Click the Images property of the Image List control in the Properties window, and then click the small button that appears. Visual Basic displays the Image Collection Editor. Notice that this editor is similar to other editors you've used in this hour.

5. Click Add to display the Open dialog box, and use this dialog box to locate and select a 16×16 pixel icon. If you don't have a 16×16 pixel icon, you can create a BMP using Microsoft Paint, or download samples I've provided at http://www. samspublishing.com/ and http://www.jamesfoxall.com/download_files/. After you've added an image, click OK to close the Image Collection Editor.

Take a look at the ImageSize property of the Image control. It should be 16, 16. If it isn't, the bitmap you selected might not be 16×16 pixels. This property should be set to the dimensions of the first picture added to the Image List, but I've seen it not be set automatically. If you're using images of a different size, you might have to manually change the ImageSize property to the correct dimensions.

You can't always rely on the background where a picture will be displayed to be white—or any other color, for that matter. The Image List control therefore has a TransparentColor property. By default, the TransparentColor property is set to Transparent. Because you used an icon file here, and icon files maintain their own transparency information, you'll leave this property alone. If you were using a BMP file, or some other format that doesn't retain transparency information, you would want to use this property to designate a color in the bitmap that would appear transparent when used with another control.

That's all there is to adding images to an Image List control. The power of the Image List lies not in properties or methods of the control itself, but in its ability to be linked to other controls so that they can access the pictures the Image List stores. You'll do this in the next section.

Building Enhanced Lists Using the `List View` Control

The `List View` control is a lot like a list box on steroids—and then some. The `List View` can be used to create simple lists, multicolumn grids, and icon trays. The right pane in Windows Explorer is a `List View`. The primary display options available for Explorer's `List View` are Extra large icons, Medium icons, Small icons, List, Details, and Tiles. These are very similar to the display options available for a `List View` by way of its `View` property. (You might not know it, but you can change the appearance of the `List View` in Explorer by right-clicking it and using the View submenu of the shortcut menu that appears.) Now you'll create a `List View` with a few items on it and experiment with the different views—including showing a picture for the items, using the `Image List` from the preceding section.

> I can only scratch the surface of this great control here. After you've learned the basics in this hour, I highly recommend that you spend some time with the `List View` control, the help text, and whatever additional material you can find. I use the `List View` all the time. It's a powerful tool to have in your arsenal, because displaying lists is a very common task.

Add a `List View` control to your form now by double-clicking the ListView item in the toolbox. Set the properties of the `List View` as follows:

Property	Value
Name	lstMyListView
Location	8, 8
Size	266, 97
SmallImageList	imgMyImages
View	Details

As you can see, you can attach an `Image List` to a control via the Properties window (and by using code as well, of course). Not all controls support the `Image List`, but those that do make it as simple as setting a property to link to an `Image List` control. The `List View` actually allows linking to two `Image Lists`: one for large icons (32×32 pixels) and one for small images. In this example, you'll use only small pictures. If you wanted to use the large format, you could hook up a second `Image List` containing larger images to the `List View` control's `LargeImageList` property.

Creating Columns

When you changed the View property to Details, the control wanted to display a header for the columns in the list. But because you haven't yet defined columns, the header doesn't appear. The contents of this header are determined by the columns defined in the Columns collection.

Follow these steps to create columns in your List View:

1. Select the Columns property in the Properties window and click the small button that appears. Visual Basic displays the ColumnHeader Collection Editor window.

2. Click Add to create a new header, and change its Text property to Name and its Width property to 120.

3. Click Add once more to create a second column, and change its Text property to State. I haven't had you change the names of the columns in this example because you won't refer to them by name.

4. Click OK to save your column settings, and close the window.

Your List View should now have two named columns, as shown in Figure 8.6.

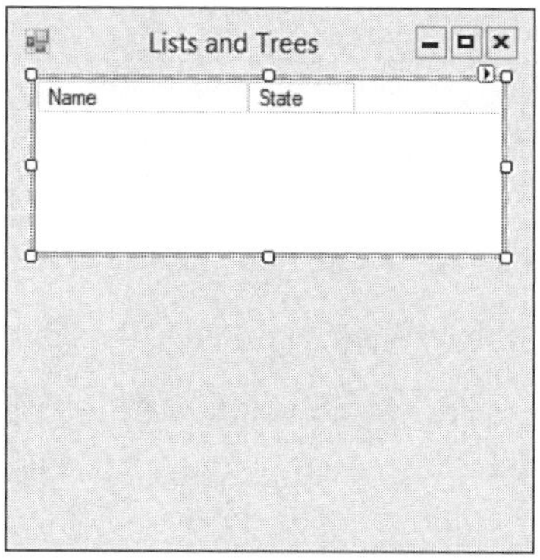

FIGURE 8.6
Use List Views to present multicolumn lists.

Adding List Items

Follow these steps to add two items to the List View:

1. Click the Items property in the Properties window, and then click the small button that appears to display the ListViewItem Collection Editor dialog box.

2. Click Add to create a new item, and change the item's Text property to James Foxall.

3. Open the drop-down list for the `ImageIndex` property. Notice how the list contains the picture in the linked `Image List` control, as shown in Figure 8.7. Select the image.

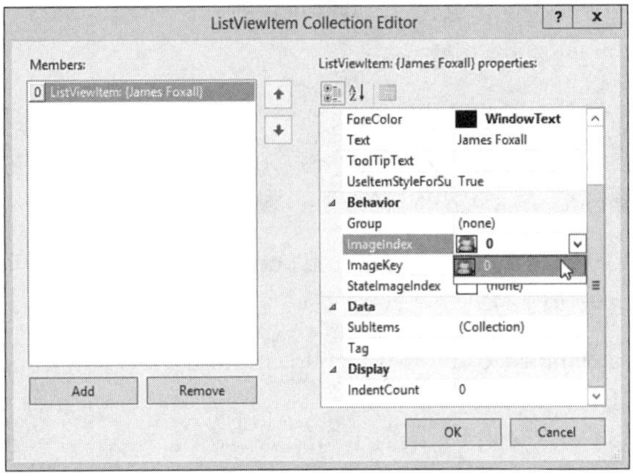

FIGURE 8.7
Pictures from a
linked Image
List are readily
available to the
control.

FIGURE 8.7
Pictures from a
linked Image
List are readily
available to the
control.

An item's `Text` property determines the text displayed for the item in the `List View`. If the `View` property is set to `Details` and multiple columns have been defined, the value of the `Text` property appears in the first column. Subsequent column values are determined by the `SubItems` collection.

4. Click the `SubItems` property (located in the Data category of the ListViewItem's properties). Then click the small button that appears, which displays the ListViewSubItem Collection Editor.

5. Click Add to create a new subitem, and change its text to Nebraska.

6. Click OK to return to the ListViewItem Collection Editor.

7. Click the Add button to create another item. This time, change the `Text` property to your name, and use the techniques you just learned to add a subitem. For the `Text` property of the subitem, enter your state of residence. Go ahead and give it an image, just as you did for my name.

8. When you're finished, click OK to close the ListViewItem Collection Editor. Your `List View` should now contain two list items, as shown in Figure 8.8.

FIGURE 8.8
List Views offer much more functionality than a standard list box.

9. Experiment with the View property of the List View control to see how the various settings affect the control's appearance. The Large Icons setting doesn't display an icon because you didn't link an Image List control to the LargeImageList property of the List View. Be sure to set the View property back to Details before continuing.

10. Press F5 to run the project, and try selecting your name by clicking your state. You can't. The default behavior of the List View is to consider only the clicking of the first column as selecting an item.

11. Stop the project, and change the FullRowSelect property of the List View to True. Then run the project once more.

12. Click your state again. This time, your name becomes selected (actually, the entire row becomes selected). I prefer to set up all my List Views with FullRowSelect set to True, but this is just a personal preference. Stop the project now, and save your work.

Manipulating a List View Using Code

You've just learned the basics of working with a List View control. Even though you performed all the steps in Design view for this example, you'll probably use code to manipulate your list items because you won't necessarily know ahead of time what to display in the list. Next, I'll show you how to work with the List View in code.

Adding List Items Using Code

Using Visual Basic code to add an item is simple—that is, if the item you're adding is simple. To add an item to your List View, you use the Add() method of the Items collection, like this:

```
lstMyListView.Items.Add("Bruce Crawford")
```

If the item is to have a picture, you can specify the index of the picture as a second parameter, like this:

```
lstMyListView.Items.Add("Monte Sothmann",0)
```

If the item has subitems, things get more complicated. The Add() method enables you to specify only the text and image index. To access the additional properties of a list item, you need to get a reference to the item in code. Remember that new items have only one subitem by default; you have to create additional items. The Add() method of the Items collection returns a reference to the newly added item. Knowing this, you can create a new variable to hold a reference to the item, create the item, and then use the variable to manipulate anything you choose to about the item. (See Hour 11, "Using Constants, Data Types, Variables, and Arrays," for information about using variables.) The following code creates a new item and appends a subitem to its SubItems collection:

```
Dim objListItem As ListViewItem
objListItem = lstMyListView.Items.Add("Rick Harber", 0)
objListItem.SubItems.Add("Georgia")
```

Determining the Selected Item in Code

The List View control has a collection that contains a reference to each selected item in the control: the SelectedItems collection. If the MultiSelect property of the List View is set to True (as it is by default), the user can select multiple items by holding down the Ctrl or Shift key when clicking items. This is why the List View supports a SelectedItems collection rather than a SelectedItem property. To gather information about a selected item, you refer to it by its index. For example, to display the text of the first selected item (or the only selected item if just one is selected), you could use code like this:

```
If lstMyListView.SelectedItems.Count > 0 Then
   MessageBox.Show(lstMyListView.SelectedItems(0).Text)
End If
```

The reason you check the Count property of the SelectedItems collection is that if no items are selected, a runtime error would occur if you attempted to reference element 0 in the SelectedItems collection.

Removing List Items Using Code

To remove a list item, use the Remove() method of the Items collection. The Remove() method accepts and expects a reference to a list item. To remove the currently selected item, for example, you could use a statement such as the following:

```
lstMyListView.Items.Remove(lstMyListView.SelectedItems(0))
```

Again, you'd want to make sure that an item is actually selected before using this statement.

Removing All List Items

If you're filling a List View using code, you'll probably want to clear the contents of the List View first. That way, if the code to fill the List View is called a second time, you won't end up with duplicate entries. To clear the contents of a List View, use the Clear() method of the Items collection, like this:

```
lstMyListView.Items.Clear()
```

The List View control is an amazingly versatile tool. As a matter of fact, I rarely use the standard List Box control; I prefer to use the List View because of its added functionality (such as displaying an image for an item). I've just scratched the surface here, but you now know enough to begin using this powerful tool in your own development.

Creating Hierarchical Lists Using the Tree View Control

The Tree View control is used to present hierarchical data. Perhaps the most commonly used Tree View control is found in Windows Explorer, where you can use the Tree View to navigate the folders and drives on your computer. The Tree View is perfect for displaying hierarchical data, such as an organizational chart of employees. In this section, I'll teach you the basics of the Tree View control so that you can use this powerful interface element in your applications.

The Tree View's items are contained in a Nodes collection, much like items in a List View are stored in an Items collection. To add items to the tree, you append them to the Nodes collection. As you can probably see by now, after you understand the basics of objects and collections, you can apply that knowledge to almost everything in Visual Basic. For instance, the skills you learned in working with the Items collection of the List View control are similar to the skills needed for working with the Nodes collection of the Tree View control. In fact, these concepts are similar to working with list boxes and combo boxes.

Add a Tree View control to your form now by double-clicking the TreeView item in the toolbox. Set the Tree View control's properties as follows:

Property	Value
Name	tvwLanguages
ImageList	imgMyImages
Location	8, 128
Size	266, 97

Adding Nodes to a `Tree View`

Working with nodes at design time is similar to working with a `List View`'s `Items` collection. So, I'll show you how to work with nodes in code. To add a node, you call the `Add()` method of the `Nodes` collection (which you'll do in this example). Add a new button to your form, and set its properties as follows:

Property	Value
Name	btnAddNode
Location	8, 231
Size	75, 23
Text	Add Node

Double-click the button to access its `Click` event, and enter the following code:

```
tvwLanguages.Nodes.Add("James")
tvwLanguages.Nodes.Add("Visual Basic")
```

Press F5 to run the project, and then click the button. Two nodes appear in the tree, one for each `Add` method call, as shown in Figure 8.9.

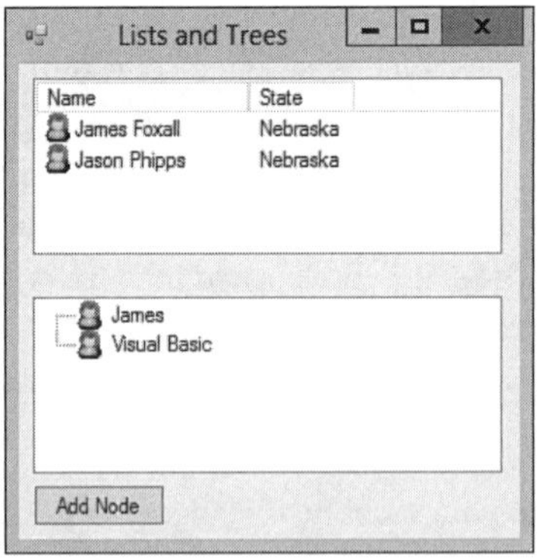

FIGURE 8.9
Nodes are the items that appear in a tree.

Notice how both nodes appear at the same level in the hierarchy; neither node is a parent or child of the other. If all your nodes will be at the same level in the hierarchy, consider using a List View control instead, because what you're creating is simply a list.

Stop the project, and return to the button's Click event. Any given node can be both a parent to other nodes and a child of a single node. (The parent node of any given node can be referenced via the Parent property of a node.) For this to work, each node has its own Nodes collection. This can be confusing, but if you keep in mind that child nodes belong to the parent node, it starts to make sense.

Now you'll create a new button that adds the same two nodes as before but makes the second node a child of the first. Return to the Design view of the form, and then create a new button and set its properties as shown:

Property	Value
Name	btnCreateChild
Location	89, 231
Size	80, 23
Text	Create Child

Double-click the new button to access its Click event, and add the following code:

```
Dim objNode As TreeNode
objNode = tvwLanguages.Nodes.Add("James")
objNode.Nodes.Add("Visual Basic")
```

This code is similar to what you created in the List View example. The Add() method of the Nodes collection returns a reference to the newly created node. Thus, this code creates a variable of type TreeNode, creates a new node whose reference is placed in the variable, and then adds a new node to the Nodes collection of the first node. To see the effect this has, press F5 to run the project and click the new button. You'll see a single item in the list, with a plus sign to the left of it. This plus sign indicates that child nodes exist. Click the plus sign, and the node is expanded to show its children, as shown in Figure 8.10.

This example is a simple one—a single parent node having a single child node. However, the principles used here are the same as those used to build complex trees with dozens or hundreds of nodes.

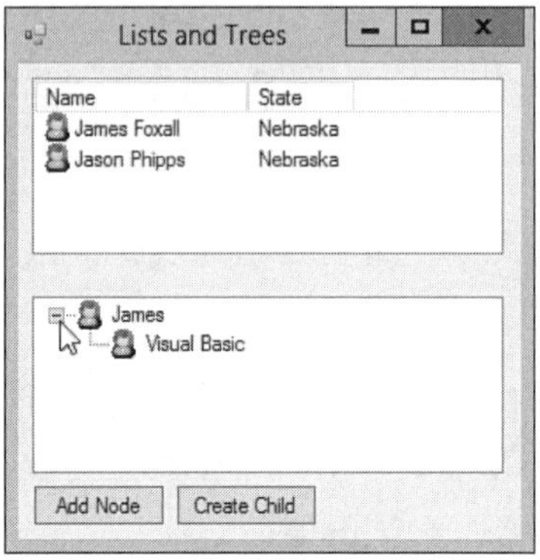

FIGURE 8.10
You can create
as deep a hierar-
chy as you need
using the Tree
View control.

Removing Nodes

To remove a node, you call the Remove() method of the Nodes collection. The
Remove() method accepts and expects a valid node, so you must know which node to
remove. Again, the Nodes collection works much like the Items collection in the List
View control, so the same ideas apply. For example, the currently selected node is
returned in the SelectedNode property of the Tree View control. So, to remove the
currently selected node, you could use this statement:

```
tvwLanguages.Nodes.Remove(tvwLanguages.SelectedNode)
```

If this statement is called when no node is selected, an error occurs. In Hour 11, you'll
learn all about data types and equalities, but here's a preview: If an object variable
doesn't reference an object, it's equivalent to the Visual Basic keyword Nothing.
Knowing this, you could validate whether an item is selected with a bit of logic, using
code like the following (note that unlike with the List View control, only one node
can be selected at a time in a Tree View control):

```
If Not (tvwLanguages.SelectedNode Is Nothing) Then
   tvwLanguages.Nodes.Remove(tvwLanguages.SelectedNode)
End If
```

By the Way

Removing a parent node causes all its children to be removed as well.

Clearing All Nodes

To clear all nodes in a Tree View, invoke the Clear() method of the Nodes collection:

```
tvwLanguages.Nodes.Clear()
```

As with the List View, I've only scratched the surface of the Tree View. Spend some
time becoming familiar with the basics of the Tree View, as I've shown here, and then
dig a bit deeper to discover the not-so-obvious power and flexibility of this control.

Summary

Visual Basic includes a number of controls that go beyond the standard functionality of the traditional controls discussed in Hour 7. In this hour, I discussed the most commonly used advanced controls. You learned how to use the Timer control to trigger events at predetermined intervals. You also learned how to use the Tab control to create the tabbed dialog boxes with which you're so familiar.

Also in this hour, you learned how to add pictures to an Image List control so that other controls can use them. The Image List makes it easy to share pictures among many controls, making it a useful tool. Finally, I taught you the basics of the List View and Tree View controls—two controls you can use to build high-end interfaces that present structured data. The more time you spend with all these controls, the better you'll become at creating great interfaces.

Q&A

Q. What if I need a lot of timers, but I'm concerned about system resources?

A. When possible, use a single timer for multiple duties. This is easy when two events occur at the same interval—why bother creating a second timer? When two events occur at different intervals, you can use some decision skills along with static variables (discussed in Hour 11) to share Timer events.

Q. What else can I do with an Image List control?

A. You can assign a unique picture to a node in a Tree View control when the node is selected. You can also display an image in the tab of a tab page in a Tab control. Image List has many uses. As you learn more about advanced controls, you'll see additional opportunities for using images from an Image List.

Workshop

Quiz

1. What unit of time is applied to the Interval property of the Timer control?

2. What collection is used to add new tabs to a Tab control?

3. What property returns the index of the currently selected tab?

4. True or false: You should use different Image List controls to store images of different sizes.

5. For you to see columns in a List View control, the View property must be set to what?

6. The additional columns of data that can be attached to an item in a List View are stored in what collection?

7. What property of what object would you use to determine how many items are in a List View?

8. What is each item in a Tree View control called?

9. How do you make a node the child of another node?

Answers

1. Milliseconds

2. The TabPages collection

3. The SelectedIndex property

4. True

5. Details

6. The SubItems collection

7. You check the Count property of the SelectedItems collection.

8. A node

9. You add it to the Nodes collection of the parent node.

Exercises

1. Add a second Image List control to your project with the List View. Place an icon (32×32 pixels) in this Image List, and set its ImageSize property to 32, 32. Next, link the Image List to the LargeImageList property of the List View control. Change the View property to Large Icons or Tile, and see how the large icons are used for these two views.

2. Create a new project, and add a List View, a button, and a text box to the default form. Create a new item in the List View, using the text entered into the text box when the button is clicked.

Adding Menus and Toolbars to Forms

What You'll Learn in This Hour:

▶ Adding, moving, and deleting menu items

▶ Creating checked menu items

▶ Programming menus

▶ Implementing context menus

▶ Assigning shortcut keys

▶ Creating toolbar items

▶ Defining toggle buttons and separators

▶ Creating a status bar

The graphical user interface (GUI) you can use to interact with and navigate programs is one of the greatest features of Windows. Despite this, a number of Windows users still rely primarily on the keyboard, preferring to use the mouse only when absolutely necessary. Data-entry people in particular never take their hands off the keyboard. Many software companies receive support calls from angry customers because a commonly used function is accessible only by using the mouse. Menus are the easiest way to navigate your program for a user who relies on the keyboard, and Visual Basic makes it easier than ever to create menus for your applications. In this hour, you'll learn how to build, manipulate, and program menus on a form. In addition, I'll teach you how to use the Toolbar control to create attractive and functional toolbars. Finally, you'll learn how to finish a form with a status bar.

Building Menus

When I said that Visual Basic makes building menus easier than ever, I wasn't kidding; building menus is an immediately gratifying process. I can't stress enough how important it is to have good menus, and because it's so easy to do, there's no excuse for not putting menus in an application.

Did you Know?

> When running an application for the first time, users often scan the menus before opening the manual. (Actually, most users never open the manual!) When you provide comprehensive menus, you make your program easier to learn and use.

Creating Top-Level Menus

You add menus to a form by way of a control: the Menu Strip control. The Menu Strip control is a bit odd. It's the only control I know of (besides the Context Menu Strip control, discussed later in this hour) that sits at the bottom of the form in the space reserved for controls without an interface (like a Timer control) even though it has a visible interface on the form.

Follow these steps to get started:

1. You'll use the Picture Viewer project that you worked on in Hour 8, "Using Advanced Controls," so open that project now.

2. Double-click ViewerForm.vb in the Solution Explorer to display the main picture viewer form in design view.

3. You'll need room at the top of the form, so change the form's Size.Height property to **375**.

4. Change the PictureBox's Location to **8, 52** and its Size to **282, 279**.

5. Select *all* the controls on the form *except the picture box* by Shift-clicking them or lassoing them. Be sure to get the X and Y labels as well! After they're all selected, click and drag the Select Picture button until its top aligns with the picture box (when you drag, all controls should move with the Select Picture button). Your form should now look like Figure 9.1. Note that once you select controls on a form, you can use the arrow keys to move them around, but the snap lines won't appear when you do so.

6. Add a new Menu Strip control to your form by double-clicking the MenuStrip item in the toolbox (located in the Menus & Toolbars category), and change its name to mnuMainMenu. As shown in Figure 9.2, the control is added to the pane at the bottom of the Form Designer. Take a look at the top of the form—you see the text Type Here.

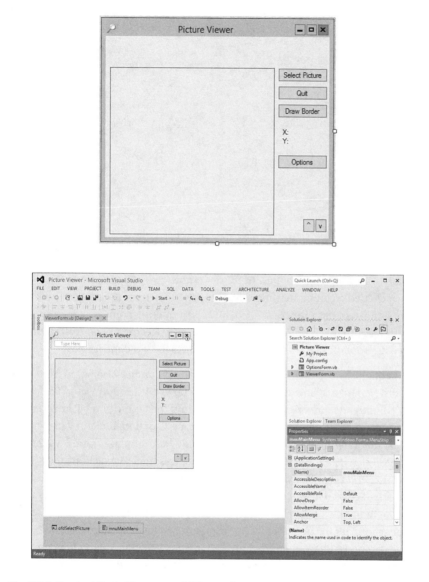

FIGURE 9.1
You'll need space for menus and toolbars at the top of your form.

FIGURE 9.2
A menu has no items when first added to a form.

7. Click the text Type Here, type **&File**, and press Enter. As you begin typing, Visual Basic displays two new boxes that say Type Here, as shown in Figure 9.3.

FIGURE 9.3
Creating a menu
item automati-
cally prepares
the control for
more items.

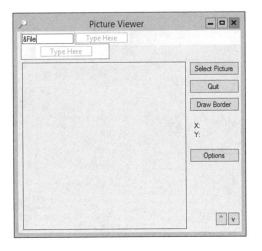

Notice the Properties window (if it's not visible, press F4 to show it). The text you just entered creates a new menu item. Each menu item is an object, and therefore, the item has properties. By default, Visual Basic names the menu FileTool-StripMenuItem. (You may need to click the new File menu item you created to see its properties.) It's a long name, but it gets the job done for now.

You might be wondering why I had you enter an ampersand (&) in front of the word *File*. Take a look at your menu now, and you'll see that Visual Basic doesn't display the ampersand; instead, it displays the text with the F underlined. The ampersand, when used in the Text property of a menu item, tells Visual Basic to underline the character immediately following it. For top-level menu items, such as the File item you just created, this underlined character is called an *accelerator key*. Pressing Alt plus an accelerator key opens the menu as if the user had clicked it. You should avoid assigning the same accelerator key to more than one top-level menu item on a form. To avoid conflicts, you can make any character the accelerator character, not just the first character (for example, typing **F&ile** would underline the i in File). When the menu item appears on a drop-down menu (as opposed to being a top-level item), the underlined character is called a *hotkey*. When a menu is visible (open), the user can press a hotkey to trigger the corresponding menu item just as if it were clicked. Again, don't use the same hotkey for more than one item on the same menu.

By the
Way

You can use the ampersand in the Text property of button controls and some other controls as well to create accelerator keys. For example, using "C&lick Me" for the Text property of a button would allow the user to "click" the button by pressing Alt+L.

8. Click the Type Here text that appears to the immediate right of the File item, enter **&Tools**, and press Enter. Visual Basic gives you two more Type Here items—the same as when you entered the File item. Adding new menu items is just a matter of clicking a Type Here box and entering the text for an item.

By the Way

If you click a Type Here box *below* an existing menu item, you add a new item to the same menu as the item above the box. If you click the Type Here box to the right of a menu item, you create a submenu that uses the menu to the left of the box as the entry point for the submenu. As you've seen, clicking the Type Here box along the top of the menu bar creates a top-level menu.

Creating Menu Items for a Top-Level Menu

You can create as many top-level menus as you have room for on a form. For the Picture Viewer, the File and Tools menus are adequate. Now you need to create the menu items that a user can select for these top-level menus. Follow these steps to create the menu items:

1. Click the File item to display a Type Here box *below* it. Click this Type Here box, enter **&Open Picture...**, and press Enter. If clicking the file item doesn't display the Type Here box, click a different control to remove the focus from the menu, click an empty area on the menu, and then click the File item once more.

2. Click the item you just created to give it the focus, and change the name of the new item to mnuOpenPicture.

3. Click the Type Here box below the Open Picture item you just created, type **&Quit**, and then press Enter. Change the name of the new item to mnuQuit. Now is a good time to save your work, so click Save All on the toolbar.

4. Click the Tools menu to select it. This displays a Type Here box to the right of and below the Tools item. Click the Type Here box *below* the Tools menu, type **&Draw Border**, and press Enter. Change the name of the new item to mnuDrawBorder.

5. This part can be tricky. Hover the pointer over the Type Here box below the Draw Border item. A small drop-down arrow appears. Click this arrow and select Separator, as shown in Figure 9.4. This drop-down is used to specify what type of item you want on the menu. You can create a combo box or a text box or, as in this case, a separator to isolate groups of unrelated menu items.

6. After you choose Separator, a line appears under Draw Border, and a new Type Here box appears. Click this box to select it, enter the text **&Options...**, and then press Enter to create the menu item. Change the name of this new item to mnuOptions.

7. Click the picture box or some other control to stop editing the menu.

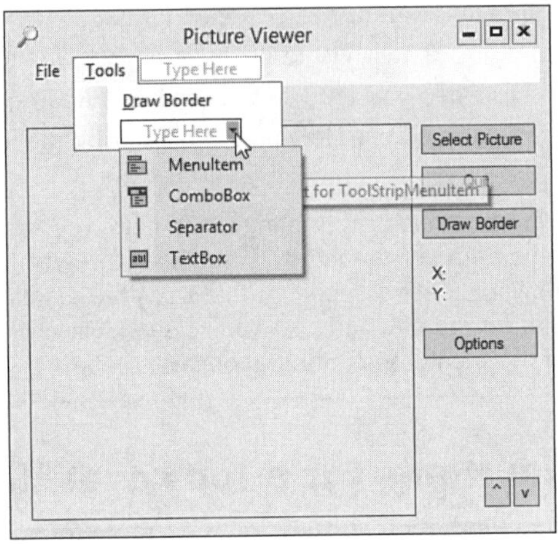

FIGURE 9.4
You can create text boxes, combo boxes, and separators in addition to regular menu items.

Moving and Deleting Menu Items

Deleting and moving menu items are even easier than adding new items. To delete a menu item, right-click it and choose Delete from the context menu that appears. To move an item, drag it from its current location and drop it in the location in which you want it placed.

Creating Checked Menu Items

A menu item that isn't used to open a submenu can display a check mark next to its text. Check marks are used to create menu items that have state—the item is either selected or it isn't. Now you'll create a checked menu item. Remember from Hour 7, "Working with Traditional Controls," the check box you created for the Options form? It was used to specify whether the user should be prompted before the Picture Viewer closes. Now you'll create a menu item for this as well. Follow these steps:

1. Click the File menu to open it.

2. Click the Type Here box below the Quit menu item, enter **Confirm on Exit**, and press Enter. Change the name of the new item to mnuConfirmOnExit.

3. Right-click Confirm on Exit, and choose Checked from the shortcut menu, as shown in Figure 9.5. If your menu is different from the one shown in Figure 9.5, click a different menu item, and then right-click the Confirm on Exit item. You also could click the menu item and change its Checked property in the Properties window.

4. Click and drag the Confirm on Exit item, and drop it on the Quit menu item. This moves the item above the Quit item. Your menu now looks like Figure 9.6.

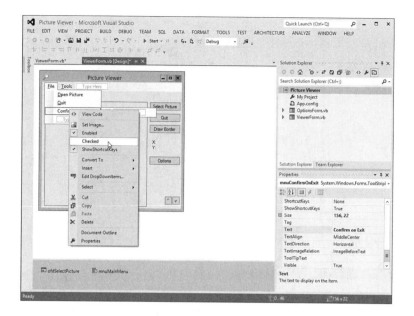

FIGURE 9.5
Menu items can be used to indicate state.

FIGURE 9.6
Menus are created in an interactive fashion.

Press F5 to run the project. The menu appears on your form, just as you designed it (see Figure 9.7). Click the File menu to open it, and then click Quit; nothing happens. In fact, the checked state of your menu item doesn't change even if you click that item. In the next section, I'll show you how to add code to menu items to make them actually do something (including changing their checked state).

Stop the project now, and save your work.

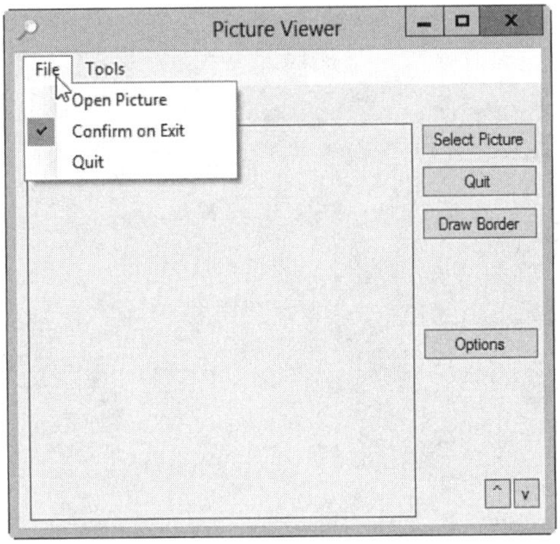

FIGURE 9.7
Menus appear at
runtime the
same as they do
at design time.

Programming Menus

Every menu item is a unique object. You could actually edit each item by clicking it to select it and then changing the item's properties in the Properties window. Although individual menu items aren't controls per se, adding code behind them is similar to adding code behind a control. Now you'll add code to menu items you created.

Follow these steps to create the code for the menus:

1. Click the File menu to open it.

2. Double-click the Open Picture menu item. Just as when you double-click a control, Visual Basic displays the code editor with the default event for the menu item you've clicked. For menu items, this is the Click event.

3. Enter the following code:

```
' Show the open file dialog box.
If ofdSelectPicture.ShowDialog = DialogResult.OK Then
    ' Load the picture into the picture box.
    picShowPicture.Image = Image.FromFile(ofdSelectPicture.FileName)
    ' Show the name of the file in the form's caption.
    Me.Text = "Picture Viewer (" & ofdSelectPicture.FileName & ")"
End If
```

This is the exact code you entered for the Select Picture button you created in Hour 1, "Jumping in with Both Feet: A Visual Basic 2012 Programming Tour," so I won't discuss it here.

4. Double-click ViewerForm.vb in the Solution Explorer window to switch back to the Form Designer for the Picture Viewer form.

5. Double-click the Confirm on Exit menu item to access its `Click` event. Enter the following code statement:

```
mnuConfirmOnExit.Checked = Not(mnuConfirmOnExit.Checked)
```

When Confirm on Exit is clicked, this code sets the item's checked state to the opposite of the item's current checked state. The function `Not()` is used to negate a Boolean (true or false) value. Don't worry; I discuss this in detail in Hour 12, "Performing Arithmetic, String Manipulation, and Date/Time Adjustments." For now, realize that if the current value of the `Checked` property is `True`, `Not()` returns `False`. If `Checked` currently is `False`, `Not()` returns `True`. Therefore, the checked value toggles between `True` and `False` each time the menu item is clicked.

6. Double-click ViewerForm.vb in the Solution Explorer window (or click the ViewerForm.vb [Design] tab) to switch back to the Form Designer for the Picture Viewer form again.

7. Double-click the Quit menu item to access its `Click` event, and enter the following code:

```
Me.Close()
```

Again, recall from Hour 1 that this statement simply closes the form. This has the effect of closing the application, because it's the only form that's loaded.

8. Return to the form designer for the viewer form yet again, click Tools to display the Tools menu, and then double-click the Draw Border menu item to access its `Click` event. Enter the following code:

```
Dim objGraphics As Graphics
objGraphics = Me.CreateGraphics
objGraphics.Clear(System.Drawing.SystemColors.Control)

objGraphics.DrawRectangle(System.Drawing.Pens.Blue, _
                    picShowPicture.Left - 1, _
                    picShowPicture.Top - 1, _
                    picShowPicture.Width + 1, picShowPicture.Height + 1)

objGraphics.Dispose()
```

This code is also directly from Hour 1, so refer to that hour for the specifics on how this code works.

9. Return to the Form Designer, double-click the Options menu item, and enter the following code in its `Click` event:

```
OptionsForm.ShowDialog()
```

You have just added all the code necessary for your menu to function. Follow these steps to test your work:

1. Press F5 to run the project. Open the File menu by pressing Alt+F (remember, the F is the accelerator key).

2. Click the Confirm on Exit menu item. The menu closes, so click File again to open it; notice that the item is no longer checked. Clicking it again would check it.

3. Click all the menu items except Quit to make sure that they work as expected. When you're finished, choose File, Quit to close the running project.

If you selected Confirm on Exit, you might have noticed that you weren't asked whether you really wanted to quit. That's because the quit code hasn't been written to consider the checked state of the Ask Before Closing button. You'll hook up this item, as well as all the other options, in Hour 11, "Using Constants, Data Types, Variables, and Arrays."

Did you Know?

> When designing your menus, look at some of the many popular Windows applications available and consider the similarities and differences between their menus and yours. Although your application might be unique and therefore have different menus from other applications, there are probably similarities as well (such as Cut, Copy, Paste, Open, and so on). When possible, make menu items in your application follow the same structure and design as similar items in the popular programs. This will shorten the learning curve for your application, reduce user frustration, and save you time.

Implementing Context Menus

Context menus (also called shortcut menus) are the pop-up menus that appear when you right-click an object on a form. Context menus get their name from the fact that they display context-sensitive choices—menu items that relate directly to the object that's right-clicked. Most Visual Basic controls have a default context menu, but you can assign custom context menus if you want. Creating context menus is much like creating regular menus. To create context menus, however, you use a different control: the `Context Menu Strip` control.

Follow these steps to implement a custom context menu in your project:

1. Display the ViewerForm.vb form in the Form Designer.

2. Add a new context menu strip to the form by double-clicking the Context Menu Strip item in the toolbox. Like the Main Menu control, the Context Menu Strip control is placed in the pane below the Form Designer. Change its name to mnuPictureContext.

3. When the Context Menu Strip control is selected, a context menu appears toward the top for editing. Click the Type Here box, enter the text **Draw Border** (see Figure 9.8), and press Enter to create the menu item. You've just created a context menu with a single menu item.

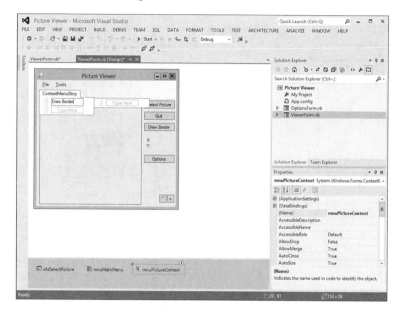

FIGURE 9.8
Context menus are edited in much the same way as regular menus.

4. Double-click the new menu item to access its Click event, and enter the following code:

```
Dim objGraphics As Graphics
objGraphics = Me.CreateGraphics
objGraphics.Clear(System.Drawing.SystemColors.Control)

objGraphics.DrawRectangle(System.Drawing.Pens.Blue, _
                    picShowPicture.Left - 1, _
                    picShowPicture.Top - 1, _
                    picShowPicture.Width + 1, picShowPicture.Height + 1)

objGraphics.Dispose()
```

Yes, this is exactly the same code you entered for the Draw Border menu item and the Draw Border button. It seems sort of redundant to enter the same code in three places, doesn't it? In Hour 10, "Creating and Calling Code Procedures,"

I'll show you how to share code so that you don't have to enter it in multiple places!

5. Double-click ViewerForm.vb in the Solution Explorer to return to the designer for the Picture Viewer form.

6. You link a control to a context menu by setting a property. Click the picture box on the form now to select it, and then change the ContextMenuStrip property of the picture box to mnuPictureContext; the context menu is now linked to the picture box.

7. Press F5 to run the project, and right-click the picture box. You see the context menu shown in Figure 9.9. Go ahead and choose Draw Border, and the border will be drawn.

FIGURE 9.9
Context menus
make handy
shortcuts.

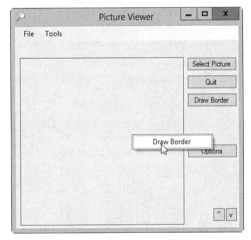

8. Stop the project, and save your work.

Assigning Shortcut Keys to Menu Items

If you've spent any time learning a Microsoft application, you've most likely learned some keyboard shortcuts. For example, pressing Ctrl+P in any application that prints has the same effect as opening the File menu and choosing Print.

Add shortcuts to your menus now by following these steps:

1. Click the File menu at the top of the form to open it, and then click Open Picture.

2. In the Properties window, click the ShortcutKeys property, and then click the down arrow that appears. This drop-down, shown in Figure 9.10, enables you to define a shortcut key for the selected menu item.

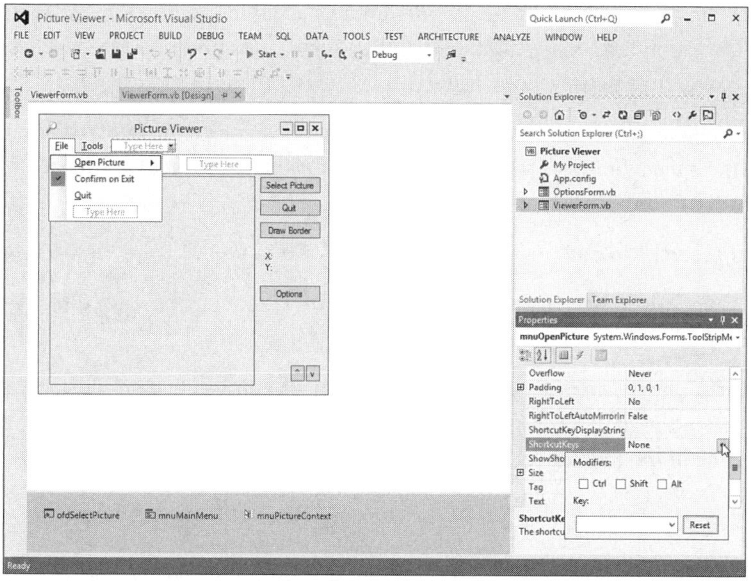

FIGURE 9.10
Use the
ShortcutKeys
property of a
menu item to
assign a short-
cut key.

3. Check Ctrl and then select O (for Open) from the Key drop-down menu; then click another property to close the drop-down.

4. Press F5 to run the project once more. Next, press Ctrl+O. The application behaves as though you opened the File menu and clicked the Open Picture item.

> Although it isn't always possible, try to assign logical shortcut key combinations. The meaning of F6 is hardly intuitive, for example. But, when assigning modifiers such as Ctrl with another character, you have some flexibility. For instance, the key combination of Ctrl+Q might be a more intuitive shortcut key for Quit than Ctrl+T. Again, if the menu item is the same as or similar to a menu item in a commercial application, use the same shortcut key as the commercial application does.

Did you Know?

Stop the running project, and save your work before continuing.

Using the Toolbar Control

Generally, when a program has a menu (as most programs should), it should also have a toolbar. Using a toolbar (called a *toolstrip* in Visual Basic for some reason) is one of the easiest ways for a user to access program functions. Unlike menu items, toolbar items are always visible and therefore are immediately available. In addition, toolbar items have ToolTips, which enable a user to discover a tool button's purpose simply by hovering the mouse pointer over the button.

Toolbar items are really shortcuts for menu items; every item on a toolbar should have a corresponding menu item. Remember, some users prefer to use the keyboard, in which case they need to have keyboard access to functions via menus.

The actual items you place on a toolbar depend on the features the application supports. However, the mechanics of creating toolbars and toolbar items are the same regardless of the buttons you choose to use. You create toolbars by using the ToolStrip control.

Follow these steps to add a toolbar to the main form in your Picture Viewer project:

1. Display the ViewerForm.vb form in the Form Designer (if it's not already displayed).

2. Add a new ToolStrip control to your form by double-clicking the ToolStrip item in the toolbox. A new toolbar is added to the top of your form. Change the name of the toolbar to tbrMainToolbar. Your form should now look like Figure 9.11.

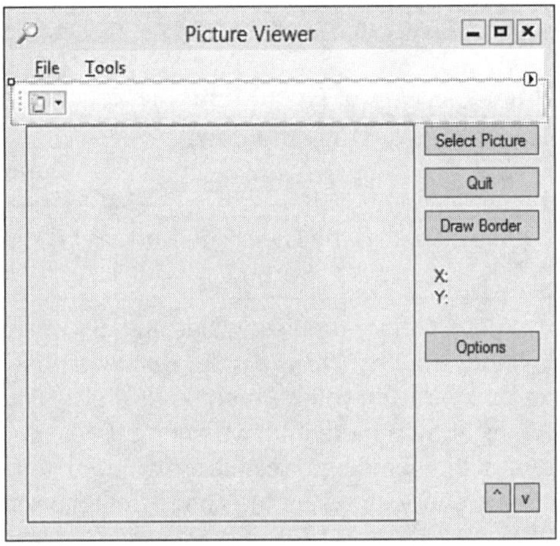

FIGURE 9.11
New toolbars have no buttons.

Adding Toolbar Buttons Using the Items Collection

Like many other controls you've already learned about, the ToolStrip control supports a special collection: Items. The Items collection contains the buttons that appear on the toolbar. Click the Items property in the Properties window, and then click the small button that appears; the Items Collection Editor appears. The list of members shows the toolbar itself, but no buttons, because new toolbars have no buttons.

You'll add three images to your toolbar: one for Open, one for Draw Border, and one for Options. You can download these images from my website, http://www.jamesfoxall.com/download_files/.

By the
Way

Open the drop-down list in the upper-left corner, as shown in Figure 9.12. This list contains the types of items that can be added to a toolbar.

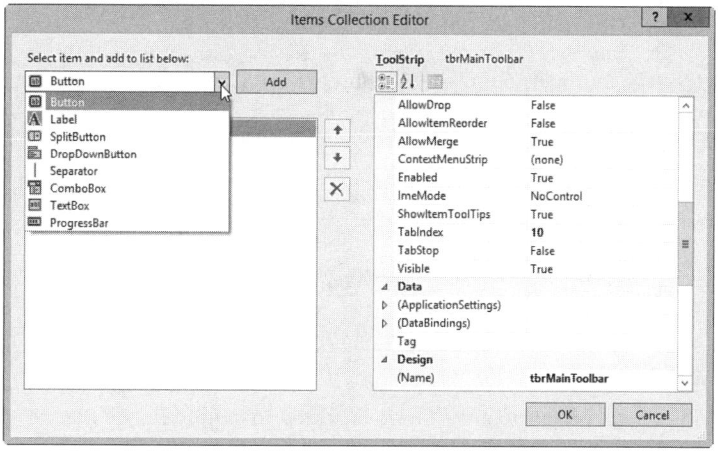

FIGURE 9.12
Toolbars may contain a number of different types of items.

For this example, you will create buttons and separators. Feel free to experiment with the different item types in another project. Follow these steps:

1. Select Button in the drop-down list and click Add to create a new button. Set its properties as follows (you might want to change the property display sort order to Alphabetical):

Property	Value
Name	tbbOpenPicture
Text	Open Picture
ToolTipText	Open Picture

2. Click the Image property for the button, and then click the Build button that appears. Click Import, and then browse and select the Open image.

3. Click OK to save the image in the button.

4. Click Add once more and click Button to create a new button. Set its properties as follows:

Property	Value
Name	tbbDrawBorder
Text	Draw Border
ToolTipText	Draw Border

5. Set the Image property of the Draw Border button to a valid image file.

6. Click Add once again to create another new button. Set its properties as follows:

Property	Value
Name	tbbOptions
Text	Options
ToolTipText	Options

7. Set the Image property of the Options button to a valid image file.

You've now created the buttons for your toolbar. There's one last thing you should do, however. Professional designers always separate related groups of tool buttons using a *separator*. A separator is a vertical line that appears between two buttons. All three of the buttons you've created are relatively unrelated, so now you'll create separators to isolate them from one another. Follow these steps:

1. Choose Separator from the drop-down list and click Add to create a separator. The separator is added at the end of the row of buttons. Click the new separator item in the Members list to select it, and then click the up arrow button twice to move the separator so that it appears in front of the Draw Border button.

2. Click Add again to create another new separator. Move this separator so that it appears between the Draw Border and Options buttons.

3. Click OK to close the Items Collections Editor dialog box, and then click the form to deselect the toolbar control. Your screen should look like Figure 9.13.

By the Way

> You can use the Items Collection Editor to add items to a toolbar, rather than adding them dynamically as shown in this example.

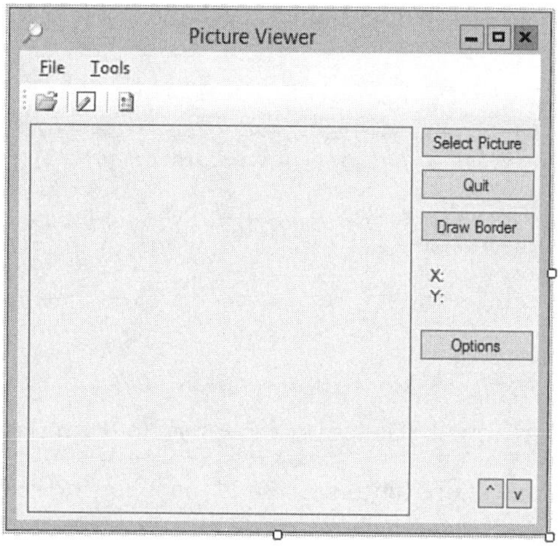

FIGURE 9.13
Your toolbar is now ready for some code to make it work.

Programming Toolbars

Programming toolbars is pretty much the same as programming menus. As you will see, Microsoft has chosen to standardize things whenever possible. For example, in early versions of .NET, you worked with a Toolbar control that had a Buttons collection. In 2005, the Toolbar control was replaced with a Toolstrip control that has an Items collection. The List View control has an Items collection, as does the Tree View control. Seeing a pattern? After you learn how to work with the Items collection of one control, it's an easy transition to work with the Items collection of other controls.

Follow these steps to make your toolbar functional:

1. Click the tbrMainToolbar control below the form to select it.

2. Double-click the Open button on the toolbar to access its Click event. Be sure to click the button and not the toolbar. Double-clicking the toolbar accesses a different event altogether. Enter the following code:

```
' Show the open file dialog box.
If ofdSelectPicture.ShowDialog = DialogResult.OK Then
    ' Load the picture into the picture box.
    picShowPicture.Image = Image.FromFile(ofdSelectPicture.FileName)
    ' Show the name of the file in the form's caption.
    Me.Text = "Picture Viewer(" & ofdSelectPicture.FileName & ")"
End If
```

3. Click the ViewerForm.vb [Design] tab to return to Form Design view.

4. Double-click the Draw Border button, and add the following code to its Click event:

```
Dim objGraphics As Graphics
objGraphics = Me.CreateGraphics
objGraphics.Clear(System.Drawing.SystemColors.Control)

objGraphics.DrawRectangle(System.Drawing.Pens.Blue, _
    picShowPicture.Left - 1, _
    picShowPicture.Top - 1, _
    picShowPicture.Width + 1, picShowPicture.Height + 1)

objGraphics.Dispose()
```

5. Click the ViewerForm.vb [Design] tab to return to Form Design view.

6. Double-click the Options button, and add the following code to its Click event:

```
OptionsForm.ShowDialog()
```

Go ahead and save your work, and then press F5 to run the project. Clicking the toolbar buttons should now perform the same actions as clicking the menu items. In Hour 10, I'll show you how the two controls can share code.

Creating Drop-Down Menus for Toolbar Buttons

Although you won't use one in this project, be aware that you can create drop-down menus on toolbars, as shown in Figure 9.14. Visual Basic 2012 uses these in a number of places. To create a menu like this, rather than add a regular button to the toolbar, you add a DropDownButton. Doing so creates a submenu just as it did when you defined regular menus earlier in this hour.

FIGURE 9.14
You can create drop-down menus like these.

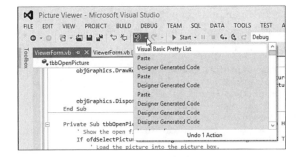

Creating a Status Bar

The last control I'll show you is the Status Bar control. The Status Bar isn't nearly as fancy, or even as useful, as other controls such as the ToolStrip or MenuStrip, but it's also not as difficult to work with, either. A status bar adds value to an application in that it makes information available in a standard location, and users have come to expect it. In its simplest form, a status bar displays a caption and *sizing grip*—the dots to the right of the control that the user can drag to change the form's size.

Add a new status bar to the form now by double-clicking the StatusStrip item in the toolbox (located in the Menus & Toolbars category). You may need to use the vertical scrollbar to the right in the designer to scroll down and see the status bar at the bottom of your form. Change the name of the StatusStrip to sbrMyStatusStrip. Because of how you have anchored your other controls, the status strip overlays a few controls at the bottom of the form. Fix this now by following these steps:

1. Click the PictureBox on the form, and change its Size property to **265, 256**.

2. Change the Location.Y property of the Shrink and Enlarge buttons to **285**. Your form should now look like Figure 9.15.

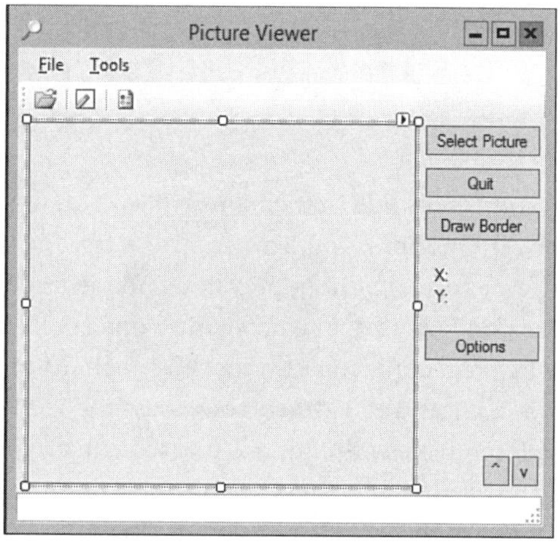

FIGURE 9.15
Status bars always appear at the bottom of a form.

Click the StatusStrip to select it, and take a look at its left edge. Does it look familiar? It's similar to the interface you have for adding menu items to MenuStrips and buttons to ToolStrips. Click the drop-down arrow, and choose Status Label. A new status label appears. Change its properties as follows:

Property	Value
Name	lblStatus
Text	No image loaded

You probably noticed when you opened the drop-down to create the status label that you can place items of other types on the status strip as well. For now, the label will do. In Hour 10, you'll write code to display the name of the opened picture in the label.

Press F5 to run the project. Move the mouse pointer over the small set of dots in the status strip's lower-right corner. The pointer changes to a sizing arrow. You can click and drag to resize the form. However, the status strip isn't smart enough to realize when a form's border can't be resized (for example, when the form's border style is set to fixed or fixed tool window). You have to change the SizingGrip property of the status strip to False to hide the grip.

Summary

Menus, toolbars, and status bars add tremendous value to an application by greatly enhancing its usability. In this hour, you learned how to use the MenuStrip control to build comprehensive menus for your applications. You learned how to add, move, and delete menu items and how to define accelerator and shortcut keys to facilitate better navigation via the keyboard. You also saw how toolbars provide shortcuts for accessing common menu items. You learned how to use the ToolStrip control to create functional toolbars, complete with bitmaps and logical groupings. Finally, you discovered how to use a status strip to dress up the application. Implementing these items is an important part of the interface design process for an application. You now have the skills necessary to start putting them into your own programs.

Q&A

Q. *I have a number of forms with nearly identical menus. Do I really need to take the time to create menus for all these forms?*

A. Not as much as you might think. Create a `MenuStrip` control that has the common items on it, and then copy and paste the control to other forms. You can then build on this menu structure, saving yourself a lot of time. Be aware, though, that when you copy and paste a control, the corresponding code does not get copied.

Q. *I've seen applications that allow the end user to customize the menus and toolbars. Can I do that with the Visual Basic menus and toolbars?*

A. No. To accomplish this behavior, you'll have to purchase a third-party component—or write a lot of code to make this happen. Personally, I think buying a component that supports this functionality is a much better option.

Workshop

Quiz

1. True or false: You use the `Context Menu Strip` control to create form menu bars.

2. To create an accelerator, or hotkey, with what do you preface the character?

3. To place a check mark next to a menu item, you set what property of the item?

4. How do you add code to a menu item?

5. Toolbar items are part of what collection?

6. True or false: Every button on a toolbar has its own `Click` event.

7. What control displays information to the user at the bottom of a form?

Answers

1. False. You use the MenuStrip control.

2. An ampersand (&)

3. The Checked property

4. Double-click the menu item.

5. The Items collection

6. True

7. The StatusStrip control

Exercises

1. Create a new project, and build a ToolStrip that has a drop-down button.

2. Using the ToolStrip control, figure out how to display status text in place of a button. (Hint: A special type of item in the Items collection does this.)

Creating and Calling Code Procedures

What You'll Learn in This Hour:

▶ Creating Visual Basic code modules

▶ Creating code procedures

▶ Calling procedures

▶ Passing parameters

▶ Exiting procedures

▶ Avoiding recursive procedures

You've now spent about nine hours building the basic skills necessary to navigate Visual Basic and to create an application interface. Creating a good interface is important, but it's only one of many steps toward creating a Windows program. After you've created the basic interface of an application, you need to enable the program to do something. The program might perform an action all on its own, or it might perform actions based on a user interacting with the GUI. Either way, you write Visual Basic code to make your application perform tasks. In this hour, you'll learn how to create sets of code (called *modules*), how to create isolated code routines that can be executed (called *procedures*), and how to invoke the procedures you create.

Creating Visual Basic Code Modules

A *module* is a place to store the code you write. Before you can begin writing Visual Basic code, you must start with a module. You've already worked with one type of module: a *form module* (refer to Hour 5, "Building Forms: The Basics," for more information). When you double-click an object on a form, you access events that reside in the form module. In addition to form modules, you can create *standard modules* or class modules.

Class modules are used as templates for the instantiation of objects. I discuss the specifics of creating such objects in Hour 16, "Designing Objects Using Classes." Most of the techniques discussed in this hour apply to class modules, but I'll focus this discussion on standard modules because they're easier to use.

Although you could place all your program's code in a single standard module or even in a class module, it's best to create different modules to group related sets of code. In addition, if code is called from within only one form, it's often best to place that code in the form's module. You'll be placing code within a form module, as well as within a new module that you'll create in this hour.

The current development trend centers on object-oriented programming (OOP, which revolves around class modules). I'll give you a primer on OOP in Hour 16, but it's an advanced topic, so I don't cover it in detail. I highly recommend that you read a dedicated object-oriented programming book, such as *Sams Teach Yourself Object-Oriented Programming with Visual Basic .NET in 21 Days*, Second Edition (Sams Publishing, 2002), after you're comfortable with the material in this book.

The primary general rule for using standard modules is that you should create modules to group related sets of code. This isn't to say that you should create dozens of modules. Rather, group related functions into a reasonably sized set of modules. For example, you might want to create one module that contains all your printing routines and another that holds your data-access routines. In addition, I like to create a general-purpose module in which to place all the various routines that don't necessarily fit in more specialized modules.

It's often preferable to create classes and instantiate objects rather than use standard modules, but no rules are set in stone. Some OOP purists suggest (strongly) that you never use a standard module. Remember that a standard module is simply a tool, and all tools have a purpose.

You'll build on the Picture Viewer application from Hour 9, "Adding Menus and Toolbars to Forms," so open that now.

Next, create a new standard module by choosing Project, Add New Item. When the Add New Item dialog box appears, scroll down and click Module (see Figure 10.1).

Note that this is the same dialog box used to add new forms. Change the name of the module to **DrawingModule.vb**, and click Add to create the new module. Visual Basic creates the new module and positions you in the code window, ready to enter code, as shown in Figure 10.2.

Save your project now by clicking Save All on the toolbar.

FIGURE 10.1
All new project items are added from within this dialog box.

FIGURE 10.2
Modules have no graphical interface, so you always work with them in the code editor.

Writing Code Procedures

After you've created the module(s) in which to store your code, you can begin to write Visual Basic code procedures. A *procedure* is a discrete set of code that can be called from other code. Procedures are much like events, but rather than being executed by a user interacting with a form or control, procedures are executed when called by a code statement.

Visual Basic has two types of procedures:

▶ Procedures that return a value (called *functions*)

▶ Procedures that do not return a value (called *subroutines*)

There are many reasons to create a procedure that returns a value. For example, a function can return True or False, depending on whether it was successful in completing its task. You could also write a procedure that accepts certain parameters (data *passed to* the procedure, in contrast to data *returned by* the procedure) and returns a value based on those parameters. For instance, you could write a procedure that enables you to pass it a sentence, and in return it passes back the number of spaces in the sentence. The possibilities are limited only by your imagination. Just keep in mind that a procedure doesn't *have to* return a value.

Declaring Procedures That Don't Return Values

To create a procedure, whether it be a Sub (a procedure that doesn't return a value) or a Function (a procedure that returns a value), you first declare it within a module. In your new module, type the following and press the Enter key:

```
Public Sub OpenPicture()
```

When you press Enter, Visual Basic automatically inserts a blank line and creates the text End Sub, as shown in Figure 10.3. You've just created a new procedure.

FIGURE 10.3
The Public Sub and End Sub statements create the basic structure of a Sub procedure.

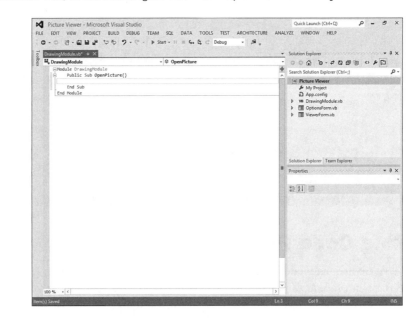

The declaration of a procedure (the statement used to define a procedure) has a number of parts. The first word, Public in this case, is a *keyword* (that is, a word with a special meaning in Visual Basic). Public defines the scope of this procedure (scope is discussed in detail in Hour 11, "Using Constants, Data Types, Variables, and Arrays"). Public specifies that the procedure can be called from code contained in modules other than the one containing the defined procedure. You can use the keyword Private in place of Public to restrict access to the procedure to code in the module in which the procedure resides. Because you'll call this code from the Picture Viewer form, you need to make the procedure Public.

> The scope designator is optional. If it's omitted, a Public procedure is created. You should always explicitly designate the scope of your procedures.

By the *Way*

The word Sub (short for *subroutine*) is another Visual Basic keyword. Sub is used to declare a procedure that doesn't return a value. Later in this hour, you'll learn how to create procedures that return values (called *functions*).

The third word, OpenPicture, is the actual name of the procedure. It can be just about any string of text you want it to be. Note, however, that you can't assign a name that's a keyword, nor can you use spaces within a name. In the example you're building, the procedure will perform the same function as the Open Picture menu item *and* the Toolstrip button—hence the name. You should always give procedures strong names that reflect their purpose. You can have two procedures with the same name *only* if they have different scope (again, scope is discussed in Hour 11).

> Some programmers prefer the readability of spaces in names, but in many instances, such as when you're naming procedures, spaces can't be used. A common technique is to use an underscore (_) in place of a space, such as in Open_Picture, but I recommend that you just use mixed case (both uppercase and lowercase letters), as you have in this example.

Did you *Know?*

Immediately following the name of the procedure is a set of parentheses. The OpenPicture() procedure doesn't accept any parameters (data passed in), so the parentheses are left empty. If you wanted calling code to pass data into this procedure, you would do so within these parentheses. I'll show you how to do that later in this hour.

> You have to supply parentheses, even when a procedure doesn't accept any parameters.

By the *Way*

Add the following code to your `OpenPicture()` procedure:

```
' Show the open file dialog box.
If ViewerForm.ofdSelectPicture.ShowDialog = DialogResult.OK Then
    ' Load the picture into the picture box.
    ViewerForm.picShowPicture.Image = _
        Image.FromFile(ViewerForm.ofdSelectPicture.FileName)
    ' Show the name of the file in the statusbar.
    ViewerForm.sbrMyStatusStrip.Items(0).Text = _
        Viewerform.ofdSelectPicture.FileName
End If
```

Notice that this code is *almost* identical to the code you entered in the Open Picture button, menu item, and Toolstrip button from previous hours. The difference is that, because this module is separate from the form, you have to explicitly name the form when referencing controls on the form or when getting or setting the form's properties (you can't use Me). Also notice that you enter code to show the selected filename in the status strip, as opposed to in the form's caption.

You've already entered this code (or a variation of it) in three places. Earlier, I alluded to the idea that this isn't optimal and that we would address it. Whenever you find yourself duplicating code, you should realize that the duplicated code should be placed in a procedure. Then, rather than duplicating the code, you can just call the procedure as needed. This approach has a number of advantages, including the following:

▶ **Reduction of errors**: Each time you enter code, you run the risk of doing something wrong. By entering code only once, you reduce the likelihood of introducing errors.

▶ **Consistency and maintainability**: When you duplicate code, you often forget all the places where that code is used. You might fix a bug in one location but not in another, or add a feature to one copy of the code but not another. By using a single procedure, you have to worry about maintaining only one instance of the code.

Now you'll create a procedure to draw a border around the picture box. Position the cursor after the words End Sub, press Enter, and type the following code where shown in Figure 10.4:

```
Public Sub DrawBorder(ByRef objPicturebox As PictureBox)
    Dim objGraphics As Graphics
    objGraphics = objPicturebox.Parent.CreateGraphics
    objGraphics.Clear(System.Drawing.SystemColors.Control)

    objGraphics.DrawRectangle(System.Drawing.Pens.Blue, objPicturebox.Left - 1, _
        objPicturebox.Top - 1, _
        objPicturebox.Width + 1, objPicturebox.Height + 1)

    objGraphics.Dispose()
End Sub
```

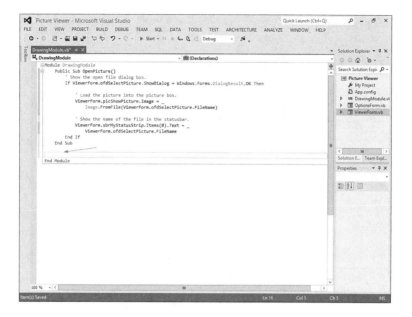

FIGURE 10.4
Start your new
procedure where
the arrow is
pointing.

A few items introduced in this procedure may look new to you. The first is that there is text within the parentheses of the procedure declaration. I mentioned earlier that this is where you can define parameters. Parameters are data passed into the procedure, as opposed to a value returned by the procedure. You've just created a parameter of type picture box. I'll cover the specifics in Hour 11, but for now I just want you to understand the following concept: Code that calls this procedure passes into it a reference to a picture box object. The procedure then can work with the reference just as though it were manipulating the object directly.

The first procedure you created *should* have been done this way, but I wanted you to see both approaches. In the first procedure (OpenPicture), you hard-coded a reference to ViewerForm. This means that the code works for only that form. Because this second procedure accepts a reference to a picture box by way of a parameter, the procedure can work with a picture box on *any* form in your project. This is an important concept to remember. You should strive to use parameters in your procedures while at the same time avoiding hard-coding references to objects that belong to other forms.

The objPicturebox parameter is used throughout the procedure in place of a hard-coded reference to the picture box object on your form. That's pretty easy to understand, but the second statement in the procedure needs a bit more clarification. Notice the reference to objPicturebox.Parent. All controls have a parent, which is the container on which the control is placed. The Parent property is an object property that returns a reference to the parent. In the case of the picture box on your form, Parent refers to the form itself. So, calling objPicturebox.Parent.CreateGraphics is the same as calling picShowPicture.CreateGraphics or Me.CreateGraphics from within the form.

Your module should now look like Figure 10.5.

FIGURE 10.5
Code must exist within proce-dures, and pro-cedures must be placed between the Module dec-laration and End Module.

Declaring Procedures That Return Values

The two procedures you've created don't return values. Now you'll declare a *function*—a procedure that returns a value. Here's the general syntax of a function declaration:

```
Scope Function functionname(parameters) As datatype
```

You'll notice two key differences between declaring a procedure that doesn't return a value and declaring one that does. First, you use the keyword Function in place of the keyword Sub. Second, you add text after the parentheses. When declaring a function, you'll always enter two words after the parentheses. The first word is always As, and the second word is a specific data type declaration. Data types are discussed in detail in Hour 11, so it's not important that you understand them now. It is important, however, that you understand what's happening.

As stated previously, functions return values. The data type entered after As denotes the type of data the function returns. You won't create a Function in your project at this time, but consider the following sample Function:

```
Public Function ComputeLength(ByVal strText As String) As Integer
    Return strText.Length
End Function
```

Note three things here:

▶ After the parentheses are the words As Integer. This denotes that the Function returns an Integer. If the function were to return a string of text, it would be declared As String. It's important that you declare the proper data type for your functions, as discussed in Hour 11.

▶ The keyword Return accomplishes two tasks. First, it causes the procedure to terminate immediately—no further code is executed in the procedure. Second, it passes back as the return value whatever you specify. In this code, the Function returns the number of characters in the supplied string.

▶ Notice that instead of End Sub, End Function is used to denote the end of the procedure. This behavior keeps the End statements consistent with their corresponding declaration statements.

Sub and Function procedures are similar—short of these three things. By remembering these key differences, you should have little trouble creating one over the other as circumstances dictate.

Calling Code Procedures

Calling a procedure is simple—much simpler than creating one! So far, I've had you create two procedures. Each of these procedures contains code like that used in no less than three places! Now you'll remove all that duplicate code, replacing it with calls to the common procedures you've just written. Follow these steps to make this happen:

1. Double-click ViewerForm.vb in the Solution Explorer to view the form in the Form Designer.

2. The first code you'll replace is the Open Picture code you entered for the Open Picture button on the toolbar. Double-click the Open Picture button to access its Click event. Delete all the code between the event declaration and End Sub, as shown in Figure 10.6.

3. With the old code deleted, enter the following statement:

```
OpenPicture()
```

That's it! To call a Sub procedure (a procedure that doesn't return a value), you simply use the procedure name followed by a pair of parentheses. If the procedure expects one or more parameters, you would enter them between the parentheses.

FIGURE 10.6
Delete this code and replace it with the procedure call.

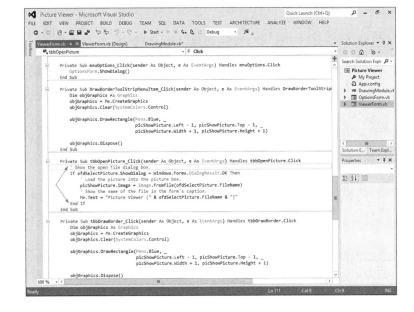

Did you Know?

When you type in the name of a valid procedure and then the left parenthesis, Visual Basic displays a ToolTip showing the parameters that the procedure expects. It can be difficult to remember the parameters expected by all procedures (not to mention the proper order in which to pass them), so this little feature will save you a great deal of time and frustration.

4. We still have two other places in which we used the Open Picture code. Double-click ViewerForm.vb in the Solution Explorer to return to the form's design view, click the File menu to display the menu, and then double-click the Open Picture button.

5. Delete the code in the Click event and replace it with the following:

```
OpenPicture()
```

Return to the Form Designer.

So far, you've created only Sub procedures—procedures that don't return values. As you now know, calling a Sub procedure is as easy as referencing the Sub's name and its parentheses. Calling Function procedures—those that return values—is a bit different. Consider this little function:

```
Public Function AddTwoNumbers(ByVal intFirst As Integer, _
    ByVal intSecond As Integer) As Long
   Return intFirst + intSecond
End Function
```

This function accepts two parameters, adds them together, and returns their sum.

When calling a `Function`, think of the function in terms of the value it returns. For example, when you set a form's `Height` property, you set it with code like this:

```
MyForm.Height = 200
```

This statement sets a form's height to 200. Suppose that you want to use the `AddTwoNumbers` procedure to determine the form's `Height`. Thinking of the procedure in terms of the value it returns, you could replace the literal value with the function, as in the following:

```
MyForm.Height = AddTwoNumbers(1, 5)
```

In this example, the form's height is set to 6, because you pass 1 and 5 to the function's parameters, and the function adds them together. In the next section, I show you how to work with parameters in more detail.

> When calling `Function` procedures, you must treat the procedure call as you would treat the literal value returned by the function. This often means placing a function call on the right side of an equals sign or embedding it in an expression.

By the Way

You've now created a procedure and called it from two locations—your application is really taking shape! Now that you have a toolbar and a menu, you no longer need the buttons that you created in Hour 1, "Jumping in with Both Feet: A Visual Basic 2012 Programming Tour."

Follow these steps to get rid of the buttons:

1. Double-click the Select Picture button on the right side of the form. Remove the entire event, including the procedure declaration that begins with `Private`, and the `End Sub` statement, as shown in Figure 10.7.

2. Go back to the Form Designer by clicking the ViewerForm.vb[Design]* tab at the top of the work area.

3. The Select Picture button should be selected, because you just double-clicked it. If it is not, click it to select it. Press Delete to delete the button.

4. Repeat steps 1 through 3 for the Quit button, the Draw Border button, and the Options button. Be sure to delete the procedures for each of them! Your screen should now look like Figure 10.8.

5. Go ahead and clean up the form further. Set the `Location` property of the X label to **336, 256**, and set the `Location` property of the Y label to **336, 269**.

FIGURE 10.7
When deleting a procedure, you must delete the declaration and the End statement as well.

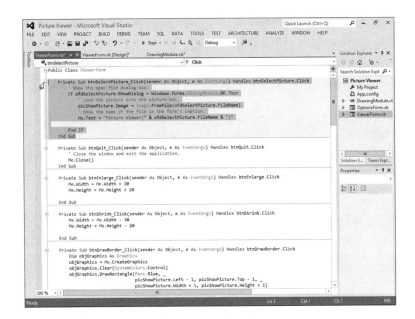

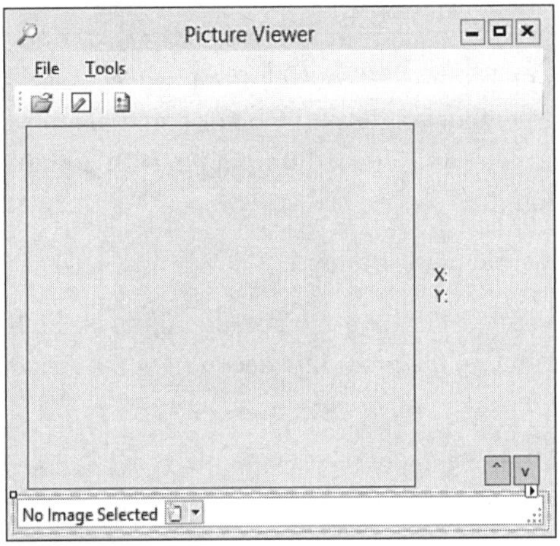

FIGURE 10.8
The buttons are no longer necessary now that you have menus and toolbars.

Finally, set the Size of the Picture box to **322, 256** and save your work. Your form should now look like Figure 10.9.

Passing Parameters

Parameters are used within a procedure to allow the calling code to pass data into the procedure. You've already seen how parameters are defined: within the parentheses

of a procedure declaration. A parameter definition consists of a name for the parameter, the word As, and a data type:

```
Public Sub MyProcedure(strMyStringParameter As String)
```

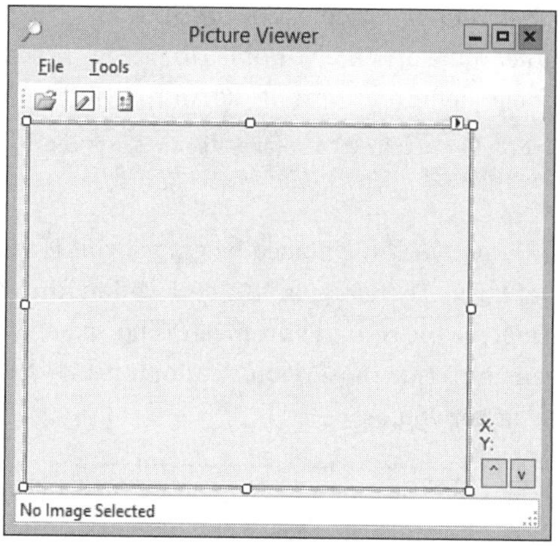

FIGURE 10.9
Much better!

> After you've read about variables in Hour 11, this structure will make much more
> sense. Here, I just want you to get the general idea of how to define and use
> parameters.

You can define multiple parameters for a procedure by separating them with a
comma, like this:

```
Public Sub MyProcedure(strMyStringParameter As String, _
                       intMyIntegerParameter as Integer)
```

A calling procedure passes data to the parameters by way of *arguments*. This is mostly
a semantics issue; when defined in the declaration of a procedure, the item is called a
parameter. When the item is part of the statement that calls the procedure, it's called
an argument. Arguments are passed within parentheses—the same way that parameters are defined. If a procedure has multiple arguments, you separate them with
commas. For example, you could pass values to the procedure just defined by using a
statement such as this:

```
MyProcedure("This is a string", 11)
```

The parameter acts like an ordinary variable within the procedure. Remember, variables are storage entities whose values can be changed. The statement just shown sends
literal values to the procedure. You could also send the values of variables this way:

```
MyProcedure(strAString, intAnInteger)
```

An important thing to note about passing variables in Visual Basic is that parameters are passed *by value* rather than *by reference*. When parameters are passed by value, the procedure receives a copy of the data; changes to the parameter *do not* affect the value of the original variable. When passed by reference, however, the parameter is actually a pointer to the original variable. Changes made to the parameter within the procedure propagate to the original variable. To pass a parameter by reference, you preface the parameter definition with the keyword ByRef, as shown here:

```
Public Sub MyProcedure(ByRef strMyStringParameter As String, _
                intMyIntegerParameter as Integer)
```

Parameters defined without ByRef are passed by value—this is the default behavior of parameters in Visual Basic. Therefore, in this declaration, the first parameter is passed by reference, whereas the second parameter is passed by value. Actually, if you typed in this statement, Visual Basic would automatically add ByVal in front of intMyIntegerParameter for you.

> The default behavior in earlier versions of Visual Basic was that parameters were passed by reference, not by value. To pass a parameter by value, you had to preface the parameter definition with ByVal.

You already created a procedure that accepts a parameter. Let's take another look:

```
Public Sub DrawBorder(ByRef objPicturebox As PictureBox)
    Dim objGraphics As Graphics
    objGraphics = objPicturebox.Parent.CreateGraphics
    objGraphics.Clear(System.Drawing.SystemColors.Control)

    objGraphics.DrawRectangle(System.Drawing.Pens.Blue, objPicturebox.Left - 1, _
            objPicturebox.Top - 1, _
            objPicturebox.Width + 1, objPicturebox.Height + 1)

    objGraphics.Dispose()
End Sub
```

Notice that the parameter is declared with ByRef. That's because you're not passing some ordinary piece of data, like a number or a string of text. This procedure accepts an object—a picture box, to be exact. Within the procedure, you reference properties of the picture box. For this to take place, the variable must be by reference (you need a pointer to the actual object to reference its properties and methods). Follow these steps to hook up the procedure:

1. Display the ViewerForm form in the Form Designer if it's not already displayed.

2. Double-click the Draw Border button on the toolbar. Delete the contents of the procedure, but not the procedure shell (the first statement, starting with Private, and the last statement, End Sub).

3. Enter the following statement in the `Click` event:

```
DrawBorder(picShowPicture)
```

4. Return to the Form Designer once more (you should know how by now), click the Tools menu on your form, and then double-click the Draw Border item.

5. Replace all the code within the procedure with this statement:

```
DrawBorder(picShowPicture)
```

You've now hooked up your menus and Toolstrip. Press F5 to run your program (see Figure 10.10), and try the various menu items and tool buttons. The Confirm on Exit button still doesn't work, but you'll hook that up in the next hour.

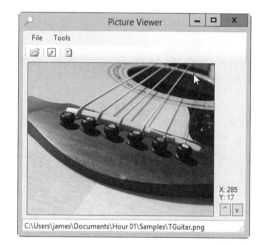

FIGURE 10.10
Professional applications demand good procedure design in addition to good interface design.

Go ahead and stop the running project, and save your work.

Exiting Procedures

Code within a procedure ordinarily executes from beginning to end—literally. When an `End Sub` or `End Function` statement is reached, execution returns to the statement that made the procedure call. You can force execution to leave the procedure at any time by using an `Exit Sub` or `Exit Function` statement. Obviously, you use `Exit Sub` in procedures declared with the keyword `Sub`, and you use `Exit Function` in procedures declared with the keyword `Function`. If Visual Basic encounters such an

exit statement, the procedure terminates immediately, and code returns to the statement that called the procedure. Take care to minimize the number of Exit statements
in any given routine. By providing too many exit points in a procedure, you will
make your code difficult to read and harder to debug.

Avoiding Infinite Recursion

It's possible to call procedures in such a way that a continuous loop occurs. Consider
the following two procedures:

```
Public Sub DoSomething()
    Call DoSomethingElse()
End Function
Public Sub DoSomethingElse()
    Call DoSomething()
End Function
```

Calling either of these procedures produces an infinite loop of procedure calls and
results in the error shown in Figure 10.11.

FIGURE 10.11
Infinite recursion
results in a
stack overflow
exception
(error).

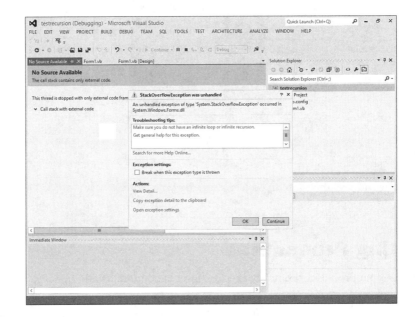

This endless loop is known as a *recursive loop*. Without getting too technical, Visual
Basic allocates some memory for each procedure call in an area known as the *stack*.
Only a finite amount of space is available on the stack, so infinite recursion eventually uses all the available stack space, and an exception occurs. This is a serious error,
and steps should be taken to avoid such recursion.

Legitimate uses exist for recursion, most notably in the use of algorithms such as those used in calculus or those used to iterate through all the folders on a hard drive. Deliberate recursion techniques don't create infinite recursion, however; there is always a point at which the recursion stops (hopefully, before the stack is consumed). If you have an interest in such algorithms, consider reading a book dedicated to the subject.

Summary

In this hour, you learned how a procedure is a discrete set of code designed to perform a task or related set of tasks. Procedures are where you write Visual Basic code. Some procedures might be as short as a single line of code, whereas others will be pages in length. You learned how to define procedures and how to call them; creating and calling procedures is critical to your success in programming with Visual Basic. Be sure to avoid creating recursive procedures! You'll use procedures so often that they'll become second nature to you in no time.

Modules are used to group related procedures. This hour focused on the standard module, which is little more than a container for procedures. Remember to group related procedures in the same module and to give each module a descriptive name. In Hour 16, you'll build on your experience with modules and work with class modules, which demands good segregation of discrete modules.

> **Did you Know?**
>
> Keep in mind that every procedure should perform a specific function. Therefore, you should avoid creating procedures that perform many different tasks. For example, suppose that you want to create a set of code that draws an ellipse on a form. You also want to clear the form. If you placed both sets of code in the same procedure, the ellipse would be drawn and then immediately erased. By placing each set of code in its own procedure, you can draw the ellipse by calling one procedure and then erase it at any time by calling the other procedure. By placing these routines in a module rather than attaching them to a specific form, you also make the procedures available to any form that needs them.

Q&A

Q. *Do I need to pay much attention to scope when defining my procedures?*

A. It might be tempting to create all your procedures as `Public`, but this is bad coding practice for a number of reasons. For one thing, you'll find that in larger projects, you have procedures with the same name that do slightly different things. Usually, these routines are relevant only within a limited scope. However, if you create all `Public` procedures, you'll run into conflicts when you create a procedure with the same name in the same scope. If the procedure isn't needed at the `Public` level, don't define it for public access.

Q. *How many modules is a reasonable number?*

A. That's hard to say. In my largest application (which is a very large application), I have had about 18 modules, but I have been reducing them over time by replacing them with class modules. Anything greater than that and the project might become difficult to manage.

Workshop

Quiz

1. What are the entities called that are used to house procedures?

2. True or false: To access procedures in a class module, you must first create an object.

3. To declare a procedure that returns a value, do you use `Sub` or `Function`?

4. True or false: You use a `Call` statement to call a procedure that returns a value.

5. Data that has been passed into a procedure by a calling statement is called what?

6. To pass multiple arguments to a procedure, with what do you separate them?

7. The situation in which a procedure or set of procedures continues to call each other in a looping fashion is called what?

Answers

1. Modules

2. True

3. `Functions` return values.

4. False. Older versions of Visual Basic had you use the word `Call` to call `Sub` procedures, but this is no longer necessary. `Call` was never used for `Functions`.

5. A parameter

6. A comma (,)

7. Infinite recursion

Exercises

1. Create a procedure as part of a form that accepts one string and outputs a different string. Add code to the `TextChanged` event of a text box to call the procedure, passing the contents of the text box as the argument. Pass back as the result of the procedure the uppercase version of the string passed into it, and display this in the text box. (Hint: Use the Visual Basic `UCase()` function.)

2. Create a single procedure that calls itself. Call this procedure from the `Click` event of a button and observe the resulting error.

Using Constants, Data Types, Variables, and Arrays

What You'll Learn in This Hour:

▶ Understanding data types

▶ Determining data type

▶ Converting data to different data types

▶ Defining and using constants

▶ Dimensioning and referencing variables

▶ Understanding explicit variable declaration and strict typing

▶ Working with arrays

▶ Determining scope

▶ Declaring static variables

▶ Using a naming convention

As you write your Visual Basic procedures, you'll regularly need to store and retrieve various pieces of information. As a matter of fact, I can't think of a single application I've written that didn't need to store and retrieve data in code. You might want to keep track of how many times a procedure has been called, for example, or store a property value and use it later. Such data can be stored as constants, variables, or arrays. *Constants* are named values that you define at design time. Constants cannot be changed after that, but they can be referenced as often as needed. *Variables*, on the other hand, are like storage bins; you can retrieve or replace the data in a variable as often as you need to. *Arrays* act like grouped variables, enabling you to store many values in a single array variable.

Whenever you define one of these storage entities, you have to decide what type of data it will contain. For example, will the new variable hold a string value (text) or a number? If it will hold a number, is the number a whole number, an integer, or something else entirely? After you determine the type of data to store, you must choose the level of visibility that the data has to other procedures within the project (this visibility is known as *scope*). In this hour, you'll learn the ins and outs of Visual Basic data types. (If you're moving up from Visual Basic 6, you'll note that even though some data types share the same names, they are different.) You'll also learn how to create and use these storage mechanisms and how to minimize problems in your code by reducing scope.

By the
Way

> In this hour, you'll build on the Picture Viewer project from Hour 10, "Creating and Calling Code Procedures." Here, you'll start the process for hooking up the features for which you created controls on your Options form.

Understanding Data Types

Every programming language has a *compiler*. The compiler is the part of the Visual Studio .NET Framework that interprets the code you write into a language the computer can understand. The compiler must understand the type of data you're manipulating in code. For example, if you asked the compiler to add the following values, it would get confused:

"Fender Strat" + 63

When the compiler gets confused, either it refuses to compile the code (which is the preferred situation, because you can address the problem before your users run the application), or it halts execution and displays an exception (error) when it reaches the confusing line of code. (These two types of errors are discussed in detail in Hour 15, "Debugging Your Code.") Obviously, you can't add the words "Fender Strat" to the number 63, because these two values are different types of data. In Visual Basic, these two values are said to have two different *data types*. Constants, variables, and arrays must always be defined to hold a specific type of information.

Determining Data Type

Data typing—the act of defining a constant, variable, or array's data type—can be confusing. To Visual Basic, a number is not just a number. A number that contains a decimal value is different from a number that doesn't. Visual Basic can perform arithmetic on numbers of different data types, but you can't store data of one type in a variable with an incompatible type. Because of this limitation, you must give careful consideration to the type of data you plan to store in a constant, variable, or array when you define it. Table 11.1 lists the Visual Basic data types and the range of values each one can contain.

TABLE 11.1 Visual Basic Data Types

Data Type	Value Range
Boolean	True or False
Byte	0 to 255 (unsigned)
Char	A single Unicode character
Date	0:00:00 (midnight) on January 1, 0001, through 11:59:59 p.m. on December 31, 9999
Decimal	0 through +/79,228,162,514,264,337,593,543,950,335, with no decimal point; +/−7.9228162514264337593543950335, with 28 places to the right of the decimal. Use this data type for currency values.
Double	−1.79769313486231570E+308 through −4.94065645841246544E-324 for negative values; 4.94065645841246544E-324 through 1.79769313486231570E+308 for positive values.
Integer	−2,147,483,648 to 2,147,483,647 (signed). This is the same as the data type Int32.
Long	−9, 223,372,036,854,775,808 to 9,223,372,036,854,775,807 (signed). This is the same as data type Int64.
Object	Any type can be stored in a variable of type Object.
SByte	-128 through 127 (signed)
Short	−32,768 to 32,767 (signed). This is the same as data type Int16.
Single	−3.4028235E+38 through −1.401298E-45 for negative values; 1.401298E-45 through 3.4028235E+38 for positive values.
String	0 to approximately 2 billion Unicode characters
UInteger	0 through 4,294,967,295 (unsigned)
ULong	0 through 18,446,744,073,709,551,615 (1.8...E+19) (unsigned)
UShort	0 through 65,535 (unsigned)

The list of data types might seem daunting at first, but you can follow some general guidelines for choosing among them. As you become more familiar with the different types, you'll be able to fine-tune your data type selection.

Following are some helpful guidelines for using data types:

▶ If you want to store text, use the `String` data type. The `String` data type can be used to store any valid keyboard character, including numbers and non-alphabetic characters.

▶ To store only the value `True` or `False`, use the `Boolean` data type.

▶ If you want to store a number that doesn't contain decimal places and is greater than –32,768 and smaller than 32,767, use the `Short` data type.

▶ To store numbers without decimal places, but with values larger or smaller than `Short` allows, use the `Integer` or `Long` (an abbreviation for "long integer") data types.

▶ If you need to store numbers that contain decimal places, use the `Single` data type. The `Single` data type should work for almost all values containing decimals, unless you're writing incredibly complex mathematical applications or need to store very large numbers. In that case, use a `Double`.

▶ To store currency amounts, use the `Decimal` data type.

▶ If you need to store a date and/or a time value, use the `Date` data type. When you use the `Date` data type, Visual Basic recognizes common date and time formats. For example, if you store the value 7/22/2012, Visual Basic doesn't treat it as a simple text string; it knows that the text represents July 22, 2012.

▶ Different data types use different amounts of memory. To preserve system resources, it's best to use the data type that consumes the least amount of memory and still enables you to store the full range of possible values. For example, if you're storing only the numbers from 1 to 10, use a `Short` instead of a `Long`.

The `Object` data type requires special attention. If you define a variable or array as an `Object` data type, you can store just about any value you care to in it; Visual Basic determines what data type to use when you set the variable's value.

Using `Object` data types has several drawbacks. First, `Object` data types take up more memory than the other data types. In addition, Visual Basic takes a little longer to perform calculations on `Object` data types. Unless you have a specific reason to do so—and there are valid reasons, such as when you don't know the type of data to be stored ahead of time—don't use the `Object` data type. Instead, become familiar with the explicit data types and use them appropriately.

Casting Data from One Data Type to Another

Under most circumstances, Visual Basic won't allow you to move data of one type into a variable of another type. The process of changing a value's data type is known as *casting*. Casting to a data type that holds a larger value or that has greater precision is called *casting upward*. Casting to a data type that holds a smaller value or that has less precision is known as *casting downward*. Visual Basic generally casts downward but not upward. For instance, you can set the value of a variable declared as Double to the value of a variable declared as Single without an explicit cast because there's no risk of losing data—Double holds more than Single. However, you can't set a variable declared as Single to the value of a variable declared as Double without explicitly casting the type by using a data type conversion function. Visual Basic makes you explicitly convert a Single to a Double because you run the risk of losing data when doing so.

Table 11.2 lists the type conversion functions you can use to cast data to a different type (think of C as standing for *cast*). The use of these functions is pretty straightforward: Pass the data to be cast as the parameter, and the function returns the value with the return type. For example, to place the value of a variable declared as Double into a variable declared as Single, you could use a statement such as the following:

```
sngVariable = CSng(dblVariable)
```

TABLE 11.2 Type Conversion Functions

Function	What It Converts To
CBool(expression)	Boolean
CByte(expression)	Byte
CChar(expression)	Char
CDate(expression)	Date
CDbl(expression)	Double
CDec(expression)	Decimal
CInt(expression)	Integer
CLng(expression)	Long
CObj(expression)	Object
CSByte(expression)	SByte
CShort(expression)	Short

TABLE 11.2   Continued

CSng(expression)	`Single`
CStr(expression)	`String`
CUInt(expression)	`UInteger`
CULng(expression)	`ULong`
CUShort(expression)	`UShort`

By the Way

> A Boolean value holds only `True` or `False`. However, it's important to understand how Visual Basic works with Boolean values under the hood. In Visual Basic, `True` is stored internally as –1 (negative 1), whereas `False` is stored as 0. Actually, any nonzero number can represent `True`, but Visual Basic always treats `True` internally as –1. When casting a numeric value to a Boolean, Visual Basic casts a value of 0 as `False` and casts any nonzero number as `True`. This becomes important when you start evaluating numeric values using Boolean logic (discussed in Hour 12, "Performing Arithmetic, String Manipulation, and Date/Time Adjustments").

Defining and Using Constants

When you hard-code numbers in your procedures (such as in `intVotingAge = 18`), a myriad of things can go wrong. Hard-coded numbers often are called *magic numbers* because they're usually shrouded in mystery. The meaning of such a number is obscure because the digits themselves don't indicate what the number represents. Constants are used to eliminate the problems of magic numbers.

You define a constant as having a specific value at design time, and that value never changes throughout the life of your program. Constants offer the following benefits:

▶ **They eliminate or reduce data-entry problems:** It's much easier to remember to use a constant named c_pi than it is to enter 3.14159265358979 everywhere that pi is needed. The compiler catches misspelled or undeclared constants, but it doesn't care one bit what you enter as a literal value.

▶ **Code is easier to update:** If you hard-coded a mortgage interest rate at 6.785, and the rate changed to 7.00, you'd have to change every occurrence of 6.785 in code. In addition to the possibility of data-entry problems, you'd run the risk of changing a value of 6.785 that had nothing to do with the interest rate—perhaps a value that represented a savings bond yield (okay, a *very* high savings bond yield). With a constant, you change the value once at the constant declaration, and all code that references the constant uses the new value right away.

▶ **Code is easier to read:** Magic numbers are often anything but intuitive. Well-named constants, on the other hand, add clarity to code. For example, which of the following statements makes more sense to you?

```
decInterestAmount = CDec((decLoanAmount * 0.075) * 12)
```

or

```
decInterestAmount = CDec((decLoanAmount * c_sngInterestRate) * _
                    c_intMonthsInTerm)
```

Constant definitions have the following syntax:

```
Const name As datatype = value
```

To define a constant to hold the value of pi, for example, you could use a statement such as this:

```
Const c_pi As Single = 3.14159265358979
```

Note how I prefix the constant name with c_. I do this so that it's easier to determine what's a variable and what's a constant when reading code. See the "Naming Conventions" section later in this hour for more information.

After a constant is defined, you can use its name in code in place of its value. For example, to output the result of 2 times the value of pi, you could use a statement like this (the * character is used for multiplication and is covered in Hour 12):

```
Debug.WriteLine(c_pi * 2)
```

Using the constant is much easier and less prone to error than typing this:

```
Debug.WriteLine(3.14159265358979 * 2)
```

Constants can be referenced only in the scope in which they are defined. I discuss scope in the section "Determining Scope" later in this hour.

You'll use what you learn in this hour to enable the options controls that you added in Hour 7, "Working with Traditional Controls." The first thing you'll do is use constants to create default values for the options. Recall from Hour 7 that you created an option form that allowed the user to manipulate the following three options:

▶ **The user's name:** This is displayed in the Picture Viewer's main form title bar.

▶ **Prompt to confirm on exit:** This is used to determine whether the user is asked whether he or she really wants to shut down the Picture Viewer application.

▶ **The default background color of the picture box:** This can be set to gray (the default) or white.

In the following steps, you'll create a constant for the default value of the Prompt on Exit option. Start by opening the Picture Viewer project from Hour 10, and then follow these steps:

1. Click ViewerForm.vb in the Solution Explorer to select it.

2. Click the View Code button at the top of the Solution Explorer to view the code behind ViewerForm.vb.

3. The constants you are about to create will be module-level constants. That is, they can be used anywhere within the module in which they are declared. This means that they won't be placed in a specific procedure. The place to put module constants is right after the declaration of the module toward the top (`Public Class classname`). Position the cursor on the line following the declaration, press Enter to create a new line, and then enter the following constant declaration (see Figure 11.1):

```
Const c_defPromptOnExit = False
```

In the next section, you'll learn how to use this constant to set the value of a variable.

Declaring and Referencing Variables

Variables are similar to constants in that when you reference a variable's name in code, Visual Basic substitutes the variable's value in place of the variable name during code execution. This doesn't happen at compile time, though, as it does with constants. Instead, it happens at runtime—the moment the variable is referenced. Variables, unlike constants, can have their values changed at any time.

Declaring Variables

The act of defining a variable is called *declaring* (sometimes *dimensioning*), which you do most often by using the keyword `Dim` (short for dimension). (Variables with scope other than local are dimensioned in a slightly different way, as discussed in the later section "Determining Scope.") You've already used the `Dim` statement in previous hours, so the basic `Dim` statement should look familiar to you:

```
Dim variablename As datatype
```

FIGURE 11.1
Module con-
stants go here.

It's possible to declare multiple variables of the same type on a single line, as in the following:

```
Dim I, J, K As Integer
```

However, this is often considered bad form because it tends to make the code more difficult to read when strong variable names are used.

Did you Know?

You don't have to specify an initial value for a variable, although being able to do so in the Dim statement is a useful feature of Visual Basic. To create a new String variable and initialize it with a value, for example, you could use two statements like this:

```
Dim strBandName As String
strBandName = "Chemical Echo"
```

However, if you know the initial value of the variable at design time, you can include it in the Dim statement, like this:

```
Dim strBandName As String = "Chemical Echo"
```

Note, however, that supplying an initial value doesn't make this a constant; it's still a variable, and the value can be changed at any time. This method of creating an initial value eliminates a code statement and makes the code a bit easier to read because you don't have to go looking to see where the variable is initialized.

It's important to note that all data types have a default initial value. For the string data type, this is the value `Nothing`. "Nothing" might sound odd; it's essentially no value—a string with no text. Empty strings are written in code as `""`. For numeric data types, the default value is 0; the output of the following statements would be 2:

```
Dim sngMyValue As Single
Debug.WriteLine (sngMyValue + 2)
```

You can't use a reserved word to name a constant or a variable. For example, you couldn't use the word Sub or Public as a variable name. There is a master list of reserved words, and you can find it by searching the Help text for "reserved keywords." You'll naturally pick up most of the common ones because you'll use them so often. For others, the compiler tells you when something is a reserved word. If you use a naming convention for your variables, which consists of giving the variable names a prefix to denote their types, you'll greatly reduce the chance of running into reserved words.

Passing Literal Values to a Variable

The syntax of assigning a *literal* value (a hard-coded value such as 6 or "guitar") to a variable depends on the variable's data type.

For strings, you must pass the value in quotation marks, like this:

```
strCollegeName = "Bellevue University"
```

For `Date` values (discussed in more detail in Hour 12), you enclose the value in # symbols, like this:

```
dteBirthDate = #7/22/1969#
```

For numeric values, you don't enclose the value in anything:

```
intAnswerToEverything = 42
```

Using Variables in Expressions

Variables can be used anywhere an expression is expected. The arithmetic functions, for example, operate on expressions. You could add two literal numbers and store the result in a variable like this:

```
intMyVariable = 2 + 5
```

In addition, you could replace either or both literal numbers with numeric variables or constants, as shown here:

```
intMyVariable = intFirstValue + 5
intMyVariable = 2 + intSecondValue
intMyVariable = intFirstValue + intSecondValue
```

Variables are a fantastic way to store values during code execution, and you'll use variables all the time—from performing decisions and creating loops to using them as a temporary place to stick a value. Remember to use a constant when you know the value at design time and the value won't change. When you don't know the value ahead of time or the value might change, use a variable with a data type appropriate to the variable's function.

Did you Know?

In Visual Basic, variables are created as objects. Feel free to create a variable and explore its members (that is, the properties and methods). You do this by entering the variable name and then a period (this works only after you've entered the statement that declares the variable). For example, to determine the length of the text within a string variable, you can use the Length property of a string variable like this:

```
strMyVariable.Length
```

Some powerful features dangle off the data type objects.

Enforced Variable Declaration and Data Typing

By default, Visual Basic forces you to declare variables before you can use them. This is called *explicit variable declaration*. In addition to this behavior, you can force Visual Basic to strictly enforce data typing. *Strict typing* means that Visual Basic performs widening conversions for you automatically if no data or precision is lost, but for other conversions, you must explicitly cast the data from one type to another.

Explicit Variable Declaration

In the past, Visual Basic's default behavior enabled you to create variables on the fly (implicit variable declaration), and it didn't even have a provision for enforcing strict data typing. Although you can turn off both these features, you shouldn't. In fact, I recommend that you turn on Strict typing, which is off by default in new projects.

Take a look at the code following this paragraph now. No, really—right *now*. There's a problem with it, and I want you to see whether you can spot it. With Visual Basic's Option Explicit project property turned on, the following code would cause a compile error because of the misspelling of the variable name on the MessageBox.Show() statement. (Did you notice it?) When you turn off explicit variable declaration, Visual Basic doesn't check at compile time for such inconsistencies, and it would gladly run this code:

```
Dim intMyVariable As Integer
intMyVariable = 10
MessageBox.Show(intMyVariabl)
```

Would an error occur at runtime? If not, what do you think would be displayed? 10? No, nothing!

Notice that in the `MessageBox.Show()` statement, an e is missing from the `intMyVariable` name. As Visual Basic compiles your code, it looks at each code entry and attempts to determine whether it's a keyword, function call, variable, constant, or another entity that it understands. If the entry is determined to be something Visual Basic knows nothing about, the default behavior is to generate a compile error.

With explicit variable declaration turned off (that is, the Option Explicit setting turned off), however, Visual Basic alters this behavior. Instead, it creates a new variable—of type `Object`, no less! As I stated earlier, all variables are initialized with some default value. New object variables are empty, which is a value of sorts. Therefore, nothing prints in this example, and no error occurs. You want to talk about hard-to-find errors? This is one of the hardest I can come up with. If you're tired and it's late, it could take you hours to notice that a variable name is misspelled (I've been there—trust me). There is simply no valid reason to turn off explicit variable declaration. Because Option Explicit is turned on for all new projects by default, there's really no reason to mess with this setting.

Strict Typing

Strict typing is the process by which Visual Basic enforces data typing; you can put a value in a variable only if the value is of the correct data type. If you want to cast a value of one type into a variable of another type that holds a smaller number or has less precision, you must use a type-conversion function. With this feature turned off (which it is for new projects by default), Visual Basic lets you move any type of data into any variable, regardless of the data types involved. To do this, it has to make a best guess about how the data should be cast, which can cause inaccuracies such as truncating a large number when moving it from a `Double` to a `Single`. There are rare circumstances in which you might need to turn off strict typing, but these only come up with advanced programming. Leaving strict typing on forces you to write better code, so I suggest that you turn it on in your projects. To turn on Option Strict in your Picture Viewer project, follow these steps:

1. Right-click the project name in the Solution Explorer and choose Properties from the context menu.

2. On the Project Properties page, click the Compile tab on the left.

3. Open the Option strict drop-down list and choose On, as shown in Figure 11.2.

4. While on the options page, change Option infer to Off.

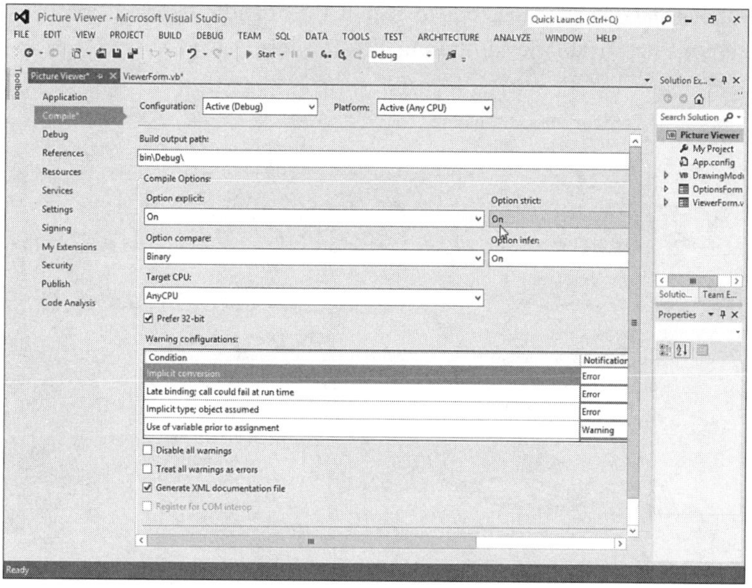

FIGURE 11.2
Using Option
Strict forces you
to write better
code.

Press F5 to run your project. Visual Basic tells you that there was a build error, as
shown in Figure 11.3.

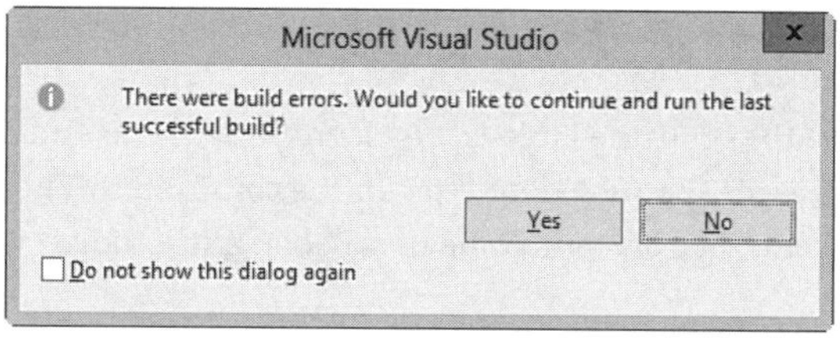

FIGURE 11.3
Simply enabling
Option Strict
broke the code.

Follow these steps to correct it:

1. Click No to stop running the project and view the error.

2. Visual Basic returns to the code window, but a new window, the Error List, has
   opened at the bottom (see Figure 11.4). Also notice that the constant you
   declared now appears with a wavy blue underline (you'll need to return to the
   ViewerForm.vb tab to see the code).

3. Notice the error message—it's an accurate one. Visual Basic is telling you that it
   wants to know the data type of every constant, variable, and array that you
   create because you are using Option Strict. Your constant declaration doesn't
   include a data type, so Visual Basic doesn't know how to handle this constant.

Double-click the error message to display the offending line of code, and then change the constant declaration to look like this:

```
Const c_defPromptOnExit As Boolean = False
```

FIGURE 11.4
The Error List window helps you pinpoint problems in your code.

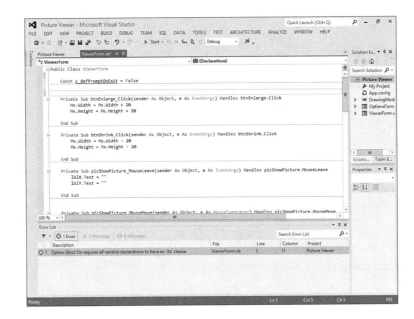

When you change the code, the Error List is cleared (go ahead and close the Error List). What you did was specify a data type for the constant, so Visual Basic now knows to always treat the constant value as a Boolean (true/false) value.

By the Way

If you would have left Option Infer turned on, the code would still run without an error. Option Infer tells Visual Basic to make a best guess at the data type based on the value put into it. I recommend that you leave this option off, as it negates the value of Option Strict.

Working with Arrays

An array is a special type of variable—it's a variable with multiple dimensions. Think of an ordinary variable as a single mail slot. You can retrieve or change the contents of the mail slot by referencing the variable. An array is like having an entire row of mail slots (called *elements*). You can retrieve and set the contents of any of the individual mail slots at any time by referencing the single array variable. You do this by using an index that points to the appropriate slot.

Dimensioning Arrays

Arrays are dimensioned in much the same way as ordinary variables, with one notable exception. Consider this statement:

```
Dim strMyArray(10) As String
```

This code is similar to the `Dim` statement of an ordinary `String` variable, with the difference being the number 10 in parentheses. The number in parentheses determines how many "mail slots" the array variable will contain, and it must be a literal value or a constant—it can't be another variable. The important point to remember is that the number you specify *isn't the exact number* of elements in the array—it's 1 less, as you'll see.

> It's possible to create arrays that can be resized at runtime. However, this topic is beyond the scope of this book.

Referencing Array Variables

To place a value in an array index, you specify the index number when referencing the variable. Most computer operations consider 0 to be the first value in a series, not 1, as you might expect. This is how array indexing behaves. For example, for an array dimensioned with 10 elements—declared using (9)—you would reference the elements sequentially by using the indexes 0, 1, 2, 3, 4, 5, 6, 7, 8, and 9.

> Notice that the upper index is the number specified when the array was declared. Because 0 is a valid element, you end up with 1 more than the number you used to declare the array. This can be confusing. To simplify your development, you might consider just ignoring element 0 and using elements 1 through the declared upper value.

To place a value in the first element of the array variable, you would use 0 as the index, like this:

```
strMyArray(0) = "This value goes in the first element"
```

To reference the second element, you could use a statement like this:

```
strMyVariable = strMyArray(1)
```

The data type specified for the array variable is used for all the elements in the array. You can use the Object type to hold any type of data in any element, but doing so isn't recommended for all the reasons discussed earlier.

Creating Multidimensional Arrays

Array variables require only one declaration, yet they can store numerous pieces of data; this makes them perfect for storing sets of related information. The array example shown previously is a single-dimension array. Arrays can be much more complex than this example and can have multiple dimensions of data. For example, a single array variable could be defined to store personal information for different people. Multidimensional arrays are declared with multiple parameters, such as the following:

```
Dim intMeasurements(3,2) as Integer
```

This Dim statement creates a two-dimensional array. The first dimension (defined as having four elements: 0, 1, 2, and 3) serves as an index to the second dimension (defined as having three elements: 0, 1, and 2). Suppose that you want to store the height and weight of three people in this array. You reference the array as you would a single-dimension array, but you include the extra parameter index. The two indexes together specify an element, much like coordinates in the game Battleship relate to specific spots on the game board. Figure 11.5 illustrates how the elements are related.

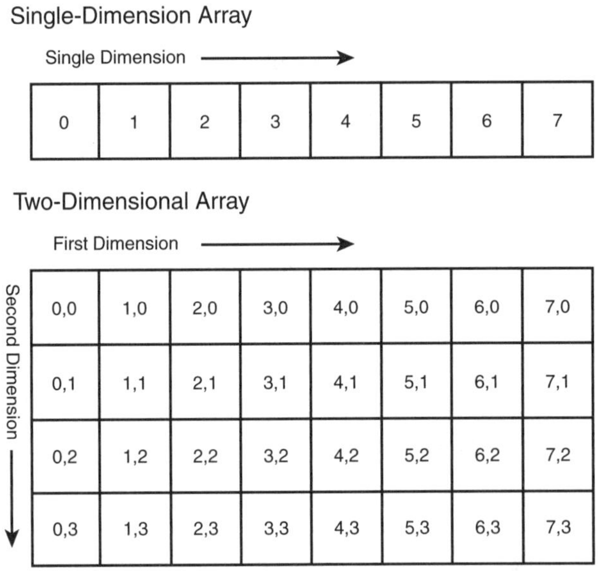

FIGURE 11.5
Two-dimensional arrays are like a wall of mail slots.

Single-Dimension Array

Single Dimension ———————→

0	1	2	3	4	5	6	7

Two-Dimensional Array

First Dimension ———————→

Second Dimension ↓

0,0	1,0	2,0	3,0	4,0	5,0	6,0	7,0
0,1	1,1	2,1	3,1	4,1	5,1	6,1	7,1
0,2	1,2	2,2	3,2	4,2	5,2	6,2	7,2
0,3	1,3	2,3	3,3	4,3	5,3	6,3	7,3

Elements are grouped according to the first index specified; think of the first set of indexes as being a single-dimension array. For example, to store the height and weight of a person in the array's first dimension (remember, arrays are 0-based), you could use code such as the following:

```
intMeasurements(0,0) = FirstPersonsHeight
intMeasurements(0,1) = FirstPersonsWeight
```

I find it helpful to create constants for the array elements, which makes array references much easier to understand. Consider this:

```
Const c_Height As Integer = 0
Const c_Weight As Integer = 1
intMeasurements(0, c_Height) = FirstPersonsHeight
intMeasurements(0, c_Weight) = FirstPersonsWeight
```

You could then store the height and weight of the second and third person like this:

```
intMeasurements(1, c_Height) = SecondPersonsHeight
intMeasurements(1, c_Weight) = SecondPersonsWeight
intMeasurements(2, c_Height) = ThirdPersonsHeight
intMeasurements(2, c_Weight) = ThirdPersonsWeight
```

In this array, I've used the first dimension to differentiate people. I've used the second dimension to store a height and weight for each element in the first dimension. Because I've consistently stored heights in the first slot of the array's second dimension and weights in the second slot of the array's second dimension, it becomes easy to work with these pieces of data. For example, you can retrieve the height and weight of a single person as long as you know the first dimension index used to store the data. You could write the total weight of all three people to the Output window using the following code:

```
Debug.WriteLine(intMeasurements (0, c_Weight) + _
             intMeasurements(1, c_Weight) + _
             intMeasurements(2, c_Weight))
```

When working with arrays, keep the following points in mind:

▶ The first element in any dimension of an array has an index of 0.

▶ Dimension an array to hold only as much data as you intend to put in it.

▶ Dimension an array with a data type appropriate to the values to be placed in the array's elements.

Arrays are a great way to store and work with related sets of data in Visual Basic code. Arrays can make working with larger sets of data much simpler and more efficient than using other methods. To maximize your effectiveness with arrays, study the For...Next loop discussed in Hour 14, "Looping for Efficiency." Using a For...Next loop, you can quickly iterate (loop sequentially) through all the elements in an array.

Determining Scope

Constants, variables, and arrays are useful ways to store and retrieve data in Visual Basic code. Hardly a program is written that doesn't use at least one of these elements. To properly use them, however, it's critical that you understand scope.

You had your first encounter with scope in Hour 10, with the keywords Private and Public. You learned that code is written in procedures and that procedures are stored in modules. *Scope* refers to the level at which a constant, variable, array, or procedure can be "seen" in code. For a constant or variable, scope can be one of the following:

▶ Block level

▶ Procedure level (local)

▶ Module level

▶ Global (also called namespace scope)

By the
Way

> Scope has the same effect on array variables as it does on ordinary variables. For the sake of clarity, I'll reference variables in this discussion on scope, but understand that what I discuss applies equally to arrays (and constants, for that matter).

Understanding Block Scope

Block scope, also called *structure scope*, is relatively new to Visual Basic .NET. Visual Basic considers whether a variable is dimensioned within a structure. If it is, Visual Basic gives the variable block scope.

Structures are coding constructs that consist of two statements, in contrast to one. For example, you've already used If...Then decision structures in previous hours. Such a structure looks like this:

```
If expression Then
    statements to execute when expression is True
End If
```

The standard Do...Loop structure, which you'll learn about in Hour 14, is used to create a loop; it looks like this:

```
Do
    statements to execute in the loop
Loop
```

If a variable is declared within a structure, the variable's scope is confined to the structure; the variable isn't created until the Dim statement occurs, and it's destroyed when the structure completes. If a variable is needed only within a structure, consider declaring it in the structure to give it block scope. Consider the following example:

```
If blnCreateLoop Then
    Dim intCounter As Integer
    For intCounter = 1 to 100
        ' Do something
    Next intCounter
End If
```

By placing the Dim statement within the If structure, you ensure that the variable is created only if it's needed. Variables consume resources, so if you only need a variable under a specific condition, placing the Dim statement in a decision construct like an If...End If block ensures that the resources are only used if necessary.

> The various structures, including looping and decision-making structures, are discussed in later hours.

By the Way

Understanding Procedure-Level (Local) Scope

When you declare a constant or variable within a procedure, that constant or variable has *procedure-level* or *local scope*. Most of the variables you'll create will have procedure scope. As a matter of fact, almost all the variables you've created in previous hours have had procedure-level scope. You can reference a local constant or variable within the same procedure, but it isn't visible to other procedures. If you try to reference a local constant or variable from a procedure other than the one in which it's defined, Visual Basic returns a compile error; to the procedure making the reference, the variable or constant doesn't exist. It's generally considered a best practice to declare all your local variables at the top of a procedure, but Visual Basic doesn't care where you place the Dim statements within the procedure. Note, however, that if you place a Dim statement within a structure, the corresponding variable has block scope, not local scope.

Understanding Module-Level Scope

When a constant or variable has module-level scope, it can be viewed by all procedures within the module containing the declaration. To procedures in all other modules, however, the constant or variable doesn't exist. To create a constant or variable with module-level scope, you must place the declaration within a module but not within a procedure. There is a section for this—called the Declarations section—at the top of each module (this is where you created your module-level constant earlier in this hour). Use module-level scope when many procedures must share the same variable and when passing the value as a parameter is not a workable solution.

Although module variables declared using Dim are private to the module, best practice dictates that you use the Private keyword to declare private module-level variables. That means it's possible to create public module variables, and you'll learn about them in the next section.

For all modules other than those used to generate forms, it's easy to add code to the Declarations section; simply add the Public/Private statements just after the module declaration line and before any procedure definitions, as shown in Figure 11.6.

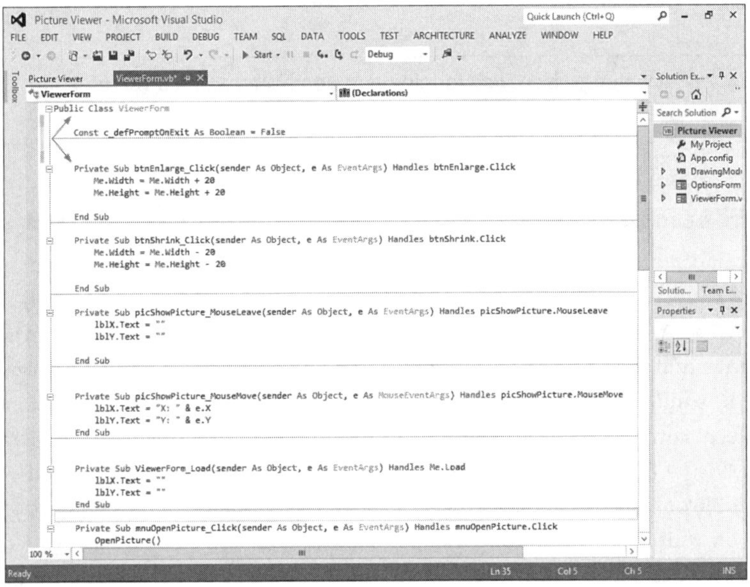

FIGURE 11.6
The Declarations section exists above all declared procedures.

A quick way to get to the Declarations section of any module is to choose (Declarations) from the procedure drop-down list in the upper-right corner of a module window.

Using Global (Namespace) Scope

A constant or variable is said to have *global scope* (or *namespace scope*) when it can be seen and referenced from any procedure, regardless of the module in which the procedure exists. One common use of a global variable is storing a reference to a database connection so that all code that needs access to the database can do so via the variable.

Creating global constants and variables is similar to declaring module-level constants and variables. Global constants and variables must be declared in a module's Declarations section, just like module-level constants and variables. The difference between a module-level declaration and a global-level declaration is the use of the keyword Public. (You must observe some restrictions to create global variables and constants; they're discussed in the following section.)

To declare a global constant, begin the constant declaration with the word Public, like this:

```
Public Const MyConstant As Integer = 1
```

To dimension a variable as a global variable, replace the keyword Dim or Private with the word Public, like this:

```
Public strMyVariable as String
```

If Visual Basic gives you the compile error The name variablename is not declared, first verify that you spelled the variable or constant reference correctly, and then verify that the variable or constant you're trying to reference is visible in the current scope.

Did you
Know?

To create a constant or variable of global scope, you must declare the constant or variable in a standard module, not a class-based module. If you declare a public variable or constant in a class module (such as a Form class module), the variable or constant behaves like a property of the class. This is a useful technique, and I discuss it in Hour 16, "Designing Objects Using Classes." Regardless, such a constant or variable does not have global scope; it has module-level scope.

Scope Name Conflicts

You can't have two variables of the same name in the same scope, but you can use the same variable name for variables with different scope. For example, if you create two public variables of the same name in standard modules (not class modules), you've created two global variables with the same name. This causes a compile error everywhere you attempt to access the variable. All variable references are ambiguous; which one should Visual Basic use? You could, however, create a local variable with the same name as a global variable (or even a module variable). Visual Basic always uses the variable with the narrowest scope. Therefore, when referencing the variable name in the procedure containing the local variable, Visual Basic would use the local variable. When accessing the variable from another procedure, the local variable is invisible, so the code would reference the global variable.

In general, the smaller (more limited) the scope, the better. When possible, make your variables block or local variables. If you have to increase scope, attempt to make the variable a module-level variable. Use global variables only when you have no other options (and you usually have other options). The larger the scope, the more the possibilities exist for problems, and the more difficult it is to debug those problems. In general, when considering a global variable, attempt to wrap the data in a class, as discussed in Hour 16.

Declaring Variables of Static Scope

When you create a variable within a procedure (local or block scope), the variable exists only during the lifetime of the procedure or block (the scope of the variable). When a variable goes out of scope, it's destroyed, and whatever value was stored in the old variable ceases to exist. The next time the procedure is called, Visual Basic creates a new variable. Consider the following procedure:

```
Public Sub MyProcedure()
   Dim intMyInteger As Integer
   intMyInteger = intMyInteger + 10
End Sub
```

If you call this procedure, it creates a new variable called intMyInteger and sets its value to its current value plus 10; then the procedure ends. Numeric variables have an initial value of 0, so when End Sub is encountered in this example, the value of intMyInteger is 10. When the procedure ends, the variable goes out of scope and therefore is destroyed. If you were to call the procedure again, it would create a new variable called intMyInteger (which again would default to 0) and increase its value by 10. Again, the procedure would end, and the variable would be destroyed.

You can create variables that persist between procedure calls by using the keyword Static. To create a static variable, use the keyword Static in place of the keyword Dim. The following code is similar to the last example, except that the variable created here is a static variable; it stays in existence and retains its value between calls to the procedure in which it resides:

```
Public Sub MyProcedure()
   Static intMyInteger As Integer
   intMyInteger = intMyInteger + 10
End Sub
```

The first time this procedure is called, the variable intMyInteger is created with a default value of 0, and then the variable is increased by 10. When the procedure ends, the variable isn't destroyed; instead, it persists in memory and retains its value (because it's declared with Static). The next time the procedure is called, Visual Basic has no need to create a new variable, so the previous variable is used, and 10 is added to its value. The variable would have a value of 20 at the conclusion of the second procedure call. Each subsequent call to the procedure would increase the value in intMyInteger by 10.

Static variables aren't nearly as common as ordinary variables, but they have their uses. For one thing, static variables enable you to minimize scope (which is a good thing). Why create a module-level variable when only one procedure will use it? As you create your Visual Basic projects, keep static variables in mind. If you ever need to create a variable that retains its value between calls, but whose scope is only procedure- or block-level, you can do so by creating a static variable.

> One scope identifier that I haven't covered is Friend. When you declare a variable or procedure by using Friend, it is given global scope within the project but is not visible to applications that are accessing your code externally via Automation. Because I don't cover how to create Automation servers, I don't have you use Friend in your Picture Viewer project, but Visual Basic uses it often.

By the Way

Naming Conventions

To make code more self-documenting (always an important goal) and to reduce the chance of programming errors, you need an easy way to determine the exact data type of a variable or the exact type of a referenced control in Visual Basic code.

Using Prefixes to Denote Data Type

Table 11.3 lists the prefixes of the common data types. Although you don't have to use prefixes, there are many advantages to doing so.

TABLE 11.3   Prefixes for Common Data Types

Data Type	Prefix	Sample Value
Boolean	bln	blnLoggedIn
Byte	byt	bytAge
Char	chr	chrQuantity
Date	dte	dteBirthday
Decimal	dec	decSalary
Double	dbl	dblCalculatedResult
Integer	int	intLoopCounter
Long	lng	lngCustomerID
Object	obj	objWord
Short	sho	shoTotalParts

Denoting Scope Using Variable Prefixes

Not only are prefixes useful for denoting type, they also can be used to denote scope, as shown in Table 11.4. In particularly large applications, a scope designator is a necessity. Again, Visual Basic doesn't care whether you use prefixes, but consistently using prefixes benefits you as well as others who have to review your code.

TABLE 11.4 Prefixes for Variable Scope

Prefix	Description	Example
g_	Global	g_strSavePath
m_	Module-level	m_blnDataChanged
s_	Static variable	s_blnInHere
No prefix	Nonstatic variable, local to procedure	

Other Prefixes

Prefixes aren't just for variables. All standard objects can use a three-character prefix. There are simply too many controls and objects to list all the prefixes here, although you'll find that I use control prefixes throughout this book. If you're interested in learning more about naming conventions and coding standards in general, I recommend that you take a look at my book *Practical Standards for Microsoft Visual Basic .NET*, Second Edition (Microsoft Press, 2002).

The prefix obj should be reserved for when a specific prefix is unavailable. The most common use of this prefix is when referencing automation libraries of other applications. For instance, when automating Microsoft Word, you create an instance of Word's Application object. Because there is no prefix specifically for Word objects, obj works just fine. Here's an example:

```
Dim objWord As Word.Application
```

You can hover the pointer over any variable in code and a ToolTip shows you the variable's declaration.

Using Variables in Your Picture Viewer Project

You added a module-level constant to your Picture Viewer project earlier in this hour. In this section, you'll create variables to hold the values for the controls on your Options form. In Hour 16, you will finish hooking up the options for your project.

Creating the Variables for the Options

In past hours, you defined three options for your Picture Viewer project. Let's consider each one now:

▶ **User Name:** This is where the user can enter her name, which appears in the form's title bar. Think for a moment about the type of data that will be stored for this option. If you said String (which is text), you're correct.

▶ **Prompt to confirm on exit:** This option has two possible values, true and false, so you need to use a Boolean value to store this option.

▶ **Default picture background color:** This is actually a special case. I told you about the common data types, but in addition to those there are dozens of other different data types, one of which is Color. You'll use a variable of the data type Color to store the user's background color preference.

Follow these steps to create the variables:

1. Display the code for the ViewerForm.vb form (not the OptionsForm.vb form). If you've sized the Solutions Explorer too small to show the button, you can right-click ViewerForm.vb and choose View Code.

2. Locate the Declarations section of the form's module—it's where you created the constant c_defPromptOnExit.

3. Enter the following three variable declarations, beginning on the line following the constant definition:

```
Private m_strUserName As String
Private m_blnPromptOnExit As Boolean
Private m_objPictureBackColor As Color
```

Your code should look like Figure 11.7.

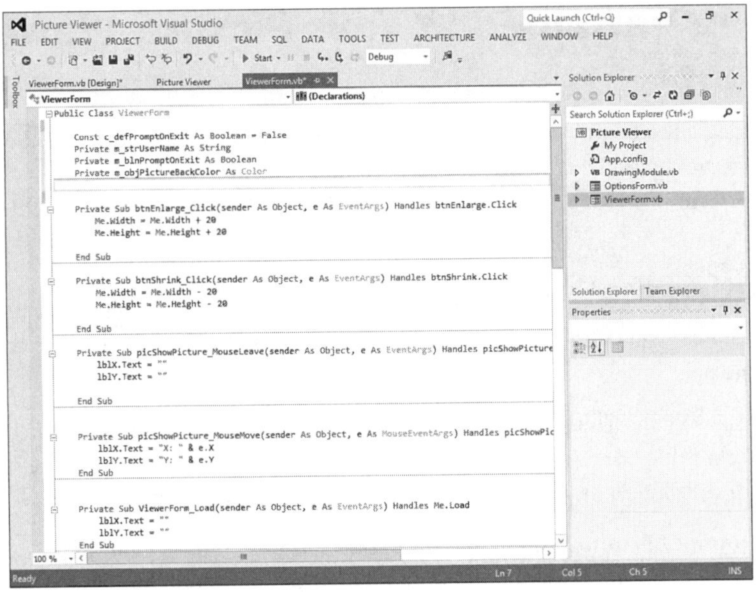

FIGURE 11.7
Public variables
go in the Decla-
rations section.

Initializing and Using the Options Variables

Now that the variables have been created, you need to initialize them. Follow
these steps:

1. The best place to set up a form is usually in the form's Load event. Getting to a
   form's events can be tricky. If you just select the form name in the object drop-
   down box (the drop-down in the upper-left corner of the code window), you see
   only a small subset of the form's events. You need to open the object drop-
   down and choose ViewerForm Events, as shown in Figure 11.8. After you've
   chosen ViewerForm Events, open the event drop-down list and choose Load to
   display the Load event.

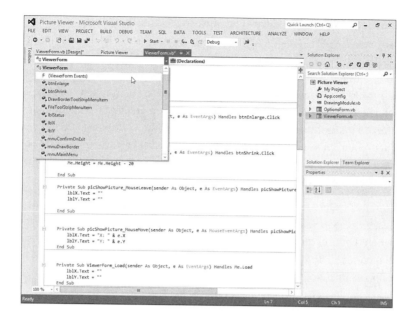

FIGURE 11.8
You need to choose this option to see all the form's events.

2. Your load event already has two lines of code: the two statements you entered to set the value of the X and Y labels. Add the following two statements below the existing code:

```
m_blnPromptOnExit = c_defPromptOnExit
m_objPictureBackColor = System.Drawing.SystemColors.Control
```

The first statement simply sets the module variable that stores the user's Prompt on Exit setting to the value of the constant you created earlier. I set up the example this way so that you can see how constants and variables work together. If you wanted to change the default behavior of the Close on Exit option, all you would have to do is change the value of the constant in the Declarations section.

The second statement sets the default back color to the default system color for controls. I've already explained how this works in Hour 2, so I won't go into detail here. Notice that I did not create an initialization statement for the module-level variable m_strUserName. This is because string variables are initialized empty, which is exactly what we need at this time.

3. So far, you've created variables for the options and initialized them in code. However, the option values aren't actually used in the project yet. The Prompt on Exit option is checked when the user closes the form, but the back color of the picture box needs to be set before the form appears. Enter the following

statement right below the two you just created:

```
picShowPicture.BackColor = m_objPictureBackColor
```

All that's left to do in this hour is to hook up the Prompt on Exit function. This takes just a tad more work, because you created a menu item that keeps track of whether the Prompt on Exit option is chosen. The first thing you'll do is make sure that the menu item is in sync with the variable; you don't want the menu item checked if the variable is set to False, because this would give the opposite response from what the user expects. Continue with these steps to hook up the Prompt on Exit variable.

4. Add this statement to your Form_Load event, right below the statement you just entered to set the picture box's back color. This statement ensures that when the form loads, the checked state of the menu item matches the state of the variable. Because Boolean variables initialize to False, the menu item appears unchecked:

```
mnuConfirmOnExit.Checked = m_blnPromptOnExit
```

5. You already created a procedure for the menu item so that it physically changes its Checked state when the user clicks it. You can scroll down the code window and locate the procedure mnuConfirmOnExit_Click, or you can switch to design view and double-click the menu item. Remember, there are usually multiple ways to approach a problem in Visual Basic. After you've found the procedure, add this statement below the existing code:

```
m_blnPromptOnExit = mnuConfirmOnExit.Checked
```

Did you notice that this statement is the exact opposite of the statement you entered in step 4? You've just told Visual Basic to set the value of the variable to the checked state of the menu item, *after* the checked state has been updated in the Click event.

6. Now that the variable will stay in sync with the menu item, you need to hook up the actual Prompt on Exit code. Open the object drop-down list and choose ViewerForm Events again. In the event drop-down list, choose FormClosing. Enter the following code exactly as it appears here:

```
If m_blnPromptOnExit Then
    If MessageBox.Show("Close the Picture Viewer program?", _
                    "Picture Viewer", MessageBoxButtons.YesNo, _
                    MessageBoxIcon.Question) = _
                    Windows.Forms.DialogResult.No Then
        e.Cancel = True
    End If
End If
```

I've already mentioned the MessageBox.Show() function (and I'll explain it in detail in Hour 17, "Interacting with Users"). All you need to understand here is that when the user closes the Picture Viewer and the variable m_blnPromptOnExit is True, the MessageBox.Show() function asks the user whether he or she really wants to quit. If the user chooses No, the e.Cancel property is set to True, which cancels the form from closing. (You can read more about the e object for the FormClosing event in the online help text.)

Press F5 to run your project, and give it a try. When you first run the application, the variable is False, and the menu item appears unchecked. If you click the Close button in the upper-right corner of the form, the Picture Viewer closes. Run the project again, but this time click the Confirm on Exit menu item to check it before you close the form. This time, when you close the form, you are asked to confirm, as shown in Figure 11.9.

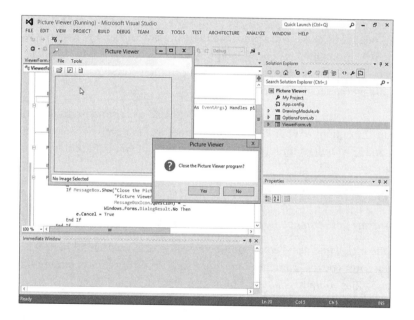

FIGURE 11.9
It's nice to give the user control over his or her experience.

Summary

In this hour, you learned how to eliminate magic numbers by creating constants. By using constants in place of literal values, you increase code readability, reduce the possibility of coding errors, and make it much easier to change a value in the future.

In addition, you learned how to create variables for data elements in which the initial value is unknown at design time, or for elements whose values will be changed at runtime. You learned how arrays add dimensions to variables and how to declare and reference them in your code.

Visual Basic enforces strict data typing, and in this hour you learned about the various data types and how they're used, as well as tips for choosing data types and functions for converting data from one type to another. Finally, you learned about scope—an important programming concept—and how to manage scope within your projects.

Writing code that can be clearly understood by those who didn't write it is a worthwhile goal. Naming prefixes goes a long way toward accomplishing this goal. In this hour, you learned the naming prefixes for the common data types, and you learned how to use prefixes to denote scope.

In the end, you utilized all these concepts and created a constant and some variables to handle the options of your Picture Viewer program. You even added code to make them work! The Options form is still not hooked up, but you'll fix that in Hour 16.

Q&A

Q. *Are any performance tricks related to the many data types?*

A. One trick when using whole numbers (values with no decimal places) is to use the data type that matches your processor. For instance, most current home and office computers have 32-bit processors. The Visual Basic Integer data type is made up of 32 bits. Believe it or not, Visual Basic can process an Integer variable faster than it can process a Short variable, even though the Short variable is smaller. This has to do with the architecture of the CPU, memory, and bus. The explanation is complicated, but the end result is that you should usually use Integer rather than Short, even when working with values that don't require the larger size of the Integer.

Q. Are arrays limited to two dimensions?

A. Although I showed only two dimensions, such as `intMeasurements(3,1)`, arrays can have many dimensions, such as `intMeasurements(3,3,3,4)`. The technical maximum is 32 dimensions, but you probably won't use more than three.

Workshop

Quiz

1. What data type would you use to hold currency values?

2. Which data type can be used to hold any kind of data and essentially serves as a generic data type?

3. What numeric values does Visual Basic internally equate to `True` and `False`?

4. What can you create to eliminate magic numbers by defining a literal value in one place?

5. What type of data element can you create in code that can have its value changed as many times as necessary?

6. What are the first and last indexes of an array dimensioned using `Dim a_strMyArray(5) As String`?

7. What term describes the visibility of a constant or variable?

8. In general, is it better to limit the scope of a variable or to use the widest scope possible?

9. What type of local variable persists data between procedure calls?

Answers

1. The Decimal data type

2. The Object data type

3. Visual Basic equates 0 to False and all nonzero values to True.

4. Constants are used to eliminate magic numbers.

5. Variables can have their values changed as often as necessary within their scope.

6. The first index is 0, and the last index is 5.

7. Scope describes the visibility of a constant, variable, or procedure.

8. It is better to use the narrowest scope possible.

9. Static variables persist their values between procedure calls.

Exercises

1. Create a project with a text box, button, and label control. When the user clicks the button, move the contents of the text box to a variable, and then move the contents of the variable to the label's Text property. (Hint: A String variable will do the trick.)

2. Rewrite the following code so that a single array variable is used rather than two standard variables. (Hint: Do not use a multidimensional array.)

```
Dim strGameTitleOne As String
Dim strGameTitleTwo As String
strGameTitleOne = "Diablo 3"
strGameTitleTwo = "Skyrim"
```

HOUR 12

Performing Arithmetic, String Manipulation, and Date/Time Adjustments

What You'll Learn in This Hour:

▶ Performing arithmetic

▶ Understanding the order of operator precedence

▶ Comparing equalities

▶ Understanding Boolean logic

▶ Manipulating strings

▶ Working with dates and times

Just as arithmetic is a necessary part of everyday life, it's also vital to developing Windows programs. You probably won't write an application that doesn't add, subtract, multiply, or divide some numbers. In this hour, you'll learn how to perform arithmetic in code. You'll also learn about order of operator precedence, which determines how Visual Basic evaluates complicated expressions (equations). After you understand operator precedence, you'll learn how to compare equalities—something that you'll do all the time.

Boolean logic is the logic Visual Basic uses to evaluate expressions in decision-making constructs. If you've never programmed before, Boolean logic might be a new concept to you. In this hour, I explain what you need to know about Boolean logic to create efficient code that performs as expected. Finally, I show you how to manipulate strings and work with dates and times.

Performing Basic Arithmetic Operations with Visual Basic

You have to have solid math skills to be a programmer; you'll be performing a lot of basic arithmetic when writing Visual Basic applications. To get the results you're looking for in any given calculation, you must

▶ Know the mathematical operator that performs the desired arithmetic function.

▶ Understand and correctly use order of precedence.

Using the correct mathematical operator is simple. Most are easy to commit to memory, and you can always look up the ones you're not quite sure of. I won't go into great detail on any of the math functions (if you've made it this far, I'm sure you have a working grasp of basic math), but I will cover them all.

Performing Addition

You perform simple addition by using the standard addition symbol, the + character. The following line prints the sum of 4, 5, and 6:

```
Debug.WriteLine(4 + 5 + 6)
```

You don't have to use a hard-coded value with arithmetic operators. You can use any of the arithmetic operators on numeric variables and constants. For example:

```
Const c_FirstValue As Integer = 4
Const c_SecondValue As Integer = 5
Debug.WriteLine(c_FirstValue + c_SecondValue)
```

This bit of code prints the sum of the constants c_FirstValue and c_SecondValue, which is 9.

Performing Subtraction and Negation

Like the addition operator, you're probably familiar with the subtraction operator, because it's the same one you would use on a calculator or when writing an equation: the – character. The following line of code prints 2 (the total of 6 – 4):

```
Debug.WriteLine(6 - 4)
```

As with written math, the – character is also used to denote a negative number. For example, to print the value –6, you would use a statement such as the following:

```
Debug.WriteLine(-6)
```

Performing Multiplication

If you work with adding machines, you already know the multiplication operator: the * character. You can enter this character by pressing Shift+8 or by pressing the * key located in the top row of the keypad section of the keyboard. Although you would ordinarily use a × when writing multiplication equations such as 3 × 2 = 6 on paper, you'll receive an error if you try this in code; you have to use the * character. The following statement prints 20 (5 multiplied by 4):

```
Debug.WriteLine(5 * 4)
```

Performing Division

You accomplish division by using the / operator. This operator is easy to remember if you think of division as fractions. For example, one-eighth is written as 1/8, which literally means 1 divided by 8. The following statement prints 8 (32 divided by 4):

```
Debug.WriteLine(32 / 4)
```

> Be sure not to confuse the division character, /, with the backslash character, \. If you use the backslash character, Visual Basic performs the division, but it returns only the integer portion (the remainder is discarded).

Did you Know?

Performing Exponentiation

Exponentiation is the process of raising a number to a certain power. An example is 10^2, which is 10 to the second power, or 100. The same equation in Visual Basic code looks like this:

```
Debug.WriteLine(10 ^ 2)
```

The number placed to the left of the ^ operator is the base, whereas the number to the right is the power/exponent. To get the ^ operator, press Shift+6.

Performing Modulus Arithmetic

Modulus arithmetic is the process of performing division on two numbers but keeping only the remainder. You perform modulus arithmetic by using the Mod keyword, rather than the / symbol. The following are examples of Mod statements and the values they would print:

```
Debug.WriteLine(10 Mod 5)        ' Prints 0
Debug.WriteLine(10 Mod 3)        ' Prints 1
Debug.WriteLine(12 Mod 4.3)      ' Prints 3.4
Debug.WriteLine(13.6 Mod 5)      ' Prints 3.6
```

The first two statements are relatively easy to understand: 5 goes into 10 twice with no remainder, and 3 goes into 10 three times with a remainder of 1. Visual Basic processes the third statement as 4.3 going into 12 two times with a remainder of 3.4. In the last statement, Visual Basic performs the Mod operation as 5 going into 13.6 twice with a remainder of 3.6.

Determining the Order of Operator Precedence

When several arithmetic operations occur within a single equation (called an *expression*), Visual Basic has to resolve the expression in pieces. The order in which these operations are evaluated is known as *operator precedence*. To fully understand operator precedence, you have to brush up a bit on your algebra skills (most of the math you perform in code will be algebraic).

Consider the following expression:

```
Debug.writeLine(6 + 4 * 5)
```

Two arithmetic operations occur in this single expression. To evaluate the expression, Visual Basic has to perform both operations: multiplication and addition. Which operation gets done first? Does it matter? Absolutely! If Visual Basic performs the addition before the multiplication, you end up with the following:

> Step 1: 6 + 4 = 10
>
> Step 2: 10 * 5 = 50

The final result would be Visual Basic printing 50. Now look at the same equation with the multiplication performed before addition:

> Step 1: 4 * 5 = 20
>
> Step 2: 20 + 6 = 26

In this case, Visual Basic would print 26—a dramatically different number from the one computed when the addition gets performed first. To prevent these types of problems, Visual Basic always performs arithmetic operations in the same order—the order of operator precedence. Table 12.1 lists the order of operator precedence for arithmetic and Boolean operators. (Boolean operators are discussed later in this hour.) If you're familiar with algebra, you'll note that the order of precedence that Visual Basic uses is the same as that used in algebraic formulas.

TABLE 12.1   Visual Basic Order of Operator Precedence

Arithmetic	Logical
Exponentiation (^)	Not
Unary identity and negation (+, –)	
Negation (–)	And
Multiplication and division (*, /)	Or
Integer division (\)	
Modulus arithmetic	(Mod)
Addition and subtraction (+, –)	
String concatenation (&)	

All comparison operators, such as >, <, and = (discussed in the next section), have equal precedence. When operators have equal precedence, they are evaluated from left to right. Notice that multiplication and division operators have equal precedence, so an expression that has both these operators would be evaluated from left to right. The same holds true for addition and subtraction. When expressions contain operators from more than one category (arithmetic, comparison, or logical), arithmetic operators are evaluated first, comparison operators are evaluated next, and logical operators are evaluated last.

Just as when writing an equation on paper, you can use parentheses to override the order of operator precedence. Operations placed within parentheses are always evaluated first. Consider the previous example:

```
Debug.WriteLine(6 * 5 + 4)
```

Using the order of operator precedence, Visual Basic evaluates the equation like this:

```
Debug.WriteLine((6 * 5) + 4)
```

The multiplication is performed first, and then the addition. If you want the addition performed before the multiplication, you could write the statement like this:

```
Debug.WriteLine(6 * (5 + 4))
```

> When writing complex expressions, you have to be conscious of the order of operator precedence and use parentheses to override the default precedence when necessary. Personally, I try to always use parentheses so that I'm sure of what's happening and my code is easier to read.

By the Way

Comparing Equalities

Comparing values, particularly variables, is even more common than performing arithmetic (but you need to know how Visual Basic arithmetic works before you can understand the evaluation of equalities).

Comparison operators are most often used in decision-making structures, as explained in Hour 13, "Making Decisions in Visual Basic Code." Indeed, the best way to understand these operators is to use a simple `If...Then` decision structure. In an `If...Then` construct, Visual Basic considers the expression on the `If` statement, and if the expression equates to `True`, the code between the `If` and `End If` statements is executed. For example, the following is an `If...Then` operation (a silly one at that) expressed in English, not in Visual Basic code:

> If dogs bark, then smile.

If this were in Visual Basic code format, Visual Basic would evaluate the `If` condition, which in this case is "dogs bark." If the condition is found to be `True`, the code following `Then` is performed. Because dogs bark, you smile. Notice how these two things (dogs barking and your smiling) are relatively unrelated. This doesn't matter; the point is that if the condition evaluates to `True`, certain actions (statements) occur.

You'll often compare the value of one variable to that of another variable or to a specific value when making decisions. The following are some basic comparisons and how Visual Basic evaluates them:

```
Debug.WriteLine(6 > 3)      ' Evaluates to True
Debug.WriteLine(3 = 4)      ' Evaluates to False
Debug.WriteLine(3 >= 3)     ' Evaluates to True
Debug.WriteLine(5 <= 4)     ' Evaluates to False
```

Performing comparisons is pretty straightforward. If you get stuck writing a particular comparison, attempt to write it in English before creating it in code.

Understanding Boolean Logic

Boolean logic is a special type of arithmetic/comparison. Boolean logic is used to evaluate expressions to either `True` or `False`. This might be new to you, but don't worry—it isn't difficult to understand. A logical operator is used to perform Boolean logic. Consider the following sentence:

> If black is a color and wood comes from trees, then print "ice cream."

At first glance, this sentence might seem nonsensical. However, Visual Basic could make sense of this statement by using Boolean logic. First, notice that three expressions are actually being evaluated within this single sentence. I've added parentheses in the following sentence to clarify the two most obvious expressions:

If (black is a color) and (wood comes from trees), then print "ice cream."

Boolean logic evaluates every expression to either True or False. Therefore, substituting True or False for each of these expressions yields the following:

If (True) and (True), then print "ice cream."

Now, for the sake of clarity, here's the same sentence with parentheses placed around the final expression to be evaluated:

If (True And True), then print "ice cream."

This is the point where the logical operators come into play. The And operator returns True if the expressions on each side of the And operator are true (see Table 12.2 for a complete list of logical operators). In the sentence we're considering, the expressions on both sides of the And operator are True, so the expression evaluates to True. Replacing the expression with True yields the following:

If True, then print "ice cream."

TABLE 12.2   Logical (Boolean) Operators

Operator	Description
And	Evaluates to True when the expressions on both sides are True.
Not	Returns the opposite of the expression on which it operates. It evaluates to True when the expression is False and False when the expression is True.
Or	Evaluates to True if an expression on either side evaluates to True.
Xor	Evaluates to True if one, and only one, expression on either side evaluates to True.

This would result in the words "ice cream" being printed. If the expression had evaluated to False, nothing would print. As you'll see in Hour 13, the decision constructs always evaluate their expressions to either True or False, executing statements according to the results.

By the Way

> As you work with Boolean logic, keep in mind that Visual Basic uses –1 to represent True and 0 to represent False, as described in Hour 11, "Using Constants, Data Types, Variables, and Arrays." You should always use True or False in your code, but just be aware of how Visual Basic treats the values internally.

Using the And Operator

The And operator is used to perform a logical conjunction. If the expressions on both sides of the And operator evaluate to True, the And operation evaluates to True. If either expression is False, the And operation evaluates to False, as illustrated in the following examples:

```
Debug.WriteLine(True And True)       ' Prints True
Debug.WriteLine(True And False)      ' Prints False
Debug.WriteLine(False And True)      ' Prints False
Debug.WriteLine(False And False)     ' Prints False
Debug.WriteLine((32 > 4) And (6 = 6))  ' Prints True
```

Using the Not Operator

The Not operator performs a logical negation. That is, it returns the opposite of the expression. Consider the following examples:

```
Debug.WriteLine(Not (True))      ' Prints False
Debug.WriteLine(Not (False))     ' Prints True
Debug.WriteLine(Not (5 = 5))     ' Prints False
Debug.WriteLine(Not (4 < 2))     ' Prints True
```

The first two statements are easy enough; the opposite of True is False, and vice versa. For the third statement, remember that Visual Basic's operator precedence dictates that arithmetic operators are evaluated first (even if no parentheses are used), so the first step of the evaluation would look like this:

```
Debug.WriteLine(Not (True))
```

The opposite of True is False, so Visual Basic prints False.

The fourth statement would evaluate to

```
Debug.WriteLine(Not (False))
```

This happens because 4 is not less than 2, which is the expression Visual Basic evaluates first. Because the opposite of False is True, this statement would print True.

Using the Or Operator

The Or operator is used to perform a logical disjunction. If the expression to the left or right of the Or operator evaluates to True, the Or operation evaluates to True. The following are examples that use Or operations, and their results:

```
Debug.WriteLine(True Or True)        ' Prints True
Debug.WriteLine(True Or False)       ' Prints True
Debug.WriteLine(False Or True)       ' Prints True
Debug.WriteLine(False Or False)      ' Prints False
Debug.WriteLine((32 < 4) Or (6 = 6)) ' Prints True
```

Using the Xor Operator

The Xor operator performs a nifty little function. I personally haven't had to use it much, but it's great for those times when its functionality is required. If one—and *only* one—of the expressions on either side of the Xor operator is True, the Xor operation evaluates to True. Take a close look at the following statement examples to see how this works:

```
Debug.WriteLine(True Xor True)        ' Prints False
Debug.WriteLine(True Xor False)       ' Prints True
Debug.WriteLine(False Xor True)       ' Prints True
Debug.WriteLine(False Xor False)      ' Prints False
Debug.WriteLine((32 < 4) Xor (6 = 6)) ' Prints True
```

Manipulating Strings

Recall from Hour 11 that a string is text. Visual Basic provides many functions for working with strings. Although string manipulation isn't technically arithmetic, the things that you do with strings are similar to things you do with numbers, such as adding two strings together; string manipulation is much like creating equations. Chances are you'll be working with strings a lot in your applications. Visual Basic includes a number of functions that enable you to do things with strings, such as retrieve a portion of a string or find one string within another. In the following sections, you'll learn the basics of string manipulation.

Concatenating Strings of Text

Visual Basic makes it possible to "add" two strings of text together to form one string. Although purists will say it's not truly a form of arithmetic, it's much like performing arithmetic on strings, so this hour is the logical place in which to present this material. The process of adding two strings together is called *concatenation*. Concatenation is very common. For example, you might want to concatenate variables with hard-coded strings to display meaningful messages to the user, such as Are you sure you wish to delete the user XXX?, where XXX is the contents of a variable.

To concatenate two strings, you use the & operator, as shown in this line of code:

```
Debug.WriteLine("This is" & "a test.")
```

This statement would print

```
This isa test.
```

Notice that there is no space between the words is and a. You could easily add a space by including one after the word is in the first string or before the a in the second string, or you could concatenate the space as a separate string, like this:

```
Debug.WriteLine("This is" & " " & "a test.")
```

Text placed directly within quotes is called a *literal*. Variables are concatenated in the same way as literals and can even be concatenated *with* literals. The following code creates two variables, sets the value of the first variable to "James," and sets the value of the second variable to the result of concatenating the variable with a space and the literal "Foxall":

```
Dim strFirstName as String
Dim strFullName as String
strFirstName = "James"
strFullName = strFirstName & " " & "Foxall"
```

The final result is that the variable strFullName contains the string James Foxall. Get comfortable concatenating strings of text—you'll do this often!

Using the Basic String Functions

Visual Basic includes a number of functions that make working with strings of text considerably easier than it might be otherwise. These functions enable you to easily retrieve a piece of text from a string, compute the number of characters in a string, and even determine whether one string contains another. The following sections summarize the basic string functions.

Determining the Number of Characters Using Len( )

The Len( ) function accepts a string (variable or literal) and returns the number of characters in the string. The following statement prints 26, the total number of characters in the literal string "Pink Floyd reigns supreme." Remember, the quotes surrounding the string tell Visual Basic that the text within them is a literal; they aren't part of the string. Len( ) is often used in support of the other string functions, as you'll learn next.

```
Debug.WriteLine(Len("Pink Floyd reigns supreme."))      ' Prints 26
```

Retrieving Text from the Left Side of a String Using Microsoft.VisualBasic.Left()

The Microsoft.VisualBasic.Left() function returns a portion of the left side of the string passed to it. The reason for the Microsoft.VisualBasic qualifier is that many objects, including controls and forms, have Left properties. Using Left on its own is ambiguous to the compiler, so it needs the full reference.

The Microsoft.VisualBasic.Left() function accepts two parameters:

▶ The string from which to retrieve a portion of the left side

▶ The number of characters to retrieve

The `Microsoft.VisualBasic.Left()` function always retrieves text starting with the leftmost character. For example, the following statement prints `Queen`, the first five characters of the string:

```
Debug.WriteLine(Microsoft.VisualBasic.Left("Queen to Queen's Level 3.", 5))
```

`Microsoft.VisualBasic.Left()` is commonly used with the `InStr()` function (discussed shortly) to retrieve the path portion of a variable containing a filename and path combination, such as c:\Myfile.txt. If you know where the \ character is, you can use `Microsoft.VisualBasic.Left()` to get the path.

By the Way

> If the number of characters requested is greater than the number of characters in the string, the entire string is returned. If you're unsure how many characters are in the string, use the `Len()` function.

Retrieving Text from the Right Side of a String Using `Microsoft.VisualBasic.Right()`

The `Microsoft.VisualBasic.Right()` function is the sister of the `Microsoft.VisualBasic.Left()` function. Instead of returning text from the left side of the string, `Microsoft.VisualBasic.Right()` returns text from the right side of the string. Note, however, that the returned characters are always in the same order in which they appear within the original string. `Microsoft.VisualBasic.Right()` doesn't retrieve the characters from right to left. Instead, it starts at the rightmost character, counts back the number of characters you specify, and returns that many characters from the right side of the string. The following statement prints `hing.`, the last five characters in the string:

```
Debug.WriteLine(Microsoft.VisualBasic.Right("Duct tape fixes everything.", 5))
```

Retrieving Text Within a String Using `Mid()`

When you need to retrieve a portion of text from within a string (from neither the left side nor the right side), use the `Mid()` function. The `Mid()` function enables you to specify where in the string to begin retrieving text, as well as how many characters to retrieve. The `Mid()` function accepts the following three parameters:

- ▶ The string from which to retrieve a portion of text
- ▶ The character position at which to begin retrieving text
- ▶ The number of characters to retrieve

The following statement prints the text look li. This occurs because the Mid() function begins at the fifth character (the l in look) and retrieves seven characters:

```
Debug.WriteLine(Microsoft.VisualBasic.Mid("You look like you could " _
    & "use a monkey.", 5, 7))
```

Not many people realize this, but you can omit the last parameter. When you do, the Mid() function returns everything from the starting character to the end of the string. The following statement prints the text ter crows at midnight.; it returns everything beginning with the ninth character:

```
Debug.WriteLine(Mid("The rooster crows at midnight.", 9))
```

Determining Whether One String Contains Another Using Instr()

At times you'll need to determine whether one string exists within another. For example, suppose that you let users enter their full name into a text box, and that you want to separate the first and last names before saving them into individual fields in a database. The easiest way to do this is to look for the space in the string that separates the first name from the last. You could use a loop to examine each character in the string until you find the space, but Visual Basic includes a native function that does this for you, faster and easier than you could do it yourself: the InStr() function. The basic InStr() function has the following syntax:

```
Instr([start, ] stringtosearch, stringbeingsought)    ' Returns an Integer
```

> The InStr() function has always been an enigma to me. For one thing, it's the only function I've ever seen in which the first parameter is optional, but the subsequent parameters are required. Second, it's documented with the second parameter, called string1, and the third parameter, called string2. This makes it difficult to remember which parameter is used for what and will probably force you to reference the Help when you use this function.

By the Way

The InStr() function searches one string for the occurrence of another. If the string is found, the character location of the start of the matching search string is returned. If the search string is not found within the other string, 0 is returned. The following code searches a variable containing the text "James Foxall", locates the space, and uses Left() and Mid() to place the first and last names in separate variables:

```
Dim strFullName As String = "James Foxall"
Dim strFirstName As String
Dim strLastName As String
Dim intLocation As Integer

intLocation = Instr(strFullName, " ")

strFirstName = Microsoft.VisualBasic.Left(strFullName, intLocation - 1)
strLastName = Mid(strFullName, intLocation + 1)
```

This code assumes that a space will be found and that it won't be the first or last character in the string. Such code might need to be more robust in a real application, such as checking to see whether InStr() returned 0, indicating that no match was found.

When this code runs, InStr() returns 6, the location in which the first space is found. Notice how I subtracted 1 from intLocation when using Microsoft.VisualBasic.Left(). If I didn't do this, the space would be part of the text returned by Microsoft.VisualBasic.Left(). The same holds true with adding 1 to intLocation in the Microsoft.VisualBasic.Mid() statement.

I omitted the first parameter in this example because it's not necessary when you want to search from the first character in the string. To search from a different location, supply the number of characters to begin searching from as the first parameter.

Trimming Beginning and Trailing Spaces from a String

In the previous example, I showed how you need to add 1 or subtract 1 from the value returned by the InStr() function to avoid getting the space that was found as part of your first or last names. As you work with strings, you'll often encounter situations in which spaces exist at the beginning or end of strings. Visual Basic includes three functions for automatically removing spaces from the beginning or end of a string (none of these functions removes spaces that exist *between* characters in a string).

Function	Description
Trim()	Removes all leading and trailing spaces from the supplied string.
LTrim()	Removes only the leading spaces from the supplied string.
RTrim()	Removes only the trailing spaces from the supplied string.

For example, consider that you didn't subtract 1 from the value of intLocation in the previous example. That is, you used a statement such as the following:

```
strFirstName = Microsoft.VisualBasic.Left(strFullName, intLocation)
```

strFirstName would contain the text "James ". Notice the space at the end of the name. To remove the space, you could use Trim() or LTrim(), like this:

```
strFirstName = Trim(Microsoft.VisualBasic.Left(strFullName, intLocation))
```

> Use `Trim()` in place of `RTrim()` or `LTrim()` unless you specifically want to keep spaces at one end of the string.

Replacing Text Within a String

It's not uncommon to have to replace a piece of text within a string with some other text. Some people still put two spaces between sentences, for example, even though this is no longer necessary because of proportional fonts. You could replace all double spaces in a string with a single space by using a loop and the string manipulation functions discussed so far, but there's an easier way: the `Replace()` function. A basic `Replace()` function call has the following syntax:

```
Replace(expression, findtext, replacetext)
```

The `expression` argument is the text to search, such as a string variable. The `findtext` argument is used to specify the text to look for within `expression`. The `replacetext` argument is used to specify the text used to replace the `findtext`. Consider the following code:

```
Dim strText As String = "Give a man a fish"
strText = Replace(strText, "fish", "sandwich")
```

When this code finishes executing, `strText` contains the string "Give a man a sandwich". `Replace()` is a powerful function that can save many lines of code, and you should use it in place of a homegrown replace function whenever possible.

Working with Dates and Times

Dates are a unique beast. In some ways, they act like strings, where you can concatenate and parse pieces. In other ways, dates seem more like numbers in that you can add to or subtract from them. You'll often perform math-type functions on dates (such as adding a number of days to a date or determining the number of months between two dates), but you won't use the typical arithmetic operations. Instead, you use functions specifically designed for working with dates.

Understanding the `Date` Data Type

Working with dates is very common. You create a variable to hold a date by using the `Date` data type. You can get a date into a `Date` variable in several ways. Recall that when you set a string variable to a literal value, the literal is enclosed in quotes.

When you set a numeric variable to a literal number, the number is not enclosed in quotes:

```
Dim strMyString As String = "This is a string literal"
Dim intMyInteger As Integer = 420
```

When setting a Date variable to a literal date, you enclose the literal in # signs, like this:

```
Dim dteMyBirthday As Date = #7/22/2012#
```

When using Option Strict, you cannot assign a string directly to a Date variable. For example, if you let the user enter a date into a text box, and you want to move the entry to a Date variable, you would have to do something like this:

```
dteMyDateVariable = CDate(txtBirthDay.Text)
```

You also have to convert a date to a string when moving it from a Date variable to a text box (again, only when Option Strict is on). For more information on the data type conversion functions, refer to Hour 11.

It's important to note that Date variables store a date *and* a time—always. For example, the following code:

```
Dim dteBirthday As Date = #7/22/2012#
Debug.WriteLine(dteBirthday)
```

produces this output:

```
7/22/2013 12:00:00 AM
```

Notice that the previous example outputs the time 12:00:00 AM, even though no time was specified for the variable. This is the default time placed in a Date variable when only a date is specified. Although a Date variable always holds a date and a time, on occasion you'll be concerned only with either the date or the time. Later, I'll show you how to use the Format() function to retrieve just the date or a time portion of a Date variable.

By the Way

Visual Basic includes a structure called DateTime. This structure has members that enable you to do many things similar to the functions I discuss here. According to Microsoft, neither method is preferred over the other. The DateTime structure can be a bit more complicated, so I've chosen to cover the Date variable.

Adding To or Subtracting From a Date or Time

To add a specific amount of time (such as one day or three months) to a specific date or time, use the `DateAdd()` function. It has the following syntax:

```
DateAdd(interval, number, date) As Date
```

Note that all three parameters are required. The first parameter is an enumeration (a predefined list of values) and determines *what* you're adding (month, day, hour, minute, and so on). Table 12.3 lists the possible values for `interval`. The second parameter is how much of the interval to add. The final parameter is a date. Supplying a negative value for `number` subtracts that much of the `interval` from the date. For example, to add 6 months to the date 7/22/69, you could use the following statements:

```
Dim dteMyBirthday As Date = #7/22/1969#
dteMyBirthday = DateAdd(DateInterval.Month, 6, dteMyBirthday)
```

After this second statement executes, `dteMyBirthday` contains the date 1/22/1970 12:00:00 AM.

TABLE 12.3   Allowable Values for the `interval` Parameter of `DateAdd()`

Enumeration Value	String	Unit of Time Interval to Add
DateInterval.Day	d	Day; truncated to integral value
DateInterval.DayOfYear	y	Day; truncated to integral value
DateInterval.Hour	h	Hour; rounded to nearest millisecond
DateInterval.Minute	n	Minute; rounded to nearest millisecond
DateInterval.Month	m	Month; truncated to integral value
DateInterval.Quarter	q	Quarter; truncated to integral value
DateInterval.Second	s	Second; rounded to nearest millisecond
DateInterval.Weekday	w	Day; truncated to integral value
DateInterval.WeekOfYear	ww	Week; truncated to integral value
DateInterval.Year	yyyy	Year; truncated to integral value

> You can use the literal string that corresponds to the enumeration (see Table 12.3), rather than using the enumerated name. For example, the previous statement could be written as
>
> ```
> dteMyBirthday = DateAdd("m", 6, dteMyBirthday)
> ```

The following code shows sample `DateAdd()` function calls and the date they would return:

```
DateAdd(DateInterval.Year, 2, #3/3/1968#)          ' Returns 3/3/1970 12:00:00 AM
DateAdd(DateInterval.Month, 5, #5/14/1998#)        ' Returns 10/14/1998 12:00:00 AM
DateAdd(DateInterval.Month, -1, #3/6/2000#)        ' Returns 2/6/2000 12:00:00 AM
DateAdd(DateInterval.Hour, -1, #6/28/1996 8:00:00 PM#) _
                                                   ' Returns 6/28/1996 7:00:00 PM
```

> Visual Basic never advances more calendar months than specified when adding months. For example, `DateAdd("m", 1, #1/31/2012#)` produces the date 2/28/2012. Because February doesn't have 31 days, Visual Basic uses the last day of the month.

Determining the Interval Between Two Dates or Times

The `DateAdd()` function enables you to easily add time to or subtract time from a date or time. You can just as easily retrieve the interval between two existing dates or times by using the `DateDiff()` function. The basic `DateDiff()` function has the following syntax:

```
DateDiff(interval, Date1, Date2) As Long
```

The `interval` parameter accepts the same values as the `interval` parameter of the `DateAdd()` function (refer to Table 12.3). The `DateDiff()` function returns a number indicating the number of specified intervals between the two supplied dates. For example, this code prints 9, the number of weeks between the two dates:

```
Dim dteStartDate As Date = #10/10/2012#
Dim dteEndDate As Date = #12/10/2012#
Debug.WriteLine(DateDiff(DateInterval.WeekOfYear, dteStartDate, dteEndDate))
```

If the second date comes before the first, the number returned is negative. The following statements help illustrate how DateDiff() works by showing you some function calls and the values they return:

```
DateDiff(DateInterval.Year, #7/22/1969#, #10/22/2001#)    ' Returns 32
DateDiff(DateInterval.Month, #3/3/1992#, #3/3/1990#)      ' Returns -24
DateDiff(DateInterval.Day, #3/3/1997#, #7/2/1997#)       ' Returns 121
```

Notice that the second function call returns -24. Whenever the first date passed to the DateDiff() function comes after the second date, a negative number is returned. This is useful in determining the order of two dates. You can simply compare them by using DateDiff() and determine which is the later date by seeing whether DateDiff() returns a positive or negative number.

Retrieving Parts of a Date

Sometimes it can be useful to know just part of a date. For example, you might have let a user enter his birth date, and you want to perform an action based on the month in which he was born. To retrieve part of a date, use the DatePart() function. The basic DatePart() function has the following syntax:

```
DatePart(interval, date) As Integer
```

Again, the possible values for interval are the same as those used for both DateAdd() and DateDiff(). The following illustrates the use of DatePart():

```
DatePart(DateInterval.Month, #7/22/2012#)    ' Returns 7
DatePart(DateInterval.Hour, #3:00:00 PM#)    ' Returns 15 (military format)
DatePart(DateInterval.Quarter, #6/9/2012#)   ' Returns 2
```

Formatting Dates and Times

As I stated earlier, at times you'll want to work with only the date or time within a Date variable. In addition, you'll probably want to control the format in which a date or time is displayed. All this is accomplished with the Format() function. The Format() function can format all sorts of items in addition to dates and times, such as monetary figures and strings. I can't possibly tell you everything about the Format() function here, but I do want to show you how to use Format() to output either the date portion or the time portion of a Date variable.

The basic Format() function has the following syntax:

```
Format(expression, style)
```

The parameter expression is the expression to format, and style is a string specifying the formatting. For example, to display the month portion of a date, you use *M* in the style. Actually, specifying a single *M* displays the month as a single digit for 1 to 9 and as a double digit for 10 to 12. Specifying two *Ms* always shows the month in double digits. Three *Ms* produce a three-digit abbreviated month, and four *Ms* return the entire month name, regardless of how many characters are in the name. (Note: lowercase *m* is used to return minutes, not months.) The following examples illustrate this function:

```
Format(#1/22/2013#, "MM")       ' Returns 01
Format(#1/22/2013#, "MMM")      ' Returns Jan
Format(#1/22/2013#, "MMMM")     ' Returns January
```

There are formatting characters for years, days, hours, minutes, and even a.m. and p.m. The list of allowable formatting characters is huge, and I encourage you to explore them in the Visual Basic Help text. Because my goal here is to show you how to extract a date or a time, I'll show you some common formatting:

```
Format(#7/22/2013#, "MMM. d, yyyy")      ' Returns Jul. 22, 2013
Format(#7/22/2013#, "MMMM yyyy")         ' Returns July 2013
Format(#9:37:00 PM#, "h:mm tt")          ' Returns 9:37 pm
Format(#5/14/2013 9:37:00 PM#, "MM/dd/yyyy h:mm tt") _
                                         ' Returns 05/14/2013 9:37 pm
```

As you can see, the comma, the colon, and the period characters are not symbolic but appear in the formatted string in the location in which they are placed within `style`.

This information should be enough to get you going, but I highly encourage you to explore the `Format()` function on your own—it's a powerful and useful function.

Retrieving the Current System Date and Time

Visual Basic lets you retrieve the current system date and time. This is accomplished by way of the `DateTime` structure. The `DateTime` structure has a number of members that mimic the functionality of many of the date functions I've discussed, as well as some additional members. One member, `Today`, returns the current system date. To place the current system date in a new `Date` variable, for example, you could use a statement such as this:

```
Dim dteToday As Date = DateTime.Today
```

To retrieve the current system date and time, use the `Now` property of `DateTime`, like this:

```
Dim dteToday As Date = DateTime.Now
```

Commit `DateTime.Today` and `DateTime.Now` to memory. You will need to retrieve the system date and/or time at some point in the future, and this is by far the easiest way to get that information.

Determining Whether a Value Is a Date

Often, I find it necessary to determine whether a value is a date. If I enable users to enter their birthdays into a text box, for example, I want to ensure that they enter a date before attempting to perform any date functions on the value. Visual Basic includes a function just for this purpose: the `IsDate()` function. `IsDate()` accepts an expression and returns `True` if the expression is a date and `False` if not.

The following statement prints `True` if the content of the text box is a date; otherwise, it prints `False`:

```
Debug.WriteLine(IsDate(txtBirthday.Text))
```

Summary

Being able to work with all sorts of data is crucial to your success as a Visual Basic developer. Just as you need to understand basic math to function in society, you need to be able to perform basic math in code to write even the simplest of applications. Knowing the arithmetic operators, as well as understanding the order of operator precedence, will take you a long way in performing math with Visual Basic code.

Boolean logic is a special form of evaluation that Visual Basic uses to evaluate simple and complex expressions down to a value of `True` or `False`. In the following hours, you'll learn how to create loops and how to perform decisions in code. What you learned here about Boolean logic is critical to your success with loops and decision structures; you'll use Boolean logic perhaps even more often than you'll perform arithmetic.

Manipulating strings and dates involves special considerations. In this hour, you learned how to work with both types of data to extract portions of values and to add together pieces of data to form a new whole. String manipulation is straightforward, and you'll get the hang of it soon enough as you start to use some of the string functions. Date manipulation, on the other hand, can be a bit tricky. Even experienced developers need to refer to the online help at times. You learned the basics in this hour, but don't be afraid to experiment.

Q&A

Q. *Should I always specify parentheses to ensure that operators are evaluated as I expect them to be?*

A. Visual Basic never fails to evaluate expressions according to the order of operator precedence, so using parentheses isn't necessary when the order of precedence is correct for an expression. However, using parentheses assures you that the expression is being evaluated the way you want it to be, and it might make the expression easier for people to read. This really is your choice.

Q. *I want to use the same custom date format whenever I work with dates. How can I best accomplish this?*

A. I'd create a global constant that represents the formatting you want to use, and use that constant in your Format() calls as shown here. This way, if you want to change your format, you have to change only the constant value, and all Format() calls that use the constant will use the new value:

```
Const gc_MyUSDateFormat As String = "MMM. d, yyyy"
Debug.WriteLine(Format(dteStartDate, gc_MyUSDateFormat))
```

Be aware that if your application will be used in a country that uses a different date format than you use, you should use the named date formats, such as "General Date," "Long Date," or "Short Date." Doing so ensures that the proper date format for the user's location will be used.

Workshop

Quiz

1. Which character is used to perform exponentiation?

2. To get only the remainder of a division operation, you use which operator?

3. Which operation is performed first in the following expression—the addition or the multiplication?

   x = 6 + 5 * 4

4. Does the following expression evaluate to `True` or `False`?

   ((True Or True) And False) = Not True

5. Which Boolean operator performs a logical negation?

6. The process of appending one string to another is called what?

7. What function can be used to return the month of a given date?

8. What function returns the interval between two dates?

Answers

1. The ^ character

2. The `Mod` operator

3. 5 * 4 is performed first.

4. This expression equates to `True`.

5. The `Not` operator

6. Concatenation

7. The `DatePart()` function

8. The `DateDiff()` function

Exercises

1. Create a project that has a single text box on a form. Assume that the user enters a first name, a middle initial, and a last name into the text box. Parse the contents into three variables—one for each part of the name.

2. Create a project that has a single text box on a form. Assume that the user enters a valid birthday into the text box. Use the date functions to tell the user exactly how many days old he or she is.

Making Decisions in Visual Basic Code

What You'll Learn in This Hour:

▶ Making decisions using `If...Then`

▶ Expanding the capability of `If...Then` using `Else` and `ElseIf`

▶ Evaluating an expression for multiple values using `Select Case`

▶ Redirecting code flow using `GoTo`

In Hour 10, "Creating and Calling Code Procedures," you learned to separate code into multiple procedures so that they can be called in any order required. This goes a long way in organizing code, but you still need a way to selectively execute code procedures or groups of statements within a procedure. You use decision-making techniques to accomplish this. Decision-making constructs are coding structures that enable you to execute or omit code based on a condition, such as the value of a variable. Visual Basic includes two constructs that enable you to make any type of branching decision you can think of: `If...Then...Else` and `Select Case`.

In this hour, you'll learn how to use the decision constructs provided by Visual Basic to perform robust yet efficient decisions in Visual Basic code. In addition, you'll learn how to use the `GoTo` statement to redirect code within a procedure (and you'll learn when it's *not* appropriate to use it). You'll probably create decision constructs in every application you build, so the quicker you master these skills, the easier it will be to create robust applications.

Making Decisions Using `If...Then`

By far the most common decision-making construct used is the `If...Then` construct. A simple `If...Then` construct looks like this:

```
If expression Then
    ...    ' code to execute when expression is True.
End If
```

The If...Then construct uses Boolean logic to evaluate an expression to either True or False. The expression might be simple (If x=6 Then) or complicated (If x=6 And Y>10 Then). If the expression evaluates to True, the code placed between the If statement and the End If statement gets executed. If the expression evaluates to False, Visual Basic jumps to the End If statement and continues execution from there, bypassing all the code between the If and End If statements.

You've already added at least one If...End construct to your Picture Viewer program. For this example, you'll create a separate sample project by following these steps:

1. Create a new Windows Application, and name it Decisions Example.

2. Right-click Form1.vb in the Solution Explorer, and choose Rename from the shortcut menu. Change the name to DecisionsForm.vb, and set the form's Text property to Decisions Example.

3. Add a new text box to the form by double-clicking the TextBox icon in the toolbox. Set the properties of the text box as follows:

Property	Value
Name	txtInput
Location	44, 44

4. Add a new button to the form by double-clicking the Button icon in the toolbox. Set the button's properties as follows:

Property	Value
Name	btnIsNumeric
Location	156, 42
Size	100, 23
Text	Is text numeric?

Your form should now look like the one shown in Figure 13.1.

Now you'll add code to the button's Click event. This code uses a simple If...Then construct and the Visual Basic function IsNumeric() to determine whether the text entered in the text box is numeric. Double-click the button now to access its Click event, and enter the following code:

```
If IsNumeric(txtInput.Text) Then
   MessageBox.Show("The text is a number.")
End If
```

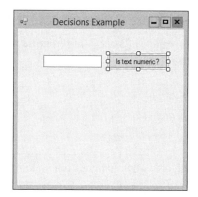

FIGURE 13.1
You'll use
If...Then to
determine
whether text
entered in the
text box is a
number.

This code is simple when examined one statement at a time. Look closely at the first statement, and recall that a simple If...Then statement looks like this:

```
If expression Then
```

In the code you entered, expression is

```
IsNumeric(txtInput.Text)
```

IsNumeric() is a Visual Basic function that evaluates a given string and returns True if the string is a number and False if it isn't. Here, you're passing the contents of the text box to the IsNumeric() function and instructing Visual Basic to make a decision based on the result. If IsNumeric() returns True, execution proceeds with the line *immediately following* the If statement, and a message is displayed. If IsNumeric() returns False, execution jumps to the End If statement, and no message is displayed.

If you have only a single line of code to execute in a simple If...Then construct, you can place the single statement of code immediately after the word Then and omit the End If statement. For example, the code you entered could have been entered like this:

```
If IsNumeric(txtInput.Text) Then MessageBox.Show("The text is a number.")
```

Although this code works, it's considered a better practice to use an End If statement, and I highly recommend that you do so because it makes the code much more readable and less prone to errors.

Executing Code When expression Is False

If you want to execute some code when expression evaluates to False, include an Else statement between If and End If:

```
If expression Then
    ...    ' code to execute when expression is True.
Else
    ...    ' code to execute when expression is False.
End If
```

If you want to execute code only when expression equates to False, not when True, use the Not operator in the expression, as in:

```
If Not(expression) Then
```

Refer to Hour 12, "Performing Arithmetic, String Manipulation, and Date/Time Adjustments," for more information on Boolean logic.

By including an Else clause, you can have one set of statements execute when expression is True and another set of statements execute when expression is False. In the example you just built, if users enter a number, they get a message. However, if they don't enter a number, they receive no feedback. Modify your code to look like the following, which ensures that the user always gets a message:

```
If IsNumeric(txtInput.Text) Then
    MessageBox.Show("The text is a number.")
Else
    MessageBox.Show("The text is not a number.")
End If
```

If the user enters a number, the message The text is a number is displayed, but nothing more. When Visual Basic encounters the Else statement, execution jumps to the End If, because code within an Else statement executes only when expression is False. Likewise, if the user enters text that isn't a number, the message The text is not a number is displayed, but nothing more; when expression evaluates to False, execution immediately jumps to the Else statement.

Click Save All on the toolbar to save your work, and then press F5 to run the project. Enter some text into the text box and click the button. A message box appears, telling you whether the text you entered is numeric, as shown in Figure 13.2.

Feel free to enter other strings of text and click the button as often as you want. When you're satisfied that the code is working, choose Debug, Stop Debugging.

Did you Know?

Get comfortable with If...Then. Odds are you'll include at least one in every project you create.

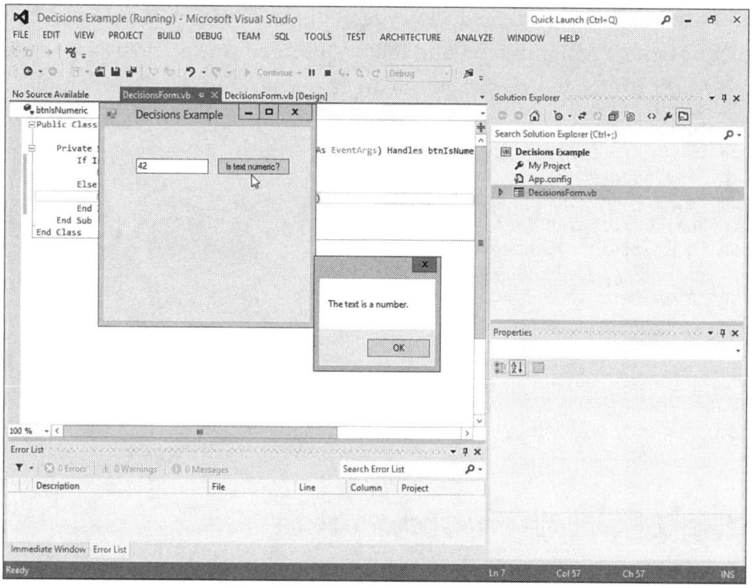

FIGURE 13.2
If...Then
gives you great
flexibility in mak-
ing decisions.

Using ElseIf for Advanced Decision-Making

If...Then...Else gives you a lot of flexibility in making decisions. Visual Basic has a statement that further expands the power of this construct and that can greatly reduce the amount of code that might otherwise be needed to nest If...Then statements. (*Nesting* involves placing one If...Then construct within another.) Specifically, the ElseIf statement enables you to evaluate a second expression when an If...Then statement equates to False.

The following shows a basic ElseIf structure:

```
If expression Then
    ...
ElseIf expression2 Then
    ...
End If
```

This code performs the same function as the following nested If...Then statements:

```
If expression Then
    ...
Else
    If expression2 Then
        ...
    End If
End If
```

The `ElseIf` statement not only reduces code, it also makes complex `If...Then` decision structures much easier to read and follow. It's important to note that you can use multiple `ElseIf` statements and even use an `Else` as a catchall. For example:

```
If optSendToPrinter.Value Then
   ' Code to print document goes here.
ElseIf optSendToScreen.Value Then
   ' Code to perform a print preview goes here.
ElseIf optSendEmail.Value Then
   ' Code to email the document goes here.
Else
   ' Code to execute if all above conditions are False.
End If
```

By the Way

> Be aware that the primary `If` statement and all its `ElseIf` statements are mutually exclusive; only one will ever execute during any one execution of the construct.

Nesting `If...Then` Constructs

As mentioned earlier, you can nest `If...Then` statements to further refine your decision-making process. The following code is an example of such a structure:

```
If optSendToPrinter.Value Then
   If blnDriverSelected Then
      ' Print the document
   Else
      ' Prompt for a printer driver.
   End If
Else
   ...
End If
```

One thing to keep in mind when nesting `If...Then` constructs is that you must have a corresponding `End If` statement for every `If...Then` statement. As mentioned earlier, there is one exception to this rule, and that is when the `If...Then` statement executes only one statement and that statement appears on the same line as `If...Then`. Personally, I recommend against putting the code to execute on the same line as the `If` statement, because it makes code more difficult to debug.

Evaluating an Expression for Multiple Values Using Select Case

At times, the `If...Then` construct can't handle a decision situation without a lot of unnecessary work. One such situation is when you need to perform different actions based on numerous possible values of a single expression, not just `True` or `False`. For example, suppose that you want to perform actions based on the user's age. The following shows what you might create using `If...Then`:

```
If lngAge < 10  Then
   ...
ElseIf lngAge < 18 Then
   ...
ElseIf lngAge < 21 Then
   ...
Else
   ...
End If
```

As you can see, this structure is a bit difficult to follow. If you don't analyze it from top to bottom (as the compiler does), you might not even get the whole picture. For example, if you looked at the last ElseIf, you might think that the code for that ElseIf would execute if the user is younger than 21. However, when you realize that the previous ElseIf statements catch all ages *up to* 18, it becomes apparent that the last ElseIf runs only when the user is between 18 and 20. If you don't see this, take a moment to follow the logic until you do.

The important thing to realize in this example is that each ElseIf is really evaluating the same expression (lngAge) but considering different values for the expression. Visual Basic includes a much better decision construct for evaluating a single expression for multiple possible values: Select Case.

A typical Select Case construct looks like this:

```
Select Case expression
   Case value1
      ...
   Case value2
      ...
   Case value3
      ...
   Case Else
      ...
End Select
```

Case Else is used to define code that executes only when expression doesn't evaluate to any of the values in the Case statements. Use of Case Else is optional.

Evaluating More Than One Possible Value in a Case Statement

The Select Case statement enables you to create some difficult expression comparisons. For example, you can specify multiple comparisons in a single Case statement by separating the comparisons with a comma (,). Consider the following:

```
Select Case strColor
   Case "Red","Purple","Orange"
      ' The color is a warm color.
   Case "Blue","Green","Blue Violet"
      ' The color is a cool color.
End Select
```

When Visual Basic encounters a comma within a `Case` statement, it evaluates the expression against each item in the comma-separated list. If `expression` matches any one of the items, the code for the `Case` statement executes. This can reduce the number of `Case` statements considerably in a complicated construct.

Another advanced comparison is the keyword `To`. When `To` is used, Visual Basic looks at the expression to determine whether the value is within a range designated by `To`. Here's an example:

```
Select Case lngAge
   Case 1 To 7
    ' Code placed here executes if lngAge is 1, 7 or any number in between.
End Select
```

The keyword `To` can be used with strings as well. For example:

```
Select Case strName
   Case "Hartman" To "White"
      ' Code placed here executes if the string is Hartman, White,
      ' or if the string falls alphabetically between these two names.
End Select
```

Here's the age example shown earlier, but this time `Select Case` is used:

```
Select Case lngAge
   Case < 10
    ...
   Case 10 To 17
    ...
   Case 18 To 20
    ...
   Case Else
    ...
End Select
```

The `Select Case` makes this decision much easier to follow. Again, the key with `Select Case` is that it's used to evaluate a single expression for more than one possible value.

Building a `Select Case` Example

Now you'll build a project that uses advanced expression evaluation in a `Select Case` structure. This simple application displays a list of animals to the user in a combo box. When the user clicks a button, the application displays the number of legs of the animal chosen in the list (if an animal is selected). Start by creating a new Windows Application named Select Case Example, and then follow these steps:

1. Right-click Form1.vb in the Solution Explorer, choose Rename, and then change the form's name to SelectCaseExampleForm.vb. Next, set the form's Text property to Select Case Example (you have to click the form to view its design properties).

2. Add a new combo box to the form by double-clicking the ComboBox item on the toolbox. Set the combo box's properties as follows:

Property	Value
Name	cboAnimals
Location	80, 100

3. Add some items to the list. Click the Items property of the combo box, and then click the Build button that appears in the property to access the String Collection Editor for the combo box. Enter the text as shown in Figure 13.3; be sure to press Enter at the end of each list item to make the next item appear on its own line.

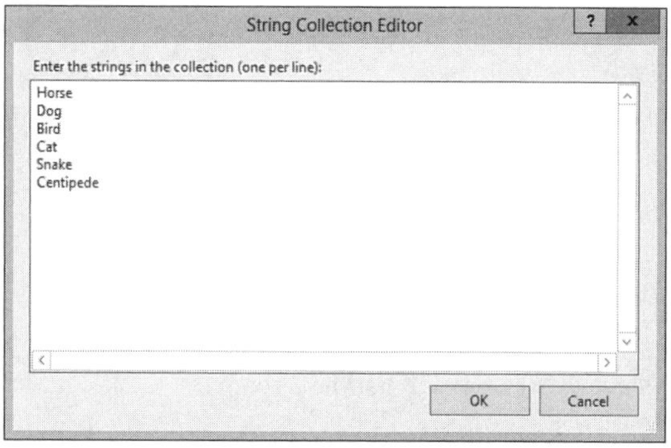

FIGURE 13.3
Each line you enter here becomes an item in the combo box at runtime.

4. Add a Button control. When the button is clicked, a Select Case construct is used to determine which animal the user selected and to tell the user how many legs the selected animal has. Add a new button to the form by double-clicking the Button tool in the toolbox. Set the button's properties as follows:

Property	Value
Name	btnShowLegs
Location	102, 130
Text	Show Legs

Your form should now look like the one shown in Figure 13.4. Click Save All on the toolbar to save your work before continuing.

FIGURE 13.4
This example uses only a combo box and a `Button` control.

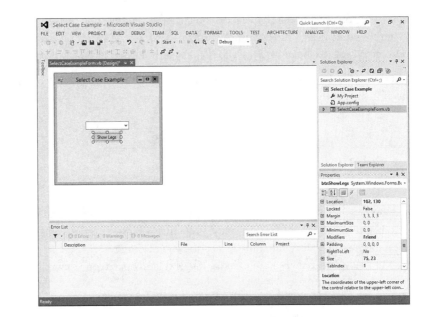

All that's left to do is add the code. Double-click the `Button` control to access its `Click` event and then enter the following code:

```
Select Case cboAnimals.Text
   Case "Bird"
      MessageBox.Show("This animal has 2 legs.")
   Case "Horse", "Dog", "Cat"
      MessageBox.Show ("This animal has 4 legs.")
   Case "Snake"
      MessageBox.Show ("This animal has no legs.")
   Case "Centipede"
      MessageBox.Show ("This animal has 100 legs.")
   Case Else
      MessageBox.Show ("You did not select from the list!")
End Select
```

Here's what's happening:

▶ The `Select Case` construct compares the content of the `cboAnimals` combo box to a set of predetermined values. Each `Case` statement is evaluated in the order in which it appears in the list. Therefore, the expression is first compared to "Bird." If the content of the combo box is Bird, the `MessageBox.Show()` statement immediately following the `Case` statement is called, and code execution then jumps to the `End Select` statement.

▶ If the combo box doesn't contain Bird, Visual Basic looks to see whether the content is "Horse," "Dog," or "Cat." If the combo box contains any of these values, the `MessageBox.Show()` statement following the `Case` statement is called, and execution then jumps to the `End Select` statement.

▶ Each successive `Case` statement is evaluated the same way. If no matches are found for any of the `Case` statements, the `MessageBox.Show()` in the `Case Else` statement is called. If there are no matches and no `Case Else` statement, no code executes.

Select Case uses case-sensitive comparisons. If the user enters **horse**, Select Case does not consider it the same as **Horse**.

By the Way

As you can see, the capability to place multiple possible values for the expression in a single `Case` statement reduces the number of `Case` statements as well as redundant code (code that would have to be duplicated for each `Case` statement in which animals had the same number of legs). Also, adding a new animal to the list can be as simple as adding the animal's name to an existing `Case` statement.

Try it now by pressing F5 to run your project, and then follow these steps:

1. Select an animal from the list and click the button.

2. Try clearing the contents of the combo box and click the button.

3. When you're finished, choose Debug, Stop Debugging to stop the project, and click Save All on the toolbar.

Creative Uses of `Select Case`

You might be surprised at what you can do with a `Select Case` statement. One of the coolest tricks I know uses `Select Case` to determine which radio button in a group is selected.

When a radio button is selected, its `Checked` property returns `True`. Essentially, this means that you have to look at the `Checked` property of each radio button in a group until you find the one that's set to `True`. The Visual Basic documentation recommends using an `If...Then` construct like this:

```
Dim strMessage As String = "You selected "
If radioButton1.Checked = True Then
    strMessage = strMessage & radioButton1.Text
ElseIf radiobutton2.Checked = True Then
    strMessage = strMessage & radioButton2.Text
ElseIf radiobutton3.Checked = True Then
    strMessage = strMessage & radioButton3.Text
End If
MessageBox.Show(strMessage)
```

In my opinion, all those `ElseIf` statements are messy. Consider this: Although you're looking at the `Checked` property of a number of radio button controls, you're comparing them all to a single value: the value `True`.

Now, if you look at `True` as the expression and the `Checked` properties of the controls as the possible values, you can replace the `If...Then` construct with a `Select Case` construct such as the following:

```
Dim strMessage As String = "You selected "
Select Case True
    Case radioButton1.Checked
        strMessage = strMessage & radioButton1.Text
    Case radioButton2.Checked
        strMessage = strMessage & radioButton2.Text
    Case radioButton3.Checked
        strMessage = strMessage & radioButton3.Text
End Select
MessageBox.Show(strMessage)
```

This seems much tidier to me. You can pretty much accomplish any decision-making task you can think of using `If...Then`, `Select Case`, or a combination of both. The skill comes in creating the cleanest and most readable decision structure possible.

> You can nest `Select Case` constructs within one another. In addition, you can nest `Select Case` constructs within `If...Then` constructs and vice versa. You can pretty much nest decision constructs in any way you see fit.

Branching Within a Procedure Using GoTo

Decision structures are used to selectively execute code. When a decision statement is encountered, Visual Basic evaluates an expression and diverts code according to the result. However, you don't have to use a decision structure to divert code because Visual Basic includes a statement that can be used to jump code execution to a predetermined location within the current procedure: the `GoTo` statement.

Before I talk about how to use `GoTo`, I want to say that under most circumstances, it's considered bad coding practice to use a `GoTo`. Code that's heavily laden with `GoTo` statements is difficult to read and debug because the execution path is so convoluted. Such code is often called *spaghetti code*, and it should be avoided at all costs. I'd say that in 99% of the situations in which `GoTo` is used, there's a better approach to the problem. I'll show an example of just such a case shortly. Nevertheless, `GoTo`, like all other statements, is a tool. Although it's not needed as often as some of the other Visual Basic statements, it's still a useful tool to have at your disposal—when used judiciously.

To jump to a specific location in a procedure, you must first define the jump location by using a *code label*. A code label is not the same as a label control that you place on a form. You create a code label by positioning the cursor on a new line in a procedure, typing in a name for the label followed by a colon, and pressing Enter. Code labels can't contain spaces, and they can't be a Visual Basic reserved word. For example, you can't create a code label called Print because Print is a reserved word in Visual Basic. However, you could create a label called PrintAll, because PrintAll isn't a reserved word. Code labels act as pointers that you can jump to when you use GoTo. The following shows an example using GoTo to jump code execution to a label:

```
Private Sub GotoExample()
    Dim intCounter As Integer = 0

IncrementCounter:
    intCounter = intCounter + 1
    If intCounter < 5000 Then GoTo IncrementCounter
End Sub
```

This procedure does the following:

▶ Dimensions an Integer variable called intCounter and initializes it with a value of 0.

▶ Defines a code label titled IncrementCounter. One or more GoTo statements can be used to jump code execution to this label at any time.

▶ Increments intCounter by 1.

▶ Uses an If...Then statement to determine whether intCounter has exceeded 5000. If it hasn't, a GoTo statement forces code execution back to the IncrementCounter label, where intCounter is incremented and tested again, creating a loop.

This code works, and you're welcome to try it. However, this is *terrible* code. Remember how I said that the use of a GoTo can often be replaced by a better coding approach? In this case, Visual Basic has specific looping constructs that you'll learn about in Hour 14, "Looping for Efficiency." These looping constructs are far superior to building your own loop under most conditions, so you should avoid building a loop that uses a GoTo statement. As a matter of fact, one of the biggest misuses of GoTo is using it in place of one of Visual Basic's internal looping constructs. In case you're interested, here's the loop that would replace the use of GoTo in this example:

```
Dim intCounter As Integer
For intCounter = 1 To 5000
    ...
Next intCounter
```

This discussion might leave you wondering why you would ever use GoTo. One situation in which I commonly use GoTo statements is to create single exit points in a procedure. As you know, you can use Exit Sub or Exit Function to force execution to leave a procedure at any time. Cleanup code is often required before a procedure exits. In a long procedure, you might have many exit statements. However, such a procedure can be difficult to debug because cleanup code might not be run under all circumstances. All procedures have a single entry point, and it makes sense to give them all a single exit point. With a single exit point, you use a GoTo statement to go to the exit point, rather than an Exit statement. The following procedure illustrates using GoTo to create a single exit point:

```
Private Sub DoSomething()
    If expression = True Then
        ' some code here that makes it necessary to exit.
        GoTo PROC_EXIT
    Else
        ' some more code here
    End If

    ' some more code here

PROC_EXIT:
    ' Put any clean up code here
    Exit Sub
End Sub
```

By the Way

An even better approach to creating a single exit point is to wrap the contents of a procedure in a Try...Catch...Finally block, as discussed in Hour 15, "Debugging Your Code." If you're interested in using industry-accepted best practices to create the soundest code possible, I suggest that you take a look at my book *Practical Standards for Microsoft Visual Basic .NET*, Second Edition (Microsoft Press, 2002).

Summary

In this hour, you learned how to use Visual Basic's decision constructs to make decisions in Visual Basic code. You learned how to use If...Then statements to execute code when an expression evaluates to True and to use Else to run code when the expression evaluates to False. For more complicated decisions, you learned how to use ElseIf statements to add further comparisons to the decision construct. You even learned how you can nest If...Then structures for more flexibility.

In addition to If...Then, you learned how to use Select Case to create powerful decision constructs that evaluate a single expression for many possible values. You learned how you can check for multiple possible values with a single Case statement, which can greatly increase legibility and reduce redundancy. Finally, you learned that mixing creativity with Select Case can yield some useful results.

Decision-making constructs are often the backbone of applications. Without the capability to run specific sets of code based on changing situations, your code would be very linear and, as a result, very limited. Become comfortable with the decision constructs, and make a conscious effort to use the best construct for any given situation. The better you are at writing decision constructs, the faster you'll be able to produce solid and understandable code.

Q&A

Q. *What if I want to execute code only when an expression in an* `If...Then` *statement is* `False`, *not* `True`? *Do I need to place the code in an* `Else` *clause with no code after the* `Then`?

A. This is where Boolean logic helps. You need to make the expression evaluate to `True` for the code you want to run. You do this by using the `Not` operator, like this:
`If Not expression Then`

Q. *How important is the order in which* `Case` *statements are created?*

A. It depends on the situation. In the earlier example in which the selected animal was considered and its number of legs was displayed, the order has no effect. If you'll perform numeric comparisons, such as the age example shown in this hour, the order is critical. If you're not careful, you can prevent a `Case` statement from ever being evaluated. For example, comparing a variable to <12 before comparing it to =6 would mean that the first comparison would evaluate to `True` if the variable were 6, so the second comparison would never take place.

Workshop

Quiz

1. Which decision construct should you use to evaluate a single expression to either `True` or `False`?

2. Evaluating expressions to `True` or `False` for both types of decision constructs is accomplished using what kind of logic?

3. If you want code to execute when the expression of an `If...Then` statement evaluates to `False`, you should include what kind of clause?

4. True or false: You don't need an `End If` statement when only one statement is to execute when an expression in an `If...Then` statement evaluates to `True`.

5. Which decision construct should you use when evaluating the result of an expression that might equate to one of many possible values?

6. To place multiple possible values on a single `Case` statement, you separate them with what?

7. Is it possible that more than one Case statement in a single Case construct might have its code execute?

8. True or false: You can use GoTo to jump code execution to a different procedure.

9. To use GoTo to jump execution to a new location in code, what must you create as a pointer to jump to?

Answers

1. The If...Then construct

2. Boolean

3. Else

4. True, but the code is less readable and more difficult to debug.

5. Select Case

6. A comma (,)

7. No, never.

8. False. GoTo can move code execution only within the current procedure.

9. A code label

Exercises

1. Create a project that enables the user to enter text into a text box. Use an If...Then construct to determine whether the text entered is a circle, triangle, square, or pentagon, and display the number of sides the entered shape has. If the text doesn't match one of these shapes, let the users know that they must enter a valid shape.

2. Rewrite the following code using only an If...Then structure; the new code should not contain a GoTo:

    ```
    ...
    If Not(blnAddToAge) Then GoTo SkipAddToAge
    intAge = intAge + 1
    SkipAddToAge:
    ```

HOUR 14

Looping for Efficiency

What You'll Learn in This Hour:

▶ Looping a specific number of times using For...Next

▶ Looping based on a condition using Do...Loop

You will often encounter situations in which you need to execute the same code statement or group of statements repeatedly. You will need to execute some of these statements a specific number of times, whereas others might need to be executed as long as a certain condition persists (an expression is True) or until a condition occurs (an expression *becomes* True). Visual Basic includes constructs that enable you to easily define and execute these repetitive code routines: *loops*. This hour shows you how to use the two major looping constructs to make your code smaller, faster, and more efficient.

Looping a Specific Number of Times Using For...Next

The simplest type of loop you can create is the For...Next loop, which has been around since the earliest forms of the BASIC language. With a For...Next loop, you instruct Visual Basic to begin a loop by starting a counter at a specific value. Visual Basic then executes the code within the loop, increments the counter by a defined incremental value, and repeats the loop until the counter reaches an upper limit you've set. The following is the general syntax for the basic For...Next loop:

```
For countervariable = start To end [Step step]
    ... [statements to execute in loop]
[Exit For]
    ... [statements to execute in loop]
Next [countervariable]
```

Initiating the Loop Using For

The For statement both sets up and starts the loop. The For statement has the components described in Table 14.1.

TABLE 14.1 Components of the For Statement

Part	Description
countervariable	A previously declared variable of a numeric data type (Integer, Long, and so on). This variable is incremented each time the loop occurs.
start	The number from which you want to start counting.
end	The number to which you want to count. When countervariable reaches the end number, the statements within the For...Next loop are executed a final time, and execution continues with the line following the Next statement.
step	The amount by which you want countervariable incremented each time the loop is performed. step is an optional parameter; if you omit it, countervariable is incremented by 1.
Exit For	A statement that can be used to exit the loop at any time. When Exit For is encountered, execution jumps to the statement following Next.

Closing the Loop with the Next Statement

Every For statement must have a corresponding Next statement. You don't have to specify the countervariable name with the Next statement, but you should because it makes the code easier to read. The following are examples of simple For...Next loops, along with explanations of what they do.

```
Dim intCounter As Integer
For intCounter = 1 To 100
   debug.WriteLine(intCounter)
Next intCounter
```

This routine declares an Integer variable named intCounter and then starts a loop with a For statement. The loop initializes intCounter at 1, prints the value of intCounter, increments intCounter by 1, and continues looping. Because step has been omitted, the variable intCounter is increased by 1 every time the loop is performed. This loop would execute 100 times, printing the numbers 1 through 100 to the Immediate window.

This next routine performs the same as the preceding example:

```
Dim intCounter As Integer
For intCounter = 1 To 100
   debug.WriteLine(intCounter)
Next
```

Note that the `Next` statement doesn't specify the name of the counter whose loop is to be executed. This is perfectly legal, but it's not good coding practice. Consider the following example:

```
Dim intCounter As Integer
Dim intSecondCounter as Integer
For intCounter = 1 To 100
   For intSecondCounter = 1 to 100
      debug.WriteLine(intSecondCounter)
   Next intSecondCounter
Next intCounter
```

This code executes a loop within a loop. If you omitted the variable names on the `Next` statements, the code would run, but from a programmer's standpoint, it would be difficult to read and understand.

Specifying an Increment Value Using `Step`

`Step` is used in a `For...Next` statement to designate the value by which to increment the counter variable each time the loop occurs. As you've seen, when `Step` is omitted, the counter variable is incremented by 1—always. If you want the counter variable incremented by 1, you don't need to use `Step` (it doesn't make the code any easier to read). However, if you need to increment the counter variable by a value other than 1, you must use `Step`.

Here's an example of a simple `For...Next` loop that uses `Step`:

```
Dim intCounter As Integer
For intCounter = 1 To 100 Step 4
   debug.WriteLine(intCounter)
Next intCounter
```

This code works much like that in the first example, except that each time `Next` is reached, `intCounter` is incremented by 4 rather than by 1. This loop would execute a total of 25 times (not 100 times). To create a `For...Next` loop that counts backward, specify a negative value for `Step`, as shown here:

```
Dim intCounter As Integer
For intCounter = 100 To 1 Step -1
   debug.WriteLine(intCounter)
Next intCounter
```

This loop initializes intCounter at a value of 100 and decrements intCounter by 1 each time Next is reached. The loop executes until intCounter is reduced to 1 (the End value). Be aware that you don't have to use whole numbers for step; you could use a number such as 0.5. If you do, the data type of the counter variable needs to support fractions, so you can't use Integer.

Exiting a Loop Early

Although you'll know the start and end of a For...Next loop when you initialize it (you have to specify a start and end, or you can't create the loop), at times you'll need to exit a loop before you reach the end value. To exit a For...Next loop at any time, use the Exit For statement, as shown in the following example:

```
Dim intCounter As Integer
For intCounter = 1 To 100
    If condition Then Exit For
    debug.WriteLine(intCounter)
Next intCounter
```

When Visual Basic encounters an Exit For statement, code execution jumps immediately to the statement *following* the Next statement of the current loop construct— the loop stops. In this example, condition could be a variable or any expression. condition is usually something that changes during the lifetime of the loop; if condition doesn't change, there's no point in evaluating it. For example, you might loop through a list of files, trying to find a specific file. After you find it, there's no need to continue looking, so you exit the loop.

Continuing Looping Before Next Is Reached

Relatively new to Visual Basic is the capability to continue a For...Next loop before encountering the Next statement. To do this, you use the statement Continue For, as shown here:

```
For countervariable = 1 to 1000
    If expression Then
        Continue For          ' Acts just like the Next statement
    End If
    ' Other code...
Next countervariable
```

Creating a For...Next Example

Now you'll create a procedure containing a For...Next loop that counts from 100 to 0 and sets the opacity of a form to the value of the counter (the form will fade out).

Create a new Windows Application named Fading Form, and then follow these steps:

1. Right-click Form1.vb in the Solution Explorer, choose Rename, and change the name of the default form to FadingFormForm.vb. Next, set the form's Text property to Fading Form (you'll need to click the form to access its design properties).

2. Add a button to the form by double-clicking the Button item in the toolbox. Set the button's properties as follows:

Property	Value
Name	btnFadeForm
Location	105, 113
Size	75, 23
Text	Fade Form

Your form should look like the one shown in Figure 14.1.

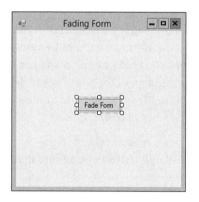

FIGURE 14.1
This simple project does something pretty cool...

All that's left to do is to write the code. Double-click the button to access its Click event, and enter the following:

```
Dim sngOpacity As Single

For sngOpacity = 1 To 0 Step -0.05
    Me.Opacity = sngOpacity
    ' Let the form repaint itself.
    Me.Refresh()
    ' Create a delay.
    System.Threading.Thread.Sleep(200)
Next

' Show the form again.
Me.Opacity = 1
```

Much of this code should make sense to you by now. Here's what's happening:

- ▶ The first statement creates a variable of type `Single`. We're using `Single` because `Opacity` works with values of 0 to 1. Integers don't support decimal places. In fact, I wasn't paying attention when I first wrote this code, used an integer, and the code didn't work. Try it and see! It took me a minute or two to figure out what was happening. If you look at a situation like this and think of it as a puzzle, you'll really enjoy programming!

- ▶ The next statement starts the `For...Next` loop. The variable is initialized to 1, and `Step` indicates that the variable will have its value decremented by .05 each time the loop starts a new iteration.

- ▶ The third line sets the form's `Opacity` to the value of the variable. The next line (after the comment) calls the form's `Refresh()` method, which forces it to repaint itself. If you don't do this, Windows might not get around to repainting the form between iterations. Comment out the `Refresh()` statement to see what happens. (In other words, put a comment character in front of the statement so that Visual Basic treats it as a comment and doesn't execute it.)

- ▶ The next statement (the `Sleep()` statement) tells Visual Basic to pause. The number in parentheses is the number of milliseconds to wait—in this case, 200. This is a nifty function! We could have used another `For...Next` loop to create a pause, but then the duration of the pause would depend on the speed of the user's computer. By using `Sleep()`, we've guaranteed that the pause will be the same on every machine that executes this code.

- ▶ The `Next` statement sends execution back to the `For` statement, where the variable is decremented and tested to make sure that we haven't reached the stop value.

- ▶ When the loop is finished, the form will be invisible. The last statement simply sets `Opacity` back to 1, showing the form.

Click Save All on the toolbar and press F5 to run the project. When the form first appears, it looks normal. Click the button, though, and watch the form fade out (see Figure 14.2)!

If you were to forgo a loop and write each line of code necessary to change the opacity, you would have to duplicate the statements 20 times each! Using a simple `For...Next` loop, you performed the same task in just a few lines of code.

Use a `For...Next` loop when you know how many times you want the loop to execute. This doesn't mean that you have to know how many times you want the loop to execute at design time. It simply means that you must know how many times you want the loop to execute when you first start the loop. You can use a variable to define any of the parameters for the For...Next loop, as illustrated in the following code:

```
Dim intCounter As Integer
Dim intUpperLimit as Integer
intUpperLimit = 100
For intCounter = 1 To intUpperLimit
    debug.WriteLine(intCounter)
Next intCounter
```

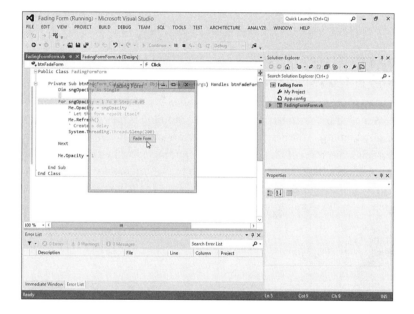

FIGURE 14.2
This would take a lot of code without a loop!

One of the keys to writing efficient code is to eliminate redundancy. If you find yourself typing the same (or a similar) line of code repeatedly, chances are it's a good candidate for a loop.

Using Do...Loop to Loop an Indeterminate Number of Times

In some situations, you won't know the exact number of times a loop must be performed—not even when the loop begins. You could start a For...Next loop specifying an upper limit that you know is larger than the number of loops needed, check for a terminating condition within the loop, and exit the loop using an Exit For statement when the condition is met. However, this approach is inefficient and usually impractical. When you need to create such a loop, using Do...Loop is the answer.

Creating a Do...Loop

Do...Loop comes in a number of flavors. Its most basic form has the following syntax:

```
Do
    [Statements]
Loop
```

Ending a Do...Loop

A Do...Loop without some sort of exit mechanism or defined condition is an endless loop. In its most basic form (shown previously), nothing is present to tell the loop when to stop looping. At times you might need an endless loop (game programming is an example), but most often you'll need to exit the loop when a certain condition is met. Like the For...Next loop, the Do...Loop has a statement you can use to exit the loop at any time: the Exit Do statement. For example, you could expand the Do...Loop we're discussing to include an Exit Do statement such as the following:

```
Do
    [Statements]
    If expression Then Exit Do
Loop
```

In this code, the loop would execute until expression evaluates to True. Generally, the expression is based on a variable that's modified somewhere within the loop. Obviously, if the expression never changes, the loop never ends.

You can build an expression into the Do...Loop structure itself by using one of two keywords: While or Until. The following is a simple Do...Loop using the While keyword:

```
Do While expression
    [Statements]
Loop
```

As long as expression evaluates to True, this loop continues to occur. If expression evaluates to False when the loop first starts, the code between the Do While and Loop statements doesn't execute—not even once.

Here's a similar Do...Loop that uses the Until keyword:

```
Do Until expression
    [Statements]
Loop
```

This loop behaves differently from the loop that uses While. When you define a loop using the keyword Until, the loop executes repeatedly until expression evaluates to True. As long as expression is False, the loop occurs. This is essentially the opposite behavior of While. If expression is True when the loop begins, the code between the Do Until and Loop statements doesn't execute—not even once.

Notice how both While and Until can prevent the loop from executing. This occurs because expression is placed on the Do statement, which means that it's evaluated before the loop is entered and again each time the loop iterates. You can put a While or Until on the Loop statement rather than on the Do statement, which means that the loop executes once before expression is evaluated for the first time. Such loops *always* occur at least once. You need to be aware of how this changes the loop's behavior. Here's the previous example with the While keyword placed on the Loop statement:

```
Do
    [Statements]
Loop While expression
```

Again, this loop executes as long as expression evaluates to True. The difference between the Do...While and Do...Loop While loops is that code between the Do and the Loop While statements always executes at least once; expression isn't evaluated until the loop has completed its first cycle. Again, such a loop always executes *at least once*, regardless of the value of expression. Here's the same code shown previously, this time with the Until keyword placed on the Loop statement rather than on the Do statement:

```
Do
    [Statements]
Loop Until expression
```

This loop executes until expression evaluates to True. However, the code within this loop always executes at least once; expression isn't evaluated until the loop completes its first cycle.

> You can use Continue Do within a Do...Loop to send execution back to the Do statement, just as though the Loop statement were reached.

By the Way

Creating a Do...Loop Example

Now you'll create an example using a Do...Loop. In this project, you'll find the first 10 numbers that are evenly divisible by 3. Although you know you want to find 10 numbers, you don't know how many numbers you will have to evaluate. Therefore, the Do...Loop is the best choice.

Create a new Windows Application named No Remainders, and then follow these steps:

1. Rename the form NoRemaindersForm.vb, and set its Text property to No Remainders.

2. Add a button to the form, and set its properties as follows:

Property	Value
Name	btnFindNumbers
Location	82, 39
Size	120, 23
Text	Find Numbers

3. Add a ListBox control to the form, and set its properties as follows:

Property	Value
Name	lstResults
Location	82, 68
Size	120, 160

Your form should look like the one shown in Figure 14.3.

FIGURE 14.3
What better con-
trol to show a
list of results
than a list box?

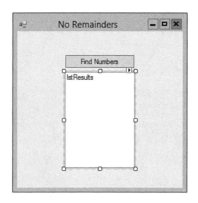

Double-click the button to access its Click event, and then enter the following code:

```
Dim intSeek As Integer = 1
Dim intFound As Integer = 0

Do Until intFound = 10
    If intSeek Mod 3 = 0 Then
        lstResults.Items.Add(CStr(intSeek))
        intFound = intFound + 1
```

```
     End If
     intSeek = intSeek + 1
Loop
```

Again, this code is more easily understood when broken down:

▶ The first two statements simply create a couple of integer variables. The variable intSeek will be the number you'll test to see whether it's evenly divisible by 3 (meaning that it has no remainder). The variable intFound will be the counter; you'll increment this by 1 each time you find a number that is evenly divisible by 3.

▶ The Do statement starts the loop. The condition ensures that the loop will continue to function until 10 numbers are found (intFound = 10).

▶ In Hour 12, "Performing Arithmetic, String Manipulation, and Date/Time Adjustments," I mentioned how the Mod operator can be used to determine a remainder. Here Mod is being used to determine whether intSeek is divisible by 3; it determines whether there is a remainder when intSeek is divided by 3.

▶ If the results of the regular division and the integer division are the same, there is no remainder. You then add the number to the results list box and increment intFound by 1.

▶ The next step is to increase intSeek so that you can test the next number.

▶ The last statement is Loop. This sends execution back to the Do statement. If intFound = 10, the loop doesn't execute; instead, the execution path is sent to the line following the Loop statement. If intFound is less than 10, the loop executes once more.

Click Save All on the toolbar to save the project, and then press F5 to run it. Click the Find Numbers button, and watch the results fill up—fast (see Figure 14.4)!

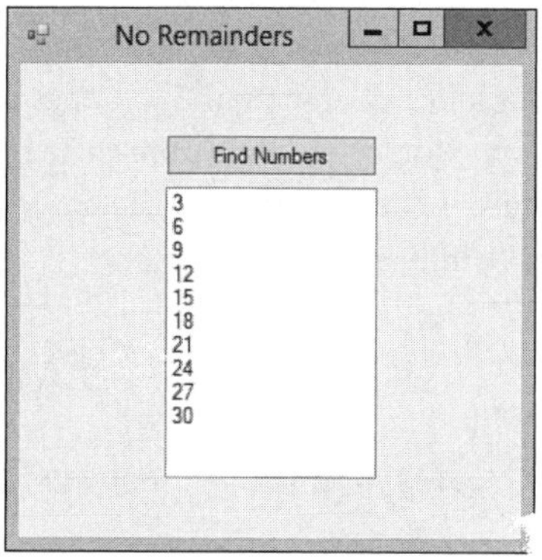

FIGURE 14.4
Visual Basic performs math functions very quickly.

The Do...Loop was the best choice here because you didn't know how many numbers you needed to evaluate (that is, how many times to iterate the loop). If you wanted to search only the numbers from 1 to 100, for example, a For...Next loop would be better.

> Visual Basic supports one more loop type: the While...End While loop. This loop is almost the same as the Do...Loop. (While...End While does the same thing as the Do...Loop but uses different syntax.) However, the Do...Loop is more widely accepted (While...End While is a holdover from earlier versions of Visual Basic). I highly recommend that you not use the While...End While loop; instead, use the Do...Loop.

Summary

Looping is a powerful technique that enables you to write tighter code. Tighter code is smaller, more efficient, and usually—but not always—more readable. In this hour, you learned to write For...Next loops for situations in which you know the precise number of times you want a loop to execute. Remember, it's not necessary to know the number of iterations at design time, but you must know the number at runtime to use a For...Next loop. You learned how to use Step to increment or decrement the counter of a For...Next loop, and even how to exit a loop prematurely by using Exit For.

In this hour, you also learned how to use the powerful Do...Loop. Do...Loop enables you to create flexible loops that can handle almost any looping scenario. Depending on your needs, you can evaluate an expression in a Do...Loop by using While or Until. You learned how evaluating expression on the Do statement makes the loop behave differently than does evaluating on the Loop statement. If a For...Next loop can't do the job, some form of the Do...Loop will.

In addition to learning the specifics about loops, you've seen firsthand how multiple solutions to a problem can exist. Often, one approach is clearly superior to all other approaches, although you might not always find it. Other times, one approach might be only marginally superior, or multiple approaches might all be equally applicable. Expert programmers consistently find the best approaches to any given problem. With time, you'll be able to do the same.

Q&A

Q. *Are there any specific cases in which one loop is more appropriate than another?*

A. Usually, when you have to walk an index or sequential set of elements (such as referencing all elements in an array), the `For...Next` loop is the best choice.

Q. *Should I be concerned about the performance differences between the two types of loops?*

A. With today's fast processors, chances are good that the performance difference between the two loop types in any given situation will be overshadowed by the readability and functionality of the best choice of loop. If you have a situation in which performance is critical, write the loop in every way you can think of, benchmark the results, and choose the fastest loop.

Workshop

Quiz

1. What keyword do you use to increment the counter variable in a `For...Next` loop by a value other than 1?

2. True or false: You have to know the start and end values of a `For...Next` loop at design time to use this type of loop.

3. What statement is used to close a loop started with a `For` statement?

4. Is it possible to nest loops?

5. What type of loop do you most likely need to create if you don't have any idea how many times the loop must occur?

6. If you evaluate the expression in a `Do...Loop` on the `Loop` statement, is it possible that the code within the loop might never execute?

7. What statement do you use to terminate a `Do...Loop` without evaluating the expression on the `Do` or `Loop` statement?

Answers

1. Step

2. False. You have to know the values only at runtime.

3. Next

4. Yes!

5. A Do loop

6. No. The code always executes at least once.

7. Exit Do

Exercises

1. Create a text box in your No Remainders project, and let the user enter a number. Find the first 10 numbers that are evenly divisible by the number the user enters.

2. Use two For...Next loops nested within each other to size a label in two dimensions. Have the outer loop change the label's Width property from 1 to 100, and have the inner loop change the Height property from 1 to 100. Don't be surprised by the end result—it's rather odd.

Debugging Your Code

What You'll Learn in This Hour:

▶ Adding comments to your code

▶ Identifying the two basic types of errors

▶ Working with break points

▶ Using the Immediate window

▶ Creating a structured error handler

No one writes perfect code. You're most certainly familiar with those problems that prevent code from executing properly—they're called *bugs*. Because you're new to Visual Basic, your code will probably contain a fair number of bugs. As you gain proficiency, the number of bugs in your code will decrease, but bugs *never* disappear entirely. This book can't teach you how to debug every possible build or runtime error you might encounter; debugging is a skill *and* an art. In this hour, however, you will learn the basic skills necessary to trace and correct most bugs in your code.

Before proceeding, create a new Windows Forms Application project named Debugging Example. Next, follow these steps to build the project:

1. Right-click Form1.vb in the Solution Explorer, choose Rename, and change the form's name to **DebuggingExampleForm.vb**. Next, set the form's Text property to Debugging Example (you will need to click the form to access its design properties).

2. Add a new text box to the form by double-clicking the TextBox item in the toolbox. Set the text box's properties as follows:

Property	Value
Name	txtInput
Location	79, 113
Size	120, 20

3. Add a new button to the form by double-clicking the Button item in the tool-box, and set its properties as follows:

Property	Value
Name	btnPerformDivision
Location	79, 139
Size	120, 23
Text	Perform Division

Your form should now look like the one shown in Figure 15.1.

This little project will divide 100 by whatever is entered into the text box. As you write the code to accomplish this, various bugs will be introduced on purpose, and you'll learn to correct them. Save your project now by clicking the Save All button on the toolbar.

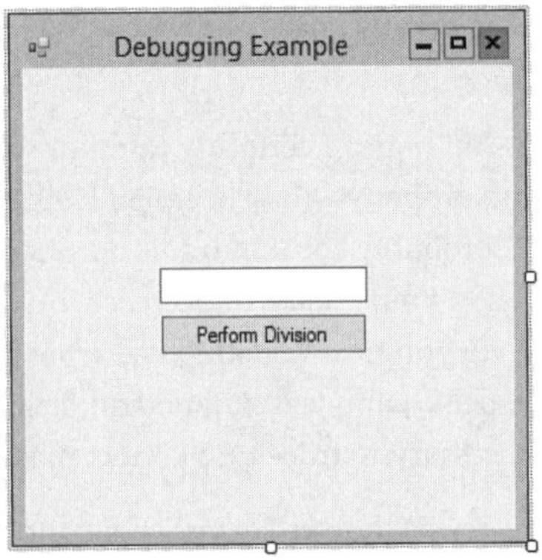

FIGURE 15.1
This simple inter-face will help you learn debugging techniques.

Adding Comments to Your Code

One of the simplest things you can do to reduce bugs —and to make tracking down existing bugs easier—is to add comments to your code. A code *comment* is simply a line of text that Visual Basic knows isn't actual code and therefore ignores. Comment lines are stripped from the code when the project is compiled to create a distributable component, so comments don't affect performance. Visual Basic's code window shows comments as green text, making it easier to read and understand procedures. Consider adding comments to the top of each procedure, stating the procedure's pur-pose. In addition, you should add liberal comments throughout all procedures, detailing what's occurring in the code.

> Comments are meant to be read by humans, not by computers. Strive to make your comments intelligible. Keep in mind that a comment that's difficult to understand isn't much better than no comment at all. Also remember that comments serve as a form of documentation. Just as documentation for an application must be clearly written, code comments should also follow good writing principles.

To create a comment, precede the comment text with the apostrophe character ('). A simple comment might look like this, for example:

```
' This is a comment because it is preceded with an apostrophe.
```

Comments can also be placed at the end of a line of code:

```
Dim intAge as Integer        ' Used to store the user's age in years.
```

Everything to the right of (and including) the apostrophe in this statement is a comment. By adding comments to your code procedures, you don't have to rely on memory to decipher a procedure's purpose or mechanics. If you've ever had to go back and work with code you haven't looked at in a while, or you've had to work with someone else's code, you probably already have a great appreciation for comments.

Double-click the Perform Division button now to access its `Click` event, and add the following two lines of code (comments, actually):

```
' This procedure divides 100 by the value entered in
' the text box txtInput.
```

Notice that after you type the `'` character, the comment text turns green.

When creating code comments, do your best to do the following:

▶ Document the code's purpose (the *why*, not the *how*).

▶ Clearly indicate the thinking and logic behind the code.

▶ Call attention to important turning points in the code.

▶ Reduce the need for readers to run a simulation of the code execution in their heads.

▶ Comment your code as you are typing it. If you wait until the code is complete, you probably won't go back and add comments.

Identifying the Two Basic Types of Errors

Two types of errors can occur in code: *build errors* and *runtime errors*. A build error is a coding error that prevents Visual Basic's compiler from being able to process the code; Visual Basic won't compile a project that has a build error in it. A statement that calls a procedure with incorrect parameters, for example, generates a build error. Runtime errors are those that don't occur at compile time but are encountered when the project is being run. Runtime errors are usually a result of trying to perform an invalid operation on a variable.

To illustrate, consider this next statement, which wouldn't generate a compile error:

```
intResult = 10 / intDenominator
```

Under most circumstances, this code wouldn't even generate a runtime error. However, what happens if the value of `intDenominator` is 0? Ten divided by 0 is undefined, which doesn't fit into `intResult` (`intResult` is an Integer variable). Attempting to run the code with the `intDenominator` variable having a value of 0 causes Visual Basic to return a runtime error. A runtime error is called an *exception*, and when an exception occurs, it's said to be *thrown* (that is, Visual Basic throws an exception when a runtime error occurs). When an exception is thrown, code execution stops at the offending statement, and Visual Basic displays an error message. You can prevent Visual Basic from stopping execution when an exception is thrown by writing special code to handle the exception, which you'll learn about later in this hour.

Add the following statements to the `Click` event, right below the two comment lines:

```
Dim lngAnswer As Long
lngAnswer = 100 / CLng(txtInput.Text)
Messagerox.Show("100/" & txtInput.Text & " = " & lngAnswer)
```

The misspelling of the function name `MessageBox` is intentional; type in the preceding line of code exactly as it appears. Although you've misspelled the function name, Visual Basic doesn't return an immediate error. Notice, however, that Visual Basic displays a wavy blue line under the function name. Move the mouse pointer over the underlined text, and leave it there for a second; Visual Basic displays a tip explaining the nature of the error, as shown in Figure 15.2.

Press F5 to run the project. When you do, Visual Basic displays a message that a build error was found, and it asks whether you want to continue by running the last successful build. Because the code won't run as is, there's no point in continuing, so click No to return to the code editor. Take a look at the Error List (if it's not displayed, use the View menu to show it). All build errors in the current project appear in the Error List, as shown in Figure 15.3. To view a particular offending line of code, double-click an item in the Error List.

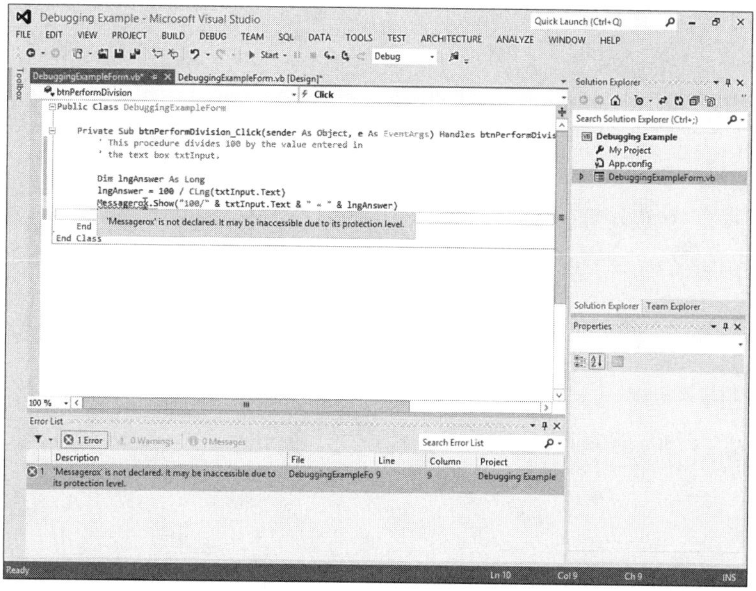

FIGURE 15.2
Visual Basic highlights build errors in the code window by using wavy lines.

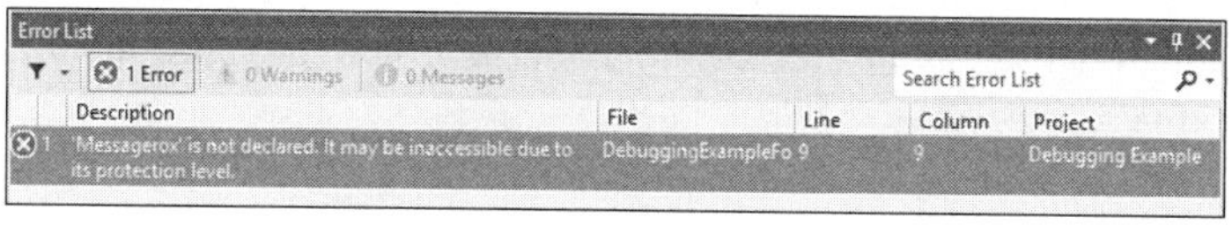

FIGURE 15.3
Build errors are easy to find using the Error List.

Build errors are very serious because they prevent code from being compiled and therefore prevent execution. Build errors must be corrected before you can run the project. Double-click the build error in the Error List to go directly to the error.

Correct the problem by changing the R to a B so that the function name is `MessageBox`. After you've made this change, press F5 to run the project. Visual Basic no longer returns a build error; you've just successfully debugged a problem!

Click the Perform Division button now, and you'll receive another error (see Figure 15.4).

This time the error is a runtime error, or exception. If an exception occurs, you know that the code compiled without a problem because build errors prevent code from compiling and executing. This particular exception is an Invalid Cast exception. Invalid Cast exceptions generally occur when you attempt to perform a function using a variable, but the variable is of an incompatible data type for the specified operation. Note that Visual Basic highlights the offending statement with a yellow background and a yellow arrow.

FIGURE 15.4
A runtime excep-
tion halts code
execution at the
offending line.

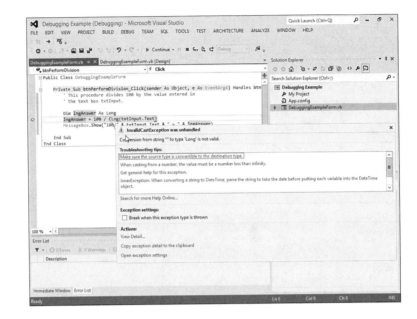

At this point, you know that the statement has a bug, and you know it's related to data typing. Choose Debug, Stop Debugging now to stop the running project and return to the code editor.

Using Visual Basic's Debugging Tools

Visual Basic includes a number of debugging tools to help you track down and elimi-nate bugs. In this section, you'll learn how to use break points and the Immediate window—two tools that form the foundation of any debugging arsenal.

Working with Break Points

Just as an exception halts the execution of a procedure, you can deliberately stop exe-cution at any statement of code by creating a *break point*. When Visual Basic encoun-ters a break point while executing code, execution is halted at the break statement *before* the statement is executed. Break points enable you to query or change the value of variables at a specific instance in time, and they let you step through code execution one line at a time.

You'll create a break point to help troubleshoot the exception in your lngAnswer = statement.

Adding a break point is simple. Just click in the gray area to the left of the statement at which you want to break code execution. When you do so, Visual Basic displays a red circle, denoting a break point at that statement (see Figure 15.5). To clear the break point, you click the red circle (but don't do this now).

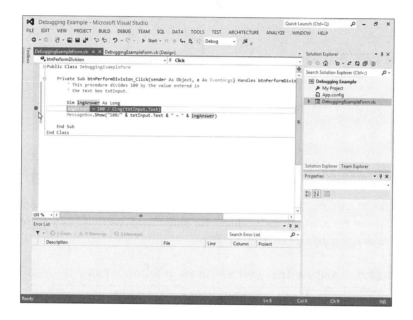

FIGURE 15.5
Break points give you control over code execution.

Break points are saved with the project. You don't have to reset all your break points each time you open the project.

By the Way

Click the gray area to the left of the lngAnswer = statement to create a break point, as shown in Figure 15.5. After you've set the break point, press F5 to run the program. Click the Perform Division button again. When Visual Basic encounters the break point, code execution is halted—right before the statement with the break point executes— and the procedure with the break point is shown. In addition, the cursor is conveniently placed at the statement with the current break point. Notice the yellow arrow overlaying the red circle of the break point (see Figure 15.6). This yellow arrow marks the next statement to be executed. It just so happens that the statement has a break point, so the yellow arrow appears over the red circle. (The yellow arrow isn't always over a red circle, but it always appears in the gray area aligned with the next statement that will execute.)

When code execution is halted at a break point, you can do a number of things.
Table 15.1 lists the most common actions. For now, press F5 to continue program execution. Again, you get an overflow exception.

TABLE 15.1   Actions That Can Be Taken at a Break Point

Action	Keystroke	Description
Continue code	F5	Continues execution at the current break execution statement.
Step into	F8	Executes the statement at the break point and then stops at the next statement. If the current statement is a function call, F8 enters the function and stops at the first statement in the function.
Step over	Shift+F8	Executes the statement at the break point and then stops at the next statement. If the current statement is a function call, the function is run in its entirety; execution stops at the statement following the function call.
Step out	Ctrl+Shift+F8	Runs all the statements in the current procedure and halts execution at the statement following the one that called the current procedure.

Using the Immediate Window

Break points themselves aren't usually sufficient to enable you to debug a procedure. In addition to break points, you'll often use the Immediate window to debug code. The Immediate window is a Visual Studio IDE window that generally appears only when your project is in Run mode. If the Immediate window isn't displayed, press Ctrl+G to display it now. Using the Immediate window, you can type in code statements that Visual Basic executes immediately (hence the name). You'll use the Immediate window now to debug the problem statement example.

Type the following statement into the Immediate window and then press Enter:

```
? txtinput.text
```

Although it isn't intuitive, the ? character has been used in programming for many years as a shortcut for the word "print." The statement you entered simply prints the contents of the Text property of the text box to the Immediate window.

Notice how the Immediate window displays " " on the line below the statement you entered. This indicates that the text box contains an empty string (also called a *zero-length string*). The statement throwing the exception is attempting to use the CLng() function to convert the contents of the text box to a Long. The CLng() function expects data to be passed to it, yet the text box has no data. (The Text property is empty.) Consequently, an overflow exception occurs because CLng() doesn't know how to convert "no data" to a number.

> Generally, when you receive an overflow exception, you should look at any variables or properties being referenced to ensure that the data they contain is appropriate data for the statement throwing the exception. You'll often find that the code is trying to perform an operation that's inappropriate for the data being supplied.

You can do a number of things to prevent this error. The most obvious is to ensure that the text box contains a value before attempting to use CLng(). You'll do this now.

Visual Basic supports on-the-fly code editing. This means that you can modify code while debugging it; you do not have to stop the project to make changes and then run it once more to test your changes.

Put the cursor at the end of the Dim statement and press Enter. Next, enter the following code statements:

```
If txtInput.Text = "" Then
    Exit Sub
End If
```

Remember the yellow arrow used to show the next statement that will execute? It indicates that if you continue code execution now, the statement that throws the exception will run once more. You want the new statements to execute. Follow these steps to designate the new code as the next code to be executed:

1. Click the yellow arrow and hold down the mouse button.

2. Drag the yellow arrow to the statement that begins with `If txtInput.Text`.

3. Release the mouse button.

Now the yellow arrow should indicate that the next statement to execute will be the `If` statement, as shown in Figure 15.7.

FIGURE 15.7
You can manually control the flow of code when debugging.

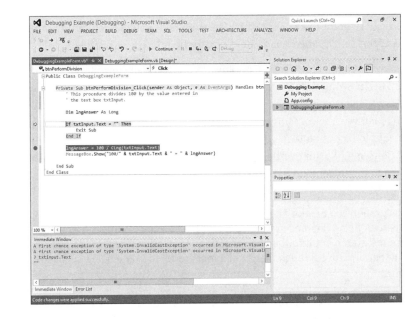

Press F5 to continue running the project. This time, Visual Basic doesn't throw an exception, and it doesn't halt execution at your break point, because the test you just created caused code execution to leave the procedure before the statement with the break point was reached.

Next, follow these steps:

1. Type your name into the text box and click the Perform Division button again. Now that the text box is no longer empty, execution passes the statement with the exit test and stops at the break point.

2. Press F5 to continue executing the code; again you'll receive an exception. Once again, you have an invalid cast exception.

3. Press Ctrl+G to display the Immediate window, and type the following into the Immediate window (be sure to press Enter when you're finished):

```
? txtinput.text
```

The Immediate window prints your name.

Well, you eliminated the problem of not supplying any data to the CLng() function, but something else is wrong.

Press F5 to continue executing the code, and take a closer look at the description of the exception. Toward the bottom of the Exception window is the text "View Detail." Click this link now. Visual Basic displays a View Detail window with more information about the exception, as shown in Figure 15.8.

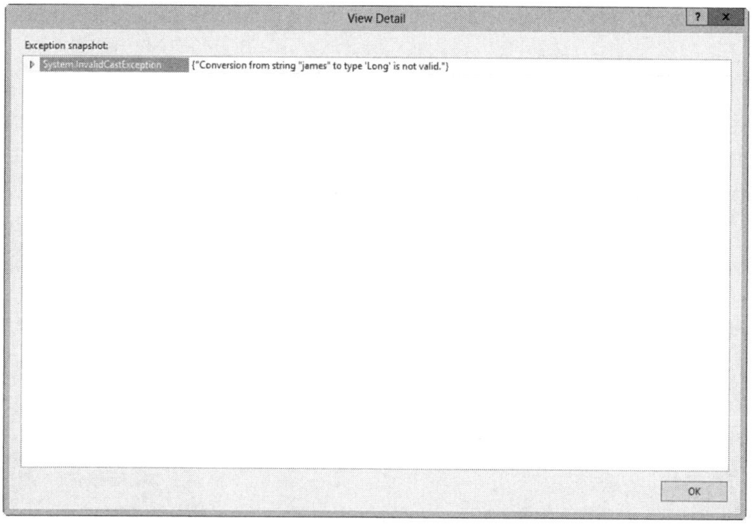

FIGURE 15.8
The View Detail window gives you important information for fixing exception problems.

The text in the View Detail window says: "Conversion from string "your name" to type 'Long' is not valid." It apparently still doesn't like what's being passed to the CLng() function.

By now, it might have occurred to you that there's no logical way to convert alphanumeric text to a number; CLng() needs a number to work with. You can easily test this by following these steps:

1. Close the View Detail dialog box.

2. Choose Debug, Stop Debugging.

3. Press F5 to run the project.

4. Enter a number into the text box, and click the button. Code execution again stops at the break point.

5. Press F8 to execute the statement. No errors this time! Press F5 to continue execution; Visual Basic displays the message box (finally). Click OK to dismiss the message box, and then close the form to stop the project.

You can use the Immediate window to change the value of a variable.

Because the CLng() function expects a number, but the text box contains no intrinsic way to force numeric input, you have to accommodate this situation in your code. Visual Basic includes a handy function called IsNumeric, which returns True if the supplied argument is a number and False if not. You can use this function to ensure that only a number is passed to the CLng() function. Add the following statement immediately below the last If...Then construct you entered (after the End...If statement):

```
If Not (IsNumeric(txtInput.Text)) Then Exit Sub
```

This statement simply passes the contents of the text box to the IsNumeric() function. If the function returns False (the text is not a number), the procedure is exited. Your procedure should now look similar to the one shown in Figure 15.9. Realize that the first If...End If statement is redundant; the new statement will catch when a user hasn't entered anything into the text box.

FIGURE 15.9
The final code, complete with data verification.

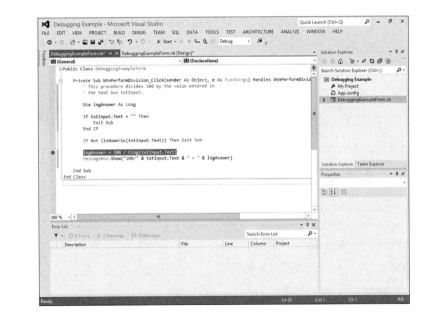

Go ahead and press F5 to run the project. Enter some nonnumeric text into the text box and click the button. If you entered the code correctly, no exception occurs; the data validation tests you've created prevent inappropriate data from being passed to the CLng() function. You just debugged the procedure!

The Immediate window is a powerful debugging tool. You can use it to get and set variables as well as view the value in a property. You can even use the Immediate window to call functions. For example, while in Break mode, you could enter the following into the Immediate window, and Visual Basic would print the result of the function call:

```
? IsNumeric(txtInput.Text)
```

You can even use the Immediate window to print data from within code during debugging. To do so, you use the WriteLine() method of the Debug object, like this:

```
Debug.WriteLine(lngInteger1 + lngInteger2)
```

Whatever you place within the parentheses of the Debug.WriteLine() method gets printed to the Immediate window. Note that you can print literal text, numbers, variables, and expressions. Debug.WriteLine() is most useful in cases where you want to know the value of a variable, but you don't want to halt code execution using a break point. For example, suppose that you had a number of statements that manipulate a variable. You could sprinkle Debug.WriteLine() statements into the code to print the variable's contents at strategic points. When you do this, you'll want to print some text along with the variable's value so that the output makes sense to you. For example:

```
Debug.WriteLine("Results of area calculation = " & sngArea)
```

You can also use Debug.WriteLine to create checkpoints in your code, like this:

```
Debug.WriteLine("Passed Checkpoint 1")
' Execute statement here
Debug.WriteLine("Passed Checkpoint 2")
' Execute another statement here
Debug.WriteLine("Passed Checkpoint 3")
```

Many creative uses exist for the Immediate window, and you should get comfortable using it; it'll help you through many tough debugging sessions. Just remember that the Immediate window isn't available to a compiled component; the compiler ignores calls to the Debug object when creating distributable components.

Writing an Error Handler Using Try...Catch...Finally

It's useful to have Visual Basic halt execution when an exception occurs. When the code is halted while running in the IDE, you receive an error message, and you're shown the offending line of code. However, when your project is run as a compiled program, an unhandled exception causes the program to terminate (crash to the desktop). This is one of the most undesirable things an application can do. Fortunately, you can prevent exceptions from stopping code execution (and terminating compiled programs) by writing code specifically designed to deal with exceptions. Exception-handling code instructs Visual Basic on how to deal with an exception instead of relying on Visual Basic's default behavior of aborting the application.

By the Way

> Visual Basic supports unstructured error handling in the way of On Error statements. This method of handling errors, although still supported by Visual Basic, is now considered antiquated. You might encounter procedures that use this form of error handling in legacy or sample code, but Microsoft strongly recommends that you use the Try...Catch...Finally structure for dealing with exceptions in all new code.

Visual Basic supports *structured error handling* (a formal way of dealing with errors) in the form of the Try...Catch...Finally structure. Creating structured error-handling code can be a bit confusing at first, and, like most coding principles, it's best understood when you do it.

Create a new Windows Application called Structured Exception Handling, and follow these steps to build the project:

1. Right-click Form1.vb in the Solution Explorer, choose Rename, and change the name of the default form to **StructuredExceptionHandlingForm.vb**. Next, set the form's Text property to Structured Exception Handling.

2. Add a new button to the form, and set its properties as follows:

Property	Value
Name	btnCatchException
Location	93, 128
Size	96, 23
Text	Catch Exception

Double-click the button, and add the following code. Be aware that when you enter the Try statement, Visual Basic automatically creates the End Try and Catch ex As Exception statements.

```
Try
   Debug.WriteLine("Try")
Catch ex As Exception
   Debug.WriteLine("Catch")
Finally
   Debug.WriteLine("Finally")
End Try
Debug.WriteLine("Done Trying")
```

As you can see, the Try...End Try structure has starting and ending statements, much like loops and decision constructs. The Try...End Try structure is used to wrap code that might cause an exception and provides you the means of dealing with thrown exceptions. Table 15.2 explains the parts of this structure.

TABLE 15.2   Sections of the `Try...End Try` Structure

Section	Description
Try	The Try section is where you place code that might cause an exception. You can place all of a procedure's code within the Try section, or just a few lines.
Catch	Code within the Catch section executes only when an exception occurs; it's the code you write to catch the exception.
Finally	Code within the Finally section occurs when the code within the Try and/or Catch sections completes. This section is where you place your *cleanup code*—code that you always want executed, regardless of whether an exception occurs.

Press F5 to run the project, and then click the button. Next, take a look at the contents of the Immediate window (Ctrl+G). The Immediate window should contain the following lines of text:

```
Try
Finally
Done Trying
```

Here's what happened:

1. The Try block begins, and code within the Try section executes.

2. Because no exception occurs, code within the Catch section is ignored.

3. When all statements within the `Try` section finish executing, the code within the `Finally` section executes.

4. When all statements within the `Finally` section finish executing, execution jumps to the statement immediately following `End Try`.

Stop the project now by choosing Debug, Stop Debugging.

Now that you understand the basic mechanics of the `Try...End Try` structure, you'll add statements within the structure so that an exception occurs and gets handled.

Change the contents of the procedure to match this code:

```
Dim lngNumerator As Long = 10
Dim lngDenominator As Long = 0
Dim lngResult As Long

Try
    Debug.WriteLine("Try")
    lngResult = lngNumerator / lngDenominator
Catch ex As Exception
    Debug.WriteLine("Catch")
Finally
    Debug.WriteLine("Finally")
End Try

Debug.WriteLine("Done Trying")
```

Again, press F5 to run the project. Click the button, and take a look at the Immediate window. This time, the text in the Immediate window should read

```
Try
A first chance exception of type 'System.OverflowException' _
occurred in Structured Exception Handling.EXE
Catch
Finally
Done Trying
```

Notice that this time, the code within the `Catch` section executes. That's because the statement that sets `lngResult` causes an overflow exception. Had this statement not been placed within a `Try` block, Visual Basic would have raised the exception, and an error dialog box would've appeared. However, because the statement is placed within the `Try` block, the exception is *caught*. Caught means that when the exception occurred, Visual Basic directed execution to the `Catch` section. (You do not have to use a `Catch` section. If you omit a `Catch` section, caught exceptions are simply ignored.) Notice also how the code within the `Finally` section executes after the code within the `Catch` section. Remember that code within the `Finally` section always executes, regardless of whether an exception occurs.

Dealing with an Exception

Catching exceptions so that they don't crash your application is a noble thing to do, but it's only part of the error-handling process. You'll usually want to tell the user (in a friendly way) that an exception has occurred. You'll probably also want to tell the user what type of exception occurred. To do this, you must have a way of knowing what exception was thrown. This is also important if you intend to write code to deal with specific exceptions. The `Catch` statement enables you to specify a variable to hold a reference to an `Exception` object. Using an `Exception` object, you can get information about the exception. The following is the syntax used to place the exception in an `Exception` object:

```
Catch variablename As Exception
```

Modify your `Catch` section to match the following:

```
Catch ex As Exception
    Debug.WriteLine("Catch")
    MessageBox.Show("An error has occurred: " & ex.Message)
```

The `Message` property of the `Exception` object contains the text that describes the specific exception that occurred. Run the project and click the button. Visual Basic displays your custom error message, as shown in Figure 15.10.

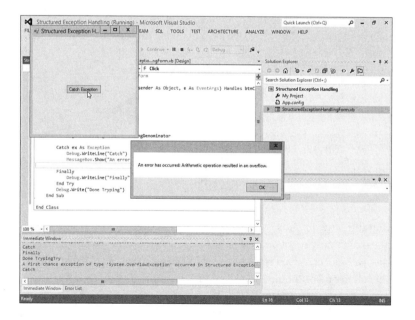

FIGURE 15.10
Structured exception handling enables you to decide what to do when an exception occurs.

Like other code structures, Visual Basic has a statement that can be used to exit a Try...End Try structure at any time: Exit Try. Note, however, that if you use Exit Try, code jumps to the Finally section (this section always executes) and then continues with the statement immediately following the End Try statement.

Handling an Anticipated Exception

At times, you'll anticipate a specific exception being thrown. For example, you might write code that attempts to open a file when the file does not exist. In such an instance, you'll probably want the program to perform certain actions when this exception is thrown. When you anticipate a specific exception, you can create a Catch section designed specifically to deal with that one exception.

Recall from the previous section that you can retrieve information about the current exception by using a Catch statement, such as

```
Catch objException As Exception
```

By creating a generic Exception variable, this Catch statement catches any and all exceptions thrown by statements within the Try section. To catch a specific exception, change the data type of the exception variable to a specific exception type. Remember the code you wrote earlier that caused a System.InvalidCastException when an attempt was made to pass an empty string to the CLng() function? You could have used a Try...End Try structure to deal with the exception, using code such as this:

```
Dim lngAnswer As Long
Try
    lngAnswer = 100 / CLng(txtInput.Text)
    MessageBox.Show("100/" & txtInput.Text & " is " & lngAnswer)

Catch objException As System.InvalidCastException
    MessageBox.Show("You must enter something in the text box.")

Catch objException As Exception
    MessageBox.Show("Caught an exception that wasn't an invalid cast.")
End Try
```

Notice that this structure has two Catch statements. The first Catch statement is designed to catch only an overflow exception; it doesn't catch exceptions of any other type. The second Catch statement doesn't care what type of exception is thrown; it catches all of them. The second Catch statement acts as a catchall for any exceptions that aren't overflow exceptions because Catch sections are evaluated from top to bottom, much as Case statements are in the Select...Case structure.

You could add more `Catch` sections to catch other specific exceptions if the situation calls for it.

In this next example, you'll build on the Picture Viewer project last edited in Hour 11, "Using Constants, Data Types, Variables, and Arrays," so go ahead and open that project now. First, I want you to see the exception that you'll catch. Follow these steps to cause an exception to occur:

1. Press F5 to run the project.

2. Click the Open Picture button on the toolbar to display the Select Picture dialog box.

3. In the File Name: box, enter *.* and press Enter. This changes your filter so that you can now select files that aren't images. Locate a file on your hard drive that you know is not an image. Files with the extension .txt, .ini, or .pdf are perfect.

4. After you've located a file that isn't an image file, click it to select it, and then click Open.

You have caused an out-of-memory exception, as shown in Figure 15.11. This is the exception thrown by the picture box when you attempt to load a file that isn't a picture. Your first reaction might be something along the lines of "Why do I have to worry about that? No one would do that." Well, welcome to programming, my friend! A lot of your time will be spent writing code to protect users from themselves. It's not fair and usually not fun, but it is a reality.

Go ahead and click Stop Debugging on the toolbar to stop the running project. Rather than take you step by step through the changes, it's easier to just show you the code for the new `OpenPicture()` procedure. Change your code to make the code shown here:

```
Try
    ' Show the open file dialog box.
    If ViewerForm.ofdSelectPicture.ShowDialog = DialogResult.OK Then
        ' Load the picture into the picture box.
        ViewerForm.picShowPicture.Image = _
            Image.FromFile(ViewerForm.ofdSelectPicture.FileName)
        ' Show the name of the file in the statusbar.
        ViewerForm.sbrMyStatusStrip.Items(0).Text = _
            ViewerForm.ofdSelectPicture.FileName
    End If

Catch ex As System.OutOfMemoryException
    MessageBox.Show("The file you have chosen is not an image file.)
End Try
```

What you've just done is wrapped the procedure in an error handler that watches for and deals with an out-of-memory exception. Press F5 to run the project, and follow the steps outlined earlier to load a file that isn't an image. Now, rather than receiving an exception from the IDE, your application displays a custom message box that is much more user-friendly and that won't crash the application to the desktop (see Figure 15.12)!

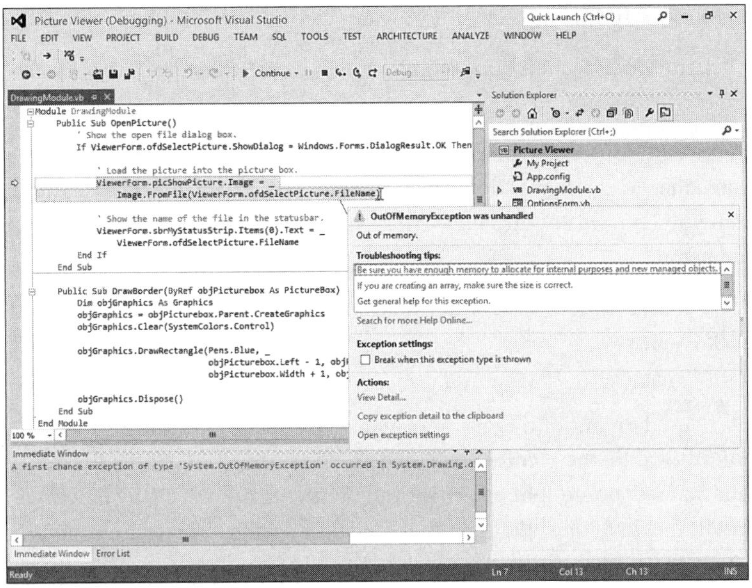

FIGURE 15.11
You never want an unhandled exception to occur—ever.

Although you have eliminated the possibility of the user's generating an out-of-memory exception by choosing a file that isn't a valid picture, you should be aware of some caveats regarding the code changes you made:

▶ If some other code in the procedure caused an out-of-memory exception, you would be misleading the user with your error message. You could address this by wrapping only the statement in a question within its own Try...End Try structure.

▶ If an exception of another type is encountered in the procedure, that error is ignored. You can prevent this by creating a generic Catch block to catch any additional exceptions.

As you can see, the mechanics of adding a Try...End Try structure to handle exceptions is relatively easy, whereas knowing what specifically to catch and how to handle the situation when an exception is caught can prove to be challenging.

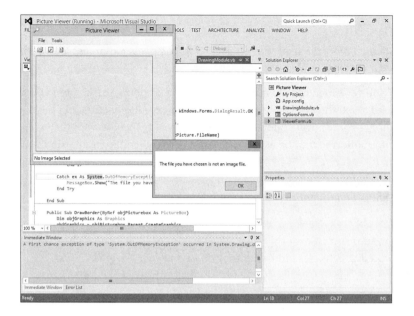

FIGURE 15.12
A useful message is much better than an unhandled exception.

Summary

In this hour, you learned the basics of debugging applications. You learned how adding useful and plentiful comments to your procedures makes debugging easier. However, no matter how good your comments are, you'll still have bugs.

You learned about the two basic types of errors: build errors and runtime errors (exceptions). Build errors are easier to troubleshoot because the compiler tells you exactly what line contains a build error and generally provides useful information about how to correct it. Exceptions, on the other hand, can crash your application if not handled properly. You learned how to track down exceptions, using break points and the Immediate window. Finally, you learned how to make your applications more robust by using the Try...End Try structure to create structured error handlers.

No book can teach you everything you need to know to write bug-free code. However, this hour taught you the basic skills you need to track down and eliminate many types of errors in your programs. As your skills as a programmer improve, so will your debugging abilities.

Q&A

Q. *Should I alert the user that an exception has occurred or just let the code keep running?*

A. If you've written code to handle the specific exception, there's probably no need to tell the user about it. However, if an exception occurs that the code doesn't know how to address, you should provide the user with the exception information so that he or she can report the problem accurately and you can fix it.

Q. *Should I comment every statement in my application?*

A. Probably not. However, consider commenting every decision-making and looping construct in your program. Such sections of code are usually pivotal to the procedure's success, and what they do isn't always obvious.

Workshop

Quiz

1. What type of error prevents Visual Basic from compiling and running code?

2. What is another name for a runtime error?

3. What character is used to denote a comment?

4. To halt execution at a specific statement in code, what do you set?

5. Explain the yellow arrow and red circles that can appear in the gray area in the code editor.

6. What IDE window would you use to poll the contents of a variable in break mode?

7. True or false: You must always specify a `Catch` section in a `Try...End Try` structure.

Answers

1. A build error

2. An exception

3. The apostrophe (')

4. A break point

5. The yellow arrow denotes the next statement to be executed during debugging. The red circles denote break points—statements where code execution halts when reached.

6. The Immediate window

7. False. If you omit a Catch section, the exception is ignored.

Exercises

1. In the code example that sets lngAnswer to the result of a division expression, change lngAnswer from a Long to a Single (call it sngAnswer). Next, remove the If statements that test the contents of the text box before performing the division. Do you get the same two exceptions that you did when the variable was a Long? Why or why not?

2. Rewrite the code that sets lngAnswer to the result of a division expression so that the code is wrapped in a Try...End Try structure. Remove the If statements that perform data validation, and create Catch sections for the exception that might be thrown.

HOUR 16

Designing Objects Using Classes

What You'll Learn in This Hour:

▶ Encapsulating data and code using classes

▶ Comparing classes to standard modules

▶ Creating an object interface

▶ Exposing object attributes as properties

▶ Exposing functions as methods

▶ Instantiating objects from classes

▶ Binding an object reference to a variable

▶ Releasing object references

▶ Understanding object lifetimes

You learned about what makes an object an object in Hour 3, "Understanding Objects and Collections." Since that hour, you've learned how to manipulate objects such as forms and controls. The real power of leveraging objects, however, comes from being able to design and implement custom objects of your own. In this hour, you'll learn how to create your own objects by using classes (in contrast to using standard modules). You'll learn how to define the template for an object and how to create your own custom properties and methods.

There is simply no way to become an expert on programming classes in a single hour. However, when you've finished with this chapter, you'll have working knowledge of creating classes and deriving custom objects from those classes; consider this hour a primer on object-oriented programming. I strongly encourage you to seek out other texts that focus on object-oriented programming after you feel comfortable with the material presented in this book.

Understanding Classes

Classes enable you to develop applications using object-oriented programming (OOP) techniques (recall that I discussed OOP briefly in Hour 3). Classes are templates that define objects. Although you might not have known it, you've been programming with classes throughout this book. When you create a new form in a Visual Basic project, you're actually creating a class that defines a form; forms instantiated at runtime are derived from the class. Using objects derived from predefined classes (such as the Visual Basic Form class) is just the start of enjoying the benefits of object-oriented programming. To truly realize the benefits of OOP, you must create your own classes.

Proper class-programming techniques can make your programs better, in both structure and in reliability. The philosophy of programming with classes is considerably different from that of traditional programming. Class programming forces you to consider the logistics of your code and data more thoroughly, causing you to create more reusable and extendable object-based code.

Encapsulating Data and Code Using Classes

An object derived from a class is an encapsulation of data and code—that is, the object comprises its code and all the data it uses. Suppose that you need to keep track of employees in an organization, for example, and that you must store many pieces of information for each employee, such as name, date hired, and title. In addition, suppose that you need methods for adding and removing employees, and that you want all this information and functionality available to many functions within your application. You could use standard modules to manipulate the data, but doing so would most likely require many variable arrays as well as code to manage those arrays.

A better approach is to *encapsulate* all the employee data and functionality (adding and deleting routines and so forth) into a single, reusable object. Encapsulation is the process of integrating data and code into one entity: an object. Your application, as well as external applications, could then work with the employee data through a consistent interface—the `Employee` object's interface. (An *interface* is a set of exposed functionality—essentially, code routines that define methods, properties, and events.)

The encapsulation of data and code is the key idea of classes. By encapsulating the data and the routines to manipulate the data into a single object by way of a class, you free application code that needs to manipulate the data from the intricacies of data maintenance. For example, suppose your company policy has changed so that when a new employee is added to the system, a special tax record must be generated and a form must be printed. If the data and code routines weren't encapsulated in a common object but instead were written in various places throughout your code, you would have to modify every module that contained code to create a new employee record. By using a class to create an object, you need to change the code in only one location: within the class. As long as you don't modify the object's interface (as discussed shortly), all the routines that use the object to create a new employee will instantly have the policy change in effect.

Comparing Classes with Standard Modules

Classes are similar to standard modules in how they appear in the Visual Studio design environment and in how you write code within them. However, the behavior of classes at runtime differs greatly from that of standard modules. With a standard module, all module-level data (static and module-level variables) is shared by all procedures within the module. In addition, there are never multiple instances of the module data. With classes, objects are instantiated from a class, and each object receives its own set of module data.

As you learned in Hour 11, "Using Constants, Data Types, Variables, and Arrays," module-level variables in a standard module exist for the lifetime of the application. However, module variables for a class exist only for the duration of an object's lifetime. Objects can be created and destroyed as needed, and when an object is destroyed, all its data is destroyed as well.

Classes differ from standard modules in more ways than just how their data behaves. When you define a standard module, its public functions and procedures are instantly available to other modules within your application. However, public functions and procedures of classes aren't immediately available to your program. Classes are templates for objects. At runtime, your code doesn't interact with the code in the class module per se, but it instantiates objects derived from the class. Each object acts as its own class "module" and thus has its own set of module data. When classes are exposed externally to other applications, the application containing the class's code is called the *server*. An application that creates and uses instances of an object is called a *client*. When you use instances of classes in the application that contains those classes, the application itself acts as both a client and a server. In this hour, I'll refer to the code instantiating an object derived from a class as *client code*.

Begin by creating a new Windows Application called Class Programming Example, and then follow these steps to create your project:

1. Rename the default form **ClassProgrammingExampleForm.vb**, and set its Text property to Class Programming Example.

2. Add a new class to the project by choosing Project, Add Class. Save the class with the name **clsMyClass.vb**, as shown in Figure 16.1.

FIGURE 16.1
Classes are added to a project just as other object files are added.

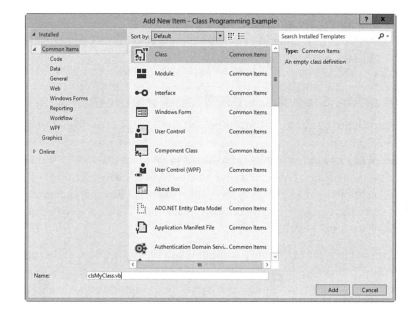

Creating an Object Interface

For an object to be created from a class, the class must expose an interface. As I mentioned earlier, an interface is a set of exposed functionality (properties, methods, and events). An interface is the means by which client code communicates with the object derived from the class. Some classes expose a limited interface, and others expose complex interfaces. The content and quantity of your class's interface are entirely up to you.

A class interface consists of one or more of the following members:

► Properties

► Methods

► Events

For example, assume that you're creating an Employee object (that is, a class used to derive employee objects). You must first decide how you want client code to interact with your object. You'll want to consider both the data contained within the object and the functions that the object can perform. You might want client code to be able to retrieve the name of an employee and other information such as sex, age, and the date of hire. For client code to get these values from the object, the object must expose an interface member for each of these items. You'll recall from Hour 3 that values exposed by an object are called *properties*. Therefore, each piece of data discussed here would have to be exposed as a property of the Employee object.

In addition to properties, you can expose functions, such as Delete or AddNew. These functions may be simple or complex. The Delete function of the Employee object, for example, might be complex. It would need to perform all the actions necessary to delete an employee, including such things as removing the employee from an assigned department, notifying the accounting department to remove the employee from the payroll, notifying the security department to revoke the employee's security access, and so on. Publicly exposed functions of an object, as you should again remember from Hour 3, are called methods.

Properties and methods are the most commonly used interface members. Although designing properties and methods might be new to you, by now using them isn't. You've used properties and methods in almost every hour so far. Here, you'll learn the techniques for creating properties and methods for your own objects.

For even more interaction between the client and the object, you can expose custom events. Custom object events are similar to the events of a form or text box. However, with custom events, you have complete control over the following:

► The name of the event

► The parameters passed to the event

► When the event occurs

Creating custom events is complicated, and I'll cover only custom properties and methods in this hour.

Properties, methods, and events together make up an object's interface. This interface acts as a contract between the client application and the object. Any and all communication between the client and the object must transpire through this interface, as shown in Figure 16.2.

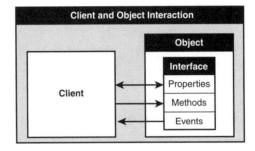

Luckily, Visual Basic handles the technical details of the interaction between the client and the object by way of the interface. Your responsibility is to define an object's properties, methods, and events so that its interface is logical and consistent and exposes all the functionality a client must have available to use the object productively.

Exposing Object Attributes as Properties

Properties are the attributes of objects. Properties can be read-only, or they can allow both reading and writing of their values. For example, you might want to let a client retrieve the value of a property containing the path of the component but not let the client change it because the path of a running component can't be changed.

You can add properties to a class in two ways. The first is to declare public variables. Any variable declared as public instantly becomes a property of the class (actually, it acts like a property, but it isn't technically a property it is a *field*). For example, suppose that you have the following statement in the Declarations section of a class:

```
Public Quantity as Integer
```

Clients could read from and write to the field, using code like the following:

```
objMyObject.Quantity = 420
```

This works, but significant limitations exist that make this approach less than desirable:

▶ You can't execute code when a field ("property") value changes. For example, what if you wanted to write the quantity change to a database? Because the client application can access the variable directly, you have no way of knowing when the value of the variable changes.

▶ You can't prevent client code from changing a field because the client code accesses the variable directly.

▶ Perhaps the biggest problem is this: How do you control data validation? For instance, how could you ensure that Quantity is never set to a negative value?

It's simply not possible to work around these issues when using a public variable. Instead of exposing public variables, you should use property procedures to create class properties.

Property procedures enable you to execute code when a property is changed, to validate property values, and to dictate whether a property is read-only, write-only, or both readable and writable. Declaring a property procedure is similar to declaring a standard Function or Sub procedure, but with some important differences. The basic structure of a property procedure looks like this:

```
Public Property propertyname() As datatype
    Get
        ' Code to return the property's value goes here.
    End Get

    Set(ByVal Value As datatype)
        ' Code that accepts a new value goes here.
    End Set
End Property
```

The first word in the property declaration simply designates the scope of the property (usually Public, Private, or Friend). Properties declared with Public are available to code outside the class. (They can be accessed by client code.) If the application exposes its objects to other applications, Public procedures are visible outside the application. Procedures declared as Friend, on the other hand, behave like Public procedures, with the exception that they are not available outside the application. Properties declared as Private are available only to code within the class. Immediately following the scope identifier is the word Property. This word tells Visual Basic that you're creating a property procedure rather than a Sub or Function procedure. Next come the property name and data type.

Type the following two statements into your class:

```
Private m_intHeight As Integer
Public Property Height() As Integer
```

Next, type the following and press Enter:

```
Get
```

After entering the Get statements, Visual Basic fills in the rest of the procedure template for you, as shown in Figure 16.3.

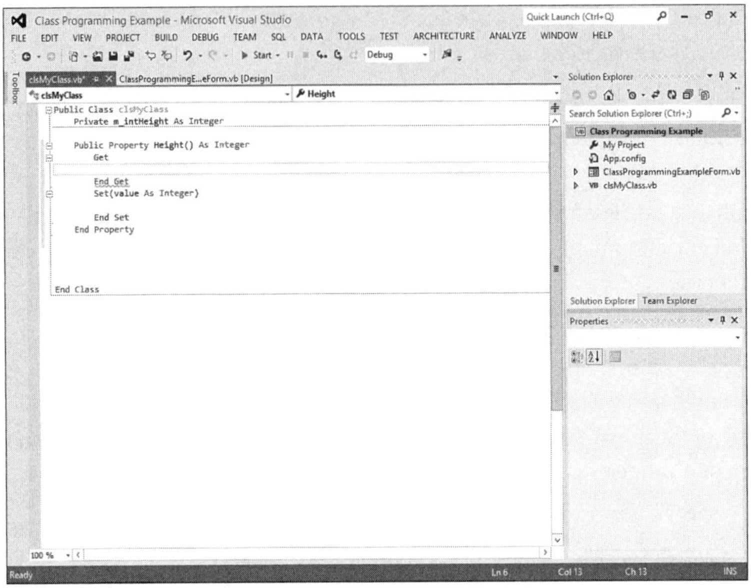

FIGURE 16.3
Visual Basic
creates property
procedure
templates.

You might be wondering why you just created a module-level variable of the same name as your property procedure (with a naming prefix, of course). After all, I just finished preaching about the problems of using a module-level variable as a property. The reason is that a property has to get its value from somewhere, and a module-level variable is usually the best place to store it. The property procedure acts as a wrapper for this variable. Notice that the variable is declared as Private rather than Public. This means that no code outside the class can view or modify the contents of this variable; as far as client code is concerned, this variable doesn't exist.

Between the property declaration statement and the End Property statement are two constructs: Get and Set. These constructs are discussed next.

Creating Readable Properties Using the Get Construct   The Get construct is used to place code that returns a value for the property when read by a client.

Think of the Get construct as a function; whatever you return as the result of the function becomes the property value. Add the following statement between the Get and End Get statements:

```
Return m_intHeight
```

All this statement does is return the value of the variable m_intHeight when client code requests the value of the Height property.

Creating Writable Properties Using the Set Construct   The Set construct is where you place code that accepts a new property value from client code.

Add the following statement between the Set and End Set statements:

```
m_intHeight = Value
```

If you look closely at the Set statement, you'll see that it's similar to a Sub declaration and that Value is a parameter. Value contains the value being passed to the property by the client code. The statement you just entered assigns the new value to the module-level variable.

As you can see, the property procedure is a wrapper around the module-level variable. When the client code sets the property, the Set construct stores the new value in the variable. When the client retrieves the value of the property, the Get construct returns the value in the module-level variable.

So far, the property procedure, with its Get and Set constructs, doesn't do anything different from what it would do if you were to simply declare a public variable (only the property procedure requires more code). However, look at this variation of the same Set construct:

```
Set(ByVal value As Integer)
    If value < 10 Then Exit Property
    m_intHeight = value
End Set
```

This Set construct restricts the client to setting the Height property to a value greater than or equal to 10. If a value less than 10 is passed to the property, the property procedure terminates without setting m_intHeight. You're not limited to performing only data validation; you can pretty much add whatever code you want and even call other procedures. Go ahead and add the verification statement to your procedure so that the Set construct looks like this one. Your code should now look like the procedure shown in Figure 16.4.

Creating Read-Only or Write-Only Properties There will be times that you will want to create properties that can be read but not changed. Such properties are called *read-only* properties. When discussing the fictitious Dog object in Hour 3, I talked about creating a property called NumberOfLegs. With such an object, you might want to expose the property as read-only—code can get the number of legs but cannot change it. To create a read-only property, you would use the ReadOnly keyword to declare the property procedure and then remove the Set...End Set section. For example, if you wanted the property procedure you just created to define a read-only procedure, you might declare it like this:

```
Public ReadOnly Property Height() As Integer
    Get
        Return m_intHeight
    End Get
End Property
```

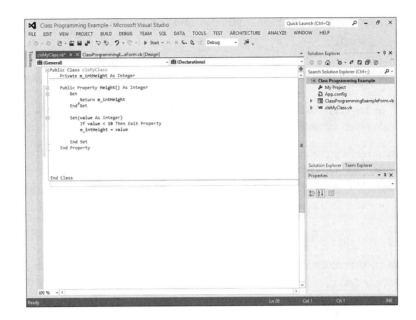

Although far more rare, it is possible to create a write-only property, in which the property can be set but not read. To do so, you would use the keyword WriteOnly in place of ReadOnly and remove the Get...End Get section instead of the Set...End Set section.

Exposing Functions as Methods

Unlike a property that acts as an object attribute, a method is a function exposed by an object. Methods are nothing more than exposed code routines. A method can return a value, but it doesn't have to. Methods are easier to create than properties because they're defined just as ordinary Sub and Function procedures are. To create a method within a class, create a public Sub or Function procedure. Create the following procedure in your class now (enter this code on the line following the End Property statement):

```
Public Function AddTwoNumbers(ByVal intNumber1 As Integer, _
                             ByVal intNumber2 As Integer) As Long
    Return = intNumber1 + intNumber2
End Function
```

Like normal Sub and Function procedures, methods defined with Function return values, whereas methods defined with Sub don't. To make a procedure private to the class and therefore invisible to client code, declare the procedure as Private rather than Public.

Instantiating Objects from Classes

After you obtain a reference to an object and assign it to a variable, you can manipulate the object by using an object variable. Let's do so now.

Click the ClassProgrammingExampleForm.vb Design tab to view the Form Designer, and add a button to the form by double-clicking the Button item in the toolbox. Set the button's properties as follows:

Property	Value
Name	btnCreateObject
Location	100, 120
Size	88, 23
Text	Create Object

Next, double-click the button to access its Click event, and enter the following code:

```
Dim objMyObject As Object
objMyObject = New clsMyClass()
MessageBox.Show(objMyObject.AddTwoNumbers(1, 2))
```

The first statement creates a variable of type Object (dimension variables were discussed in Hour 11). The second statement needs an explanation. Because the variable appears on the left side of the equals sign, you can deduce that the variable is being set to some value.

However, what appears on the right side of the equals sign might look foreign to you. You want to place a reference to an object in the variable, but no object has yet been created. The New keyword tells Visual Basic to create a new object, and the text following New is the name of the class to use to derive the object (remember, classes are object templates). The last statement calls the AddTwoNumbers() method of your class and displays the result in a message box.

Go ahead and run the project by pressing F5, and then click the button to make sure that everything is working correctly. When finished, stop the project and save your work.

Binding an Object Reference to a Variable

An object can contain any number of properties, methods, and events; every object is different. When you write code to manipulate an object, Visual Basic has to understand the object's interface, or your code won't work. The interface members (the object's properties, methods, and events) are resolved when an object variable is bound to an object. The two forms of binding are *early binding*, which occurs at compile time, and *late binding*, which occurs at runtime. It's important that you have at least a working understanding of binding if you're to create code based on classes. Although I can't explain the intricacies and technical details of early binding versus late binding in this hour, I'll teach you what you need to know to perform each type of binding.

> Both types of binding have advantages, but early binding generally is superior to late-binding. Code that uses late-bound objects requires more work by Visual Basic than code that uses early-bound objects.

Late-Binding an Object Variable

When you dimension a variable as data type `Object`, as shown in the following code sample, you're late-binding to the object:

```
Dim objMyObject As Object
objMyObject = New clsMyClass()
MessageBox.Show(objMyObject.AddTwoNumbers(1, 2))
```

> You cannot use late-binding in a project with Option Strict turned on (refer to Hour 11 for information on Option Strict).

When you late-bind an object, the binding occurs at runtime when the variable is set to reference an object. For a member of the object to be referenced, Visual Basic must determine and use an internal ID of the specified member. Fortunately, because Visual Basic handles all the details, you don't need to know the ID of a member. Just be aware that Visual Basic *does* need to know the ID of a member to use it. When you late-bind an object variable (dimension the variable As `Object`), the following occurs behind the scenes:

1. Visual Basic obtains a special ID (the Dispatch ID) of the property, method, or event that you want to call. This takes time and resources.

2. An internal array containing the parameters of the member, if any, is created.

3. The member is invoked, using the ID obtained in step 1.

The preceding steps require a great deal of overhead and adversely affect an application's performance. Therefore, late-binding isn't the preferred method of binding. Late binding does have some attractive uses, but most of them are related to using objects outside your application, not to using objects derived from classes within the project.

One of the main drawbacks of late binding is the compiler's inability to check the syntax of the code manipulating an object. Because a member's ID and the parameters it uses aren't determined until runtime, the compiler has no way of knowing whether you're using a member correctly—or even if the member you're referencing exists. This can result in a runtime exception or some other unexpected behavior. Change the third statement in your code to look like the following (deliberately misspell the AddTwoNumbers method):

```
MessageBox.Show(objMyObject.AddtoNumbers(1, 2))
```

Press F5 to run the project. No problems—well, so far, at least. Even though the method name is misspelled, Visual Basic compiles the project without raising a build error. This happens because the variable is declared As Object, and Visual Basic has no idea what will eventually be placed in the variable. Therefore, it can't perform any syntax checking at compile time and just assumes that whatever action you perform with the variable is correct. Click the button to create the object and call the method. When you do, you get the exception shown in Figure 16.5.

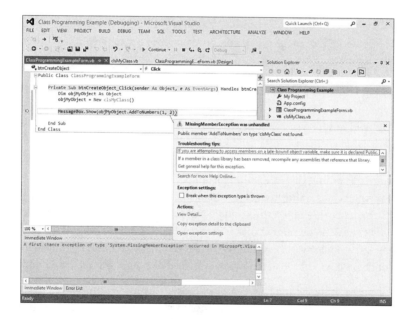

FIGURE 16.5
Exceptions such as this are a risk of late binding.

As explained in Hour 15, "Debugging Your Code," runtime exceptions are more problematic than build errors because they're usually encountered by end users and under varying circumstances. When you late-bind objects, it's easy to introduce these types of problems; therefore, late binding has a real risk of throwing exceptions. As you'll see in the next section, early binding reduces many of these risks.

Go ahead and choose Debug, Stop Debugging before continuing.

Early-Binding an Object Variable

If Visual Basic can determine a Dispatch ID for a member at compile time, there's no need to look up the ID when the member is referenced at runtime. This results in considerably faster calls to object members. Not only that, but Visual Basic can also validate the member call at compile time, reducing the chance of errors in your code.

Early binding occurs when you dimension a variable as a specific type of object, rather than just As Object. When a variable is early-bound, Visual Basic looks up the Dispatch IDs of the object's members at compile time, rather than at runtime.

The following are important reasons to use early binding:

- ► Speed.

- ► More speed.

- ► Objects, their properties, and their methods appear in IntelliSense drop-down lists.

- ► The compiler can check for syntax and reference errors in your code so that many problems are found at compile time, rather than at runtime.

For early binding to take place, an object variable must be declared as a specific object type (that is, not As Object). Change the Dim statement in the code you've entered to read as follows:

```
Dim objMyObject As clsMyClass
```

As soon as you commit this statement, Visual Basic displays a wavy blue line under the bad method call, as shown in Figure 16.6. This occurs because Visual Basic now knows the exact type of object the variable will contain; therefore, it can and does perform syntax checking on all member references. Because it can't find a member with the name AddtoNumbers, it flags this as a build error. Try running the project by pressing F5, and you'll see that Visual Basic does indeed recognize this as a build problem.

Place the cursor at the period between the words objMyObject and AddtoNumbers. Delete the period and then type a period once more. This time, Visual Basic displays an IntelliSense drop-down list with all the members of the class, as shown in Figure 16.7. Go ahead and select the AddTwoNumbers member to fix your code.

Creating a New Object When Dimensioning a Variable

You can instantiate a new object on the declaration statement by including the keyword New, like this:

```
Dim objMyObject As New clsMyClass()
```

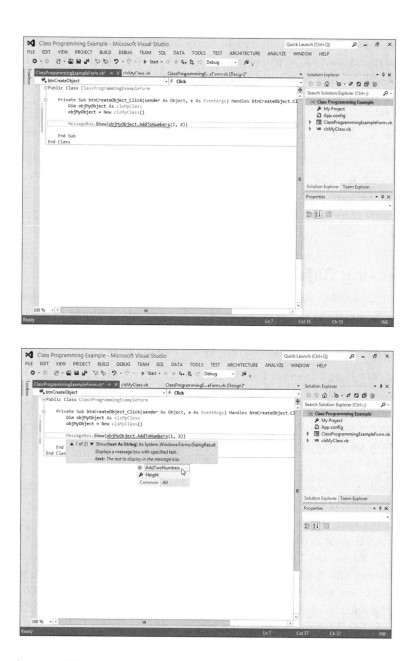

FIGURE 16.6
With early-bound objects, Visual Basic performs syntax checking for you.

FIGURE 16.7
Visual Basic displays IntelliSense drop-down lists of members for early-bound objects.

Note that I could have used two statements—one to declare the variable and another to set it, but putting them on the same line when possible is preferred. This approach alleviates the need for a second statement to create a new instance of the object.

However, if you do this, the variable will always contain a reference to an object. If there's a chance that you might not need the object, you should probably avoid using the New keyword on the Dim statement. Consider the following:

```
Dim objMyObject As clsMyClass
If condition Then
   objMyObject = New clsMyObject
   ' Code to use the custom object would go here.
End If
```

Remember that instantiating an object takes resources. In this code, no object is created when condition is False. If you were to place the word New on the Dim statement, a new object would be instantiated whenever this code was executed, regardless of the value of condition.

Releasing Object References

When an object is no longer needed, it should be destroyed so that all the resources used by the object can be reclaimed. Objects are destroyed automatically when the last reference to the object is released. Although there are two primary ways to release an object reference, one is clearly better than the other.

One way to release a reference to an object is simply to let the object variable holding the reference go out of scope. As you might recall from Hour 11, variables are destroyed when they go out of scope. This is no less true for object variables. However, you can't necessarily be assured that an object is fully released and that all the memory being used by the object is freed by letting the object's variable go out of scope. Therefore, relying on scope to release objects isn't a good idea.

To explicitly release an object, set the object variable equal to Nothing, like this:

```
objMyObject = Nothing
```

When you set an object variable equal to Nothing, you're assured that the object reference is fully released. The object won't be destroyed, however, if other variables are referencing it. After the last reference is released, the garbage collector eventually destroys the object. (I talk about the garbage collector in Hour 24, "The 10,000-Foot View.") Go ahead and add the statement just shown to your procedure, right after the statement that shows the message box.

If you don't correctly release object references, your application might experience resource leaks, become sluggish, and consume more resources than it should.

Understanding the Lifetime of an Object

An object created from a class exists as long as a variable holds a reference to it. Fortunately, Visual Basic (or, more specifically, the .NET Framework, as discussed in Hour 24) handles the details of keeping track of the references to a given object; you don't have to worry about this when creating or using objects. When all the references to an object are released, the object is flagged and eventually destroyed by the garbage collector.

The following are key points to remember about an object's lifetime and what they mean to your application:

▶ An object is created (and hence referenced) when an object variable is *declared* by the keyword New. For example:

```
Dim objMyObject = New clsMyClass()
```

▶ An object is created (and hence referenced) when an object variable is *assigned* an object by the keyword New. For example:

```
objMyObject = New clsMyClass()
```

▶ An object is referenced when an object variable is assigned an existing object. For example:

```
objThisObject = objThatObject
```

▶ An object reference is released when an object variable is set to Nothing, as discussed in the preceding section.

▶ An object is destroyed sometime after the last reference to it is released. This is handled by the garbage collector, as discussed in Hour 24.

Understanding the lifetime of objects is important. You've now seen how and when object references are created, but you also need to know how to explicitly release an object reference. Only when all references to an object are released is the object flagged for destruction and the resources it uses are reclaimed.

Summary

Object-oriented programming is an advanced methodology that enables you to create more robust applications, and programming classes is the foundation of OOP. In this hour, you learned how to create classes, which are the templates used to instantiate objects. You also learned how to create a custom interface consisting of properties and methods, and how to use the classes you've defined to instantiate and manipulate objects by way of object variables.

Visual Basic is on par with languages such as C++ for OOP capabilities. In this hour, you learned the basic mechanics of programming objects with classes. Object-oriented programming takes considerable skill, and you'll need to master the concepts in this book before you can really begin to take advantage of what OOP has to offer. Nevertheless, what you learned in this hour will take you further than you might think. Using an OOP methodology is as much a way of thinking as it is a way of programming. Consider how things in your projects might work as objects, and before you know it, you'll be creating robust classes.

Q&A

Q. *Should I always try to place code in classes rather than standard modules?*

A. Not necessarily. As with most things, there are no hard-and-fast rules. Correctly programming classes takes some skill and experience, and programming standard modules is easier for beginners. If you want to experiment with classes, I encourage you to do so. However, don't feel as though you have to place everything in a class.

Q. *I want to create a general class with many miscellaneous procedures—sort of a catchall class. What's the best way to do this?*

A. If you want to create some sort of utility class, I recommend calling it something like clsUtility. Create a global variable to hold a reference to an object instantiated from this class. In your program's startup code, set the global variable to a new instance of the class. Then you can use the global variable throughout your application to access the utility functions instead of having to instantiate a new object each time you want to use the functions.

Workshop

Quiz

1. To create objects, you must first create a template. What is this template called?

2. One of the primary benefits of object-oriented programming is that objects contain both their data and their code. What is this capability called?

3. With standard modules, public variables and routines are always available to code in other modules. Is this true with public variables and routines in classes?

4. True or false: Each object derived from a class has its own set of module-level data.

5. What must you do to create a property that can be read but not changed by client code?

6. What's the best way to store the internal value of a property within a class?

7. Which is generally superior, early binding or late binding?

8. If an object variable is declared As Object, is it early-bound or late-bound?

9. What's the best way to destroy an object reference?

Answers

1. Class

2. Encapsulation

3. No. An object would have to be instantiated before the public variables and routines would be available.

4. True

5. Declare the property procedure by using the ReadOnly modifier, and remove the Set...End Set section.

6. Store the internal value in a private module-level variable.

7. Early binding is almost always superior to late binding.

8. The object is late-bound.

9. Set the object variable equal to Nothing.

Exercises

1. Add a new property to your class called DropsInABucket. Make this property an Integer, and set it up so that client code can read the property value but not set it. Finally, add a button to the form that, when clicked, prints the value of the property to the Immediate window (it will be 0 by default). When this is working, modify the code so that the property always returns 1,000,000.

2. Add a button to your form that creates two object variables of type clsMyClass(). Use the New keyword to instantiate a new instance of the class in one of the variables. Then set the second variable to reference the same object and print the contents of the Height property to the Output window or display it in a message box.

HOUR 17

Interacting with Users

What You'll Learn in This Hour:

▶ Displaying messages using the `MessageBox.Show()` function

▶ Creating custom dialog boxes

▶ Using `InputBox()` to get information from a user

▶ Interacting with the keyboard

▶ Using the common mouse events

Forms and controls are the primary means by which users interact with an application, and vice versa. However, program interaction can and often does go deeper than that. For example, a program can display customized messages to a user, and it can be fine-tuned to deal with certain keystrokes or mouse clicks. In this hour, you'll learn how to create functional and cohesive interaction between your application and the user. In addition, you'll learn how to program the keyboard and mouse so that you can expand your program's interactivity beyond what a form and its controls natively support.

Displaying Messages Using the `MessageBox.Show()` Function

A message box is a small dialog box that displays a message to the user (just in case that's not obvious). Message boxes are often used to tell the user the result of some action, such as "The file has been copied" or "The file could not be found." A message box is dismissed when the user clicks one of its available buttons. Most applications have *many* message boxes, but developers often don't display messages correctly. It's important to remember that when you display a message to a user, you're communicating with the user. In this section, I'll teach you not only how to use the `MessageBox.Show()` function to display messages, but also how to use the statement to communicate effectively.

The `MessageBox.Show()` function can be used to tell the user something or ask the user a question. In addition to displaying text, which is its primary purpose, you can use this function to display an icon and display one or more buttons that the user can click. Although you're free to display whatever text you want, you must choose from a predefined list of icons and buttons.

The `MessageBox.Show()` method is an overloaded method. This means that it was written with numerous constructs supporting various options. When you code in Visual Basic, IntelliSense displays a drop-down scrolling list displaying any of the 21 overloaded `MessageBox.Show()` method calls to aid in coding. The following are a few ways to call `MessageBox.Show()`:

To display a message box with specified text, a caption in the title bar, and an OK button, use this syntax:

```
MessageBox.Show(MessageText, Caption)
```

To display a message box with specified text, a caption, and one or more specific buttons, use this syntax:

```
MessageBox.Show(MessageText, Caption, Buttons)
```

To display a message box with specified text, a caption, buttons, and an icon, use this syntax:

```
MessageBox.Show(MessageText, Caption, Buttons, Icon)
```

In all these statements, `MessageText` is the text to display in the message box, `Caption` determines what appears in the message box's title bar, `Buttons` determines which buttons the user sees, and `Icon` determines what icon (if any) appears in the message box. Consider the following statement, which produces the message box shown in Figure 17.1:

```
MessageBox.Show("This is a message.", "Hello There")
```

You should always ensure that the buttons displayed are appropriate for the message. As you can see, if you omit `Buttons`, Visual Basic displays only an OK button.

FIGURE 17.1
A simple
message box.

> The older-style basic `MsgBox()` function (which is still supported, although not recommended) defaults the caption for the message box to the name of the project. There is no default for `MessageBox.Show()`, so you should always specify a caption, or you'll get an empty title bar for the dialog box.

Specifying Buttons and an Icon

Using the `Buttons` parameter, you can display one or more buttons in the message box. The `Buttons` parameter type is `MessageBoxButtons`. Table 17.1 shows the allowable values.

TABLE 17.1   Allowable Enumerators for `MessageBoxButtons`

Member	Description
AbortRetryIgnore	Displays Abort, Retry, and Ignore buttons.
OK	Displays an OK button only.
OKCancel	Displays OK and Cancel buttons.
YesNoCancel	Displays Yes, No, and Cancel buttons.
YesNo	Displays Yes and No buttons.
RetryCancel	Displays Retry and Cancel buttons.

Because the `Buttons` parameter is an enumerated type, Visual Basic gives you an IntelliSense drop-down list when you specify a value for this parameter. Therefore, committing these values to memory isn't all that important; you'll commit to memory the ones you use most often fairly quickly.

The `Icon` parameter determines the symbol displayed in the message box. The `Icon` parameter is an enumeration from the `MessageBoxIcon` type. Table 17.2 shows the most commonly used values of `MessageBoxIcon`.

TABLE 17.2   Common Enumerators for `MessageBoxIcon`

Member	Description
Exclamation	Displays a symbol consisting of an exclamation point in a triangle with a yellow background.
Information	Displays a symbol consisting of a lowercase letter i in a circle.
None	Displays no symbol.
Question	Displays a symbol consisting of a question mark in a circle.

TABLE 17.2   Continued

Member	Description
Stop	Displays a symbol consisting of a white X in a circle with a red background.
Warning	Displays a symbol consisting of an exclamation point in a triangle with a yellow background.

The Icon parameter is also an enumerated type; therefore, Visual Basic gives you an IntelliSense drop-down list when you specify a value for this parameter. You may have noticed that Exclamation and Warning have the same icon. As best I can tell, this is a throwback to early versions of Visual Basic, and either work just fine. Whichever you choose, I suggest you pick one and stick with it for the sake of consistency.

The message box shown in Figure 17.2 was created with the following statement:

```
MessageBox.Show("I'm about to do something...","MessageBox sample", _
    MessageBoxButtons.OKCancel,MessageBoxIcon.Information)
```

FIGURE 17.2
Assign the Information icon to general messages.

The message box shown in Figure 17.3 was created with a statement almost identical to the previous one, except that the second button is designated as the default button. If a user presses the Enter key with a message box displayed, the message box acts as though the user clicked the default button. You'll want to give careful consideration to the default button in each message box. For example, suppose the application is about to do something that the user probably doesn't want to do. It's best to make the Cancel button the default button in case the user is a bit quick when pressing the Enter key. Following is the statement used to generate the message box shown in Figure 17.3:

```
MessageBox.Show("I'm about to do something irreversible...", _
    "MessageBox sample", _
    MessageBoxButtons.OKCancel,MessageBoxIcon.Information, _
    MessageBoxDefaultButton.Button2)
```

The Error icon is shown in Figure 17.4. The Error icon is best used in rare circumstances, such as when an exception has occurred. Overusing the Error icon is like crying wolf—when a real problem emerges, the user might not notice. Notice here how I display only the OK button. If something has already happened and there's nothing the user can do about it, don't bother giving the user a Cancel button. The following statement generates the message box shown in Figure 17.4:

```
MessageBox.Show("Something bad has happened!","MessageBox sample", _
    MessageBoxButtons.OK, MessageBoxIcon.Error)
```

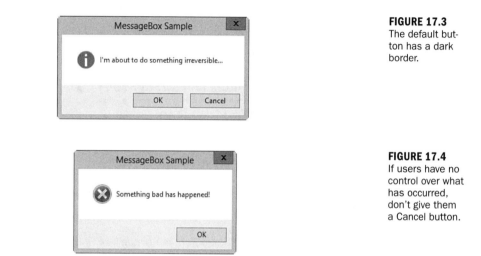

FIGURE 17.3
The default button has a dark border.

FIGURE 17.4
If users have no control over what has occurred, don't give them a Cancel button.

In Figure 17.5, a question is posed to the user, so the message displays the Question icon. Also note how the message box assumes that the user would probably choose No, so the second button is set as the default. In the next section, you'll learn how to determine which button the user clicks. Here's the statement used to generate the message box shown in Figure 17.5:

```
MessageBox.Show("Would you like to format your hard drive now?", _
    "MessageBox sample",MessageBoxButtons.YesNo,MessageBoxIcon.Question, _
    MessageBoxDefaultButton.Button2)
```

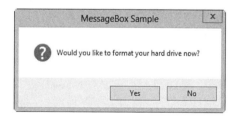

FIGURE 17.5
A message box can be used to ask a question.

As you can see, designating buttons and icons isn't all that difficult. The real effort comes in determining which buttons and icons are appropriate for a given situation.

Determining Which Button Is Clicked

You'll probably find that many of your message boxes are simple, containing only an OK button. For other message boxes, however, you must determine which button a user clicks. Why give the user a choice if you won't act on it?

The `MessageBox.Show()` method returns the button clicked as a `DialogResult` enumeration. The `DialogResult` has the values shown in Table 17.3.

TABLE 17.3   Enumerators for `DialogResult`

Member	Description
Abort	The return value is `Abort`. Usually sent from a button labeled Abort.
Cancel	The return value is `Cancel`. Usually sent from a button labeled Cancel.
Ignore	The return value is `Ignore`. Usually sent from a button labeled Ignore.
No	The return value is `No`. Usually sent from a button labeled No.
None	Nothing is returned from the dialog box. The model dialog continues running.
OK	The return value is `OK`. Usually sent from a button labeled OK.
Retry	The return value is `Retry`. Usually sent from a button labeled Retry.
Yes	The return value is `Yes`. Usually sent from a button labeled Yes.

> Note the phrase "Usually sent from" in the descriptions of the `DialogResult` values. When you create custom dialog boxes (as shown later in this hour), you can assign a `DialogResult` to any button of your choosing.

Performing actions based on the button clicked is a matter of using one of the decision constructs. For example:

```
If (MessageBox.Show("Would you like to do X?","MessageBox sample", _
    MessageBoxButtons.YesNo,MessageBoxIcon.Question) = _
    Windows.Forms.DialogResult.Yes) Then
  ' Code to do X would go here.
End If
```

As you can see, the `MessageBox.Show()` method gives you a lot of bang for your buck; it offers considerable flexibility.

Creating Good Messages

The `MessageBox.Show()` method is surprisingly simple to use, considering all the different forms of messages it lets you create. The real trick is providing appropriate messages to users at appropriate times. In addition to considering the icon and buttons to display in a message, you should follow these guidelines for crafting message text:

- **Use a formal tone.** Don't use large words, and avoid using contractions. Strive to make the text immediately understandable and not overly fancy; a message box is not a place to show off your literary skills.

- **Limit messages to two or three lines.** Not only are lengthy messages more difficult for users to read, but they also can be intimidating. When a message box is used to ask a question, make the question as succinct as possible.

- **Never make users feel as though they've done something wrong.** Users will, and do, make mistakes, but you should craft messages that take the sting out of the situation.

- **Spell-check all message text.** The Visual Basic code editor doesn't spell-check for you, so you should type your messages in a program such as Microsoft Word and spell-check the text before pasting it into your code. Spelling errors have an adverse effect on a user's perception of a program.

- **Avoid technical jargon.** Just because someone uses software doesn't mean that he is a technical person. Explain things in plain English (or whatever the native language of the GUI happens to be).

- **Be sure that the buttons match the text!** For example, don't show the Yes/No buttons if the text doesn't present a question to the user.

Creating Custom Dialog Boxes

Most of the time, the `MessageBox.Show()` method should be a sufficient means to display messages to a user. At times, however, the `MessageBox.Show()` method is too limited for a given purpose. Suppose that you want to display a lot of text to the user, such as a log file of some sort, for example, so you want a message box that the user can size.

Custom dialog boxes are nothing more than standard modal forms, with one notable exception: One or more buttons are designated to return a dialog result, just as the buttons on a message box shown with the `MessageBox.Show()` method return a dialog result.

Now you'll create a custom dialog box. Begin by creating a new Windows Application titled Custom Dialog Example, and then follow these steps to build the project:

1. Rename the default form **MainForm.vb**, and set its `Text` property to `Custom Dialog Box Example`.

2. Add a new button to the form, and set its properties as follows:

Property	Value
Name	btnShowCustomDialogBox
Location	67, 180
Size	152, 23
Text	Show Custom Dialog Box

3. Now you'll create the custom dialog box. Add a new form to the project by choosing Project, Add Windows Form. Save the new form with the name **CustomDialogBoxForm.vb**.

4. Change the `Text` property of the new form to `This is a custom dialog box`, and set its `FormBorderStyle` to `FixedDialog`.

5. Add a new text box to the form, and set its properties as follows:

Property	Value
Name	txtCustomMessage
Location	8, 8
Multiline	True
ReadOnly	True
Size	268, 220
Text	Custom message goes here

For a custom dialog box to return a result as a standard message box does, it must have buttons that are designated to return a dialog result. You do this by setting a button's `DialogResult` property, as shown in Figure 17.6.

6. Add a new button to the form, and set its properties as shown in the following table. This button will act as the custom dialog box's Cancel button.

7. You need to create an OK button for the custom dialog box. Create another button and set its properties as follows:

Property	Value
Name	btnCancel
DialogResult	Cancel
Location	201, 234
Size	75, 23
Text	Cancel

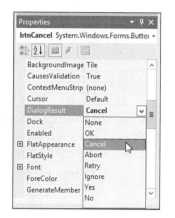

Specifying a dialog result for one or more buttons is the first step in making a form a custom dialog box. The second part of the process is in how the form is shown. As you learned in Hour 5, "Building Forms: The Basics," you display forms by calling the Show() method of a form variable. However, to show a form as a custom dialog box, you call the ShowDialog() method instead. When ShowDialog() is used to display a form, the following occurs:

Property	Value
Name	btnOK
DialogResult	OK
Location	120, 234
Size	75, 23
Text	OK

▶ The form is shown modally.

▶ If the user clicks a button that has its DialogResult property set to return a value, the form is immediately closed, and that value is returned as a result of the ShowDialog() method call.

Notice how you don't have to write code to close the form; clicking a button with a dialog result closes the form automatically. This simplifies the process of creating custom dialog boxes.

8. Return to the first form in the Form Designer by double-clicking MainForm.vb in the Solution Explorer.

9. Double-click the button you created, and add the following code:

```
If CustomDialogBoxForm.ShowDialog() = Windows.Forms.DialogResult.OK Then
    MessageBox.Show("You clicked OK.")
Else
    MessageBox.Show("You clicked Cancel.")
End If
```

When you typed the equals sign after ShowDialog(), did you notice that Visual Basic gave you an IntelliSense drop-down list with the possible dialog results? These results correspond directly to the values you can assign to a button when you use the DialogResult property. Press F5 to run the project, click the button to display your custom dialog box (see Figure 17.7), and then click one of the available dialog box buttons. When you're satisfied that the project is working correctly, stop the project and save your work.

FIGURE 17.7
The ShowDialog() method enables you to create custom message boxes.

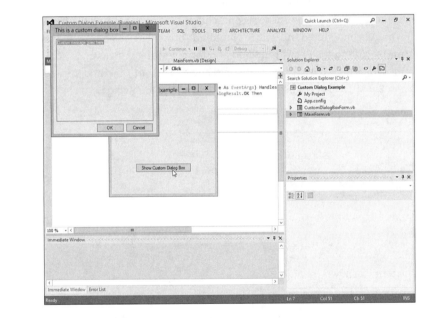

If you click the Close (X) button in the upper-right corner of the form, the form is closed, and the code behaves as if you've clicked Cancel because the Else code occurs.

The ability to create custom dialog boxes is a powerful feature. A call to MessageBox.Show() is usually sufficient, but when you need more control over the appearance and contents of a message box, creating a custom dialog box is the way to go.

Using `InputBox()` to Get Information from a User

The `MessageBox.Show()` method enables you to ask the user simple Yes/No, OK/Cancel–type questions, but it doesn't let you get specific input from a user, such as text or a number. When you need input from a user, you have two choices:

▶ Create a form with one or more controls to capture the data.

▶ Use the `InputBox()` function to gather data from the user.

The `InputBox()` function can capture only one piece of data, so it's not appropriate for most data-entry situations. However, in some circumstances, you might find that you need only one piece of data, and creating a custom form in such a situation would be overkill. For example, suppose that you have a simple application and you want the user to enter a name when he or she first starts the application. You could use the `InputBox()` function to have the user enter his or her name, rather than designing a special form.

The basic syntax of the `InputBox()` function looks like this:

```
InputBox(prompt, [title], [defaultresponse])
```

The first two parameters are similar to the corresponding parameters in `MessageBox.Show()`. The first parameter is the prompt to display to the user. This is where you specify the instructions or question that you want posed to the user. The `title` parameter determines the text that appears in the title bar. Again, if you omit `title`, the name of the project is shown. The following statement creates the input box shown in Figure 17.8:

```
strResult = InputBox("What is your favorite color?", "Enter Color")
```

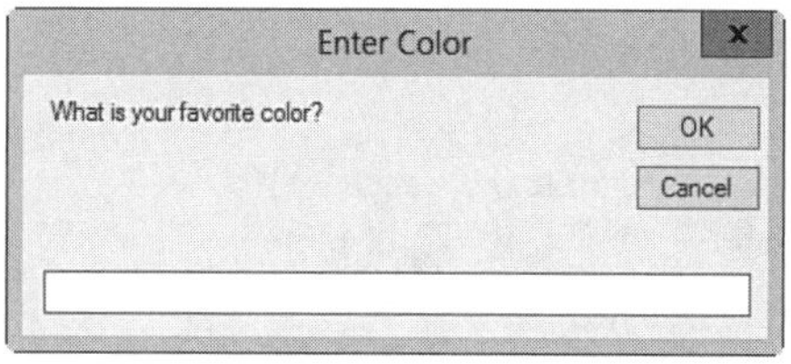

FIGURE 17.8
The input box enables a user to enter a single piece of information.

The last parameter, `defaultresponse`, enables you to specify text that appears by default in the text box portion of the input box. For example, the following statement produces the input box shown in Figure 17.9:

```
strResult = InputBox("How many eggs do you want to order?", "Order Eggs", "12")
```

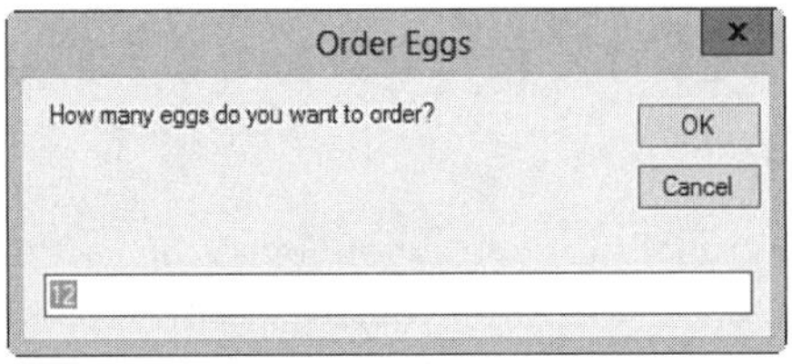

FIGURE 17.9
You can specify
a default value
for the user.

You should keep in mind two things about the return value of InputBox(). The first is that the result is *always* a string. The second is that an empty string is returned if the user clicks Cancel. The fact that InputBox() can return only a string and not a number data type is a limitation, but it's one that you can work around.

Now you'll create a project that uses an InputBox() to get the user's age. If the user clicks Cancel or enters something other than a number, the program behaves accordingly. Begin by creating a new Windows Application titled InputBox Example, and then follow these steps to build the project:

1. Rename the default form **MainForm.vb**, and then set its Text property to InputBox Example.

2. Add a new button to the form, and set its properties as follows:

Property	Value
Name	btnGetAge
Location	105, 109
Size	75, 23
Text	Enter Age

3. Double-click the button to access its Click event, and enter the following code:

```
Dim strResult As String
Dim intAge As Integer

strResult = InputBox("Please enter your age.", "Enter Age")

If strResult = "" Then
   MessageBox.Show("You clicked cancel!")
ElseIf IsNumeric(strResult) Then
   ' The user entered a number, store the age as a number.
   intAge = CInt(strResult)
   MessageBox.Show("You entered " & intAge & ".")
Else
   MessageBox.Show("You did not enter a number.")
End If
```

Nothing in this procedure, short of the call to InputBox(), should be new to you. What happens here is that the InputBox() function is used to ask the user to enter his or her age. Because InputBox() always returns a string, you use a string variable to hold the result. Next, an If...Else If...Else...End If construct is used to evaluate the result of the InputBox() call. The first test looks to see whether the result is a zero-length string. If it is, the code assumes that the user clicked Cancel. Next, the result is evaluated to see whether it is a number. If it is a number, the result is converted to an integer and displayed to the user. Go ahead and Press F5 and test the project.

If the user doesn't enter anything, an empty string is returned, just as though he or she clicked Cancel. There's no way to know the difference between clicking Cancel and not entering any text when using InputBox().

By the Way

InputBox() is a useful function for gathering a single piece of information. As you can see, it's possible to work around the limitation of the function's returning only a string. Keep the InputBox() function in mind; at times, it will come in handy.

Interacting with the Keyboard

Although most every control on a form handles its own keyboard input, on occasion you'll want to handle keyboard input directly. For example, you might want to perform an action when the user presses a specific key or releases a specific key. Most controls support three events that you can use to work directly with keyboard input. These are listed in Table 17.4.

TABLE 17.4 Events That Handle Keyboard Input

Event Name	Description
KeyDown	Occurs when a key is pressed while the control has the focus.
KeyPress	Occurs when a key is pressed while the control has the focus. If the user holds down the key, this event fires multiple times.
KeyUp	Occurs when a key is released while the control has the focus.

These events fire in the same order in which they appear in Table 17.4. For example, suppose that the user presses a key while a text box has the focus. The following list shows how the events would fire for the text box:

1. When the user presses a key, the KeyDown event fires.

2. While the key is down, the KeyPress event fires. This event repeats as long as the key is held down.

3. When the user releases the key, the KeyUp event fires, completing the cycle of keystroke events.

If you were creating a text editor and needed to perform an action for every keystroke entered by a user, for example, you would need to use the KeyPress event. This is the only event that would work because when a user holds down a key, Windows repeats the key in a text box or other data entry control. The KeyPress event fires for each repetition of the key, whereas KeyDown and KeyUp fire only once for each physical press of a key, regardless of how long the key is held down.

Now you'll create a project that illustrates handling keystrokes. This project has a text box that refuses to accept any character that isn't a number. Basically, you'll create a numeric text box. Start by creating a new Windows Application titled Keyboard Example, and then follow these steps to build the project:

1. Right-click Form1.vb in the Solution Explorer, choose Rename, change the name of the default form to **KeyboardExampleForm.vb**, and set its `Text` property to `Keyboard Example`.

2. Add a new text box to the form, and set its properties as shown in the following table:

Property	Value
Name	txtInput
Location	23, 56
Multiline	True
Size	238, 120

3. You'll add code to the `KeyPress` event of the text box to "eat" keystrokes that aren't numbers. Double-click the text box now to access its default event.

4. We're not interested in the `TextChanged` event, so choose `KeyPress` from the event list in the upper right of the code window.

5. Go ahead and delete the `TextChanged` event because you won't be using it. Your code editor should now look like Figure 17.10.

As you learned in Hour 4, "Understanding Events," the e parameter contains information specific to the occurrence of this event. In keyboard-related events, the e parameter contains information about the key being pressed; it's what you'll use to work with the user's keystrokes.

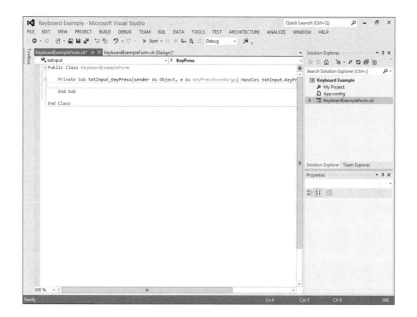

FIGURE 17.10
The KeyPress event is a good place to handle keyboard entry.

The key being pressed is available as the KeyChar property of the e parameter. You'll write code that handles the keystroke when the pressed key is anything other than a number.

Add the following code to the KeyPress event:

```
If Not (IsNumeric(e.KeyChar)) Then
    e.Handled = True
End If
```

You're probably curious about the Handled property of the e object. When you set this property to True, you're telling Visual Basic that you handled the keystroke and that Visual Basic should ignore it (that is, not add it to the text box). To see the effect this has, press F5 to run the project, and enter text into the text box. Try entering both numbers and letters; you'll find that only the numbers appear in the text box (see Figure 17.11).

When you paste data from the Clipboard, the KeyPress event isn't fired for each keystroke. Therefore, it's possible that a nonnumeric character could appear in the text box. If you absolutely needed to keep nonnumeric characters out of the text box, you'd need to use the TextChanged event as well.

FIGURE 17.11
The keyboard events enable you to handle keystrokes as you see fit.

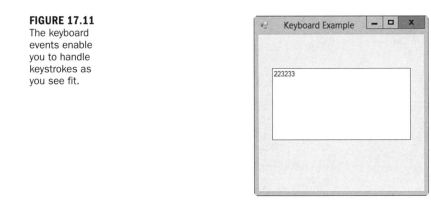

By the Way

It's not often that I need to catch a keypress, but every now and then I do. The three keystroke events listed in Table 17.4 have always made it easy to do what I need to do, but if there's one caveat I've discovered, it's that you need to give careful consideration to which event you choose (such as KeyPress or KeyUp, for example). Different events work best in different situations, and the best thing to do is to start with what seems like the most logical event, test the code, and change the event if necessary.

Using the Common Mouse Events

As with keyboard input, most controls support mouse input natively; you don't have to write code to deal with mouse input. At times, you might need more control than that offered by a control's native functionality, however. Visual Basic supports seven events that enable you to deal with mouse input directly. These events are listed in Table 17.5 in the order in which they occur.

TABLE 17.5 Events That Handle Mouse Input

Event Name	Description
MouseEnter	Occurs when the pointer enters a control.
MouseMove	Occurs when the pointer moves over a control.
MouseHover	Occurs when the pointer hovers over a control.
MouseDown	Occurs when the pointer is over a control and a button is pressed.
MouseUp	Occurs when the pointer is over a control and a button is released.
MouseLeave	Occurs when the pointer leaves a control.
Click	Occurs between the MouseDown and MouseUp events.

Now you'll build a project that illustrates using the MouseMove event to interact with the mouse. This project enables a user to draw on a form, much like you can draw in a paint program. Begin by creating a new Windows Application titled Mouse Paint, and then follow these steps to create the project:

1. Right-click Form1.vb in the Solution Explorer and choose Rename. Then change the name of the default form to **MainForm.vb** and set its Text property to Paint with the Mouse.

2. Double-click the form to access its default event, the Load event. Enter the following statement into the Load event:

```
m_objGraphics = Me.CreateGraphics
```

You've already used a graphics object a few times. What you're doing here is setting a graphics object to the client area of the form; any drawing performed on the object appears on the form. Because you'll draw to this graphics object each time the mouse moves over the form, there's no point in creating a new graphics object each time you need to draw to it. Therefore, you'll make m_objGraphics a module-level variable, which is instantiated only once—in the form's Load event.

3. Enter this statement into the Declarations section of your form class (between the Public Class MainForm statement and the Private Sub statement for your event procedure):

```
Private m_objGraphics As Graphics
```

As mentioned previously, always destroy objects when you're done with them. In this case, you want the object to remain in existence for the life of the form. Therefore, you'll destroy it in the form's FormClosed event, which occurs when the form is unloaded.

4. Open the object drop-down list (the upper-left drop-down list) and choose (MainForm Events). Next, open the procedure drop-down list (the drop-down list in the upper right), and select FormClosed. Enter the following statement in the FormClosed event:

```
m_objGraphics.Dispose()
```

Your procedure should now look like the one shown in Figure 17.12.

The last bit of code you need to add is the code that will draw on the form. You'll place code in the form's MouseMove event to do this. First, the code makes sure that the left mouse button is held down. If it isn't, no drawing takes place;

the user must hold down the mouse button to draw. Next, a rectangle is created. The coordinates of the mouse pointer are used to create a small rectangle that is passed to the DrawEllipse method of the graphics object. This has the effect of drawing a tiny circle where the mouse pointer is positioned.

FIGURE 17.12
Code in many places often works together to achieve one goal.

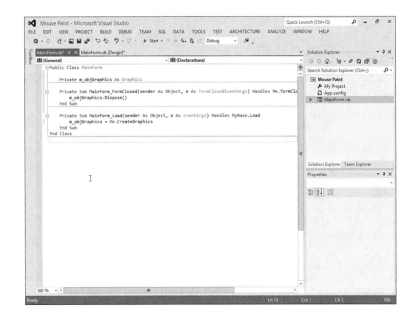

5. Again, select (MainForm Events) from the object drop-down list, and this time select MouseMove from the list of event procedures. Add the following code to the MouseMove event:

```
Dim rectEllipse As Rectangle

If e.Button <> Windows.Forms.MouseButtons.Left Then Exit Sub

With rectEllipse
    .X = e.X - 1
    .Y = e.Y - 1
    .Width = 2
    .Height = 2
End With

m_objGraphics.DrawEllipse(System.Drawing.Pens.Blue, rectEllipse)
```

Like all events, the e object contains information related to the event. In this example, you're using the X and Y properties of the e object, which are the coordinates of the pointer when the event fires. In addition, you're checking the Button property of the object to make sure that the user is pressing the left button.

Your project is now complete! Save your work by clicking Save All on the toolbar, and then press F5 to run the project. Move the mouse over the form—nothing happens. Now, hold down the left mouse button and move the mouse. This time, you draw on the form, as shown in Figure 17.13.

FIGURE 17.13
Capturing mouse events opens many exciting possibilities.

Notice that the faster you move the mouse, the more space appears between circles. This shows you that the user can move the mouse faster than the MouseMove event can fire, so you can't catch every single movement of the mouse. This is important to remember.

Summary

Forms and controls allow a lot of flexibility in how a user interacts with an application. However, solid interactivity goes beyond just what is placed on a form. In this hour, you learned how to use the MessageBox.Show() function to create informational dialog boxes. You learned how to specify an icon and buttons, and even how to designate a specific button as the default button. You also learned some valuable tips to help create the best messages possible. You'll create message boxes frequently, so mastering this skill is important.

Sometimes a simple OK/Cancel or Yes/No question isn't applicable—you need more data from the user. In this hour, you learned how to use the InputBox() function to get a single piece of data from the user and how to create custom dialog boxes. Although InputBox() always returns a string, you learned how to use it to gather numeric input as well.

Finally, you learned how to interact with the keyboard and mouse directly through numerous events. A control's mouse or keyboard capabilities sometimes fall short of what you want to accomplish. By understanding the concepts presented in this hour, you can go beyond the native capabilities of controls to create a rich, interactive experience for your users.

Q&A

Q. *Is it possible to capture keystrokes at the form level, rather than capturing them in control events?*

A. Yes. For the form's keyboard-related events to fire when a control has the focus, however, you must set the form's `KeyPreview` property to `True`. The control's keyboard events still fire, unless you set `KeyPressEventArgs.Handled` to `True` in the control's `KeyPress` event.

Q. *If I need to gather two or three pieces of information from the user, is it okay to use multiple* `InputBox` *statements?*

A. Probably not. In this case, a form or custom dialog box is probably a better choice.

Workshop

Quiz

1. What argument must you always supply a value for when calling `MessageBox.Show()`?

2. If you don't supply a value for the `Caption` parameter of `MessageBox.Show()`, what is displayed in the title bar of the message box?

3. How many icons can you show in a message box at once?

4. What type of data does the `InputBox()` function always return?

5. What does `InputBox()` return when the user clicks Cancel?

6. Which event fires first, `KeyUp` or `KeyPress`?

7. How do you determine which button is being pressed in a mouse-related event?

Answers

1. The prompt and the dialog title (caption). Actually, technically the caption is optional, but it's such a bad idea to leave it off that I consider it required.

2. Nothing gets displayed—the title bar is empty.

3. Only one icon can be shown at a time.

4. The InputBox() function always returns a string.

5. An empty string is returned when the user clicks Cancel.

6. The KeyPress event fires before the KeyUp event.

7. By using the e.Button property in the event.

Exercises

1. Modify your custom dialog box project so that the OK button is the form's Accept button. That way, the user must only press Enter to dismiss the dialog box. Next, make the Cancel button the form's Cancel button so that the user can also press the Escape key to dismiss the form.

2. Modify your mouse paint project so that the form clears each time the user starts drawing. Hint: Clear the graphics object in the MouseDown event to the form's BackColor.

HOUR 18

Working with Graphics

Visual Basic provides an amazingly powerful array of drawing capabilities. However, this power comes at the price of a relatively steep learning curve. Drawing isn't intuitive; you can't sit down for a few minutes with the online Help text and start drawing graphics. However, after you learn the basic principles involved, you'll find that drawing isn't that complicated. In this hour, you'll learn the basic skills for drawing shapes and text to a form or other graphical surface. You'll learn about pens, colors, and brushes (objects that help define graphics that you draw). In addition, you'll learn how to persist graphics on a form—and even how to create bitmaps that exist solely in memory.

Understanding the Graphics Object

At first, you might not come up with many reasons to draw to the screen, preferring to use the many advanced controls found within Visual Basic to build your interfaces. However, as your applications increase in size and complexity, you'll find more and more occasions to draw your own interfaces directly to the screen; when you need this functionality, you *really* need this functionality. You might even choose to design your own controls (which you can do with Visual Basic). In this hour, you'll learn the basics of drawing and printing to the screen. Using the skills you'll acquire in this hour, you'll be able to build incredibly detailed interfaces that look exactly how you want them to look.

The code within the Windows operating system that handles drawing everything to the screen, including text, lines, and shapes, is called the *Graphical Device Interface (GDI)*. The GDI processes all drawing instructions from applications, as well as from Windows itself, and generates the output for the current display. Because the GDI generates what you see onscreen, it is responsible for dealing with the particular display driver installed on the computer and the driver's settings, such as resolution and color depth. This means that applications (and their developers) don't have to worry about these details; you write code that tells the GDI what to output, and the GDI does whatever is necessary to produce that output. This behavior is called *device independence* because applications can instruct the GDI to display text and graphics, using code that's independent of the particular display device.

Visual Basic code communicates with the GDI primarily via the `Graphics` object. The basic process is as follows:

▶ An object variable is created to hold a reference to a `Graphics` object.

▶ The object variable is set to a valid `Graphics` object (new or existing).

▶ To draw or print, you call methods of the `Graphics` object.

Creating a `Graphics` Object for a Form or Control

If you want to draw directly to a form or control, you can easily get a reference to the drawing surface by calling the `CreateGraphics()` method of the object in question. For example, to create a `Graphics` object that draws to a text box, you could use code such as this:

```
Dim objGraphics As Graphics = TextBox1.CreateGraphics
```

When you call `CreateGraphics()`, you're setting the object variable to hold a reference to the `Graphics` object of the form or control's client area. The client area of a form is the gray area within the form's borders and title bar, whereas the client area of a control is usually the entire control. All drawing and printing done using the `Graphics` object are sent to the client area. In the code shown previously, the `Graphics` object references the client area of a text box, so all drawing methods executed on the `Graphics` object would draw directly to the text box.

By the Way

When you draw directly to a form or control, the object in question doesn't persist what's drawn on it. If the form is obscured in any way, such as by a window covering it or the form's being minimized, the next time the form is painted, it won't contain anything that was drawn on it. Later in this hour, I'll teach you how to persist graphics on a form.

Creating a Graphics Object for a New Bitmap

You don't have to set a Graphics object to the client area of a form or control; you can also set a Graphics object to a bitmap that exists only in memory. For performance reasons, you might want to use a memory bitmap to store temporary images or as a place to build complex graphics before sending them to a visible element (such as a form or control). To do this, you first have to create a new bitmap.

To create a new bitmap, you dimension a variable to hold a reference to the new bitmap, using the following syntax:

```
variable = New Bitmap(width, height, pixelformat)
```

The width and height arguments are exactly what they appear to be: the width and height of the new bitmap. The pixelformat argument, however, is less intuitive. This argument determines the bitmap's color depth and might also specify whether the bitmap has an alpha layer (used for transparent portions of bitmaps). Table 18.1 lists a few of the common values for pixelformat. (See Visual Basic's online Help for the complete list of values and their meanings.)

TABLE 18.1 Common Values for `pixelformat`

Value	Description
Format16bppGrayScale	The pixel format is 16 bits per pixel. The color information specifies 65,536 shades of gray.
Format16bppRgb555	The pixel format is 16 bits per pixel. The color information specifies 32,768 shades of color, of which 5 bits are red, 5 bits are green, and 5 bits are blue.
Format24bppRgb	The pixel format is 24 bits per pixel. The color information specifies 16,777,216 shades of color, of which 8 bits are red, 8 bits are green, and 8 bits are blue.

To create a new bitmap that's 640 pixels wide by 480 pixels tall and that has a pixel depth of 24 bits, for example, you could use this statement:

```
objMyBitMap = New Bitmap(640, 480, Drawing.Imaging.PixelFormat.Format24bppRgb)
```

After the bitmap is created, you can create a `Graphics` object that references the bitmap by using the `FromImage()` method, like this:

```
objGraphics = Graphics.FromImage(objMyBitMap)
```

Now any drawing or printing done using `objGraphics` would be performed on the memory bitmap. For the user to see the bitmap, you'd have to send the bitmap to a form or control. You'll do this later in this hour in the section "Persisting Graphics on a Form."

By the Way

> When you're finished with a `Graphics` object, call its `Dispose()` method to ensure that all resources used by the `Graphics` object are freed.

Working with Pens

A *pen* is an object that defines characteristics of a line. Pens are used to define color, line width, and line style (solid, dashed, and so on). Pens are used with almost all the drawing methods you'll learn about in this hour.

Visual Basic supplies a number of predefined pens, and you can also create your own. To create your own pen, use the following syntax:

```
penVariable = New Pen(color, width)
```

After a pen is created, you can set its properties to adjust its appearance. For example, all `Pen` objects have a `DashStyle` property that determines the appearance of lines drawn with the pen. Table 18.2 lists the possible values for `DashStyle`.

TABLE 18.2   Possible Values for `DashStyle`

Value	Description
Dash	Specifies a line consisting of dashes.
DashDot	Specifies a line consisting of a pattern of dashes and dots.
DashDotDot	Specifies a line consisting of alternating dashes and double dots.
Dot	Specifies a line consisting of dots.
Solid	Specifies a solid line.
Custom	Specifies a custom dash style. The Pen object contains properties that can be used to define the custom line.

The enumeration for DashStyle is part of the Drawing.Drawing2D namespace. Therefore, to create a new, dark blue pen that draws a dotted line, you would use code like the following:

```
Dim objMyPen As Pen
objMyPen = New Pen(Drawing.Color.DarkBlue, 3)
objMyPen.DashStyle = Drawing.Drawing2D.DashStyle.Dot
```

The 3 passed as the second argument to create the new pen defines the pen's width—in pixels.

Visual Basic includes many standard pens, which are available via the System.Drawing.Pens class, as in

```
objPen = System.Drawing.Pens.DarkBlue
```

When drawing using the techniques discussed shortly, you can use custom pens or system-defined pens—it's your choice.

Using System Colors

At some point, you might have changed your Windows theme, or perhaps you changed the image or color of your desktop. What you might not be aware of is that Windows enables you to customize the colors of almost all Windows interface elements. The colors that Windows allows you to change are called *system colors*. To change your system colors, right-click the desktop, and choose Personalize from the shortcut menu to display the Personalization page. Next, click the Window Color link to display the Window Color and Appearance dialog box shown in Figure 18.1. You can click a color on this dialog box to change the border color of windows, and if you are running Windows 7, you can click the Advanced Appearance Settings link to further customize the colors of various elements such as buttons and text boxes.

When you change a system color by using the Window Color and Appearance dialog box, all loaded applications should change their appearance to match your selection. In addition, when you start any new application, it should also match its appearance to your selection. If you had to write code to manage this behavior, you'd have to write a lot of code, and you'd be justified in avoiding the whole mess. However, making an application adjust its appearance to match the user's system color selections is actually easy, so there's no reason not to do it. For the most part, it's automatic, with controls that you add to a form.

To specify that an interface color should stay in sync with a user's system colors, you assign a system color to a color property of the item in question, as shown in Figure 18.2. If you wanted to ensure that the color of a button matches the user's system color, for example, you would assign the system color Control to the BackColor property of the Button control. Table 18.3 lists the most common system colors you can use. For a complete list, consult the online Help.

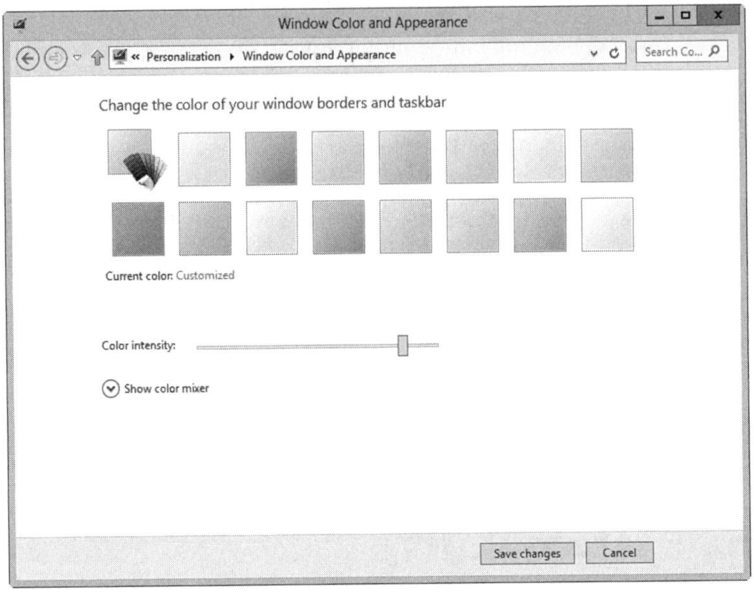

FIGURE 18.1
The Window
Color and
Appearance dia-
log box lets you
customize your
desktop colors.

FIGURE 18.2
System colors
are assigned
from within the
System pal-
ette tab.

TABLE 18.3 System Colors

Enumeration	Description
ActiveCaption	The color of the background of the active caption bar (title bar).
ActiveCaptionText	The color of the text of the active caption bar (title bar).
Control	The color of the background of push buttons and other 3D elements.
ControlDark	The color of shadows on a 3D element.

TABLE 18.3 System Colors

Enumeration	Description
ControlLight	The color of highlights on a 3D element.
ControlText	The color of the text on buttons and other 3D elements.
Desktop	The color of the Windows desktop.
GrayText	The color of the text on a user interface element when it's disabled or dimmed.
Highlight	The color of the background of highlighted text. This includes selected menu items as well as selected text.
HighlightText	The color of the foreground of highlighted text. This includes selected menu items as well as selected text.
InactiveBorder	The color of an inactive window border.
InactiveCaption	The color of the background of an inactive caption bar.
InactiveCaptionText	The color of the text of an inactive caption bar.
Menu	The color of the menu background.
MenuText	The color of the menu text.
Window	The color of the background in a window's client area.

When a user changes a system color using the Window Color and Appearance dialog box, Visual Basic automatically updates the appearance of objects that use system colors. You don't have to write a single line of code to do this. Fortunately, when you create new forms and add controls to forms, Visual Basic automatically assigns the proper system color to the appropriate properties, so you don't usually have to mess with them.

Be aware that you aren't limited to assigning system colors to their logically associated properties. You can assign system colors to any color property you want, and you can also use system colors when drawing. This enables you to draw custom interface elements that match the user's system colors, for example. Be aware, however, that if you do draw with system colors, Visual Basic doesn't update the colors automatically when the user changes system colors; you would have to redraw the elements with the new system colors. In addition, if you apply system colors to properties that aren't usually assigned system colors, you run the risk of displaying odd color combinations, such as black on black, depending on the user's color settings.

Users don't change their system colors just for aesthetic purposes. I work with a programmer who is color-blind. He's modified his system colors so that he can see things better on the screen. If you don't allow your applications to adjust to the user's color preferences, you might make using your program unnecessarily difficult, or even impossible, for someone with color blindness or visual acuity issues.

Working with Rectangles

Before learning how to draw shapes, you need to understand the concept of a rectangle as it relates to Visual Basic programming. A rectangle is a structure used to hold bounding coordinates used to draw a shape. A rectangle isn't necessarily used to draw a rectangle (although it can be). Obviously, a square can fit within a rectangle. However, so can circles and ellipses. Figure 18.3 illustrates how most shapes can be bound by a rectangle.

FIGURE 18.3
Rectangles are used to define the boundaries of most shapes.

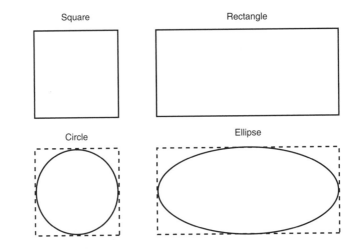

To draw most shapes, you must have a rectangle. The rectangle you pass to a drawing method is used as a bounding rectangle. The proper shape (circle, ellipse, and so on) is always drawn within the confines of the bounding rectangle. Creating a rectangle is easy. First, you dimension a variable as `Rectangle`, and then you set the X, Y, `Width`, and `Height` properties of the object variable. The X, Y value is the coordinate of the upper-left corner of the rectangle. The `Height` and `Width` properties are self-explanatory.

The following code creates a rectangle that has its upper-left corner at coordinate 0,0, has a width of 100, and height of 50. Note that this code simply defines a rectangle in code; it doesn't draw a rectangle to the screen:

```
Dim rectBounding As New Rectangle()
rectBounding.X = 0
rectBounding.Y = 0
rectBounding.Width = 100
rectBounding.Height = 50
```

The Rectangle object enables you to send the X, Y, Height, and Width values as part of its initialize construct. Using this technique, you could create the same rectangle with only a single line of code:

```
Dim rectBounding as New Rectangle(0,0,100,50)
```

You can do a number of things with a rectangle after it's defined. Perhaps the most useful is the capability to enlarge or shrink the rectangle with a single statement. You enlarge or shrink a rectangle using the Inflate() method. Here's the most common syntax of Inflate():

```
object.Inflate(changeinwidth, changeinheight)
```

When called this way, the rectangle width is enlarged (the left side of the rectangle remains in place), and the height is enlarged (the top of the rectangle stays in place). To leave the height or width unchanged, pass 0 as the appropriate argument. To shrink a side, specify a negative number.

If you're planning to do much drawing, you'll use a lot of Rectangle objects, so I strongly suggest that you learn as much about them as you can.

Drawing Shapes

Now that you've learned about the Graphics object, pens, and rectangles, you'll probably find drawing shapes to be fairly simple. You draw shapes by calling methods of a Graphics object. Most methods require a rectangle, which is used as the shape's bounding rectangle, as well as a pen. In this section, you'll learn what you need to do to draw different shapes.

> I've chosen to discuss only the most commonly drawn shapes. The Graphics object contains many methods for drawing additional shapes.

Drawing Lines

To draw lines, you use the DrawLine() method of the Graphics object. DrawLine() is one of the few drawing methods that doesn't require a rectangle. The syntax for DrawLine() is

```
object.DrawLine(pen, x1, y1, x2, y2)
```

As previously discussed, object refers to a Graphics object, and pen refers to a Pen object. x1, y1 is the coordinate of the line's starting point, whereas x2, y2 is the coordinate of the ending point; Visual Basic draws a line between the two points, using the specified pen.

Drawing Rectangles

To draw rectangles (and squares, for that matter), you use the DrawRectangle() method of a Graphics object. As you might expect, DrawRectangle() accepts a pen and a rectangle. Here's the syntax for calling DrawRectangle() in this way:

```
object.DrawRectangle(pen, rectangle)
```

If you don't have a Rectangle object (and you don't want to create one), you can call DrawRectangle() by using the following format:

```
object.DrawRectangle(pen, X, Y, width, height)
```

Drawing Circles and Ellipses

You draw circles and ellipses by calling the DrawEllipse() method. If you're familiar with geometry, you know that a circle is simply an ellipse that has the same height and width. This is why no specific method exists for drawing circles: DrawEllipse() works perfectly. Like the DrawRectangle() method, DrawEllipse() accepts a pen and a rectangle. The rectangle is used as a bounding rectangle. The width of the rectangle is the width of the ellipse, and the height of the rectangle is the height of the ellipse. DrawEllipse() has the following syntax:

```
object.DrawEllipse(pen, rectangle)
```

If you don't have a Rectangle object defined (and you don't want to create one), you can call DrawEllipse() with this syntax:

```
object.DrawEllipse(pen, X, Y, Width, Height)
```

Clearing a Drawing Surface

To clear the surface of a Graphics object, call the Clear() method, passing it the color to paint the surface like this:

```
objGraphics.Clear(Drawing.SystemColors.Control)
```

Drawing Text

Drawing text on a Graphics object is similar to drawing a shape. The method name even contains the word Draw, in contrast to Print. To draw text on a Graphics object, call the DrawString() method. The basic format for DrawString() looks like this:

```
object.DrawString(stringoftext, font, brush, topX, leftY)
```

A few of these items are probably new to you. The argument stringoftext is self-explanatory: It's the string you want to draw on the Graphics object. The topX and leftY arguments represent the coordinate at which drawing will take place; they represent the upper-left corner of the string, as illustrated in Figure 18.4.

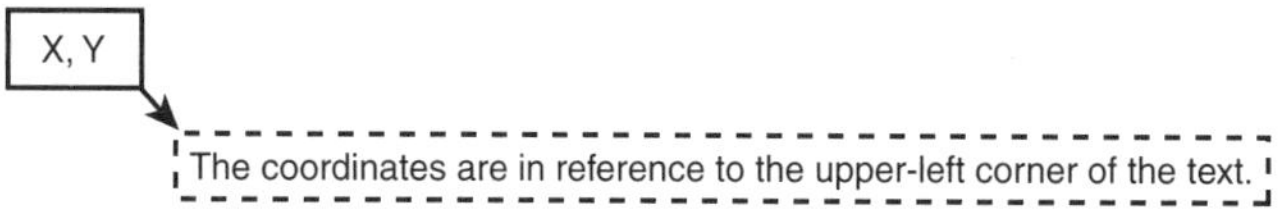

FIGURE 18.4
The coordinate specified in DrawString() represents the upper-left corner of the printed text.

The arguments brush and font aren't so obvious. Both arguments accept objects. A brush is similar to a pen, but whereas a pen describes the characteristics of a line, a brush describes the characteristics of a fill. For example, both pens and brushes have a color. But where pens have an attribute for defining a line style such as dashed or solid, a brush has an attribute for a fill pattern such as solid, hatched, weave, or trellis. When you draw text, a solid brush is usually sufficient. You can create brushes in much the same way as you create pens, or you can use one of the standard brushes available from the System.Drawing.Brushes class.

A Font object defines characteristics used to format text, including the character set (Times New Roman, Courier, and so on), size (point size), and style (bold, italic, normal, underlined, and so on). To create a new Font object, you could use code such as the following:

```
Dim objFont As Font
objFont = New System.Drawing.Font("Arial", 30)
```

The text Arial in this code is the name of a font installed on my computer. In fact, Arial is one of the few fonts installed on *all* Windows computers. If you supply the name of a font that doesn't exist on the machine at runtime, Visual Basic uses a default font that it thinks is the closest match to the font you specified. The second parameter is the point size of the text. If you want to use a style other than normal, you can provide a style value as a third parameter, like this (note the logical or, as discussed in Hour 12, "Performing Arithmetic, String Manipulation, and Date/Time Adjustments"):

```
objFont = New System.Drawing.Font("Arial Black", 30, _
                            FontStyle.Bold or FontStyle.Italic)
```

In addition to creating a Font object, you can use the font of an existing object, such as a form. For example, the following statement prints text to a Graphics object, using the font of the current form:

```
objGraphics.DrawString("This is the text that prints!", Me.Font, _
                    System.Drawing.Brushes.Azure, 0, 0)
```

Persisting Graphics on a Form

Sometimes you will find it necessary to use the techniques discussed in this hour to draw to a form. However, you might recall from earlier hours that when you draw to a form (actually, you draw to a Graphics object that references a form), the things you draw aren't persisted. The next time the form paints itself, the drawn elements disappear. If the user minimizes the form or obscures the form with another window, for example, the next time the form is painted, it will be missing all drawn elements that were obscured. You can use a couple of approaches to deal with this behavior:

- ▶ Place all code that draws to the form in the form's Paint event.

- ▶ Draw to a memory bitmap, and copy the contents of the memory bitmap to the form in the form's Paint event.

If you're drawing only a few items, placing the drawing code in the Paint event might be a good approach. However, consider a situation in which you have a lot of drawing code. Perhaps the graphics are drawn in response to user input, so you can't re-create them all at once. In these situations, the second approach is clearly better.

Building a Graphics Project Example

Now you'll build a project that uses the skills you've learned to draw to a form. In this project, you'll use the technique of drawing to a memory bitmap to persist the graphics each time the form paints itself.

By the Way

The project you're about to build is perhaps the most difficult yet. I'll explain each step of the process, but I won't spend time explaining the objects and methods that have already been discussed.

To make things interesting, I've used random numbers to determine font size as well as the X, Y coordinate of the text you'll draw to the form. By far the easiest way to create a random number in Visual Basic is to use the `System.Random` class. To generate a random number within a specific range (such as a random number between 1 and 10), you follow these steps:

1. Create a new object variable of type `System.Random`.

2. Create a new instance of the `Random` class, passing a value to be used as the seed to generate random numbers. I use `Now.Millisecond`, which causes a pseudorandom number to be used as the seed, because this value changes every millisecond and probably won't be the same across repeated runs of the application.

3. Call the `Next()` method of the `Random` class, passing it minimum and maximum values. The `Random` class returns a random number that falls within the specified range.

Start by creating a new Windows Application titled Persisting Graphics, and then follow these steps to build the project:

1. Right-click Form1.vb in the Solution Explorer and choose Rename. Change the name of the default form to **MainForm.vb**, and set the form's `Text` property to `Persisting Graphics Example`.

2. Your form's interface will consist of a text box and a button. When the user clicks the button, the contents of the text box will be drawn on the form in a random location and with a random font size. Add a new text box to your form, and set its properties as follows:

Property	Value
Name	txtInput
Location	56, 184
Size	100, 20

3. Add a new button to the form, and set its properties as follows:

Property	Value
Name	btnDrawText
Location	162, 182
Text	Draw Text

Time for the code to fly!

As mentioned earlier, all drawing will be performed through the use of a memory bitmap, which then will be copied to the form. You'll reference this bitmap in multiple places, so you'll make it a module-level variable.

4. Double-click the form to access its Load event. Then add the following statement above the Form_Load procedure declaration; do not place this in the form's Load event!

```
Private m_objDrawingSurface As Bitmap
```

5. For the bitmap variable to be used, it must reference a Bitmap object. A good place to initialize things is in the form's Load event, so put your cursor back in the Load event now, and enter the following code:

```
Randomize()
' Create a drawing surface with the same dimensions as the client
' area of the form.
m_objDrawingSurface = New Bitmap(Me.ClientRectangle.Width, _
                  Me.ClientRectangle.Height, _
                  Drawing.Imaging.PixelFormat.Format24bppRgb)
InitializeSurface()
```

Your procedure should now look like the one shown in Figure 18.5.

FIGURE 18.5
Make sure that your code appears exactly as it does here.

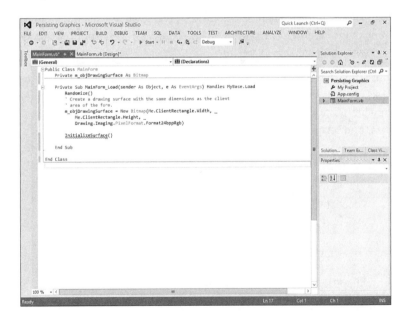

The first statement in this procedure initializes the random-number generator (you'll be using random numbers in another procedure). The next statement creates a new bitmap in memory. Because the contents of the bitmap are to be sent to the form, it makes sense to use the dimensions of the form's client area as the size of the new bitmap—which is exactly what you've done. The final statement calls a procedure that you haven't yet created.

6. Position the cursor at the end of the End Sub statement, and press Enter a few times to create a few new lines. Now you'll write code to initialize the bitmap. The code clears the bitmap to the system color Control and then draws an ellipse that has the dimensions of the bitmap. (I've added comments to the code so that you can follow along with what's happening; all the concepts in this procedure have been discussed already.) Enter the following procedure in its entirety:

```
Private Sub InitializeSurface()
    Dim objGraphics As Graphics
    Dim rectBounds As Rectangle

    ' Create a Graphics object that references the bitmap and clear it.
    objGraphics = Graphics.FromImage(m_objDrawingSurface)
    objGraphics.Clear(System.Drawing.SystemColors.Control)

    ' Create a rectangle the same size as the bitmap.
    rectBounds = New Rectangle(0, 0, m_objDrawingSurface.Width, _
                               m_objDrawingSurface.Height)
    ' Reduce the rectangle slightly so the ellipse won't appear on the
    ' border.
    rectBounds.Inflate(-1, -1)

    ' Draw an ellipse that fills the form.
    objGraphics.DrawEllipse(System.Drawing.Pens.Orange, rectBounds)
End Sub
```

Your procedure should now look like the one shown in Figure 18.6.

If you run your project now, you'll find that nothing is drawn to the form. The drawing is being done to a bitmap in memory, and you haven't yet added the code to copy the bitmap to the form. The place to do this is in the form's Paint event so that the contents of the bitmap are sent to the form every time the form paints itself. This ensures that the items you draw always appear on the form.

7. Create an event handler for the form's Paint event. First, choose MainForm Events from the object drop-down list in the upper-left corner of the code editor. Then select Paint from the event drop-down list in the upper-right corner. Add the following code to the Paint event:

```
Dim objGraphics As Graphics
' You can't modify e.Graphics directly.
objGraphics = e.Graphics
' Draw the contents of the bitmap on the form.
objGraphics.DrawImage(m_objDrawingSurface, 0, 0, _
                      m_objDrawingSurface.Width, _
                      m_objDrawingSurface.Height)
```

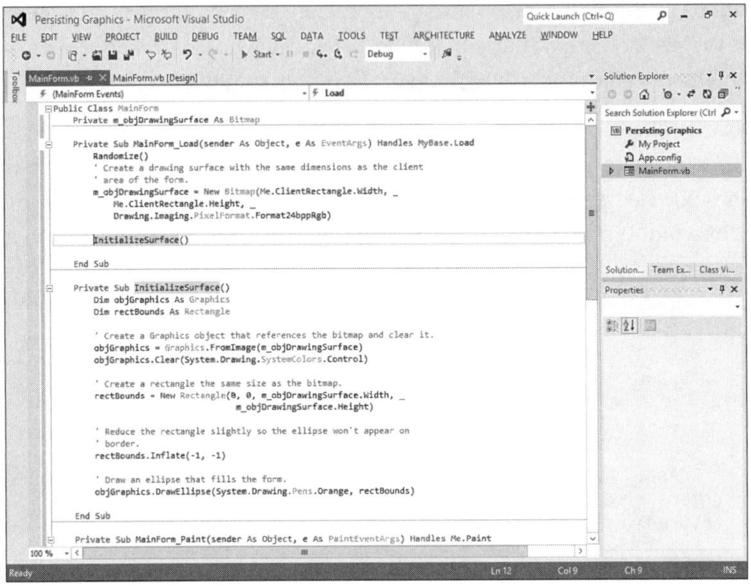

FIGURE 18.6
Verify that your
code is entered
correctly.

The e parameter of the `Paint` event has a property that references the form's `Graphics` object. You can't modify the `Graphics` object by using the e parameter, however, because it's read-only. This is why you've created a new `Graphics` object to work with and then set the object to reference the form's `Graphics` object. The method `DrawImage()` draws the image in a bitmap to the surface of a `Graphics` object, so the last statement simply sends the contents of the bitmap that exists in memory to the form.

If you run the project now, you'll find that the ellipse appears on the form. Furthermore, you can cover the form with another window, or even minimize it, and the ellipse will always appear on the form when it's displayed again—the graphics persist.

8. The last thing you'll do is write code that draws the contents entered into the text box on the form. The text will be drawn with a random size and location. Return to the Form Designer, and double-click the button to access its `Click` event. Add the following code:

```
Dim objGraphics As Graphics
Dim objFont As Font
Dim intFontSize As Integer
Dim intTextX As Integer
Dim intTextY As Integer
Dim objRandom As System.Random

' If no text has been entered, get out.
```

```
If txtInput.Text .Length = 0 Then Exit Sub

' Create a graphics object using the memory bitmap.
objGraphics = Graphics.FromImage(m_objDrawingSurface)

' Initialize the Random object.
objRandom = New Random(Now.Millisecond)

' Create a random number for the font size. Keep it bet
intFontSize = objRandom.Next(8, 48)
' Create a random number for X coordinate of the text.
intTextX = objRandom.Next(0, Me.ClientRectangle.Width
' Create a random number for Y coordinate of the text.
intTextY = objRandom.Next(0, Me.ClientRectangle.Height - 20)
' Create a new font object.
objFont = New System.Drawing.Font("Arial", intFontSize, _
                              FontStyle.Bold Or FontStyle.Italic)
' Draw the user's text.
objGraphics.DrawString(txtInput.Text, objFont, _
                    System.Drawing.Brushes.Red, intTextX, intTextY)
' Clean up.
objGraphics.Dispose()
' Force the form to paint itself. This triggers the Paint event.
Me.Invalidate()
```

The comments I've included should make the code self-explanatory. However, the last statement bears discussing. The Invalidate() method of a form invalidates the client rectangle. This operation tells Windows that the form's appearance is no longer accurate and that the form needs to be repainted. This, in turn, triggers the form's Paint event. Because the Paint event contains the code that copies the contents of the memory bitmap to the form, invalidating the form causes the text to appear. If you don't call Invalidate() here, the text doesn't appear on the form (but it is still drawn on the memory bitmap).

> If you draw elements that are based on the form's size, you need to call Invalidate() in the form's Resize event; resizing a form doesn't trigger the form's Paint event.

By the Way

Your project is now complete! Click Save All on the toolbar to save your work, and then press F5 to run the project. You'll notice immediately that the ellipse is drawn on the form. Type something into the text box and click the button. Click it again.

ach time you click the button, the text is drawn on the form by the same brush, but with a different size and location, as shown in Figure 18.7.

Summary

You won't need to add drawing capabilities to every project you create. However, when you need the capabilities, *you need the capabilities*. In this hour, you learned the basic skills for drawing to a graphics surface, which can be a form, control, memory bitmap, or one of many other types of surfaces. You learned that all drawing is done with a Graphics object. You now know how to create a Graphics object for a form or control, and even how to create a Graphics object for a bitmap that exists in memory.

Most drawing methods require a pen and a rectangle, and you can now create rectangles and pens using the techniques you learned in this hour. After learning about pens and rectangles, you've found that the drawing methods themselves are pretty easy to use. Even drawing text is simple when you have a Graphics object to work with.

Persisting graphics on a form can be a bit complicated, and I suspect this will confuse many new Visual Basic programmers who try to figure it out on their own. However, you've now built an example that persists graphics on a form, and you'll be able to leverage the techniques involved when you have to do this in your own projects.

I don't expect you to be able to sit down for an hour and create an Adobe Photoshop knockoff. However, you now have a solid foundation on which to build. If you want to attempt a project that performs a lot of drawing, dig deeper into the Graphics object.

Q&A

Q. *What if I need to draw a lot of lines, one starting where another ends? Do I need to call* `DrawLine()` *for each line?*

A. The `Graphics` object has a method called `DrawLines()`, which accepts a series of points. The method draws lines connecting the sequence of points.

Q. *Is there a way to fill a shape?*

A. The `Graphics` object includes methods that draw filled shapes, such as `FillEllipse()` and `FillRectangle()`.

Workshop

Quiz

1. What object is used to draw to a surface?

2. To set a `Graphics` object to draw to a form directly, you call what method of the form?

3. What object defines the characteristics of a line? A fill pattern?

4. How do you make a color property adjust with the user's Windows settings?

5. What object is used to define the boundaries of a shape to be drawn?

6. What method do you call to draw an ellipse? A circle?

7. What method do you call to print text on a graphics surface?

8. To ensure that graphics persist on a form, they must be drawn on the form in what event?

Answers

1. The `Graphics` object

2. The `CreateGraphics()` method

3. Lines are defined by `Pen` objects; fill characteristics are defined by `Brush` objects.

4. Use System Colors.

5. A Rectangle object

6. Both shapes are drawn with the DrawEllipse() method.

7. The DrawString() method

8. The form's Paint event

Exercises

1. Modify the example in this hour to use a font other than Arial. If you're not sure what fonts are installed on your computer, click the Start menu and choose Settings, Control Panel. Click the Appearance and Personalization link, and you'll find a link to the system fonts.

2. Create a project that draws an ellipse that fills the form, much like the one you created in this hour. However, draw the ellipse directly to the form in the Paint event. Make sure that the ellipse is redrawn when the form is sized. (Hint: Invalidate the form in the form's Resize() event.)

HOUR 19

Performing File Operations

What You'll Learn in This Hour:

▶ Using the OpenFileDialog and SaveFileDialog controls

▶ Manipulating files with System.IO.File

▶ Manipulating directories with System.IO.Directory

It's difficult to imagine any application other than a tiny utility program that doesn't use the file system. In this hour, you'll learn how to use controls to make it easy for a user to browse and select files. In addition, you'll learn how to use the System.IO.File and System.IO.Directory objects to manipulate the file system more easily than you might think. Using these objects, you can delete files and directories, move them, rename them, and more. These objects are powerful, so remember: Play nice!

Using the OpenFileDialog and SaveFileDialog Controls

In Hour 1, "Jumping in with Both Feet: A Visual Basic 2012 Programming Tour," you used the OpenFileDialog control to enable a user to browse for pictures to display in your Picture Viewer program. In this section, you'll move beyond those basics to learn important details about working with the OpenFileDialog, as well as its sister control, the SaveFileDialog.

You'll build a project to illustrate most of the file-manipulation concepts discussed in this hour. Begin by creating a new Windows application called Manipulating Files, and then follow these steps:

1. Right-click Form1.vb in the Solution Explorer, choose Rename, and change the name of the default form to **MainForm.vb**. Next, set the form's Text property to Manipulating Files.

2. Add a new text box to the form, and set its properties as shown in the following table:

Property	Value
Name	txtSource
Location	95, 8
Size	184, 20

Using the `OpenFileDialog` Control

The `OpenFileDialog` control is used to display a dialog box that enables the user to browse and select a file, as shown in Figure 19.1. It's important to note that usually the `OpenFileDialog` doesn't actually open a file, but it enables a user to select a file so that it can be opened by code within the application.

Add a new `OpenFileDialog` control to your project now by double-clicking the `OpenFileDialog` item in the toolbox. The `OpenFileDialog` doesn't have an interface per se, so it appears in the area below the form rather than on it, as shown in Figure 19.2. For the user to browse for files, you have to manipulate the `OpenFileDialog`, using its properties and methods.

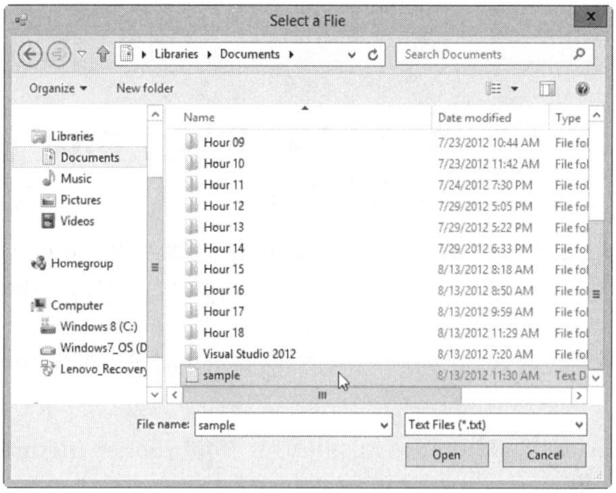

FIGURE 19.1
The `OpenFileDialog` control is used to browse for a file.

You'll add a button to the form that, when clicked, enables a user to locate and select a file. If the user selects a file, the filename is placed in the text box you've created.

1. Add a button to the form, and set its properties as follows:

Property	Value
Name	btnOpenFile
Location	9, 6
Size	80, 23
Text	Source:

2. Double-click the button, and add the following code to its Click event:

```
OpenFileDialog1.InitialDirectory = "C:\"
OpenFileDialog1.Title = "Select a File"
OpenFileDialog1.FileName = ""
```

The first statement specifies the directory to display when the dialog box is first shown. If you don't specify a directory for the InitialDirectory property, the active system directory is used (for example, the last directory browsed to with a different Open File dialog box).

> I have you start in the root of the C: drive for consistency, but be aware that if you are using Windows 8, you will have to use a different folder—such as Documents, because Windows 8 won't allow you to modify files in the root.

The Title property of the OpenFileDialog determines the text displayed in the title bar of the Open File dialog box. If you don't specify text for the Title property, Visual Basic displays the word Open in the title bar.

The FileName property is used to return the name of the chosen file. If you don't set this to an empty string before showing the Open File dialog box, the name of the control is used by default—not a desirable result.

Creating File Filters

Different types of files have different extensions. The Filter property determines what types of files appear in the Open File dialog box (refer to Figure 19.1). A filter is specified in the following format:

```
Description¦*.extension
```

The text that appears before the pipe symbol (|) describes the file type on which to filter, whereas the text after the pipe symbol is the pattern used to filter files. For example, to display only Windows bitmap files, you could use a filter such as the following:

```
control.Filter = "Windows Bitmaps¦*.bmp"
```

You can specify more than one filter type. To do so, add a pipe symbol between the filters, like this:

```
control.Filter = "Windows Bitmaps¦*.bmp¦JPEG Files¦*.jpg"
```

You want to restrict your Open File dialog box to show only text files, so enter this statement in your procedure:

```
OpenFileDialog1.Filter = "Text Files (*.txt)¦*.txt"
```

When you have more than one filter, you can specify which filter appears selected by default by using the FilterIndex property. Although you've specified only one filter type in this example, it's still a good idea to designate the default filter, so add this statement to your procedure:

```
OpenFileDialog1.FilterIndex = 1
```

By the Way

> Unlike most other collections, the FilterIndex property is 1-based, not 0-based, so 1 is the first filter listed.

Showing the Open File Dialog Box

Finally, you need to show the Open File dialog box and take action based on whether the user selects a file. The `ShowDialog()` method of the `OpenFileDialog` control acts much like the method of forms by the same name, returning a result that indicates the user's selection in the dialog box.

Enter the following statements into your procedure:

```
If OpenFileDialog1.ShowDialog() <> Windows.Forms.DialogResult.Cancel Then
    txtSource.Text = OpenFileDialog1.FileName
Else
    txtSource.Text = ""
End If
```

This code just places the selected filename into the text box `txtSource`. If the user clicks Cancel, the contents of the text box are cleared.

Press F5 to run the project, and click the button. You get the same dialog box shown earlier in Figure 19.1 (with different files and directories, of course). Select a text file and click Open. Visual Basic places the name of the file into the text box.

By default, the `OpenFileDialog` doesn't let the user enter a filename that doesn't exist. You can override this behavior by setting the `CheckFileExists` property of the `OpenFileDialog` to `False`.	**Did you Know?**

The `OpenFileDialog` control can allow the user to select multiple files. It's rare that you need to do this (I don't recall ever needing this capability in one of my projects), so I won't go into the details here. If you're interested, take a look at the `Multiselect` property of the `OpenFileDialog` in the Help text.	**By the Way**

The `OpenFileDialog` control makes allowing a user to browse and select a file almost trivial. Without this component, you would have to write an astounding amount of difficult code and probably still wouldn't come up with all the functionality supported by this control.

Using the `SaveFileDialog` Control

The `SaveFileDialog` control is similar to the `OpenFileDialog` control, but it's used to allow a user to browse directories and specify a file to save, rather than open. Again, it's important to note that the `SaveFileDialog` control doesn't actually save a file; it's used to allow a user to specify a filename to save. You have to write code to do something with the filename returned by the control.

You'll use the `SaveFileDialog` control to let the user specify a filename. This file-name will be the target of various file operations that you'll learn about later in this hour. Follow these steps to create the Save File dialog box:

1. Create a new text box on your form, and set its properties as follows:

Property	Value
Name	txtDestination
Location	95, 34
Size	184, 20

2. Now you'll create a button that, when clicked, enables the user to specify a file-name by which to save a file. Add a new button to the form, and set its proper-ties as shown in the following table:

Property	Value
Name	btnSaveFile
Location	9, 31
Size	80, 23
Text	Destination:

3. Of course, none of this will work unless you add a Save File dialog box. Double-click the SaveFileDialog item in the toolbox to add a new control to the project.

4. Double-click the new button you just created (`btnSaveFile`), and add the fol-lowing code to its `Click` event:

   ```
   SaveFileDialog1.Title = "Specify Destination Filename"
   SaveFileDialog1.Filter = "Text Files (*.txt)¦*.txt"
   SaveFileDialog1.FilterIndex = 1

   SaveFileDialog1.OverwritePrompt = True
   ```

   The first three statements set properties identical to those of the `OpenFileDialog`. The `OverwritePrompt` property, however, is unique to the `SaveFileDialog`. When this property is set to `True`, Visual Basic asks users to confirm their selections when they choose a file that already exists, as shown in Figure 19.3. I highly recommend that you prompt the user about replacing files by ensuring that the `OverwritePrompt` property is set to `True`.

By the Way

If you want the Save File dialog box to prompt users when the file they specify *doesn't* exist, set the `CreatePrompt` property of the `SaveFileDialog` control to `True`.

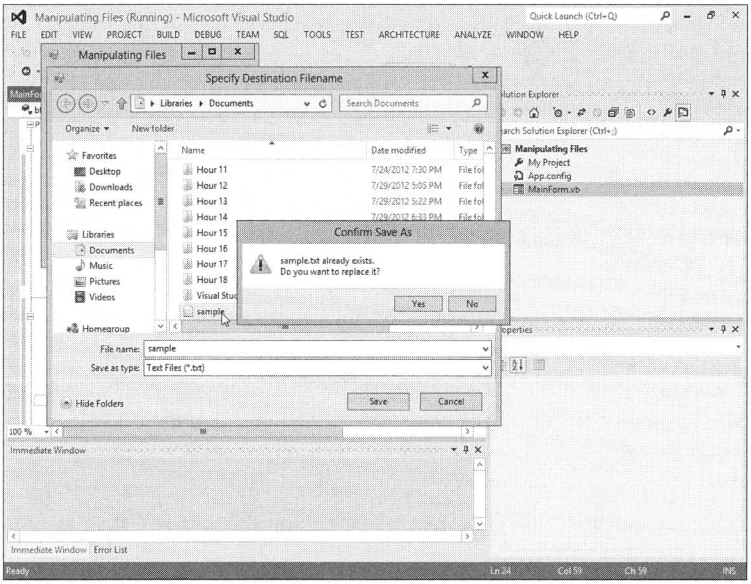

FIGURE 19.3
It's a good idea
to get confirma-
tion before
replacing an
existing file.

5. The last bit of code you need to add places the selected filename in the
`txtDestination` text box. Enter the code as shown here:

```
If SaveFileDialog1.ShowDialog() <> Windows.Forms.DialogResult.Cancel Then
    txtDestination.Text = SaveFileDialog1.FileName
End If
```

Press F5 to run the project, and then click each of the buttons and select a file.
When you're satisfied that your selections are being sent to the appropriate text
box, stop the project and save your work. If your selected filenames aren't being
sent to the proper text box, compare your code against the code I've provided.

The `OpenFileDialog` and `SaveFileDialog` controls are similar in design and
appearance, but each serves a specific purpose. You'll be using the interface you've
just created throughout the rest of this hour.

Manipulating Files with the `File` Object

Visual Basic includes a powerful namespace called `System.IO` (the `IO` object acts like
an object property of the `System` namespace). Using various properties, methods, and
object properties of `System.IO`, you can do just about anything you can imagine with
the file system. In particular, the `System.IO.File` and `System.IO.Directory` objects
provide you with extensive file and directory (folder) manipulation capabilities.

In the following sections, you'll continue to expand the project you've created. You'll
write code that manipulates the selected filenames by using the `OpenFileDialog` and
`SaveFileDialog` controls.

> The code you're about to write in the following sections is "the real thing." For example, the code for deleting a file really does delete a file. Don't forget this as you test your project; the files selected as the source and destination *will* be affected by your actions. I provide the cannon, and it's up to you not to shoot yourself with it.

Determining Whether a File Exists

Before attempting any operation on a file, such as copying or deleting it, it's a good idea to make certain the file exists. For example, if the user doesn't click the Source button to select a file but instead types the name and path of a file into the text box, the user could type an invalid or nonexistent filename. Attempting to manipulate a nonexistent file could result in an exception—which you don't want to happen. Because you'll work with the source file selected by the user in many routines, you need to create a central function that can be called to determine whether the source file exists. The function uses the `Exists()` method of the `System.IO.File` object to determine whether the file exists.

Add the following function to your form class:

```
Private Function DoesSourceFileExist() As Boolean
    If Not (System.IO.File.Exists(txtSource.Text)) Then
        MessageBox.Show("The source file does not exist!")
        Return False
    Else
        Return True
    End If
End Function
```

The `DoesSourceFileExist()` method looks at the filename specified in the text box. If the file exists, `DoesSourceFileExist()` returns `True`; otherwise, it returns `False`.

Copying a File

Copying files is a common task. For example, you might want to create an application that backs up important data files by copying them to another location. For the most part, copying is pretty safe—as long as you use a destination filename that doesn't already exist. To copy files, you use the `Copy()` method of the `System.IO.File` class.

Now you'll add a button to your form. When the user clicks this button, the file specified in the source text box is copied to a new file with the name given in the destination text box. Follow these steps to create the copy functionality:

1. Add a button to your form, and set its properties as shown in the following table:

Property	Value
Name	btnCopyFile
Location	95, 71
Size	75, 23
Text	Copy

2. Double-click the Copy button, and add the following code:

```
If Not Does(SourceFileExist()) Then Exit Sub

System.IO.File.Copy(txtSource.Text, txtDestination.Text)
MessageBox.Show("The file has been successfully copied.")
```

The Copy() method has two arguments. The first is the file that you want to copy, and the second is the name and path of the new copy of the file. In this example, you're using the filenames selected in the two text boxes.

Press F5 to run the project, and test your copy code by following these steps:

1. Click the Source button and select a text file.

2. Click the Destination button to display the Save File dialog box. Don't select an existing file. Instead, type a new filename into the File Name text box and click Save. If you're asked whether you want to replace a file, click No and change your filename; don't use the name of an existing file.

3. Click Copy to copy the file.

After you see the message box telling you the file was copied, you can use Explorer to locate the new file and open it. Stop the project and save your work before continuing.

Moving a File

When you move a file, it's taken out of its current directory and placed in a new one. You can specify a new name for the file or use its original name. You use the Move() method of the System.IO.File object to move a file. Follow the steps listed next to create a button on your form that moves the selected source file to the path and the filename selected as the destination.

Did you Know?

I recommend that you use Notepad to create a text file, and use this temporary text file when testing from this point forward. This code, as well as the rest of the examples presented in this hour, can permanently alter or destroy a file.

1. Add a new button to the form, and set its properties as follows:

Property	Value
Name	btnMove
Location	95, 100
Size	75, 23
Text	Move

2. Double-click the Move button, and add the following code to its Click event:

```
If Not (DoesSourceFileExist()) Then Exit Sub

System.IO.File.Move(txtSource.Text, txtDestination.Text)
MessageBox.Show("The file has been successfully moved.")
```

Go ahead and press F5 to test your project. Select a file to move (again, I recommend that you create a dummy file in Notepad) and supply a destination filename. When you click Move, the file is moved to the new location and given the new name. Remember, if you specify a filename for the destination that isn't the same as that of the source, the file is given the new name when it's moved.

Renaming a File

When you rename a file, it remains in the same directory, and nothing happens to its contents—the name is just changed to something else. Because the original file isn't altered, renaming a file isn't as risky as performing an action such as deleting it. Nevertheless, it's frustrating trying to determine what happened to a file when it was mistakenly renamed. To rename a file, use the Move() method of System.IO.File, specifying a new filename but keeping the same path.

Deleting a File

Deleting a file can be a risky proposition. The Delete() method of System.IO.File deletes a file permanently—*it does not send the file to the Recycle Bin*. For this reason, take great care when deleting files. First and foremost, this means testing your code. When you write a routine to delete a file, be sure to test it under many conditions. For example, if you reference the wrong text box in this code, you would inadvertently delete the wrong file! Users aren't forgiving of such mistakes.

Follow these steps to add a button to your project that deletes the source file when clicked. Remember: Be careful when testing this code.

1. Add a button to the form, and set its properties as follows:

Property	Value
Name	btnDelete
Location	95, 129
Size	75, 23
Text	Delete

2. Double-click the button, and add the following code to its `Click` event:

```
If Not (SourceFileExists()) Then Exit Sub

If MessageBox.Show("Are you sure you want to delete the source file?", _
        "MyApp", MessageBoxButtons.YesNo , MessageBoxIcon.Question) = _
        Windows.Forms.DialogResult.Yes Then
    System.IO.File.Delete(txtSource.Text)
    MessageBox.Show("The file has been successfully deleted.")
End If
```

Notice that you've included a message box to confirm the user's intentions. It's a good idea to do this *whenever* you're about to perform a serious action that can't be undone. In fact, the more information you can give the user, the better. For example, I suggest that if this was production code (code meant for end users), you should include the name of the file in the message box so that the user knows *without a doubt* what the program intends to do. If you're feeling brave, press F5 to run the project, and then select a file and delete it.

Instead of permanently deleting a file, you can send it to the Recycle Bin by using the My object like this:

```
My.Computer.FileSystem.DeleteFile("C:\test.txt", _
    FileIO.UIOption.AllDialogs, FileIO.RecycleOption.SendToRecycleBin)
```

Did you Know?

Retrieving a File's Properties

Although many people don't realize it, files have a number of properties, such as the date the file was last modified. The easiest way to see these properties is to use the Explorer. View the attributes of a file now by starting the Explorer, right-clicking any file displayed in the Explorer, and choosing Properties. Explorer shows the File Properties window, with information about the file (see Figure 19.4).

The `System.IO.File` object provides ways to get at most of the data displayed on the General tab of the File Properties dialog box, shown in Figure 19.4. Some of this data is available directly from the `File` object, whereas the `FileAttributes` object is used to access other data.

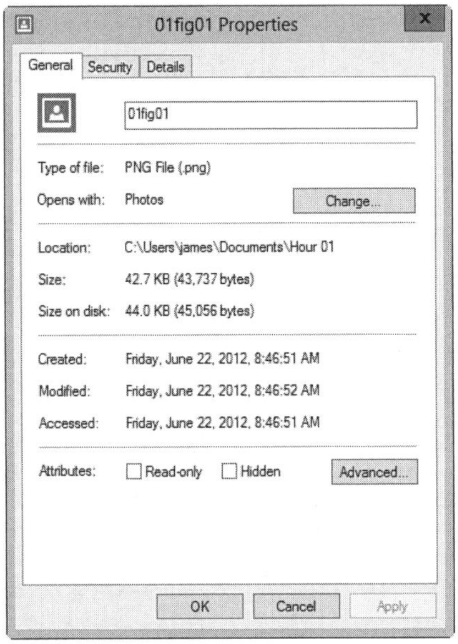

FIGURE 19.4
Visual Basic
provides a
means to easily
obtain most file
properties.

Getting Date and Time Information About a File

Getting the date the file was created, the last date it was accessed, and the last date it was modified is easy. The `System.IO.File` object supports a method for each of these dates. Table 19.1 lists the applicable methods and what they return.

TABLE 19.1   File Object Methods to Retrieve Data Information

Property	Description
GetCreationTime	Returns the date and time the file was created.
GetLastAccessTime	Returns the date and time the file was last accessed.
GetLastWriteTime	Returns the date and time the file was last modified.

Getting a File's Attributes

A file's attributes (see the bottom of the dialog box shown in Figure 19.4) aren't available as properties of the `System.IO.File` object. How you determine an attribute is complicated. The `GetAttributes()` method of `System.IO.File` returns a Long. This Long, in turn, acts as a set of flags for the various attributes. The method used to store these values is called *bit packing*. Bit packing is pretty complicated and has to do with the binary method in which values are stored in memory and on disk. Teaching bit packing is beyond the scope of this book. What I want to show you is how to determine whether a certain flag is set in a value that is bit-packed.

The first step in determining the attributes is to get the Long containing the flags for the file attributes. To do this, you would create a Long variable and call GetAttributes(), like this:

```
Dim lngAttributes As Long
lngAttributes = System.IO.File.GetAttributes("c:\test.txt")
```

or use the short form, like this:

```
Dim lngAttributes As Long = System.IO.File.GetAttributes("c:\test.txt")
```

After you retrieve the file attributes flag into the variable lngAttributes, perform a logical And on lngAttributes with one of the flags shown in Table 19.2 to determine whether a particular attribute is set. This is sometimes called "Anding" a variable. For example, to determine whether a file's ReadOnly flag is set, you would use a statement like this:

```
lngAttributes And IO.FileAttributes.ReadOnly
```

TABLE 19.2   Common File Attribute Flags

Attribute	Meaning
Archive	The file's archive status. Applications use this attribute to mark files for backup and removal.
Directory	The file is a directory.
Hidden	The file is hidden and therefore isn't included in an ordinary directory listing.
Normal	The file is normal and has no other attributes set.
ReadOnly	The file is a read-only file.
System	The file is part of the operating system or is used exclusively by the operating system.
Temporary	The file is a temporary file.

When you logically And a flag value with a variable, you get True if the variable contains the flag and False otherwise.

Writing Code to Retrieve a File's Properties

Now that you know how to retrieve an object's properties, you'll modify your Picture Viewer project so that the user can view file properties of a picture file he or she has displayed. Start by opening the Picture Viewer project you last modified in Hour 15, "Debugging Your Code," and then follow these steps to add the file attributes functionality:

1. Add a new tool button to the Toolstrip (the toolbar) of the ViewerForm.vb form, and set its name to tbbGetFileAttributes.

2. If you have downloaded the sample code, set the image to Properties.png. Next, set the `ToolTipText` property to `Get File Attributes`.

The code you enter into the `Click` event of this button is a bit longer than most of the code you've entered so far. Therefore, I'll show the code in its entirety and then explain what it does.

3. Double-click the new toolbar button, and add the following code to the button's `Click` event:

```
Dim strProperties As String
Dim lngAttributes As Long

If ofdSelectPicture.FileName = "" Then Exit Sub

' Get the dates.
strProperties = "Created: " & _
    System.IO.File.GetCreationTime(ofdSelectPicture.FileName)

strProperties = strProperties & vbCrLf
strProperties = strProperties & "Accessed: " & _
    System.IO.File.GetLastAccessTime(ofdSelectPicture.FileName)
strProperties = strProperties & vbCrLf
strProperties = strProperties & "Modified: " & _
    System.IO.File.GetLastWriteTime(ofdSelectPicture.FileName)

' Get the file attributes.
lngAttributes = System.IO.File.GetAttributes(ofdSelectPicture.FileName)

' Use a binary AND to extract the specific attributes.
strProperties = strProperties & vbCrLf
strProperties = strProperties & "Normal: " & _
    CBool(lngAttributes And IO.FileAttributes.Normal)

strProperties = strProperties & vbCrLf
strProperties = strProperties & "Hidden: " & _
    CBool(lngAttributes And IO.FileAttributes.Hidden)

strProperties = strProperties & vbCrLf
strProperties = strProperties & "ReadOnly: " & _
    CBool(lngAttributes And IO.FileAttributes.ReadOnly)

strProperties = strProperties & vbCrLf
strProperties = strProperties & "System: " & _
    CBool(lngAttributes And IO.FileAttributes.System)

strProperties = strProperties & vbCrLf
strProperties = strProperties & "Temporary File: " & _
    CBool(lngAttributes And IO.FileAttributes.Temporary)

strProperties = strProperties & vbCrLf
strProperties = strProperties & "Archive: " & _
    CBool(lngAttributes And IO.FileAttributes.Archive)

MessageBox.Show(strProperties, "Picture Viewer")
```

Did you Know?

A quick way to determine a file's size is to use the built-in Visual Basic function `FileLen()`, as in `lngFileSize = FileLen("c:\temp\test.txt")`.

The first thing this procedure does is see whether the user is viewing a file. The place to look is the `OpenFileDialog` control because that is where the filename was obtained from the user. If the `OpenFileDialog` control has no filename, the user hasn't viewed a file yet.

All the file's various properties are concatenated with the `strProperties` variable. The system constant `vbCrLf` denotes a carriage return and a line feed, and concatenating this into the string ensures that each property appears on its own line.

The first set of statements simply calls the `GetCreateTime()`, `GetLastAccessTime()`, and `GetLastWriteTime()` methods to get the values of the date-related properties. Next, the attributes are placed in a variable by way of the `GetAttributes()` method, and the state of each attribute is determined. The `CBool()` functions are used so that the words `True` and `False` appear, rather than the numeric results of the And operations.

Press F5 to run the project, open a picture file to display it, and then click the Get File Attributes button on the toolbar. If you entered the code exactly as shown, the attributes of the image file should appear in the text box as they do in Figure 19.5.

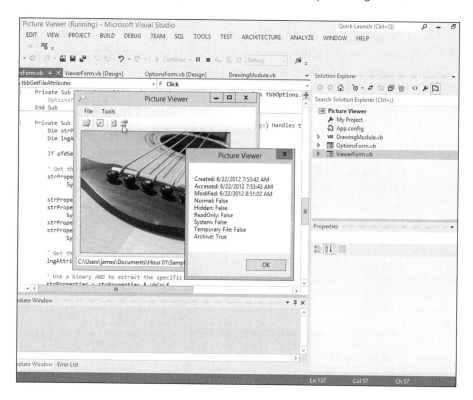

FIGURE 19.5
The `System. IO.File` object enables you to look at a file's properties.

Manipulating Directories with the Directory Object

Manipulating directories (folders) is similar to manipulating files. However, instead of using `System.IO.File`, you use `System.IO.Directory`. If any of these method calls confuse you, refer to the previous section on `System.IO.File` for more detailed information. The following are the method calls:

▶ To create a directory, call the `CreateDirectory()` method of `System.IO.Directory`, and pass the name of the new folder, like this:

```
System.IO.Directory.CreateDirectory("c:\my new directory")
```

▶ To determine whether a directory exists, call the `Exists()` method of `System.IO.Directory` and pass it the directory name in question, like this:

```
MsgBox(System.IO.Directory.Exists("c:\temp"))
```

▶ To move a directory, call the `Move()` method of `System.IO.Directory`. The `Move()` method takes two arguments. The first is the current name of the directory, and the second is the new name and path of the directory. When you move a directory, its contents are moved as well. The following illustrates a call to `Move()`:

```
System.IO.Directory.Move("c:\current directory name", _
        "c:\new directory name")
```

▶ Deleting directories is even more perilous than deleting files because when you delete a directory, you also delete all files and subdirectories within the directory. To delete a directory, call the `Delete()` method of `System.IO.Directory`, and pass it the directory to delete. *I can't overstate that you have to be careful when calling this method;* it can get you in a lot of trouble. The following statement illustrates deleting a directory:

```
System.IO.Directory.Delete("c:\temp")
```

Did you Know?

To send a directory to the Recycle Bin, rather than permanently delete it, use the My object like this:

```
My.Computer.FileSystem.DeleteDirectory("D:\OldDir", _
    FileIO.UIOption.AllDialogs, FileIO.RecycleOption.SendToRecycleBin, _
    FileIO.UICancelOption.ThrowException)
```

Summary

The `OpenFileDialog` and `SaveFileDialog` controls, coupled with `System.IO`, enable you to do many powerful things with a user's file system. In this hour, you learned how to let a user browse and select a file for opening and how to let a user browse and select a file for saving. Determining a user's file selection is only the first part of the process, however. You also learned how to manipulate files and directories, including renaming, moving, and deleting, by using `System.IO`. Finally, you learned how to retrieve a file's properties and attributes.

With the techniques shown in this hour, you should be able to do most of what you'll need to do with files and directories. None of this material is difficult, but don't be fooled by the simplicity; use care whenever manipulating a user's file system.

Q&A

Q. *What if I want to perform an operation on a file, but something is preventing the operation, such as the file being open or me lacking rights to the file?*

A. All the method calls have one or more exceptions that can be thrown if the method fails. These method calls are listed in the online Help. You can use the techniques discussed in Hour 15 to trap the exceptions.

Q. *What if the user types a filename into one of the file dialog boxes but doesn't include the extension?*

A. By default, both file dialog controls have their `AddExtension` properties set to `True`. When this property is set to `True`, Visual Basic automatically appends the extension of the currently selected filter.

Workshop

Quiz

1. True or false: The Open File dialog box automatically opens a file.

2. What symbol is used to separate a filter description from its extension?

3. What object is used to manipulate files?

4. What arguments does `System.IO.File.Copy()` expect?

5. How would you rename a file?

6. True or false: Files deleted with `System.IO.File.Delete()` are sent to the Recycle Bin.

7. What object is used to manipulate folders?

Answers

1. False

2. The pipe symbol (|)

3. `System.IO`

4. The name and path of the source file and a name and path for the copy

5. Use the `Move()` method while retaining the path.

6. False. The files are permanently deleted.

7. `System.IO.Directory`

Exercises

1. Create a project that enables the user to select a file with the `OpenFileDialog` control. Store the filename in a text box. Provide another button that, when clicked, creates a backup of the file by making a copy of it with the extension `.bak`.

2. Create a project with a text box on a form in which the user can type in a three-character file extension. Include a button that shows an Open File dialog box when clicked, with the filter set to the extension that the user entered.

Working with the Registry and Text Files

What You'll Learn in This Hour:

▶ Using My.Computer.Registry to create and delete Registry keys and values

▶ Using a StreamWriter object to open, read, and edit text files

▶ Modifying your Picture Viewer program to use a text file and the Registry

Text files have been around since the early days of computing, and even today they are useful for storing data. For robust applications, a database is the way to go, but for storing simple sets of data, it doesn't get much easier than using a text file. In the first edition of this book, I neglected to cover working with text files, thinking that most users were moving to databases. After many emails from readers, I got the point: Text files are still used regularly, and they aren't going anywhere. This hour teaches you the basics of creating, opening, reading, and editing text files.

Another common method of storing data—particularly user settings and program configuration options—is the Windows Registry. The Registry is a database-like storage entity in Windows that resembles a tree with nodes. Accessing the Registry is fast, is handled through a consistent interface, and is often preferred over the old method of using INI text files. In this hour, you'll learn how to store data in and get data from the Windows Registry.

Working with the Registry

The Windows Registry is a repository used to store application, user, and machine-specific information. It's the perfect place to store configuration data such as user preferences, database connection strings, file locations, and more.

Don't pollute the Registry! I'm constantly amazed by the amount of junk that a program will store in the Registry. Keep in mind that the Registry is not your personal database. In fact, if your application uses a database, it's often a better idea to store information in the database.

Understanding the Structure of the Windows Registry

The Registry is organized in a hierarchical structure—like a tree. The top nodes in the tree (called *hives*) are predefined—you can't add to, modify, or delete them. Table 20.1 lists the hives (top levels) of the Registry.

TABLE 20.1   Top Nodes of the Windows Registry

Node	Description
HKEY_CLASSES_ROOT	Contains information that associates file types with programs and configuration data for COM components.
HKEY_CURRENT_USER	Contains configuration information for the user currently logged on to Windows.
HKEY_LOCAL_MACHINE	Contains configuration information specific to the computer, regardless of the user logged in.
HKEY_USERS	Contains all user profiles on the computer. When a user logs in, HKEY_CURRENT_USER is set as an alias to a specific user in HKEY_USERS.
HKEY_CURRENT_CONFIG	Contains information about the hardware profile used by the local computer during startup.

Under each hive listed in Table 20.1 are a number of keys. Figure 20.1 shows what the Registry looks like on my computer. Notice how NETFramework is a subkey that belongs to the Microsoft key, which is a subkey that belongs to the Software key, which belongs to the HKEY_LOCAL_MACHINE hive. Note that while you can't see the higher levels in the tree, you can see the entire path in the status bar.

Keys can contain one or more values. In Figure 20.1, notice that the NETFramework key has many values (they appear in the list view on the right). Keys are used to provide a framework for storing data; values actually hold the data in question. Value items have specific data types, although they are different from the data types in Visual Basic. Table 20.2 lists the possible data types for Registry values.

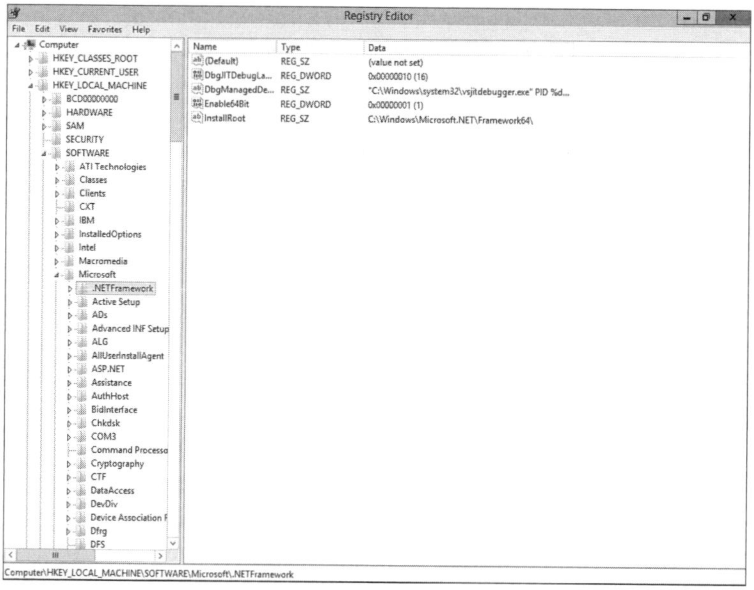

FIGURE 20.1
The Registry is a hierarchical structure of hives, keys, and values.

TABLE 20.2 Common Registry Value Data Types

Data Type	Description
REG_SZ	The primary type of string data. It is used to store fixed-length string data or other short text values.
REG_EXPAND_SZ	An expandable string value that can hold system variables whose values get resolved at runtime.
REG_MULTI_SZ	Holds multiple text strings formatted as an array. Each "element" string is terminated by a null character.
REG_BINARY	Used to store binary data.

By far, the most commonly used data type is the REG_SZ string data type. You can store all sorts of things in a REG_SZ value, such as text (obviously), True, False, 0, 1, and more. In fact, this is usually the only data type I use for my applications. When saving Boolean values, I just format them as either 1 or 0.

Accessing the Registry with My.Computer.Registry

You can access the Windows Registry in two ways. The first (and easiest) is to use the built-in Visual Basic functions GetSetting() and SaveSetting(). These functions have serious limitations, however, including only letting you manipulate keys and values in specific Visual Basic keys within the Registry. No self-respecting commercial application would do this, and neither should your applications. I won't teach you these two functions. Instead, you'll learn how to use the Registry object to manipulate the Windows Registry like a pro.

The Registry object is an object property of My.Computer. When Microsoft first released .NET, people were amazed by the power but confused by the complexity. Harnessing the power of the .NET Framework often required digging through poorly written Help text or exploring objects using the Object Browser. Microsoft realized this was a problem and consequently added the My object. The My object is basically a shortcut to other useful objects that aren't so easy to get to on their own. The My object makes it easy to retrieve information about your running application and the user's computer. One of the object properties available to the My object is the Computer object, which is used to access objects that let you work with the user's computer. The Computer object has an object property called Registry, which gives you direct access to the Windows Registry. You will use My.Computer.Registry to perform all your Registry tasks.

Creating Registry Keys

The My.Computer.Registry object has a number of properties. Among these are object properties that relate to the hives of the Registry already shown in Table 20.1. Table 20.3 lists the properties that reference the Registry's hives.

TABLE 20.3 Common Top-Node Properties of the Registry Object

Property	What It's Used to Access
ClassesRoot	HKEY_CLASSES_ROOT
CurrentConfig	HKEY_CURRENT_CONFIG
CurrentUser	HKEY_CURRENT_USER
LocalMachine	HKEY_LOCAL_MACHINE
Users	HKEY_USERS

Creating Registry keys using My.Computer.Registry is a snap. First, you have to identify the hive under which you want to create the key. When you know the hive, you just call the CreateSubKey() method of the corresponding hive object property, passing it the name of the key to create. For example, consider this statement:

```
My.Computer.Registry.CurrentUser.CreateSubKey("UserSettings")
```

This statement would create the key UserSettings under HKEY_CURRENT_USER. Realize that an application rarely creates a key directly under a hive. You can use many subkeys for each hive, but perhaps the most common is the \Software key. Most applications create a corporate-named key under \Software and then create product keys below the corporate subkey. For example, suppose that your company name is CleverSoftware, you're planning to ship the Picture Viewer program, and you want to store some application settings in the Registry. (In fact, you will modify your Picture Viewer to do this later in this hour.) You want to end up with a key structure that looks like this:

```
HKEY_CURRENT_USER\Software\CleverSoftware\PictureViewer
```

Fortunately, the CreateSubKey() method enables you to specify multiple levels of keys in one method call. To create this structure, you would use the following statement:

```
My.Computer.Registry.CurrentUser.CreateSubKey _
    ("Software\CleverSoftware\PictureViewer")
```

Visual Basic would parse this statement by first locating the hive HKEY_CURRENT_USER and then looking for a \Software key. It would find one, because all Windows machines have this key, but it would not overwrite this key. It would then look for CleverSoftware. Assuming that it does not find this key, it would create it and the subkey that you specified. Note that if Visual Basic finds an existing subkey that you defined in your statement (all subkeys are separated by a backslash [\]), it does not overwrite it.

Why HKEY_CURRENT_USER instead of HKEY_LOCAL_MACHINE? In general, it's best to save application settings in HKEY_CURRENT_USER so that each user who uses your application can have his or her own settings. If you store your settings in HKEY_LOCAL_MACHINE, the settings will be global to all users who run the application from the computer in question. Also, some administrators restrict access to HKEY_LOCAL_MACHINE, and your application will fail if it attempts to access restricted keys.

By the Way

Deleting Registry Keys

You can use two methods to delete a Registry key: DeleteSubKey() and DeleteSubKeyTree(). DeleteSubKey() deletes a key and all its values *as long as the key contains no subkeys.* `DeleteSubKeyTree()` deletes a key, its values, and all subkeys and values found below it. Use this one with care!

Here's a statement that could be used to delete the key created with the previous sample code:

```
My.Computer.Registry.CurrentUser.DeleteSubKey _
        ("Software\CleverSoftware\PictureViewer")
```

> DeleteSubKey throws an exception if the key you specify does not exist. Whenever you write code to work with the Registry, try to account for the unexpected.

Getting and Setting Key Values

Creating and deleting keys is useful, but only in the sense that keys provide the structure for the important data: the value items. You've already learned that keys can have one or more value items and that value items are defined as a specific data type. All that's left is to learn the code used to manipulate Registry values.

Unfortunately, getting and setting key values isn't as easy as defining keys. When you define keys, the `My.Computer.Registry` object makes it easy to work with hives by giving you an object property for each hive. There are properties for getting and setting values for each of these hive properties, but they don't work as expected. To create a new value item, or to set the value of an existing value item, you use `My.Computer.Registry.SetValue()`. The `SetValue()` method has the following syntax:

```
SetValue(keypath, itemname, value)
```

Unfortunately, you have to specify the hive name in `keypath`, as you will see. Notice that you do not specify the data type; Visual Basic sets the data type according to the value that is passed to the method. For example, to create a `UserName` value item for the Registry key discussed in the preceding section, you would use a statement like this:

```
My.Computer.Registry.SetValue _
        ("HKEY_CURRENT_USER\Software\CleverSoftware\PictureViewer\", _
        "UserName", "James")
```

This statement would produce a value item, as shown in Figure 20.2.

To change the value, you would call `SetValue` again, passing it the same key and item name, but a different value—nice and easy!

To retrieve a value from the Registry, you use the `GetValue` method. This method also requires a full hive/key path. The format of `GetValue()` is this:

```
GetValue(keypath, itemname, defaultvalue)
```

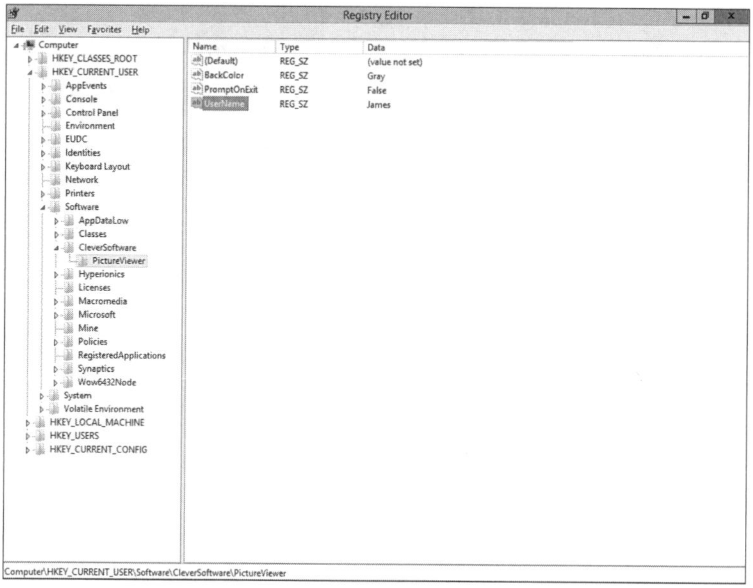

FIGURE 20.2
Values appear
attached to
keys.

The parameters `keypath` and `itemname` are the same as those used with `SetValue()`. Sometimes, when you go to retrieve a value from the Registry, the value and perhaps even the key don't exist. There are a number of reasons for this. Another application might have deleted the value, the user might have manually deleted the value, or the user might have restored a backup of his or her Registry from before the value was created. The `defaultvalue` parameter is used to define what `GetValue()` returns if it is unable to find the value item. This eliminates the need to catch an exception if the value item is missing. The following statement displays the value in the `RegistrationName` as created in the previous example:

```
MessageBox.Show(My.Computer.Registry.GetValue _
    ("HKEY_CURRENT_USER\Software\CleverSoftware\PictureViewer\", _
    "RegistrationName", ""))
```

Modifying Your Picture Viewer Project to Use the Registry

In this section, you'll modify your Picture Viewer project so that the user's settings in the Options dialog box are saved to the Registry. When the user first starts the Picture Viewer program, the settings are loaded from the Registry. Start by opening the Picture Viewer project you last worked on in Hour 19, "Performing File Operations."

Displaying Options from the Registry

The first thing you need to do is show the current user's settings when the Options form is displayed. Follow these steps to display the options stored in the Registry:

1. Double-click OptionsForm.vb in the Solution Explorer to display the Options form, and then double-click the form to access its Load event.

2. Right above the statement that declares the Load procedure, add the following statement to declare a module-level constant:

```
Const c_strKeyName As String =
"HKEY_CURRENT_USER\Software\CleverSoftware\PictureViewer\"
```

3. Put the cursor back in the Load procedure. Notice that the Load event already includes a statement to set the form's icon. Add the following code statements to the Load event, immediately following the existing statement:

```
txtUserName.Text = CStr(My.Computer.Registry.GetValue _
    (c_strKeyName, "UserName", ""))

chkPromptOnExit.Checked = CBool(My.Computer.Registry.GetValue _
    (c_strKeyName, "PromptOnExit", "0"))

If CStr(My.Computer.Registry.GetValue _
    (c_strKeyName, "BackColor", "Gray")) = "Gray" Then
    optBackgroundDefault.Checked = True
Else
    optBackgroundWhite.Checked = True
End If
```

All this code should be familiar to you by now. The first statement you enter simply creates a module-level constant with the full key path you'll use to access the Registry. Since you need this three times in this procedure alone, and it won't change during runtime, it makes sense to use a constant rather than hard-code the value on each line. It should be a module-level constant because you'll need it again in another procedure.

The first statement you enter into the Load event sets the value of the txtUserName text box to the username stored in the Registry. The first time the Options form loads, there is no entry in the Registry, so an empty string is used. Notice that the Registry call is wrapped in CStr() so that whatever value you pull from the Registry will be converted to a string, which is what a text box accepts. Because I had you turn on Options Strict in Hour 11, "Using Constants, Data Types, Variables, and Arrays," this is required.

The second statement in the Load event sets the checked state of the Prompt on Exit check box to the value stored in the Registry. If no value is found, as is the case the first time the Options form is loaded, the Checked property is set to False. Again, you have to wrap the result of GetValue() with a conversion function—in this case, CBool()—to convert the value to a Boolean.

The next statement starts an If...End If construct that looks for a color name in the Registry and sets the appropriate option button's Checked property to True. Because you're comparing the Registry result to text, wrap the result in CStr() to cast the result as a string.

Saving Options to the Registry

Now that the Options form displays the current values stored in the Registry, you can add the code to save the changes the user makes to these values. Follow these steps:

1. Choose btnOK from the object drop-down list in the upper-left corner of the code window.

2. Choose Click from the list of events in the upper-right corner of the code window.

3. Enter the following code into the btnOK_Click event. Be sure to put the code before the existing statement Me.Close():

```
My.Computer.Registry.SetValue _
    (c_strKeyName, "UserName", txtUserName.Text)

My.Computer.Registry.SetValue _
    (c_strKeyName, "PromptOnExit", chkPromptOnExit.Checked)

If optBackgroundDefault.Checked Then
   My.Computer.Registry.SetValue _
        (c_strKeyName, "BackColor", "Gray")
Else
   My.Computer.Registry.SetValue _
       (c_strKeyName, "BackColor", "White")
End If
```

This code is essentially the opposite of the code you entered in the Load event; it stores the values of the controls in the Registry. You should be able to follow this code on your own.

Using the Options Stored in the Registry

You're now allowing the user to view and change the settings stored in the Registry, but you're not actually using the user's preferences. Follow these steps to use the values stored in the Registry:

1. Double-click ViewerForm.vb in the Solution Explorer window to display the main Picture Viewer form in the designer.

2. Double-click the form to access its Load event.

3. The Load event currently contains six lines of code. Add the following statement right after the third statement (place it right below the two statements that set the X and Y label text):

```
Const c_strKeyName As String = _
    "HKEY_CURRENT_USER\Software\CleverSoftware\PictureViewer\"
```

Notice how you've duplicated a constant. That's fine for this example, but if you wanted to ship this as a real product, you should declare the constant in a global module so that it could be declared only once and be used throughout the application.

4. The first statements to change are the following:

```
m_blnPromptOnExit = c_defPromptOnExit
mnuConfirmOnExit.Checked = m_blnPromptOnExit
```

Recall that you keep track of the Prompt on Exit flag as a module variable. The first statement sets this flag to the constant you defined as the default value. The second statement sets the checked state of the menu item to the variable.

5. Delete the statement m_blnPromptOnExit = c_defPromptOnExit, and replace it with this:

```
m_blnPromptOnExit = CBool(My.Computer.Registry.GetValue _
    (c_strKeyName, "PromptOnExit", "0"))
```

This is almost identical to the statement you created in the Load event of the Options form. It retrieves the Prompt on Exit flag from the Registry, but this time it sets the module variable instead of a check box on the form.

6. Here's the next statement you'll replace:

```
m_objPictureBackColor = System.Drawing.SystemColors.Control
```

This sets the default back color of the picture box to the system color Control, which by default is a shade of gray. Replace this statement with the following code:

```
If CStr(My.Computer.Registry.GetValue _
    (c_strKeyName, "BackColor", "Gray")) = "Gray" Then
    m_objPictureBackColor = System.Drawing.SystemColors.Control
Else
    m_objPictureBackColor = System.Drawing.Color.White
End If
```

Testing and Debugging Your Picture Viewer Project

Press F5 to run the project. Next, click the Options button on the toolbar to display the Options form. Nothing looks different yet. Follow these steps to see the effect of your new code:

1. In the User Name text box, enter your name.

2. Click the Prompt to Confirm Exit check box to check it.

3. Click the Appearance tab, and then click the White option button to select it.

4. Click OK to close the Options dialog box.

5. Click the Options button on the toolbar again to display the Options dialog box. Notice that White is now chosen as the Default Picture Background color.

6. Click the General tab. Notice that your name is in the User Name text box and that the Prompt to Confirm on Exit check box is selected.

7. Click OK to close the Options dialog box.

8. Close the Picture Viewer.

Notice that you weren't prompted to confirm exiting. This occurs because the main Picture Viewer form is not being updated to reflect the changes made to the Registry. Now you'll use the skills you learned for creating procedures to make your code work properly. Follow these steps:

1. Double-click ViewerForm.vb in the Solution Explorer window to show the form in the designer.

2. Double-click the form to show its Load event.

3. Highlight all the code except the first two statements, as shown in Figure 20.3, and press Ctrl+X to cut the code.

4. Enter the following statement:

   ```
   LoadDefaults()
   ```

5. Position the cursor at the end of the End Sub statement that completes the definition of the frmViewer_Load event, and press Enter to create a new line.

6. Type the following statement, and press Enter:

   ```
   Public Sub LoadDefaults()
   ```

7. Press Ctrl+V to paste the code you deleted from the Form_Load event. Your code window should look like Figure 20.4.

   You now have a procedure that you can call when the user saves new settings to the Registry.

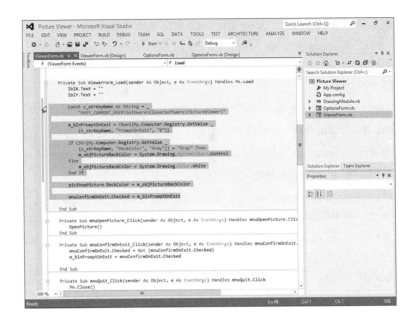

8. Double-click OptionsForm.vb in the Solution Explorer to display it in the designer.

9. Double-click OK to access its Click event.

10. Enter the following statement right before the `Me.Close()` statement (after all the code that saves the user's values to the Registry):

```
ViewerForm.LoadDefaults()
```

11. Press F5 to run the project.

12. Click the Options button on the toolbar to display the Options form, and change the default background color to Gray on the Appearance tab. When you click OK to save the settings and close the Options form, the background of the picture box changes to gray immediately.

The Registry is a powerful tool to have at your disposal—*if used properly!* In this section, you learned all the necessary techniques to implement Registry functionality in your applications.

To view your Registry, hold down the Shift key and right-click the desktop. You see a shortcut menu with the item Open Command Window Here. (If you don't see this item, you probably aren't holding down the Shift key.) When you click this menu item, a command prompt appears. Type **regedit** and press Enter to launch the Registry Editor. Be careful. Making inappropriate changes to the Registry can foul up your computer to the point where it won't boot!

Did you Know?

Reading and Writing Text Files

The Registry is a handy place to store user options and program configuration settings. It's not a good place, however, to store a lot of data such as a text document. If you have a lot of text data to store and retrieve, a good old-fashioned text file is probably the best place to put it (assuming that a real database such as Microsoft SQL is not an option). Visual Basic includes classes that make it relatively easy to manipulate text files: `StreamWriter` and `StreamReader`. Notice that reading and writing text files are performed by two different objects, only one of which can access a file at any given time. If you want to simultaneously read and write to a single file, you're probably better off using a real database.

Writing to a Text File

You write to text files by using the `StreamWriter` class. The first step of using this class is to declare an object of type `StreamWriter`, like this:

```
Dim objFile As New System.IO.StreamWriter("c:\temp\test.txt")
```

or like this:

```
Dim objFile As New System.IO.StreamWriter("c:\temp\test.txt", True)
```

> There are actually at least seven different forms of StreamWriter usage. I'm showing you the most common, but if you plan to do serious work with text files, you should read the Microsoft Developer Network (MSDN) document on the StreamWriter class.

As you can see, the second parameter is optional (it is omitted in the first example), and it determines whether you want to append to the text file if it already exists. If you omit this second parameter or supply False as its value, a new text file is created. If the text file already exists, it gets replaced with a new file of the same name. If you pass True, as in the second example, the file is opened, and any write operations you perform on the file are tacked on to the end of the file.

Did you Know?

> If you pass a file path/filename that doesn't exist, Visual Basic creates a new text file for you when you write data to the StreamWriter object. Also, be aware that you need access to the folder you specify when you run this code or you will receive an error.

After you have an object that points to a StreamWriter object, you can store data in the text file, using one of the following two methods:

- ▶ WriteLine() sends a single line of text to the file and automatically appends a carriage return to the end of the line. Each call to WriteLine() creates a new line.

- ▶ Write() sends data to the file but does not automatically append a carriage return to create a new line.

These two methods are best understood by example. Consider the following code snippet:

```
Dim objFile As New System.IO.StreamWriter("c:\temp\test.txt")
objFile.WriteLine("text1")
objFile.WriteLine("text2")
objFile.WriteLine("text3")
objFile.Close()
```

This snippet would produce the following data in the text file:

```
text1
text2
text3
```

By the Way

> Notice the last statement, objFile.Close(). It's vital that you close a text file when you're finished with it, and the Close() method does this. In addition, you should also call objFile.Dispose() to make sure that the file is fully released.

Now, consider the same code snippet that uses Write() instead of WriteLine():

```
Dim objFile As New System.IO.StreamWriter("c:\temp\test.txt")
objFile.Write("text1")
objFile.Write("text2")
objFile.Write("text3")
objFile.Close()
```

This snippet produces a text file that contains the following:

```
text1text2text3
```

See how WriteLine() creates lines of data, whereas Write() simply streams the data into the file? This is an incredibly important distinction, and understanding the difference is crucial to your success with writing text files. Which method you choose depends on what you are trying to accomplish. I think perhaps WriteLine() is the more common way. The following code illustrates how you could use WriteLine() to store a list of albums (assuming that you have the list in a list box titled lstAlbums):

```
Dim objFile As New System.IO.StreamWriter("c:\:\albums\albums.txt")
Dim intCounter As Long = lstAlbums.Items.Count
For intCounter = 0 To lstAlbums.Items.Count - 1
    objFile.WriteLine(lstAlbums.Items(intCounter).ToString)
Next intCounter
objFile.Close()
```

Reading a Text File

Reading a text file is handled by the StreamReader class, which behaves similarly to the StreamWriter class. First, you need to define an object of type StreamReader, like this:

```
Dim objFile As New System.IO.StreamReader("c:\temp\test.txt")
```

A key difference in declaring a StreamReader object versus a StreamWriter object is how the code behaves if the file is not found. The StreamWriter object is happy to create a new text file for you if the specified file isn't found. If StreamReader can't find the specified file, it throws an exception—something you need to account for in your code.

Just as StreamWriter lets you write the data to the file in one of seven ways, StreamReader also has multiple ways to read the data. The first of the two most common ways is to use the ReadToEnd() method, which reads the entire file and is used to place the contents of the file into a variable. You would use ReadToEnd() like this:

```
Dim objFile As New System.IO.StreamReader("c:\:\temp\test5.txt")
Dim strContents As String
strContents = objFile.ReadToEnd()
objFile.Close()
objFile.Dispose()
MessageBox.Show(strContents)
```

The ReadToEnd() method can be handy, but sometimes you just want to get a single line of text at a time. For example, consider the text file created by the previous example, the one with a list of albums. Say that you wanted to read the text file and place all the albums found in the text file into a list box named lstAlbums. The ReadToEnd() method would allow you to get the data, but then you would have to find a way to parse each album name. The proper solution for reading one line at a time is to use the ReadLine() method. The following code shows how you could load the Albums.txt text file, one line at a time, and place each album name in a list box:

```
Dim objFile As New System.IO.StreamReader("c:\:\albums\albums.txt")
Dim strAlbumName As String
strAlbumName = objFile.ReadLine()
Do Until strAlbumName Is Nothing
    lstAlbums.Items.Add(strAlbumName)
    strAlbumName = objFile.ReadLine()
Loop
objFile.Close()
objFile.Dispose()
```

A couple of important concepts in this example need discussing. The first is how you know when you've reached the end of a text file. The answer is that the return result will be Nothing. So, the first thing this code does (after creating the StreamReader object and the String variable) is get the first line from the text file. It's possible that the text file could be empty, so the Do loop tests for this. If the string is Nothing, the file is empty, so the loop doesn't execute. If the string is not Nothing, the loop begins. The first statement in the loop adds the string to the list box. The next statement gets the next line from the file. This sends execution back to the Do statement, which again tests to see whether we're at the end of the file. One thing this code doesn't test for is a zero-length string (" "). If the text file has a blank line, the string variable holds a zero-length string. You might want to test for a situation like this when working with text files in your code.

That's it! Text files are not database files; you'll never get the power and flexibility from a text file that you would from a real database. With that said, text files are easy to work with and provide amazing and quick results within the context of their design.

Modifying Your Picture Viewer Project to Use a Text File

In this section, you'll modify your Picture Viewer project to use a text file. You'll have your Picture Viewer update a log (a text file) every time the user views a picture. You'll then create a simple dialog box that the user can open to view the log file. If you no longer have the Picture Viewer project open from earlier, open it now.

Creating the Picture Viewer Log File

In this section, you'll modify the Picture Viewer project to create the log file. Follow these steps to implement the log functionality:

1. Double-click ViewerForm.vb in the Solution Explorer window to display the form in the designer.

2. Recall that you created a single procedure that is called from both the menu and the toolbar to open a picture. This makes it easier, because you have to add the log code in only one place. Double-click the Open Picture button on the toolbar to access its Click event.

3. You now need to go to the OpenPicture() function. Here's an easy way to do this: Right-click the code OpenPicture(), and choose Go To Definition from the shortcut menu, as shown in Figure 20.5. Whenever you do this to a procedure call, Visual Basic displays the code of the procedure being referenced.

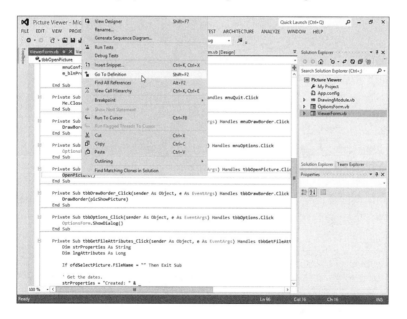

FIGURE 20.5
Go To Definition is a quick way to view a procedure being called in code.

4. Take a look at the OpenPicture() procedure. Where would you place the code to create a log file? Would you enter all the log file code right into this procedure? First, the log file should be updated only when a picture is successfully loaded, which would be in the Try block, right after the statement that updates the sbrMyStatusStrip control. Second, the log code should be isolated from this procedure, so you'll add just a single function call. Add this statement between the code to update the status bar and the End If:

```
UpdateLog(ViewerForm.ofdSelectPicture.FileName)
```

Your code should look like Figure 20.6. Note that it currently has an error (the procedure UpdateLog doesn't exist), but you're about to correct that.

FIGURE 20.6
It's always a
good idea to
isolate code
into cohesive
procedures.

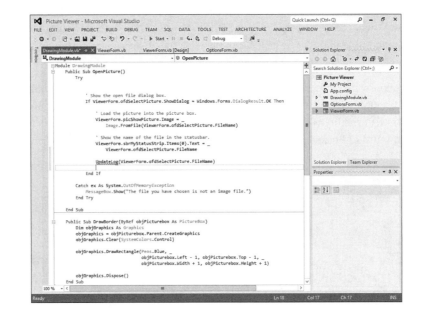

5. Position the cursor between the End Sub of OpenPicture() and the declaration of the DrawBorder() procedure. Press Enter to create a new line, and then enter the following procedure code:

```
Private Sub UpdateLog(ByVal strFileName As String)
    Dim objFile As New System.IO.StreamWriter( _
        System.AppDomain.CurrentDomain.BaseDirectory() & "\PictureLog.txt", _
        True)
    objFile.WriteLine(Today() & " " & strFileName)
    objFile.Close()
    objFile.Dispose()
End Sub
```

Most of this code should be recognizable, but consider this snippet:

```
System.AppDomain.CurrentDomain.BaseDirectory() & "\PictureLog.txt"
```

The method BaseDirectory() returns the path of the running program. This is a great trick to know! What you've done here is append the filename PictureLog.txt to the application path so that the log file is always created in the application path. This makes it easy for the user to find the log file. In a robust application, you might let the user specify a path, perhaps storing it in the Registry. For our purposes, the application path works just fine.

By the Way

When you're debugging an application in the Visual Basic IDE, the application path might not be exactly what you expect. When you compile and test your application, Visual Basic creates a `bin\Debug` folder under the folder containing your project. This is where it places the temporary `.exe` file it creates for debugging, and this is your application path. If you go looking for the log file in your project folder, you won't find it. You need to drill down into the `\bin\Debug` folder to get it.

Displaying the Picture Viewer Log File

In this section, you'll modify the Picture Viewer project to include a dialog box that the user can display to view the log file. Follow these steps to implement the log viewer functionality:

1. Choose Project, Add Windows Form to display the Add New Item dialog box. Enter **LogViewerForm.vb** as the new form name, and click Add to create the form.

2. Set the properties of the new form as follows:

Property	Value
MaximizeBox	False
MinimizeBox	False
Size	520, 344
Text	Picture Viewer History Log

3. Add a new button to the form, and set its properties as follows:

Property	Value
Name	btnOK
Anchor	Top, Right
Location	425, 275
Size	75, 23
Text	OK

4. Add a new text box to the form, and set its properties as follows:

Property	Value
Name	txtLog
Anchor	Top, Bottom, Left, Right

Location	3, 12
Multiline	True
ReadOnly	True
Size	497, 257

5. Double-click the OK button to access its `Click` event, and enter the following statement:

```
Me.Close()
```

6. Add the code that actually displays the log. Choose (LogViewerForm Events) from the object drop-down list in the upper-left corner of the code window. Then choose Load from the Event drop-down list in the upper right of the code window. Enter the following code into the `Form_Load` event:

```
Try
    Dim objFile As New System.IO.StreamReader( _
        System.AppDomain.CurrentDomain.BaseDirectory() & _
        "\PictureLog.txt")
    txtLog.Text = objFile.ReadToEnd()
    objFile.Close()
    objFile.Dispose()
Catch ex As Exception
    txtLog.Text = "The log file could not be found."
End Try
```

This code is just like the code discussed earlier on reading text files. It uses `ReadToEnd()` to load the entire log into the text box. The whole thing is wrapped in a `Try...End Try` block to handle the situation of there being no log file.

7. All that's left is to add a button to the toolbar of the Picture Viewer to display the log. Double-click ViewerForm.vb in the Solution Explorer to display the form in the designer.

8. Click the Toolstrip to select it, and then click the `Items` property in the Properties window.

9. Click the Build button in the `Items` property in the Property window to access the Items Collection Editor, and then create a new button on the toolbar. Set the new button's properties as follows:

Property	Value
Name	tbbShowLog
Image	Log.png (found with the samples on my website)

Property	Value
Text	View Picture Log
ToolTipText	View Picture Log

10. Click OK to save the new button; then double-click the new button on the toolbar and add the following code:

```
LogViewerForm.ShowDialog()
```

Testing Your Picture Viewer Log

Save your project, and press F5 to run it. Follow these steps to test the project:

1. Click the View Picture Log button on the toolbar to display the Picture Viewer History Log. Notice that the text box displays The log file could not be found. This means the Try block worked!

2. Click OK to close the form.

3. Click the Open Picture button on the toolbar, browse to a picture file, and display it.

4. Click the View Picture Log button again. Notice that the log now displays a log entry, as shown in Figure 20.7.

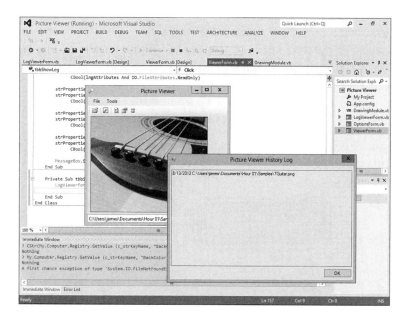

FIGURE 20.7
Text files make creating logs easy.

Summary

In this hour, you learned how to use the Registry to store and retrieve user settings. You learned about the structure of the Registry and how to use hives, keys, and values. The Registry is a powerful tool, and you should use it when applicable. Remember: The Registry isn't your personal repository; respect the Registry! Windows relies on certain data in the Registry, and if you mess up the Registry, you can actually prevent a computer from booting to Windows. As you saw firsthand with the Picture Viewer project, saving data to and retrieving data from the Registry is relatively easy, but how you handle the data is the real trick.

Next, you learned about the power (and limitations) of working with text files. You can read and write text files, but you can't do both to a single text file at the same time. If you need that functionality, a database is the way to go. However, you learned that it's relatively easy to store and retrieve sequential information in a text file, such as a log file. Finally, you used what you learned to implement log functionality for the Picture Viewer project.

Q&A

Q. *Can I use a text file to save configuration information?*

A. Yes, you could do that. You would need some way to denote the data element. How would you know that the first line was the `BackColor` setting, as opposed to a default file path, for example? One method would be to append the data element to a caption, as in `BackColor=White`. You would then have to parse the data as you read it from the text file. The Registry is probably a better solution for something like this, but a text file could be useful if you wanted to transfer settings to a different computer.

Q. *Can I store binary data instead of text to a file?*

A. Visual Basic includes classes designed to work with binary files: `BinaryWriter` and `BinaryReader`. You would need to use objects based on these classes, instead of using `StreamWriter` and `StreamReader` objects.

Workshop

Quiz

1. Why should you use the Registry object instead of the built-in Visual Basic functions to work with the Registry?

2. Under what hive should you store a user's configuration information in the Registry?

3. What full object/method is used to create a key in the Registry?

4. What two methods are used to delete a key from the Registry, and what is the difference between the two?

5. What classes do you use to write and read text files?

6. What method of the `StreamReader` class do you use to read the entire contents of a text file at once?

7. What happens if you attempt to use the `StreamReader` class to open a file that doesn't exist?

Answers

1. The built-in functions restrict you to working with keys and values under specific Visual Basic keys only.

2. You should store user configuration in the `HKEY_CURRENT_USER` hive.

3. `My.Computer.Registry.CurrentUser.CreateSubKey()`

4. The method `DeleteSubKey()` deletes a key, but only if no subkeys exist for the specified key. The method `DeleteSubKeyTree()` deletes a key and any subkeys of the specified key.

5. The `StreamWriter` class is used to write to a text file, whereas the `StreamReader` class is used to read data from a text file.

6. The `ReadToEnd()` method

7. An exception is thrown.

Exercises

1. Every toolbar item should have a corresponding menu item. Create a menu item on the Tools menu for displaying the log. While you're at it, create one for viewing the file properties to match the toolbar item you created in Hour 19. (You should move the code in `tbbGetFileAttributes_Click` to its own procedure so that it can be called from both the menu and the toolbar.) Finally, go back and add images to your menu items so that they match the toolbar items.

2. Create a button on the Log Viewer form called `btnClearLog`. Change the text of the button to Clear. When the user clicks the button, delete the log file from the hard drive and close the Log Viewer form.

HOUR 21

Working with a Database

What You'll Learn in This Hour:

- ▶ Introduction to ADO.NET
- ▶ Connecting to a database
- ▶ Understanding DataTables
- ▶ Creating a DataAdapter
- ▶ Referencing fields in a DataRow
- ▶ Navigating records
- ▶ Adding, editing, and deleting records
- ▶ Building an ADO.NET example

You've heard it so many times that it's almost a cliché: This is the Information Age. Information is data, and managing information means working with databases. Database design is a skill unto itself, and entire books are devoted to database design and management. In this hour, you'll learn the basics of working with a database using ADO.NET, Microsoft's newest database technology. High-end solutions are built around advanced database technologies such as Microsoft's SQL Server, which is the database technology used in this chapter. If you don't have Microsoft SQL Server 2008 or SQL Server 2012 installed on your computer, you can download it at http://www.microsoft.com/express/sql/default.aspx. You will have to have Microsoft SQL Server 2008 or 2012 installed for the code in this chapter to work. Don't let the installation process for SQL Express confuse you—you can probably accept all of the defaults in the installation wizard and be just fine.

> You'll learn a lot in this hour, but realize that this material is really the tip of the iceberg. Database programming is often complex. This hour is intended to get you writing database code as quickly as possible, but if you plan to do a lot of database programming, you'll want to consult a book (or two) dedicated to the subject.

Begin by creating a new Windows Forms Application named Database Example. Right-click Form1.vb in the Solution Explorer window, choose Rename, and then change the name of the default form to **MainForm.vb**. Next, set the form's Text property to Database Example.

Now that the project has been created, follow the steps in the next sections to build your database project.

Introducing ADO.NET

ADO.NET is the .NET platform's database technology, and it builds on the older ADO (Active Data Objects) technology. ADO.NET provides DataSet and DataTable objects that are optimized for moving disconnected sets of data across the Internet and intranets, including through firewalls. At the same time, ADO.NET includes the traditional connection and command objects, as well as an object called a DataReader (which resembles a forward-only, read-only ADO RecordSet, in case you're familiar with ADO). Together, these objects provide the best performance and throughput for retrieving data from a database.

In short, you'll learn about the following objects as you progress through this hour:

- ▶ SqlConnection is used to establish a connection to a SQL Server data source.

- ▶ DataSet is a memory-resident representation of data. There are many ways of working with a DataSet, such as through DataTables.

- ▶ DataTable holds a result set of data for manipulation and navigation.

- ▶ DataAdapter is used to populate a DataReader.

All the ADO.NET objects, except the DataTable, are part of the System.Data namespace. The DataTable is part of System.Xml. Follow these steps to add references to both namespaces so that you can use the namespaces without having to type the full namespace qualifier:

1. Choose Project, Database Example Properties to display the Project Properties.

2. Click the References tab to display the active references for the project, as shown in Figure 21.1.

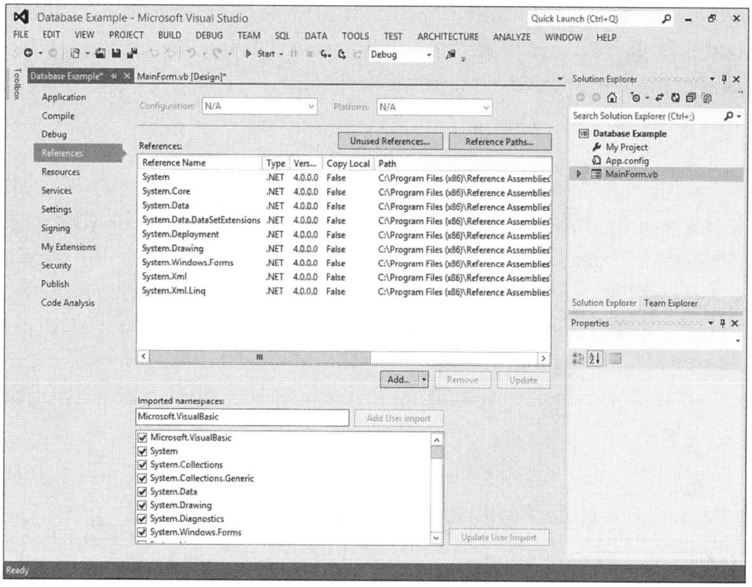

FIGURE 21.1
You use Project
Properties to
import name-
spaces.

3. In the lower part of this page is a check box list of imported namespaces. Use the scrollbar for this list box (not the main scrollbar for the page) to locate and check `System.Data`, `System.Data.SqlClient`, and `System.Xml`. `System.Data` is probably already checked and will appear toward the top of the list. If not, locate it and check it. `System.Data.SqlClient` and `System.Xml` will most likely not be checked, and will be toward the bottom of the list. Sometimes clicking once doesn't check the box, so make sure you get these selected before continuing.

4. Click Save All on the toolbar.

5. Click MainForm.vb [Design] to return to the Form Designer.

Connecting to a Database

To access data in a database, you must first establish a connection, using an ADO.NET connection object. Multiple connection objects are included in the .NET Framework, such as the `OleDbConnection` object (for working with the same OLE DB data providers you would access through traditional ADO) and the `SqlConnection` object (for optimized access to Microsoft SQL Server). Because these examples connect to a Microsoft SQL Database, you'll be using the `SqlConnection` object. To create an object variable of type `SqlConnection` and initialize the variable to a new connection, you could use a statement like this:

```
Dim cnADONetConnection As New SQLConnection()
```

You'll create a module-level variable to hold the connection. Double-click the form now to access its events, and place the cursor below the class definition statement at the top of the module. Enter the following statement:

```
Private m_cn As New SQLConnection()
```

Before using this connection, you must specify the data source to which you want to connect. This is done through the ConnectionString property of the ADO.NET connection object. The ConnectionString contains connection information such as the name of the provider, username, and password. The ConnectionString might contain many connection parameters; the set of parameters available varies, depending on the source of data to which you're connecting. Table 21.1 lists some of the parameters used in the SQL ConnectionString. If you specify multiple parameters, separate them with a semicolon.

TABLE 21.1   Possible Parameters for **ConnectionString**

Parameter	Description
Provider	The name of the data provider (Jet, SQL, and so on) to use.
Data Source	The name of the data source (database) to connect to.
User ID	A valid username to use when connecting to the data source.
Password	A password to use when connecting to the data source.
DRIVER	The name of the database driver to use. This isn't required if a data source name (DSN) is specified.
SERVER	The network name of the data source server.

The Provider= parameter is one of the most important at this point; it is governed by the type of database you're accessing. For example, when accessing a SQL Server database, you specify the provider information for SQL Server, and when accessing a Jet (Microsoft Access) database, you specify the provider for Jet. In this example, you access a Microsoft SQL database, so you use the provider information for Microsoft SQL.

In addition to specifying the provider, you also need to specify the database. I've provided a sample database on this book's website. This code assumes that you've placed the database in a folder called C:\Temp. If you're using a different folder, you need to change the code accordingly. Follow these steps:

1. Specify the `ConnectionString` property of your ADO.NET connection by placing the following statement in your form's `Load` event:

```
m_cn.ConnectionString = "Data Source=.\SQLEXPRESS; AttachDbFilename = " & _
     "C:\Temp\Test.mdf;Integrated Security=True; Connect Timeout=30;" & _
     "User Instance=True"
```

2. After the connection string is defined, you establish a connection to a data source by using the `Open()` method of the connection object. Add the following statement to the `Load` event, right after the statement that sets the connection string:

```
m_cn.Open()
```

<table>
<tr><td>Refer to the online documentation for information on connection strings for providers other than Microsoft SQL Server.</td><td>**By the**
Way</td></tr>
</table>

When you attach to an unsecured Microsoft SQL Server database, it isn't necessary to provide a username and password. When attaching to a secured database, however, you must provide a username and a password. You do so by passing the username and password as parameters in the `ConnectionString` property. The sample database I've provided isn't secured, so you don't need to provide a username and password.

Closing a Connection to a Data Source

You close a connection to a data source. That means you shouldn't rely on a variable going out of scope to close a connection. Instead, you should force an explicit disconnect via code. You do so by calling the `Close()` method of the connection object.

Now you'll write code to explicitly close the connection when the form is closed.

Start by opening the object drop-down list in the code window and selecting Main-Form Events if it isn't already selected. Next, choose `FormClosed` from the event drop-down list to create an event handler for the `FormClosed` event. Enter the following statements in the `FormClosed` event:

```
m_cn.Close()
m_cn.Dispose()
```

Manipulating Data

The easiest way to manipulate data when using ADO.NET is to create a `DataTable` object containing the result set of a table, query, or stored procedure. Using a `DataTable` object, you can add, edit, delete, find, and navigate records. The following sections explain how to use `DataTables`.

Understanding `DataTables`

`DataTables` contain a snapshot of data in the data source. You generally start by filling a `DataTable`, manipulating its results, and finally sending the changes back to the data source. You populate the `DataTable` by using the `Fill()` method of a `DataAdapter` object, and changes are sent back to the database through use of the `Update()` method of a `SqlDataAdapter`. Any changes made to the `DataTable` appear only in the local copy of the data until you call the `Update` method. Having a local copy of the data reduces contention by preventing users from blocking others from reading the data while it's being viewed. If you're familiar with ADO, you'll note that this is similar to the Optimistic Batch Client Cursor in ADO.

Creating a `DataAdapter`

To populate a `DataTable`, you must create a `SqlDataAdapter`. The `DataAdapter` you'll create uses the connection you've already defined to connect to the data source and then executes a query you provide. The results of that query are pushed into a `DataTable`.

As mentioned earlier, the .NET Framework has multiple connection objects. It has multiple ADO.NET DataAdapter objects as well. You'll use the `SqlDataAdapter` because you will be connecting to Microsoft SQL Server.

The constructor for an `SqlDataAdapter` optionally takes the command to execute when filling a `DataTable` or `DataSet`, as well as a connection specifying the data source (you could have multiple connections open in a single project). This constructor has the following syntax:

```
Dim daSqlDataAdapter As New SqlDataAdapter([CommandText],[Connection])
```

To add an `SqlDataAdapter` to your project, follow these steps:

1. Add the following statement immediately below the statement you entered to declare the m_cn object (in the class header, not in the Load event) to create a module-level variable:

```
Private m_DA As SqlDataAdapter
```

2. Add the following statement at the bottom of the form's Load event (immediately following the statement that opens the connection):

```
m_DA = New SqlDataAdapter("Select * From Contacts", m_cn)
```

Because you'll use the `SqlDataAdapter` to update the original data source, you must specify the insert, update, and delete statements to use to submit changes from the `DataTable` to the data source. ADO.NET lets you customize how updates are submitted by enabling you to manually specify these statements as database commands or stored procedures. In this case, you'll have ADO.NET generate these statements automatically by creating a `CommandBuilder` object.

3. Enter this statement in the class header to create the `CommandBuilder` module-level variable:

```
Private m_CB As SqlCommandBuilder
```

The `CommandBuilder` is an interesting object in that after you initialize it, you no longer work with it directly. It works behind the scenes to handle the updating, inserting, and deleting of data. To make this work, you have to attach the `CommandBuilder` to a `SqlDataAdapter`. You do so by passing a `SqlDataAdapter` to the `CommandBuilder`. The `CommandBuilder` then registers for update events on the `SqlDataAdapter` and provides the insert, update, and delete commands as needed.

4. Add the following statement to the end of the Form_Load event to initialize the `CommandBuilder` object:

```
m_CB = New SqlCommandBuilder(m_DA)
```

Your code should now look like Figure 21.2.

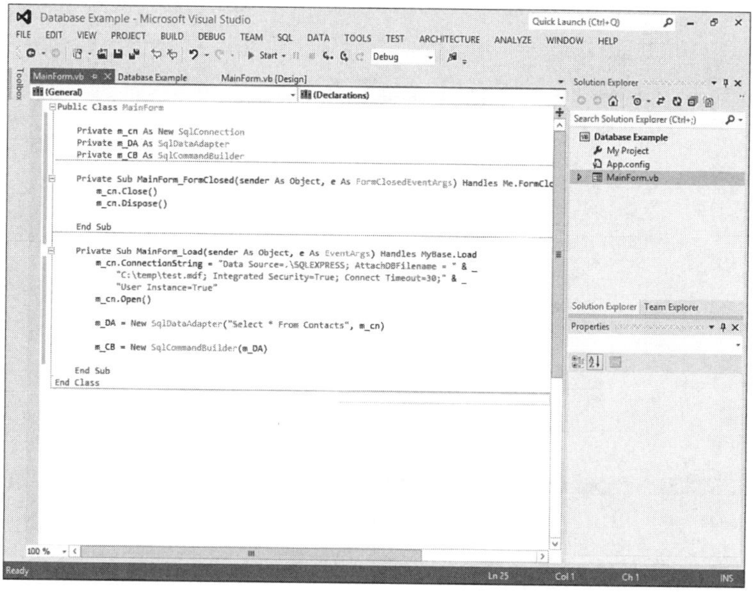

FIGURE 21.2
You jump around a lot in this example. Be sure to follow the steps exactly!

Creating and Populating `DataTables`

You need to create a module-level `DataTable` in your project. Follow these steps:

1. Create the `DataTable` variable by adding the following statement on the class header to create another module-level variable:

    ```
    Private m_DataTable As New DataTable
    ```

2. You use an integer variable to keep track of the user's current position (row) within the `DataTable`. To do this, add the following statement immediately below the statement you just entered to declare the new `DataTable` object:

    ```
    Private m_intRowPosition As Integer = 0
    ```

3. You now have a `SqlDataAdapter` that allows access to a data source via the connection. You've declared a `DataTable` that will hold a reference to data. Next, add the following statement to the form's `Load` event, after the existing code, to fill the `DataTable` with data:

    ```
    m_DA.Fill(m_DataTable)
    ```

Because the `DataTable` doesn't hold a connection to the data source, you don't need to close it when you're finished. Your class should now look like the one shown in Figure 21.3.

FIGURE 21.3
This code accesses a database and creates a `DataTable` that can be used anywhere in the class.

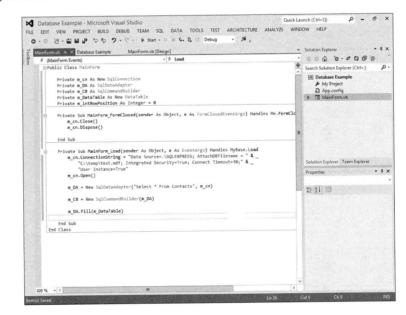

Referencing Fields in a `DataRow`

`DataTables` contain a collection of `DataRows`. To access a row within the `DataTable`, you specify the ordinal (index) of that `DataRow`. For example, you could access the first row of your `DataTable` like this:

```
Dim m_DataRow As DataRow = m_DataTable.Rows(0)
```

Data elements in a `DataRow` are called *columns*. For example, the Contacts table I've created has two columns: `ContactName` and `State`. To reference the value of a column, you can pass the column name to the `DataRow` like this:

```
' Change the value of the column.
m_DataRow("ContactName") = "Bob Brown"
```

or

```
' Get the value of the column.
strContactName = m_DataRow ("ContactName")
```

> If you misspell a column name, an exception occurs when the statement executes at runtime; no errors are raised at compile time.

Now you create a procedure that's used to display the current record in the data table. Follow these steps:

1. Position the cursor *after* the End Sub for the `MainForm_FormClosed` event (after its End Sub statement), and press Enter a few times to create some blank lines.

2. Enter the following procedure in its entirety:

```
Private Sub ShowCurrentRecord()
    If m_DataTable.Rows.Count = 0 Then
        txtContactName.Text = ""
        txtState.Text = ""
        Exit Sub
    End If

    txtContactName.Text = _
        m_DataTable.Rows(m_rowPosition)("ContactName").ToString()
    txtState.Text = _
        m_DataTable.Rows(m_rowPosition)("State").ToString()
End Sub
```

3. Make sure that the first record is shown when the form loads by adding this statement to the Form_Load event, *after* the existing statements:

```
Me.ShowCurrentRecord()
```

You've now ensured that the first record in the `DataTable` is shown when the form first loads. To display the data, you must add a few controls to the form.

4. Create a new text box, and set its properties as follows:

Property	Value
Name	txtContactName
Location	48, 112
Size	112, 20

5. Add a second text box to the form, and set its properties according to the following table:

Property	Value
Name	txtState
Location	168, 112
Size	80, 20

6. Press F5 to run the project. The first contact in the Contacts table is displayed in the text box, as shown in Figure 21.4.

FIGURE 21.4
It takes quite a bit of prep work to display data from a database.

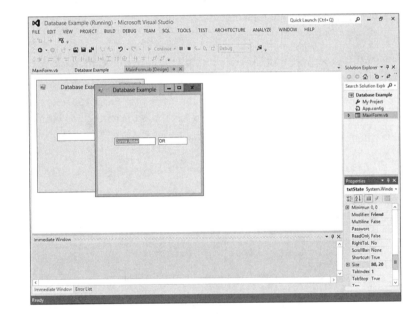

Navigating Records

The ADO.NET DataTable object supports a number of methods that can be used to access its DataRows. The simplest of these is the ordinal accessor that you used in your ShowCurrentRecord() method. Because the DataTable has no dependency on the source of the data, this same functionality is available regardless of where the data comes from.

Now you need to create buttons that the user can click to navigate the `DataTable`. The first button is used to move to the first record in the `DataTable`. Follow these steps:

1. Stop the running project and display the Form Designer for `MainForm.vb`.

2. Add a new button to the form, and set its properties as follows:

Property	Value
Name	btnMoveFirst
Location	12, 152
Size	32, 23
Text	<<

3. Double-click the button, and add the following code to its `Click` event:

```
' Move to the first row and show the data.
m_intRowPosition = 0
Me.ShowCurrentRecord()
```

4. A second button is used to move to the previous record in the `DataTable`. Add another button to the form, and set its properties as shown in the following table:

Property	Value
Name	btnMovePrevious
Location	86, 152
Size	32, 23
Text	<

5. Double-click the button, and add the following code to its `Click` event:

```
' If not at the first row, go back one row and show the record.
If m_intRowPosition > 0 Then
   m_intRowPosition = m_intRowPosition - 1
   Me.ShowCurrentRecord()
End If
```

6. A third button is used to move to the next record in the `DataTable`. Add a third button to the form, and set its properties as shown in the following table:

Property	Value
Name	btnMoveNext
Location	86, 152

Size	32, 23
Text	>

7. Double-click the button, and add the following code to its `Click` event:

```
' If not on the last row, advance one row and show the record.
If m_intRowPosition < (m_DataTable.Rows.Count - 1) Then
    m_intRowPosition = m_intRowPosition + 1
    Me.ShowCurrentRecord()
End If
```

8. A fourth button is used to move to the last record in the `DataTable`. Add yet another button to the form, and set its properties as shown in the following table:

Property	Value
Name	btnMoveLast
Location	124, 152
Size	32, 23
Text	>>

9. Double-click the button, and add the following code to its `Click` event:

```
' If there are any rows in the data table, move to the last and show
' the record.
If m_DataTable.Rows.Count > 0 Then
    m_intRowPosition = m_DataTable.Rows.Count - 1
    Me.ShowCurrentRecord()
End If
```

Editing Records

To edit records in a `DataTable`, you change the value of a particular column in the desired `DataRow`. Remember, though, that changes aren't made to the original data source until you call `Update()` on the `SqlDataAdapter`, passing in the `DataTable` containing the changes.

Now it's time to add a button that the user can click to update the current record. Follow these steps:

1. Add a new button to the form, and set its properties as follows:

Property	Value
Name	btnSave
Location	162, 152

Size	40, 23
Text	Save

2. Double-click the Save button, and add the following code to its Click event:

```
' If there is existing data, update it.
If m_DataTable.Rows.Count <> 0 Then
    m_DataTable.Rows(m_intRowPosition)("ContactName") = txtContactName.Text
    m_DataTable.Rows(m_intRowPosition)("State") = txtState.Text
    m_DA.Update(m_DataTable)
End If
```

Creating New Records

You add records to a DataTable much as you edit records. However, to create a new row in the DataTable, you must first call the NewRow() method. After creating the new row, you can set its column values. The row isn't actually added to the DataTable, however, until you call the Add() method on the DataTable's RowCollection.

Now you need to modify your interface so that the user can add new records. One text box is used for the contact name and a second text box for the state. When the user clicks the button you provide, the values in these text boxes are written to the Contacts table as a new record. Follow these steps:

1. Start by adding a group box to the form and setting its properties as shown in the following table:

Property	Value
Name	grpNewRecord
Location	16, 192
Size	256, 58
Text	New Contact

2. Add a new text box to the group box (not to the form), and set its properties as follows:

Property	Value
Name	txtNewContactName
Location	8, 24
Size	112, 20

3. Add a second text box to the group box, and set its properties as shown:

Property	Value
Name	txtNewState
Location	126, 24
Size	80, 20

4. Finally, add a button to the group box, and set its properties as follows:

Property	Value
Name	btnAddNew
Location	210, 22
Size	40, 23
Text	Add

5. Double-click the Add button, and add the following code to its Click event:

```
Dim drNewRow As DataRow = m_DataTable.NewRow()

drNewRow("ContactName") = txtNewContactName.Text
drNewRow("State") = txtNewState.Text
m_DataTable.Rows.Add(drNewRow)
m_DA.Update(m_DataTable)
m_intRowPosition = m_DataTable.Rows.Count - 1
Me.ShowCurrentRecord()
```

Notice that after the new record is added, the position is set to the last row, and the ShowCurrentRecord() procedure is called. This causes the new record to appear in the display text boxes you created earlier.

Deleting Records

To delete a record from a DataTable, you call the Delete() method on the DataRow to be deleted. Follow these steps:

1. Add a new button to your form (not to the group box), and set its properties as shown in the following table:

Property	Value
Name	btnDelete
Location	208, 152
Size	56, 23
Text	Delete

2. Double-click the Delete button, and add the following code to its `Click` event:

```
' If there is data, delete the current row.
If m_DataTable.Rows.Count <> 0 Then
    m_DataTable.Rows(m_intRowPosition).Delete()
    m_DA.Update(m_DataTable)
    m_intRowPosition = 0
    Me.ShowCurrentRecord()
End If
```

Your form should now look like the one shown in Figure 21.5.

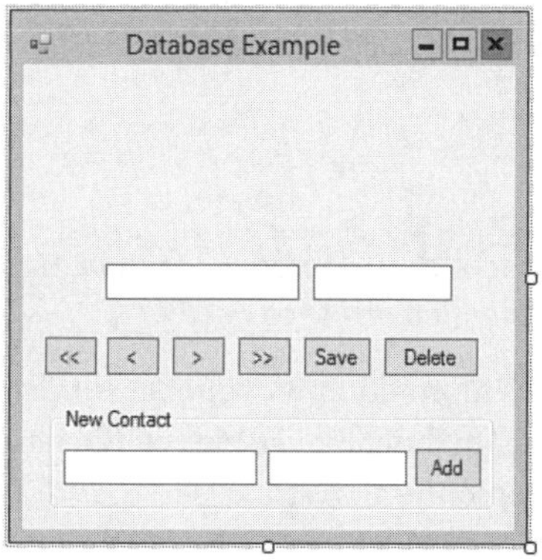

FIGURE 21.5
A basic data-entry form.

Running the Database Example

Press F5 to run the project. If you entered all the code correctly and you placed the Contacts database in the C:\Temp folder (or modified the path used in code), the form should be displayed without errors, and the first record in the database appears. Click the navigation buttons to move forward and backward. Feel free to change a contact's information; click the Save button, and your changes are made to the underlying database. Next, enter your name and state into the New Contact section of the form, and click Add. Your name is then added to the database and displayed in the appropriate text boxes.

Summary

Most commercial applications use some sort of database. Becoming a good database programmer requires extending your skills beyond just being a good Windows programmer. There's so much to know about optimizing databases and database code, creating usable database interfaces, creating a database schema—the list goes on. Writing any database application, however, begins with the basic skills you learned in this hour. You learned how to connect to a database, create and populate a `DataTable`, and navigate the records in the `DataTable`. In addition, you learned how to edit records and how to add and delete records. Although this just scratches the surface of database programming, it is all you need to begin writing your own small database application.

Q&A

Q. *If I want to connect to a data source other than Microsoft SQL Server, how do I know what connection string to use?*

A. Different connection information is available not only for different types of data sources but also for different versions of different data sources. The best way to determine the connection string is to consult the documentation for the data source to which you want to attach.

Q. *What if I don't know where the database will be at runtime?*

A. For file-based data sources such as Jet or Microsoft SQL Server, you can add an Open File Dialog control to the form and let the user browse and select the database. Then concatenate the filename with the rest of the connection information (such as the provider string).

Workshop

Quiz

1. What is the name of the data access namespace used in the .NET Framework?

2. What is the name given to a collection of `DataRows`?

3. How do you get data into and out of a `DataTable` of a Microsoft SQL Server database?

4. What object is used to connect to a data source?

5. What argument of a connection string contains information about the type of data being connected to?

6. What object provides update, delete, and insert capabilities to a `DataAdapter`?

7. What method of a `DataTable` object do you call to create a new row?

Answers

1. `System.Data`

2. A `DataSet`

3. You use a `SqlDataAdapter`.

4. There are multiple connection objects. You have to use the connection object appropriate for the type of data you are accessing.

5. The `Provider` argument

6. A `CommandBuilder` object

7. The `Add()` method is used to create the row. The `Update()` method saves your changes to the new row.

Exercises

1. Create a new project that connects to the same database used in this example. Rather than displaying a single record in two text boxes, put a list box on the form, and fill the list box with the names of the people in the database.

2. Right now, the code you created in this hour saves an empty name to the database. Add code to the `Click` event of the Add button so that it first tests to see whether the user entered a contact name. If not, tell the user that a name is required, and then exit the procedure.

HOUR 22

Controlling Other Applications Using Automation

What You'll Learn in This Hour:

▶ Creating a reference to an automation library

▶ Creating an instance of an automation server

▶ Manipulating the objects of an automation server

▶ Automating Microsoft Word

▶ Automating Microsoft Excel

In Hour 16, "Designing Objects Using Classes," you learned how to use classes to create objects. In that hour, I mentioned that objects could be exposed to outside applications. Excel, for example, exposes most of its functionality as a set of objects. The process of using objects from another application is called *automation*. The externally accessible objects of an application comprise its *object model*. Using automation to manipulate a program's object model enables you to reuse components. For example, you can use automation with Excel to perform complex mathematical functions, using the code that's been written and tested within Excel rather than writing and debugging the complex code yourself.

Programs that expose objects are called *servers*, and programs that consume objects are called *clients*. Creating automation servers requires advanced skills, including a thorough understanding of programming classes. On the other hand, creating clients to use objects from other applications is relatively simple. In this hour, you'll learn how to create a client application that uses objects of an external server application.

To understand automation, you'll build two projects. The first is a Microsoft Excel client—a program that automates Excel via Excel's object model. The second project automates Microsoft Word.

By the Way

These exercises are designed to work with Microsoft Excel 2007 or newer and Microsoft Word 2007 or newer. You must have these programs installed for the examples to work.

Automating Microsoft Excel

Begin by creating a new Windows Forms Application named Automate Excel. Right-click Form1.vb in the Solution Explorer, choose Rename, and then change the name of the default form to **MainForm.vb**. Next, set the form's Text property to Automate Excel.

Add a button to the form by double-clicking the Button item in the toolbox, and set the button's properties as follows:

Property	Value
Name	btnAutomateExcel
Location	90, 128
Size	104, 23
Text	Automate Excel

Creating a Reference to an Automation Library

To use the objects of a program that supports automation (a server), you have to reference the program's *type library*. A program's type library (also called its *object library*) is a file containing a description of the program's object model. After you've referenced the type library of an automation server (also called a *component*), you can access the server's objects as though they were internal Visual Basic objects.

You create the reference to Excel's automation library much as you created a reference to the System.Data namespace in Hour 21, "Working with a Database." To create a reference to the Excel library, follow these steps:

1. Choose Project, Automate Excel Properties to display the Project Properties.

2. Click the References tab to display the active references for the project, as shown in Figure 22.1.

3. Below the list of existing references (and above the imported namespaces), click the Add button to display the list of available references.

4. On the COM tab, shown in Figure 22.2, locate Microsoft Excel 14.0 Object Library and double-click it to select it. Click Close to close the Add Reference dialog box and save your change. The COM reference appears in the References list in the Project Properties window. Note, if you see version 12 of Microsoft Excel, you have Excel 2007 and the code will still work.

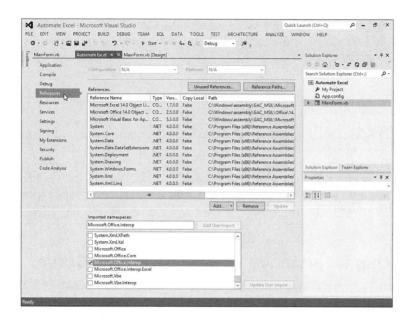

FIGURE 22.1
You use Project Properties to add references to COM servers.

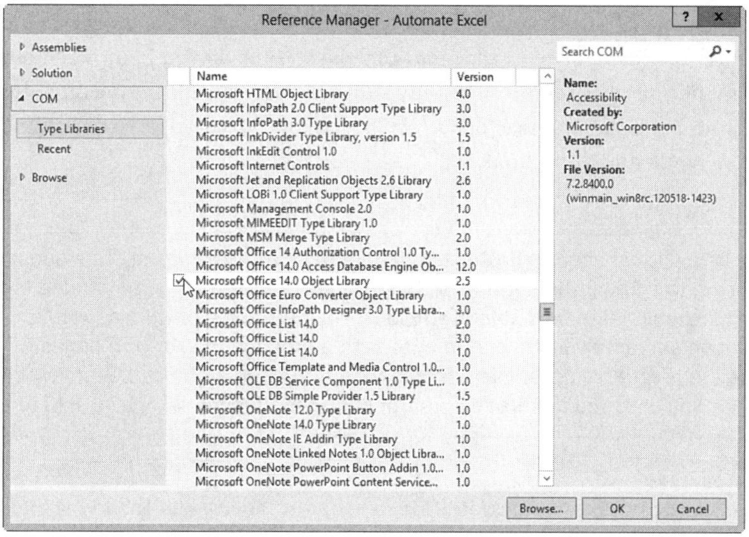

FIGURE 22.2
You have to add a reference to the Excel library before you can use it in code.

If you don't see Microsoft Excel 14.0 Object Library in your list of available COM references, you probably don't have Excel 2012 installed. If you see version 10.0 listed, you have Microsoft Excel 2007 and the code will still work.

By the Way

5. In the lower part of the References page is a check box list of imported name-spaces. Use the scrollbar for this list box (not the main scrollbar for the page) to

locate and check Microsoft.Office.Interop. This most likely is one of the last items in the list. Again, clicking once doesn't always select the item, so make sure you have it selected before continuing.

6. Click Save All on the toolbar.

7. Click MainForm.vb [Design] to return to the Form Designer.

> Visual Basic doesn't work directly with COM components (as did previous versions of Visual Basic). Instead, it interacts through a wrapper, a set of code and objects that works as an intermediary between Visual Basic and a COM component. When you add the reference to a COM component, .NET automatically creates this wrapper for you.

Creating an Instance of an Automation Server

Referencing a type library enables Visual Basic to integrate the available objects of the type library with its own internal objects. After this is done, you can create object variables based on object types found in the type library. Excel has an object called Application, which acts as the primary object in the Excel object model. In fact, most Office programs have an Application object. How do you know what objects an automation server supports? The only sure way is to consult the documentation of the program in question or use the Object Browser, as discussed in Hour 3, "Understanding Objects and Collections."

By the Way

> This example uses about a half-dozen members of an Excel object. This doesn't even begin to scratch the surface of Excel's object model, nor is it intended to. What you should learn from this example is the mechanics of working with an automation server. If you choose to automate a program in your own projects, consult the program's developer documentation to learn as much about its object model as you can. You're sure to be surprised at the functionality available to you.

Double-click the button to access its Click event, and then enter the following code, which creates a new Excel Application object:

```
Dim objExcel As New Excel.Application
```

Notice that Visual Basic includes Excel in its IntelliSense drop-down list of available objects. It can do this because you referenced Excel's type library. Excel is the reference to the server, and Application is an object supported by the server. This statement creates a new Application object based on the Excel object model.

Manipulating the Server

After you have an instance of an object from an automation server, you manipulate the server (create objects, set properties, call methods, and so forth) by manipulating the object. In the following sections, you manipulate the new Excel object by setting properties and calling methods, and in so doing you manipulate Excel itself.

Forcing Excel to Show Itself

When you use automation to start Excel, it's loaded hidden—the user can't see the user interface. By remaining hidden, Excel allows the developer to use Excel's functionality and then close it without the user even knowing what happened. For example, you could create an instance of an Excel object, perform a complicated formula to obtain a result, close Excel, and return the result to the user—all without the user seeing Excel. In this example, you *want* to see Excel so that you can see what your code is doing. Fortunately, showing Excel couldn't be any easier. Add the following statement to make Excel visible:

```
ObjExcel.Visible = True
```

Creating an Excel Workbook

In Excel, a workbook is the file in which you work and store your data; you can't manipulate data without a workbook. When you first start Excel from the Start menu, an empty workbook is created. When you start Excel via automation, however, Excel doesn't create a workbook; you have to do it yourself. To create a new workbook, you use the Add method of the Workbooks collection. Enter the following statement to create a new workbook:

```
objExcel.Workbooks.Add()
```

Working with Data in an Excel Workbook

Workbooks contain a single worksheet by default. In this section, you manipulate data in the worksheet. The following describes what you do:

1. Add data to four cells in the worksheet.

2. Select the four cells.

3. Total the selected cells, and place the sum in a fifth cell.

4. Bold all five cells.

To manipulate cells in the worksheet, you manipulate the `ActiveCell` object, which is an object property of the `Application` object. Entering data into a cell involves first selecting a cell and then passing data to it. You select a cell by calling the `Select` method of the `Range` object; the `Range` object is used to select one or more cells. The `Select` method accepts a starting column and row and an ending column and row. If you want to select only a single cell, as we do here, you can omit the ending column and row. After the range is set, you pass data to the `FormulaR1C1` property of the `ActiveCell` object (which references the cell specified by the `Range` object). Setting the `FormulaR1C1` property has the effect of sending data to the cell. Sound confusing? Well, it is to some extent. Programs that support automation are often vast and complex, and programming them is usually far from intuitive.

If the program you want to automate has a macro builder (as most Microsoft products do), you can save yourself a lot of time and headaches by creating macros of the tasks you want to automate. Macros are actually code, and in the case of Microsoft products, they're VBA code, which is similar to Visual Basic 6 code. Although this code won't port directly to Visual Basic 2012, it's rather easy to migrate in most cases, and the macro builder does all or most of the work of determining objects and members for you.

The following section of code uses the techniques just described to add data to four cells. Follow these steps now to automate sending the data to Excel:

1. Enter this code into your procedure:

```
objExcel.Range("A1").Select()
objExcel.ActiveCell.FormulaR1C1 = "75"
objExcel.Range("B1").Select()
objExcel.ActiveCell.FormulaR1C1 = "125"
objExcel.Range("C1").Select()
objExcel.ActiveCell.FormulaR1C1 = "255"
objExcel.Range("D1").Select()
objExcel.ActiveCell.FormulaR1C1 = "295"
```

The next step is to have Excel total the four cells. You do this by using the `Range` object to select the cells, activating a new cell in which to place the total, and then using `FormulaR1C1` again to create the total by passing it a formula rather than a literal value.

2. Enter this code into your procedure:

```
objExcel.Range("A1:D1").Select()
objExcel.Range("E1").Activate()
objExcel.ActiveCell.FormulaR1C1 = "=SUM(RC[-4]:RC[-1])"
```

3. Select all five cells and bold them. Enter the following statements to accomplish this:

```
objExcel.Range("A1:E1").Select()
objExcel.Selection.Font.Bold = True
```

The last thing you need to do is destroy the object reference by setting the object variable to Nothing. Excel remains open even though you've destroyed the automation instance (not all servers do this).

4. Add this last statement to your procedure:

```
objExcel = Nothing
```

To help ensure that you entered everything correctly, Listing 22.1 shows the procedure in its entirety.

LISTING 22.1   Code to Automate Excel

```
Private Sub btnAutomateExcel_Click(ByVal sender As System.Object, _
                                    ByVal e As System.EventArgs) _
                                    Handles btnAutomateExcel.Click
    Dim objExcel As New Excel.Application
    objExcel.Visible = True
    objExcel.Workbooks.Add()
    objExcel.Range("A1").Select()
    objExcel.ActiveCell.FormulaR1C1 = "75"
    objExcel.Range("B1").Select()
    objExcel.ActiveCell.FormulaR1C1 = "125"
    objExcel.Range("C1").Select()
    objExcel.ActiveCell.FormulaR1C1 = "255"
    objExcel.Range("D1").Select()
    objExcel.ActiveCell.FormulaR1C1 = "295"
    objExcel.Range("A1:D1").Select()
    objExcel.Range("E1").Activate()
    objExcel.ActiveCell.FormulaR1C1 = "=SUM(RC[-4]:RC[-1])"
    objExcel.Range("A1:E1").Select()
    objExcel.Selection.Font.Bold = True
    objExcel = Nothing
End Sub
```

Testing Your Client Application

Now that your project is complete, press F5 to run it, and click the button to automate Excel. If you entered the code correctly, Excel starts, data is placed in four cells, the total of the four cells is placed in a fifth cell, and all cells are made bold, as shown in Figure 22.3.

FIGURE 22.3
You can control almost every aspect of Excel when using its object model.

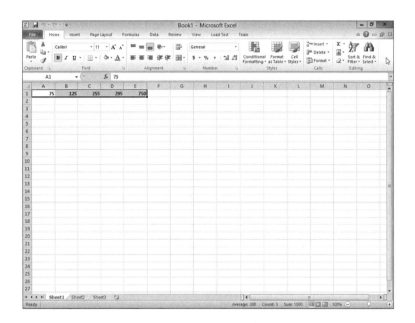

Automating Microsoft Word

Now you'll build another simple application that automates Microsoft Word 2010 or 2012. Begin by creating a new project titled Automate Word. Right-click Form1.vb in the Solution Explorer, choose Rename, and then change the default form's name to **MainForm.vb**. Next, change the form's Text property to `Automate Word`.

Creating a Reference to an Automation Library

To automate Microsoft Word, you have to reference Word's object library, just as you did for Excel. Follow these steps to reference the library:

1. Choose Project, Automate Word Properties to display the Project Properties.

2. Click the References tab to display the active references for the project.

3. Below the list of existing references (and above the list of imported namespaces), click the Add button to display the list of available references.

4. On the COM tab, locate Microsoft Word 12.0 Object Library, and double-click it to select it. Then click OK to save your selection and close the Add Reference dialog box. The COM reference appears in the References list in the Project Properties window.

If you don't see Microsoft Word 12.0 Object Library in your list of available COM references, you probably don't have Word 2012 installed. If you see version 10.0 listed, you have Microsoft Word 2007 and the code will still work.

By the Way

5. In the lower part of the References page is a check box list of Imported Namespaces. Use the scrollbar for this list box (not the main scrollbar for the page) to locate and check Microsoft.Office.Interop. This most likely is one of the last items in the list.

6. Click Save All on the toolbar.

7. Click MainForm.vb [Design] to return to the Forms Designer.

Creating an Instance of an Automation Server

As with the previous example, all the code for automating Word is placed in a button's `Click` event. Follow these steps to create the button and instantiate a Word object:

1. Add a button to the form by double-clicking the Button item in the toolbox, and set the button's properties as follows:

Property	Value
Name	btnAutomateWord
Location	90, 128
Size	104, 23
Text	Automate Word

2. Double-click the button to access its `Click` event.

3. To work with Word's object model, you need an instance of Word's `Application` object. Enter the following statement to create a variable that contains an instance of Word's `Application` object:

   ```
   Dim objWord As New Word.Application
   ```

4. As with Excel, Word starts hidden, so the user doesn't know it's running. Because you'll want to see the fruits of your labor, add this statement to force Word to show itself:

   ```
   objWord.Visible = True
   ```

5. Next, have Word create a new document by adding this statement to your procedure:

```
objWord.Documents.Add()
```

6. There are many ways to send text to Word. Perhaps the easiest is the `TypeText()` method of the `Selection` object. The `Selection` object refers to currently selected text in the Word document. When a new document is created, it has no text, and the selection object simply refers to the edit cursor at the start of the document. Sending text to Word using `Select.TypeText()` inserts the text at the top of the document. Enter this statement to send text to Word:

```
objWord.Selection.TypeText("This is text from a VB 2012 application.")
```

7. The last statement you need to enter sets the Word object to `Nothing`:

```
objWord = Nothing
```

8. Press F5 to run the program. You should see Word start, and then a new document is created using the text you specified with `TypeText()`, as shown in Figure 22.4.

FIGURE 22.4
A simple but effective demonstration of automating Word.

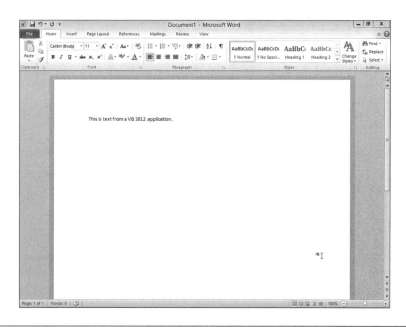

Summary

In this hour, you learned how a program can make available an object model that client applications can use to manipulate the program. You learned that the first step in automating a program (server) is to reference the server's type library. After the type library is referenced, the server's objects are available as though they're internal Visual Basic objects. As you've seen, the mechanics of automating a program aren't that difficult—they build on the object-programming skills you've already learned in this book. The real challenge comes in learning the object model of a given server and in making the most productive use of the objects available.

Q&A

Q. *What are some applications that support automation?*

A. All the Microsoft Office products, as well as Microsoft Visio, support automation. You can create a robust application by building a client that uses multiple automation servers. For example, you could calculate data in Excel and then format and print the data in Word.

Q. *Can you automate a component without creating a reference to a type library?*

A. Yes, but this is considerably more complicated than when you use a type library. First, you can't early-bind to objects because Visual Basic doesn't know anything about the objects without a type library. This means that you have no IntelliSense drop-down list to help you navigate the object model, and Visual Basic doesn't perform any syntax checking on your automation code; the chances for bugs in this situation are almost unbearably large. To create a reference to a server using late binding, you use Visual Basic's `CreateObject()` function.

Workshop

Quiz

1. Before you can early-bind objects in an automation server, you must do what?

2. What is the most likely cause of not seeing a type library listed in the Add References dialog box?

3. For Visual Basic to use a COM library, what must it create?

4. To manipulate a server via automation, what do you manipulate?

5. To learn about the object library of a component, what should you do?

Answers

1. Add a reference to the server's type library.

2. The application is not installed.

3. A wrapper around the COM library

4. An object that holds an instantiated object from the server

5. Consult the programmer's help file for the component.

Exercises

1. Modify the Excel example to prompt the user for a filename to use to save the workbook. Hint: Consider the `Save()` method of the `Application` object. Note, if you cancel saving the document, you will crash your application. As the old doctor joke says, "don't do that!"

2. Modify your Excel example so that after summing the four cells, you retrieve the sum from Excel and then send the value to a new Word document.

HOUR 23

Deploying Applications

What You'll Learn in This Hour:

▶ Understanding ClickOnce technology

▶ Using the Publish Wizard to create a ClickOnce program

▶ Testing a ClickOnce install program

▶ Uninstalling an application you've distributed

▶ Setting Advanced options when creating ClickOnce programs

Now that you've learned how to create a Visual Basic application, you're probably itching to create a project and send it to the world. Fortunately, Visual Basic includes the tools you need to create a setup program for your applications. In this hour, you'll learn how to use these tools to create a setup program that a user can run to install an application you've developed. In fact, you'll create a setup program for the Picture Viewer application you've been working on since Hour 1, "Jumping in with Both Feet: A Visual Basic 2010 Programming Tour."

Understanding ClickOnce Technology

Microsoft can't seem to settle on a deployment technology. Before .NET, serious developers were forced to use third-party applications to build installation programs. Then Microsoft introduced Windows Installer Technology, in which developers created an MSI file that installed an application. With Visual Basic 2005, Microsoft introduced yet another technology: ClickOnce. ClickOnce technology has its drawbacks, mostly in its lack of flexibility, but it does have some significant improvements over earlier technologies, and Microsoft has continued to improve it. Many of the improvements will be appreciated mostly by experienced developers who have been battling install technology for some time. This hour covers the highlights of ClickOnce technology. After you understand what the ClickOnce technology offers, I'll walk you through creating a ClickOnce program that installs your Picture Viewer program on a user's computer.

The following points are highlights of the new ClickOnce technology:

▶ ClickOnce is designed to bring the ease of deploying a web application to the deployment of desktop applications. Traditionally, to distribute a desktop application you had to touch every client computer, running the setup program and installing the appropriate files. Web applications, on the other hand, need to be updated in only one place: on the web server. ClickOnce provides desktop applications with update functionality similar to that of web applications.

▶ Applications deployed with ClickOnce can update themselves. They can check the Web for a newer version and install the newer version automatically.

▶ ClickOnce programs update only necessary files. With previous installation technologies, entire applications had to be reinstalled to be updated.

▶ ClickOnce allows applications to install their components in such a way that they don't interfere with other installed applications. In other words, they are *self-contained* applications. With Windows Installer deployments (that is, the "old way"), applications shared components such as custom controls. If one application mistakenly installed an older version of a component, deleted a component, or installed an incompatible version of a component, it would break other installed applications that used the shared component.

▶ ClickOnce programs do not require the user to have administrative permissions. With Windows Installer deployments, users needed administrative permissions to install an application. Trust me—this is a serious issue, and I'm glad to see ClickOnce address it.

▶ A ClickOnce application can be installed in one of three ways: from a web page, from a network file share, or from media such as a CD-ROM.

▶ A ClickOnce application can be installed on a user's computer, so it can be run when the user is offline. Or it can be run in an online-only mode, where it doesn't permanently install anything on the user's computer.

Using the Publish Wizard to Create a ClickOnce Application

Now you'll create a ClickOnce program that installs the Picture Viewer program you've been building throughout this book. Begin by opening the Picture Viewer project from Hour 20, "Working with the Registry and Text Files," and then follow these steps:

1. Choose Build, Publish Picture Viewer. This displays the Publish Wizard, shown in Figure 23.1. This page is used to specify where you want the ClickOnce file created.

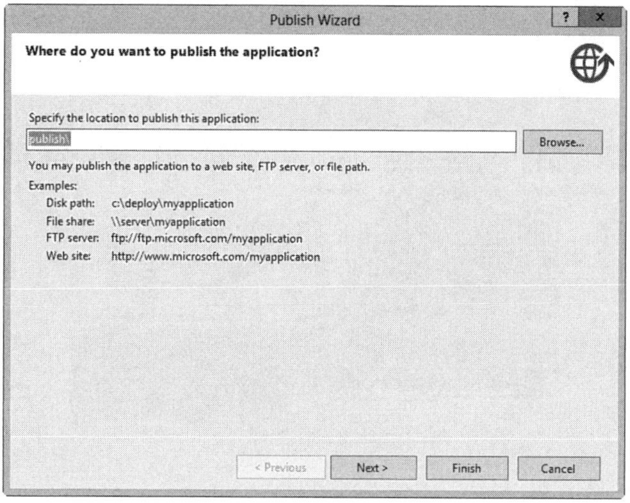

FIGURE 23.1
The Publish Wizard is used to create ClickOnce programs.

2. Specify the location for the ClickOnce install files. Be aware that you must enter a path that already exists; Visual Basic does not create a path for you. If you specify an invalid path, you get a Build error at the end of the wizard.

3. On the next page of the Publish Wizard, shown in Figure 23.2, specify the method users are to employ to install your program. Although you can specify a website or UNC share, choose From a CD-ROM or DVD-ROM for this example and click Next.

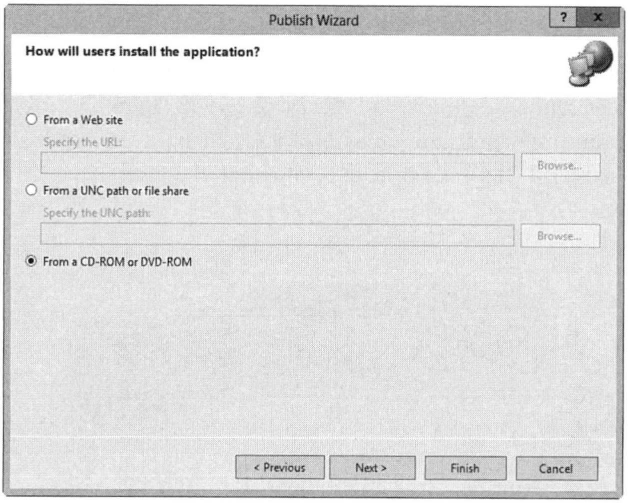

FIGURE 23.2
Users can install your application in one of three ways.

4. The next page of the Publish Wizard, shown in Figure 23.3, asks you whether the application will check for updates. If your application supports this feature, select the appropriate option button and specify a location where the update files will be placed. The Picture Viewer is a simple application and does not need this level of functionality, so leave the option The Application Will Not Check for Updates selected and click Next.

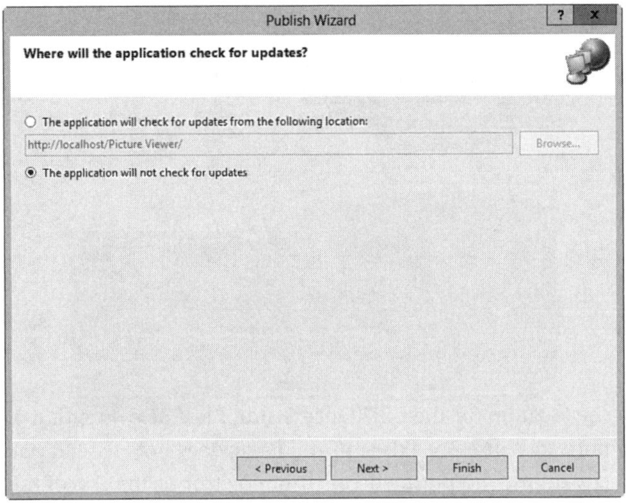

FIGURE 23.3
ClickOnce applications can update themselves if you design them to do so.

Publish Wizard	? X

Where will the application check for updates?

○ The application will check for updates from the following location:

http://localhost/Picture Viewer/   Browse...

◉ The application will not check for updates

< Previous   Next >   Finish   Cancel

5. The final page of the Publish Wizard, shown in Figure 23.4, is simply a confirmation page. Verify that the information displayed is how you want it. Don't be concerned about the formatting applied to your path. Visual Basic modifies it to create a valid UNC path. Click Finish to create the install.

When you click Finish, the Publish Wizard creates the ClickOnce application and opens the folder containing the install files, as shown in Figure 23.5. To distribute this application, you simply burn the contents of this folder, including the subfolder and its contents, to a CD-ROM or DVD-ROM and send it to a user.

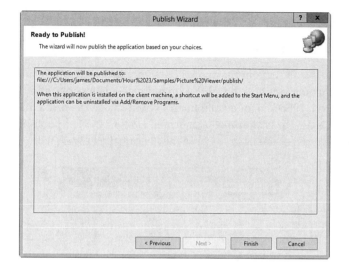

FIGURE 23.4
Make sure that everything is correct before you finish the wizard.

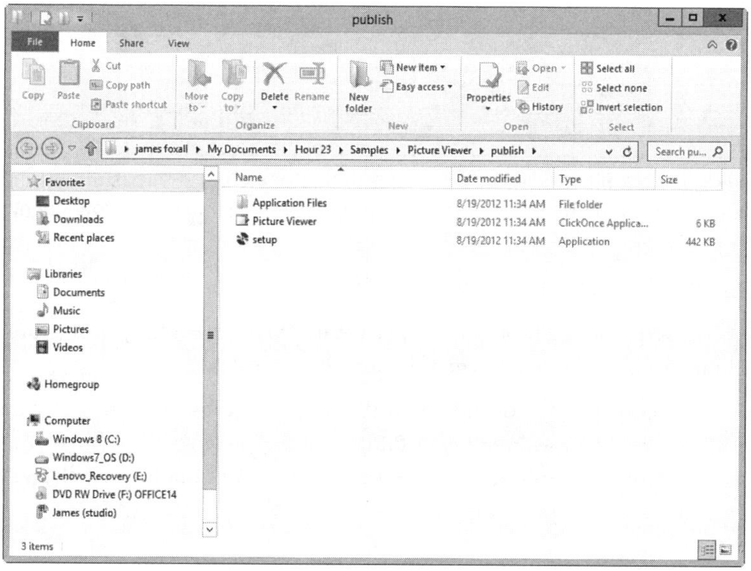

FIGURE 23.5
These files (and the subfolder) make up the ClickOnce program.

Testing Your Picture Viewer ClickOnce Install Program

Run the Setup.exe file in your designated ClickOnce folder to start the install. You might notice a quick window that shows an animated dialog indicating that the computer is being checked for a valid Internet connection. The first dialog you can interact with is a security warning, as shown in Figure 23.6. The publisher of the component is listed as unknown because the file isn't digitally signed.

FIGURE 23.6
All ClickOnce programs launch with a security warning.

Did you Know?

> Digitally signing a file is beyond the scope of this book, but if this is important to you, you can learn more at http://www.verisign.com/. (Search for "code signing.")

Click Install to install the Picture Viewer.

That's it! There are no additional dialog boxes to deal with. In fact, the Picture Viewer launches automatically when the install completes.

Now, when you open your Start menu on Windows 7 or look at the tiles on your Start page in Windows 8, you will see a new folder. It most likely will be titled Picture Viewer (see Figure 23.7). In that folder is the Picture Viewer application shortcut the user can click to run the program.

Uninstalling an Application You've Distributed

All Windows applications should provide a facility to easily be removed from the user's computer. Most applications provide this functionality in the Add/Remove Programs dialog box, and yours is no exception. In fact, all ClickOnce programs automatically create an entry in the Uninstall or Change a Program dialog box. Follow these steps to uninstall the Picture Viewer program:

FIGURE 23.7
Users can find your program in their Program Files, just as with commercial applications.

If you are running Windows 7, follow these steps to uninstall the Picture Viewer program:

1. Choose Start, Control Panel.

2. Locate the Uninstall a program link, and click it.

3. Scroll down in the dialog box until you find the Picture Viewer program, as shown in Figure 23.9.

4. To uninstall the program, click to select it and then click Uninstall/Change. You are given an opportunity to confirm or cancel. If you select OK, the program is uninstalled.

If you are running Windows 8, follow these steps to uninstall the Picture Viewer program:

1. Locate the Picture Viewer on your Start Page and right-click it to display options (see Figure 23.8).

2. Locate the Uninstall link at the bottom of the screen and click it.

3. Scroll down in the dialog box until you find the Picture Viewer program, as shown in Figure 23.9.

4. To uninstall the program, click to select it and then click Uninstall/Change. You are given an opportunity to confirm or cancel. If you select OK, the program is uninstalled.

FIGURE 23.8
Your program can be uninstalled from the Windows 8 Start page.

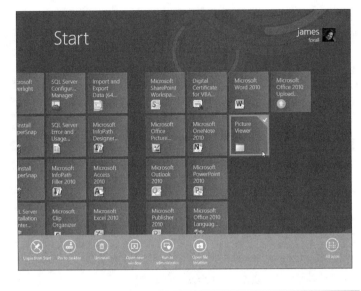

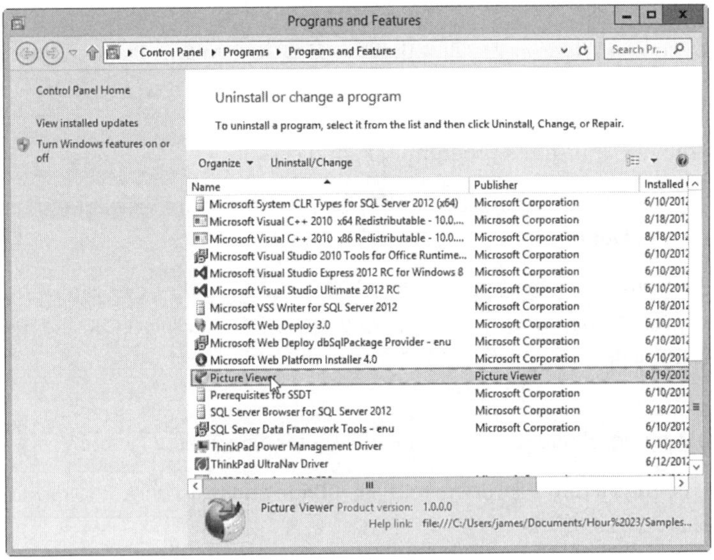

FIGURE 23.9
You cannot undo an uninstall—you must reinstall the application to use it again.

Setting Advanced Options for Creating ClickOnce Programs

The Publish Wizard is the easiest way to create a ClickOnce program, but it doesn't give you access to all the features of ClickOnce. To view all the available settings, right-click the project name in the Solution Explorer and choose Properties. Next, click the Publish tab, and you see a page of publishing options, as shown in Figure 23.10. Using this page, you can specify prerequisites, such as whether to install the

.NET Framework, which is required to run any .NET application. (By default, the Publish Wizard creates your ClickOnce application such that it installs the .NET Framework from the Web if the user performing the install doesn't have the Framework installed.) The Publish Wizard walks you through many of these options, but you gain the most control by setting your options here and clicking the Publish Now button, which appears at the bottom right of the Publish page.

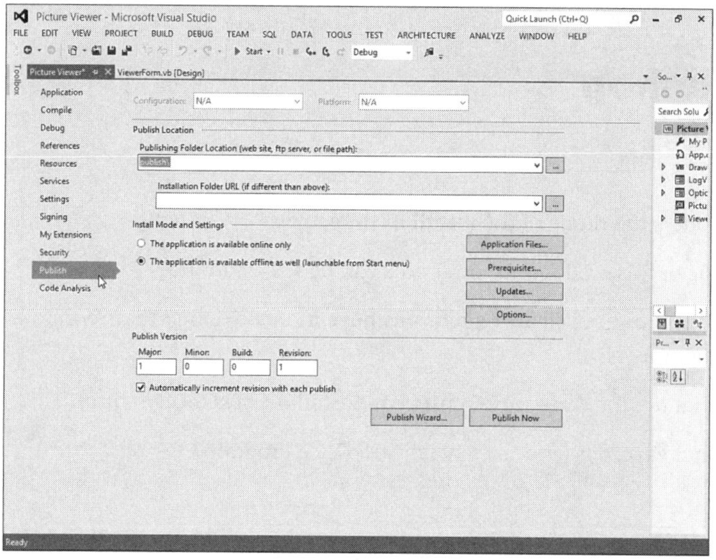

FIGURE 23.10
Advanced Click-Once settings can be set on the Publish tab of the Project Properties.

Summary

In this hour, you learned about ClickOnce and why Microsoft has moved to Click-Once from Windows Installer technology. You also learned how to use the Publish Wizard to create a ClickOnce program to distribute an application you've built using Visual Basic. Creating installs for robust applications requires a lot more effort and, in many cases, more tools. But the skills you learned in this hour enable you to distribute most projects that you'll build as a beginner with Visual Basic 2010.

Q&A

Q. How can I create the great installation wizards I see other install applications use?

A. If you want to create robust installations that gather user input in wizards, make changes to the Registry, enable you to include additional files, create shortcuts, and so on, you need to use a tool that uses the Windows Installer technology.

Q. *Should I assume that a user will always have the .NET Framework on her computer?*

A. If you plan on distributing to users running Windows 7 or Windows 8, this might be a safe assumption. Older versions of Windows might not have the Framework installed. If you are unsure, you should specify the .NET Framework as a prerequisite (note that this is set by default).

Workshop

Quiz

1. What is the name of the install technology?

2. True or false: ClickOnce programs can be self-updating.

3. True or false: ClickOnce programs have more flexibility than Windows Installer programs.

4. What are the three ways a user can install a ClickOnce program?

5. What wizard is used to create a ClickOnce program?

Answers

1. ClickOnce

2. True

3. False. Windows Installer technology provides much more flexibility than Click-Once programs.

4. From a web page, from a network file share, or from media such as a CD-ROM

5. The Publish Wizard

Exercises

1. Use the Publish Wizard to create an install for the Automate Excel project in Hour 22, "Controlling Other Applications Using Automation." Try installing the ClickOnce program on a computer that doesn't have Excel, and see what happens when you run the program.

2. If you have access to a web server, use the Publish Wizard to deploy the Picture Viewer to the web server, and then install the application on a different computer from the web server.

The 10,000-Foot View

What You'll Learn in This Hour:

▶ Understanding the .NET Framework

▶ Understanding the common language runtime

▶ How Visual Basic 2012 uses the Microsoft intermediate language

▶ Using Visual Studio .NET namespaces

▶ Understanding the common type system

▶ Understanding garbage collection

You know a lot about Visual Basic 2012 now. You can create projects, you can use forms and controls to build an interface, and you know how to add menus and toolbars to a form. You've also learned how to create modules and procedures and how to write code to make things happen. You can use variables, make decisions, perform looping, and even debug your code. Now you might be wondering, "Where to next?" In fact, this is the number-one question I receive from readers via emails.

Throughout this book, I've focused my discussions on Visual Basic. When it comes to Microsoft's .NET Framework, however, Visual Basic is just part of the picture. This hour provides an overview of Microsoft's .NET Framework so that you can see how Visual Basic relates to .NET as a whole. After completing this hour, you'll understand the various pieces of .NET and how they're interrelated. I hope you'll be able to combine this information with your current personal and professional needs to determine the facets of .NET that you want to explore in more detail.

The .NET Framework

The components and technology that make up Microsoft .NET are collectively called the *.NET Framework*. The .NET Framework is composed of numerous classes and includes components such as the Common Language Runtime, Microsoft Intermediate Language, and ADO.NET. The following sections explain the various pieces that make up the .NET Framework.

Common Language Runtime

A *language runtime* allows an application to run on a target computer; it consists of code that's shared among all applications developed using a supported language. A runtime contains the "guts" of language code, such as code that draws forms to the screen, handles user input, and manages data. The runtime of .NET is called the *common language runtime*.

Unlike runtimes for other languages, the common language runtime is designed as a multilanguage runtime. For example, both C# and Visual Basic use the common language runtime. In fact, currently more than 15 language compilers are being developed to use the common language runtime.

Because all .NET languages share the common language runtime, they also share the same IDE, forms engine, exception-handling mechanism, garbage collector (discussed shortly), and much more. One benefit of the multilanguage capability of the common language runtime is that programmers can leverage their knowledge of a given .NET language.

For example, some developers on a team might be comfortable with Visual Basic, whereas others are more comfortable with C#. Because both languages share the same runtime, both can be integrated to deliver a single solution. In addition, a common exception-handling mechanism is built into the common language runtime so that exceptions can be thrown from code written in one .NET language and caught in code written in another.

Code that runs within the common language runtime is called *managed* code because the code and resources that it uses (variables, objects, and so on) are fully managed by the common language runtime. Visual Basic is restricted to working only in managed code, but some languages (such as C++) can drop to *unmanaged* code—code that isn't managed by the common language runtime.

Another advantage of the common language runtime is that all .NET tools share the same debugging and code-profiling tools. In the past, Visual Basic was limited in its debugging tools, whereas applications such as C++ had many third-party debugging tools available. All languages now share the same tools. This means that as advancements are made to the debugging tools of one product, they're made to tools of all products because the tools are shared. This goes beyond debugging tools. Add-ins to the IDE such as code managers, for example, are just as readily available to Visual Basic as they are to C#—or any other .NET language, for that matter.

By the Way

Although Microsoft hasn't announced any official plans to do so, it's possible that it could produce a version of the common language runtime that runs on other operating systems, such as Macintosh OS or Linux. If this occurs, the applications that you've written for Windows should run on a newly supported operating system with little or no modification.

Microsoft Intermediate Language

As you can see in Figure 24.1, all .NET code, regardless of the language syntax used, compiles to Intermediate Language (IL) code. IL code is the only code that the common language runtime understands; it doesn't understand C#, Visual Basic, or any other developer syntax. IL gives .NET its multilanguage capabilities; as long as an original source language can be compiled to IL, it can become a .NET program. For example, people have developed a .NET compiler for COBOL—a mainframe language with a long history. This compiler takes existing COBOL code and compiles it to IL so that it will run within the .NET Framework, using the common language runtime. COBOL itself isn't a Windows language and doesn't support many of the features found in a true Windows language (such as a Windows Forms engine), so you can imagine the excitement of COBOL programmers when they first learned of being able to leverage their existing code and programming skills to create powerful Windows applications.

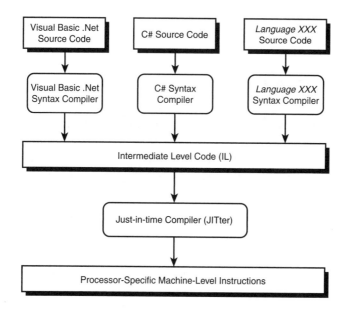

FIGURE 24.1
These are the steps taken to turn developer code into a running component.

By the Way

A potential drawback of IL is that it can be susceptible to reverse compilation. This has many people questioning the security of .NET code and the security of the .NET Framework in general. If code security is a serious concern for you, I encourage you to research this matter on your own.

Generating IL code isn't the final step in the process of compiling and running an application. For a processor (CPU) to execute programmed instructions, those instructions must be in *machine language* format. When you run a .NET application, a just-in-time compiler (called a *JITter*) compiles the IL to machine-language instructions that the processor can understand. IL code is *processor independent*, which again brings up the possibility that JITters could be built to create machine code for computers that are using something other than Intel-compatible processors. If Microsoft were to offer a common language runtime for operating systems other than Windows, many of the differences would lie in how the JITter would compile IL.

As .NET evolves, changes made to the common language runtime will benefit all .NET applications. For example, if Microsoft finds a way to further increase the speed at which forms are drawn to the screen by making improvements to the common language runtime, all .NET applications will immediately benefit from the improvement. However, optimizations made to a specific syntax compiler, such as the one that compiles Visual Basic code to IL, are language specific. This means that even though all .NET languages compile to IL code and use the common language runtime, it's possible for one language to have small advantages over another because of how the language's code is compiled to IL.

Namespaces

As mentioned earlier in this book, the .NET Framework is composed of classes—many classes. Namespaces are the way .Net creates a hierarchical structure of all these classes, and they help prevent naming collisions. A naming collision occurs when two classes have the same name. Because namespaces provide a hierarchy, it's possible to have two classes with the same name, as long as they exist in different namespaces. Namespaces, in effect, create scope for classes.

The base namespace in the .NET Framework is the `System` namespace. The `System` namespace contains classes for garbage collection (discussed shortly), exception handling, data typing, and much more. The `System` namespace is just the tip of the iceberg. There are literally dozens of namespaces. Table 24.1 lists some of the more common namespaces, many of which you've used in this book. All the controls you've placed on forms and even the forms themselves belong to the System.Windows.Forms namespace. Use Table 24.1 as a guide; if a certain namespace interests you, I suggest that you research it further in the Visual Studio .NET online help.

TABLE 24.1 Commonly Used Namespaces

Namespace	Description
Microsoft.VisualBasic	Contains classes that support compilation and code generation using Visual Basic.
System	Contains fundamental classes and base classes that define commonly used value and reference data types, event handlers, interfaces, attributes, and exceptions. This is the base namespace of .NET.
System.Data	Contains classes that constitute the ADO.NET architecture.
System.Diagnostics	Contains classes that enable you to debug your application and to trace the execution of your code.
System.Drawing	Contains classes that provide access to the Graphical Device Interface (GDI+) basic graphics functionality.
System.IO	Contains classes that allow reading from and writing to data streams and files.
System.Net	Contains classes that provide a simple programming interface to many of the protocols found on the network.
System.Security	Contains classes that provide the underlying structure of the common language runtime security system.
System.Web	Contains classes that provide interfaces that enable browser/server communication.
System.Windows.Forms	Contains classes for creating Windows-based applications that take advantage of the rich user interface features available in the Microsoft Windows operating system.
System.XML	Contains classes that provide standards-based support for processing XML.

> **By the Way**
>
> All Microsoft-provided namespaces begin with either System or Microsoft. Other vendors can provide their own namespaces, and it's possible for you to create your own custom namespaces as well, but that's beyond the scope of this book.

Common Type System

The common type system in the common language runtime is the component that defines how data types are declared and used. The common language runtime's capability to support cross-language integration to the level it does is largely due to the common type system. In the past, each language used its own data types and managed data in its own way. This made it difficult for applications developed in different languages to communicate because no standard way existed for passing data between them.

The common type system ensures that all .NET applications use the same data types. It also provides for self-describing type information (called *metadata*) and controls all the data manipulation mechanisms so that data is handled (stored and processed) in the same way among all .NET applications. This allows data (including objects) to be treated the same way in all .NET languages.

Garbage Collection

Although I've talked a lot about objects (you can't talk about anything .NET-related without talking about objects), I've avoided discussing the underlying technical details of how .NET creates, manages, and destroys objects. Although you don't need to know the complex minutiae of how .NET works with objects, you do need to understand a few details of how objects are destroyed.

As discussed in previous hours, setting an object variable to Nothing or letting it go out of scope destroys the object. However, as mentioned in Hour 16, "Designing Objects Using Classes," this isn't the whole story. The .NET platform uses a *garbage collector* to destroy objects. The specific type of garbage collection that .NET implements is called *reference-tracing garbage collection*. Essentially, the garbage collector monitors the resources a program uses. When consumed resources reach a defined threshold, the garbage collector looks for unused objects. When the garbage collector finds an unused object, it destroys it, freeing all the memory and resources the object was using.

An important thing to remember about garbage collection is that releasing an object by setting it to Nothing or letting an object variable go out of scope doesn't mean that the object is destroyed immediately. The object isn't destroyed until the garbage collector is triggered to go looking for unused objects.

Further Reading

Readers often ask me what books they should read next. I do not have a specific answer to this question because it depends entirely on who is asking. Chances are you're learning .NET for one of the following reasons:

- School
- Professional requirements
- Personal interest or as a hobby

Your reasons for learning Visual Basic have a lot to do with where you should proceed from here. If you're just learning Visual Basic as a hobby, take a route that interests you, such as web development or database development. If you're looking to advance your career, consider the companies you want to work for. What types of things are they doing—security, databases, web development? How can you make yourself more valuable to those companies? Instead of just picking a direction, choose a goal and move in that direction.

If a subject simply does not jump out at you, my recommendation is that you learn how to program databases. Get a book dedicated to your database of choice (mine is Microsoft SQL Server). Most applications these days use databases, and database skills are *always* a plus! Database programming and database design are really two different subjects. If you really want to make yourself valuable, you should learn how to properly design, normalize, and optimize databases, in addition to programming them for users to access.

Summary

Now that you've completed this book, you should have a solid working understanding of developing applications with Visual Basic. Nevertheless, you've just embarked on your journey. One of the things I love about developing applications for a living is that there's always something more to learn, and there's always a better approach to a development problem. In this hour, you saw the bigger picture of Microsoft's .NET platform by seeing the .NET Framework and its various components. Consider the information you learned in this hour a primer; what you do with this information and where you go from here is entirely up to you.

I wish you the best of luck with your programming endeavors!

HOUR 25

Printing

What You'll Learn in This Hour:

▶ Using the PrintDocument, PrintPreviewDialog, and PageSetupDialog controls

▶ Printing and previewing a document

▶ Changing printer and page settings

▶ Scaling images to fit a page

Printing is something that most users take for granted; you can find a Print and Print Preview button on almost every toolbar and File menu in almost every program. From a user's perspective, printing is a piece of cake—click a button and watch the document print to the screen or printer. Writing the code to print a document, on the other hand, is actually a bit of a challenge.

In this hour, you will learn about the System.Drawing.Printing namespace that contains the .NET printing functionality, as well as three non-visual controls that you can add to a form to print: PrintDocument, PrintPreviewDialog, and PageSetupDialog. You will learn how to print a document to the printer, as well as show the document in a Print Preview window to let the user see the document as it would print, without committing to using paper and toner. There are myriad printers on the market, as well as many different paper sizes. You will learn how to let the user choose the printer to print to, as well as the paper size and page margins. Because of the different printers, page sizes, and margins involved, you have to control the scaling of what you send to the printer or images and text appear distorted. You will learn how to scale an image so it prints with the proper proportions, regardless of the settings chosen by the user.

> If you are writing complex applications that will be run by a lot of users, you should consider using a third-party printing component, such as Crystal Reports. You want to spend your time creating value in your application, not writing code to print a document. My company Tigerpaw's flagship product ships with over 600 reports, all developed in Crystal Reports. We use Crystal Reports so that we can focus on creating usable reports instead of writing code to talk to printers.

By the Way

Preparing the Picture Viewer Project

You're going to be adding print and print preview functionality to the Picture Viewer project you completed in Hour 23. You'll be adding items to the toolbar as well as three controls that are used to print the image currently being displayed.

Adding Print and Print Preview Buttons to the Form

Start by opening the Picture Viewer project and then follow these steps to add Print and Print Preview buttons to the toolbar:

1. Double-click ViewerForm.vb in the Solutions Explorer to display the Viewer Form in the designer.

2. Click the toolbar on the form to select it and then click the Items property in the Property window.

3. Click the Build button in the Items property to display the Items Collection Editor shown in Figure 25.1.

FIGURE 25.1
The Items Collection Editor makes it easy to create useable toolbars.

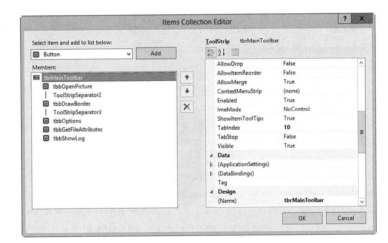

4. Click Add to create a new button and set its properties as follows:

Property	Value
Name	tbbPrint
Image	*(Use the file Print.png supplied at www.jamesfoxall.com/books.aspx or a 16×16 pixel image of your choice.)*
Text	Print
ToolTipText	Print

5. Use the positioning arrow buttons to move the new tbbPrint button so that it is located right above the tbbDrawBorder button.

6. Click Add to create another button and set its properties as follows:

Property	Value
Name	tbbPrintPreview
Image	(Use the file PrintPreview.png supplied at my website or a 16x16 pixel image of your choice.)
Text	Print Preview
TooltipText	Print

7. Use the Up positional arrow button to move the tbbPrintPreview item so that it appears right after the tbbPrint button.

8. Open the drop-down and choose Separator; then click the Add button to create a new separator.

9. Move the separator so that it appears after the tbbPrintPreview button (see Figure 25.2).

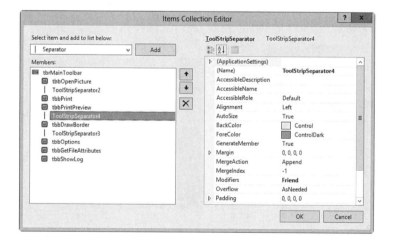

FIGURE 25.2
Users expect to find Print and Print Preview buttons here on a toolbar.

10. Click OK to save your changes and close the Items Collection Editor.

Adding the `PrintDocument`, `PrintPreviewDialog`, and `PageSetupDialog` Controls

Strictly speaking, the PrintDocument control is all you need to print something to the printer. However, while the `PrintDocument` control lets you dump something directly to the printer, it does not provide print preview functionality, nor can you use it to let users change their printer or page settings. To show a preview of a document to be printed, you use the `PrintPreviewDialog` control, and to let the user choose a printer and set page options such as margins, you use the `PageSetupDialog` control. Rather than have you add these controls one at a time as you progress through this chapter, you're going to add them all to the form now.

Follow these steps to adding the printing controls to your form:

1. Double-click ViewerForm.vb in the Solution Explorer window to show the viewer form (if it's not already visible).

2. Click the Toolbox tab to open the Toolbox and scroll down to the Printing category. Double-click PrintDocument to add it to the form.

3. Double-click PrintPreviewDialog to add one to the form. (Be careful not to double-click PrintPreview by mistake.)

4. Double-click PageSetupDialog to add a page setup dialog control to the form.

5. Click the form to close the toolbox.

All three of these controls are non-visual controls and will appear in the bottom area below the form, as shown in Figure 25.3.

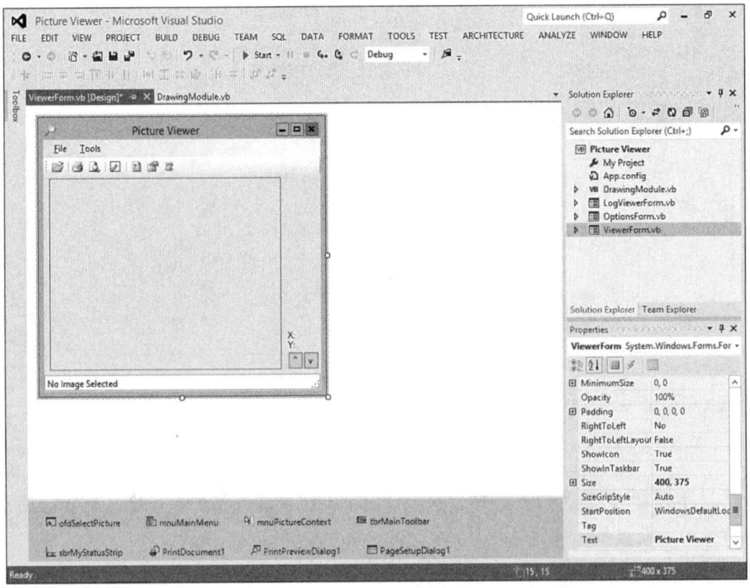

FIGURE 25.3
These three non-visual controls allow you to print, print preview, and change printer and page settings.

Printing and Previewing a Document

The basics of printing a document are handled by the `PrintDocument` control. The behavior of this control, however, is not intuitive. You don't actually pass a document to the `PrintDocument` control; instead, you tell the `PrintDocument` to print. This causes the control's `PrintPage` event to fire, and it is in this event that you place code that does the actual printing.

In Hour 18, you learned how to draw using the graphics methods of GDI+. To print a document, you have to draw to a Graphics object in the `PrintPage` event—much as you draw on a form. Whatever you draw to this Graphics object prints on the printer. You will start by adding basic printing functionality to your Picture Viewer project, using the PrintDocument control. Then, you will add the `PrintPreviewDialog` control to the mix to generate a print preview window so that the user can see what is to be printed before actually sending the image to the printer.

Printing a Document

Rather than create separate procedures for printing and print previewing, you are going to create a single procedure that accepts a parameter that determines whether to send the document to the printer or display it in a print preview window. You are going to use an enumeration for the parameter that determines the destination of the image. By now, you've created many message boxes and are familiar with enumerations. Enumerations are the lists of potential values that you can use in code. They appear in Intellisense drop-downs, as shown in Figure 25.4.

When passing data to a variable declared as an enumeration, you specify the name of the value in code. At compile time, Visual Basic resolves this name to an underlying number associated with it; enums are actually Integer values. You're going to create a simple enumeration for your print procedure. The enumeration you will define consists of two values—one to designate sending the image to the printer, and another to designate sending the image to a print preview window. To create your enumeration, follow these steps:

1. Click the View Code button in the Solution Explorer to view the code behind ViewerForm.vb.

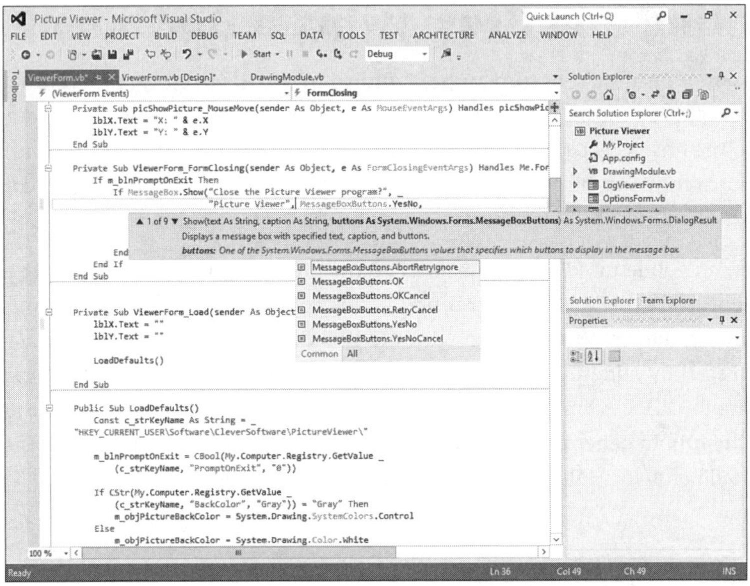

FIGURE 25.4
Enumerations
make coding
easier, and
enable you to
use named
values rather
than cryptic
numbers.

2. Scroll to the top of the procedure and locate the Private module variables. Immediately below these variables and in front of the first procedure, enter the following code:

```
Private Enum PrintDestination
    Printer = 0
    PrintPreview = 1
End Enum
```

Your code now looks like that shown in Figure 25.5.

You know that `Private` indicates scope, so this enumeration is visible and valid only when called within this form. The keyword `Enum` is used to create an enumeration and the text `PrintDestination` specifies the name of the enumeration. Within the `Enum` structure, you entered two values: `Printer` and `PrintPreview`. Notice that each value equates to a number. In code, you reference the named text, making your code easier to read and reducing the chance for errors. At compile time, the value associated with the name (0 for printer and 1 for print preview) is substituted in your code. With the enumeration defined, you can now declare variables as type `PrintDestination`, which you'll do next.

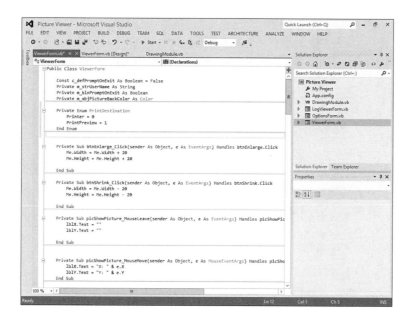

FIGURE 25.5
Enumerations
reduce coding
complexities and
chances for
error.

Creating the `PrintImage` Procedure

In this section, you're going to create the basic framework for the `PrintImage` procedure that will be used to print the currently viewed image. Scroll to the bottom of the
form module and enter the following code after the last procedure and before the End
Class statement:

```
Private Sub PrintImage(ByVal Destination As printDestination)

    If ofdSelectPicture.FileName = "" Then
        MessageBox.Show("There is no image to print.", "Picture Viewer", _
            MessageBoxButtons.OK, MessageBoxIcon.Exclamation)
        Exit Sub
    End If

    PrintDocument1.Print()

End Sub
```

Your code should now look like that in Figure 25.6.

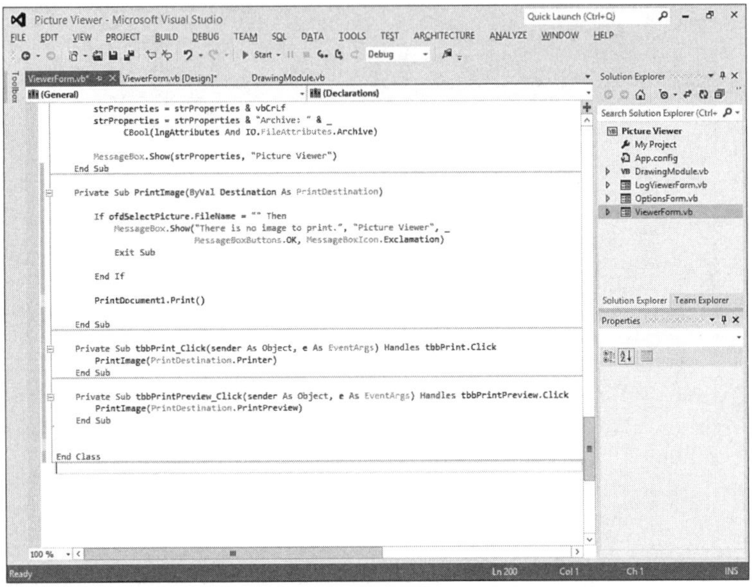

FIGURE 25.6
This basic procedure shell doesn't actually print—not yet.

Notice how Visual Basic allowed you to create the `Destination` variable as type `PrintDestination`; it's that easy. When you write code to call this procedure, you'll get a drop-down list of the two values in your enumeration. You're going to do that now by hooking up code to your Print and Print Preview buttons. Follow these steps to add the code:

1. Click the ViewerForm.vb [Design] tab to return to the form designer and then double-click the Print button on the toolbar to access its click event.

2. Enter the following code in the Click event:

```
PrintImage(PrintDestination.Printer)
```

When you entered the open parenthesis of the procedure, did you notice that Visual Basic gave you a drop-down with your enumerated values (see Figure 25.7)? Enumerations are easy to create and use, and they do a wonderful job of improving readability of code.

3. Click the ViewerForm.vb [Design] tab to return to the form designer and double-click the Print Preview button to access its `Click` event.

4. Enter the following code in the `Click` event:

```
PrintImage(PrintDestination.PrintPreview)
```

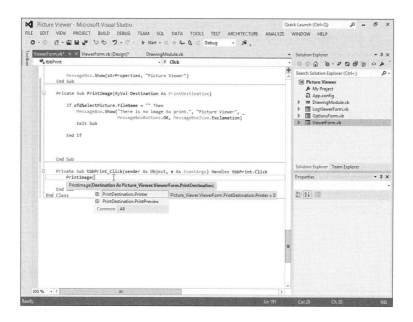

FIGURE 25.7
Custom enumerations work just like the standard enumerations found in Visual Basic.

Printing the Currently Viewed Image

At this time, you've made a call to the PrintDocument but haven't specified what to print. As I mentioned earlier, printing is done using a Graphics object—you literally draw to a Graphics object and the contents of that object are printed on the printer. When you call the `Print` method of the `PrintDocument` control, you initiate the printing of a document. This triggers the `PrintPage` event of the `PrintDocument` control. It is in this event that you place the code to draw to the `Graphics` object of the page. Follow these steps to create the code to actually print to the printer:

1. Open the object dropdown list located in the upper-left corner of the code window and choose `PrintDocument1`.

2. Open the events dropdown list in the upper-right corner of the code window and choose `PrintPage` to access the PrintPage event.

3. Enter the following code:

```
' Create a rectangle the size of the printable area of the page
Dim recPrintable As New Rectangle( _
    e.MarginBounds.Left, e.MarginBounds.Top, _
    e.MarginBounds.Width, e.MarginBounds.Height)

' Create a rectangle used for the actual drawing dimensions of the image.
' Default it to the printable area.
Dim recDraw As Rectangle = recPrintable

' Load the image in a bitmap object we can use.
Dim bmSource As New Bitmap(ofdSelectPicture.FileName)
```

```
' Draw the bitmap on the Graphics object of the PrintDocument control.
e.Graphics.DrawImage(bmSource, recDraw)

' This is the last page to be printed.
e.HasMorePages = False

' Free up resources used.
bmSource.Dispose()
```

Your procedure should look like Figure 25.8.

FIGURE 25.8
Printing a document takes a fair bit of code.

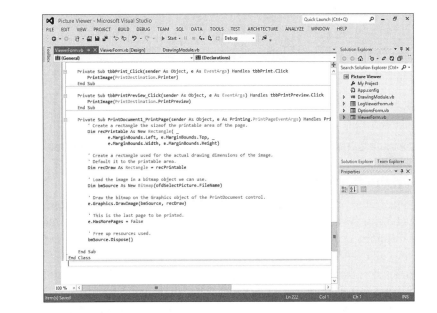

Go ahead and run the project, open an image, and click the Print button. The image you are viewing should be printed to your printer. You might notice that the image is stretched to fit the page dimensions—we'll be addressing this shortly.

Most of this code should make sense to you, but I'm going to explain it step by step:

1. A rectangle variable called recPrintable is created with the dimensions of the printable area of the page. At present, the values held in the variable are the default margin values for the default printer. Notice that MarginBounds is part of the e parameter, and it contains the margin settings of the page.

2. A rectangle variable called recDraw is created and set to the values of the printable rectangle. This is the rectangle that is used in the actual drawing of the image to the Graphics object. In the current state of the code, you could just use recPrintable as the rectangle to print. However, I mentioned earlier (and you probably saw it on your printed page) that the image is stretched to

fit the page. We'll address this shortly, and it will require using a rectangle variable different from the one holding the printable dimensions; hence the creation of recDraw.

3. A bitmap variable called bmSource is created and filled with the image that is shown on the viewer form. Rather than copy from the picture box, you should load the image straight from the file to make sure you're working with a pure source image.

4. We copy the contents of the bitmap (the source file to print) to the Graphics object (the image that the printer can understand) by using the DrawImage() method. This method accepts a bitmap object and a rectangle. Keep in mind that the Graphics object is created automatically by the event and has the same dimensions as the full page (margin space is included in the full page). The rectangle parameter tells Visual Basic the location and the size to use when copying the image. In this case, it uses recDraw, which is set to the margins of the page.

5. If you had more pages to print, you would set the HasMorePages property to True and this event would fire again. It would be up to you to track what page is being printed and draw the appropriate graphics to send to the printer. Because you're printing just one page, set this to False so the event doesn't fire a second time.

6. The final statement simply frees up resources used by the bitmap object.

Actually, the code isn't all that difficult but it is all required. If you miss a step, it can be confusing to figure out where you went wrong. If you have complicated images to print or require multiple pages, the complexity of required code grows considerably, but for our purposes this is all you need to print your image.

Previewing a Document

You might have noticed that when you printed your image, the image took almost the entire page. Also, if you have more than one printer installed, the default printer was used, as well as the default paper tray. Users often want to see what is being printed before committing to using paper and toner, and the way to give them this capability is by showing the page to be printed in a print preview window. To show a print preview window, you use the PrintPreviewDialog control. Follow these steps to add preview capability to your Picture Viewer project:

1. Stop your project if it is running and return to the code window of ViewerForm.vb.

2. Locate the `PrintImage()` procedure (not the PrintPage event) and replace the statement `PrintDocument1.Print()` with the following code:

```
If Destination = printDestination.PrintPreview Then
    'Specify document for print preview dialog box and show
    PrintPreviewDialog1.Document = PrintDocument1

    PrintPreviewDialog1.ShowDialog()
Else
    PrintDocument1.Print()
End If
```

Your code should now look like that in Figure 25.9.

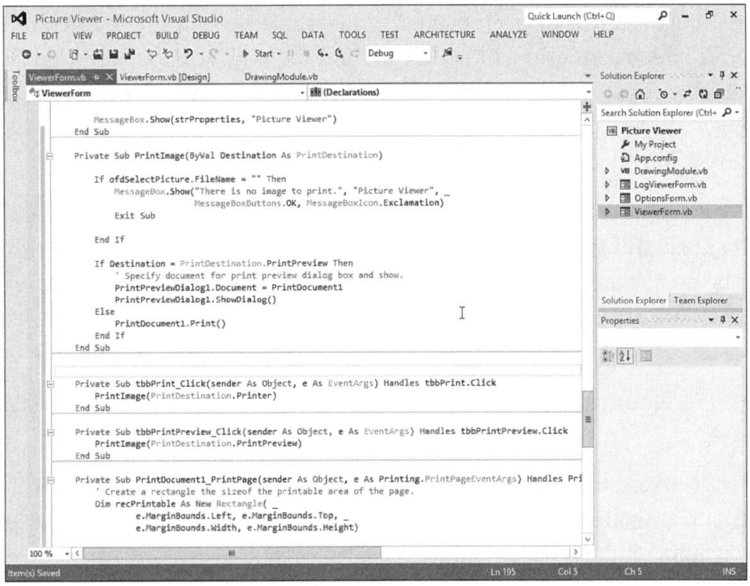

FIGURE 25.9
It takes just a
few lines of
code (and the
PrintPreview
Dialog control)
to add print
preview
capabilities.

Notice that the enumeration was used again to determine whether the calling procedure wanted to send the image to the printer or to a print preview window. You only added two lines of print code to this procedure to change the behavior. First, you set the `Document` property of the `PrintPreviewDialog` control to the `PrintDocument` object. You've already entered code in the `PrintPage` event to draw the page, and all this statement does is tell the `PrintPreviewDialog` control that you want to use the same printing code to generate the page. The second statement simply calls the `ShowDialog()` method to show the print preview window.

Go ahead and run the project now. Click the Open button to browse and select an image file; then click the Print Preview button on the toolbar. Visual Basic displays the image in a print preview window (see Figure 25.10). Using this dialog box, a user can see exactly what is to be printed before committing to actually printing the document.

It's possible to zoom in to the page, print the document, close the dialog, and even view multiple pages (if you've written code to generate multiple pages). Feel free to print the image again or click the Close button to close the print preview window without actually printing the image.

FIGURE 25.10
The Print Preview window lets a user see what is to be printed before printing it.

Changing Printer and Page Settings

You have now added printing and previewing capability to your Picture Viewer project. These are fantastic additions, but you still have two problems to deal with. The first is the limitation of printing to only the default printer, using the default page size and margin values. The second issue is the stretching of your source image. You'll tackle the page setup issues in this section, and address the scaling problem in the next section.

Just as the `PrintPreviewDialog` control added the capability to preview a document before printing it, the `PrintPageSettings` control allows you to enable your users to change printer and page settings. Follow these steps to add this capability:

1. Stop the project if it's running.

2. Click the ViewerForm.vb [Design] tab to display the code window for the Viewer Form.

3. Create a new procedure using the following code:

```
Private Sub ChangePageSettings()
    ' Let the user change the printer settings
    Dim PrintPageSettings As New System.Drawing.Printing.PageSettings
```

```
PageSetupDialog1.PageSettings = PrintPageSettings
PageSetupDialog1.ShowDialog()

'Specify current page settings
PrintDocument1.DefaultPageSettings = PrintPageSettings
End Sub
```

This code creates a new variable called `PrintPageSettings`, which is of type `PageSettings`. This object is part of the System.Drawing.Printing namespace and it contains things such as a selected printer, page size, and print margins. When `New` is used to declare the variable, its values are initialized to the default printer and its page settings. This object is passed to the `PageSetupDialog` control and then the `ShowDialog()` method is called to show the page setup dialog box modally. When the user closes the dialog box, code returns to the procedure. The user's choices are stored in the `PrintPageSettings` variable, which is then passed to the `PrintDocument` object by way of its `DefaultPageSettings` property.

All that's left is to call this code. Locate the `PrintImage()` procedure you created earlier and add the call to `ChangePageSettings()`, as shown in Figure 25.11.

FIGURE 25.11
Call the ChangePage Settings procedure to let the user choose the printer and page settings before sending the document to the printer or a preview window.

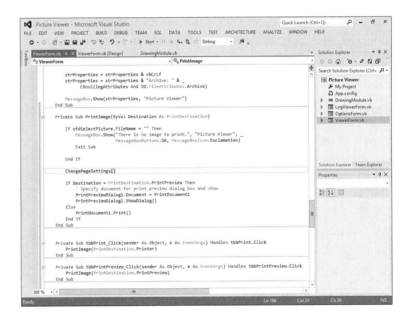

Now, save your work and run the project. Follow these steps to test the page setup code:

1. Click the Open button to browse and select an image to display.

2. Click Print Preview on the toolbar. The Page Setup window appears (see Figure 25.12).

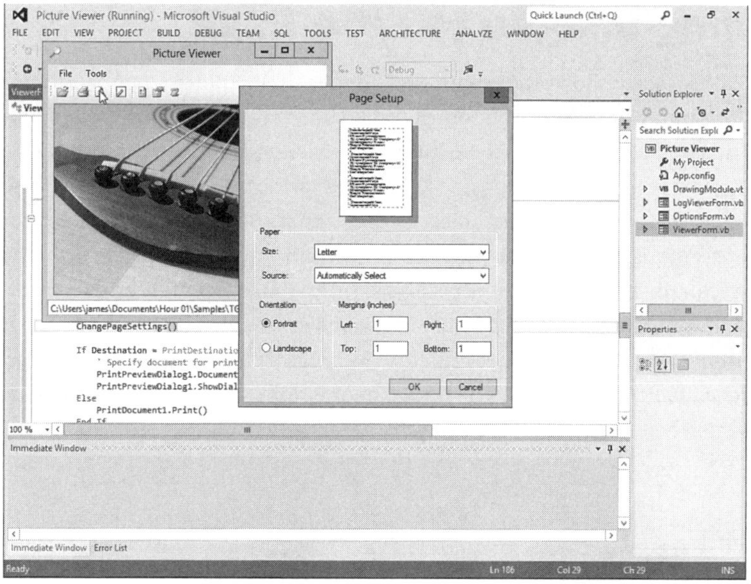

FIGURE 25.12
The Page Setup dialog box can be used to change printers, paper sources, and margins.

3. Click the Landscape radio button to print in landscape mode and change the Top property to 5.

4. Click OK to commit your changes and display the Print Preview window.

Visual Basic does exactly what you ask it to: It renders the page in landscape mode and puts the image in the specified margins. As you can tell from Figure 25.13, you've still got one more issue to solve.

FIGURE 25.13
When printing images, Visual Basic renders them in the specified margins, even if that means stretching the image.

Scaling Images to Fit a Page

Figure 25.13 clearly shows that some stretching is taking place when rending the image for print. Here's why: The source image has very specific dimensions, say 800 pixels wide by 600 pixels tall. The actual printable area within the margins of the page also has specific dimensions, say 400 pixels wide by 800 pixels high. When you draw the image in the Graphics object in the `PrintPage` event, Visual Basic stretches the image so that it takes up the exact space within the margins, even if that destination rectangle has a different aspect ratio (the ratio of height to width) than the dimensions of the bitmap itself. Figure 25.14 shows this effect. The image on the left represents a typical portrait page. The arrows indicate the directions the image will be stretched to fit the margins. The image on the right shows how the image actually prints—stretched to fit within the margins.

FIGURE 25.14
Without specific code to prevent it, images are stretched to fit the destination rectangle.

Correcting this problem actually requires some tricky code. The short of it is you must determine a rectangle to be used for drawing the image on the Graphics object, and this rectangle must have the following constraints:

▶ Either the height or the width of the printable region must be shortened to compensate for the dimensions of the original image.

▶ Neither the height nor width of the rectangle can exceed the printable height or width region, respectively.

Stop the project if it's currently running and return to the code window of the Viewer form. Create the following new procedure:

```
Private Sub ResizeToPrintableArea(ByRef img As Bitmap, _
    ByRef recDraw As Rectangle, ByRef recPrintable As Rectangle)

  ' Which is bigger in the source image, the height or width?
  If img.Width > img.Height Then
     ' Which is bigger on destination rectangle, height or width?
     If recPrintable.Width > recPrintable.Height Then
        ' Height is the constraint.
        recDraw.Width = CInt(recDraw.Height * (img.Width / img.Height))
     Else
        ' Width is the constraint.
        recDraw.Height = CInt(recDraw.Width * (img.Height / img.Width))
     End If

  Else
     ' The height is greater than or equal to the width.
     ' Which is bigger on destination rectangle, height or width?
     If recPrintable.Height > recPrintable.Width Then
        ' Width is the constraint.
        recDraw.Height = CInt(recDraw.Width * (img.Height / img.Width))
     Else
        ' Height is the constraint.
        recDraw.Width = CInt(recDraw.Height * (img.Width / img.Height))
     End If
  End If

End Sub
```

Next, you need to call this procedure in the `PrintPage` event. Locate the `PrintPage` event and add the call as shown in Figure 25.15.

Rather than try to explain every detail, allow me to walk you through an example. Consider Figure 25.14:

▶ The first thing the code does is determine whether the height or width of the image is greater. Because the picture of this beautiful Jamaican sunset is landscape, the width is greater than the height.

▶ The destination rectangle is then considered. This is a portrait page, so the height is greater than the width.

From looking at the two rectangles, you can see that width is the constraint—after the source image is stretched to the width, it can go no further even though there is space to continue to stretch the height. So, leave the destination rectangle width as it is, and determine a new height for the destination rectangle by determining the aspect ratio of the height to width in the source rectangle and applying that to the width of the destination rectangle. The code is a bit complicated, but you don't have to fully understand it to use it.

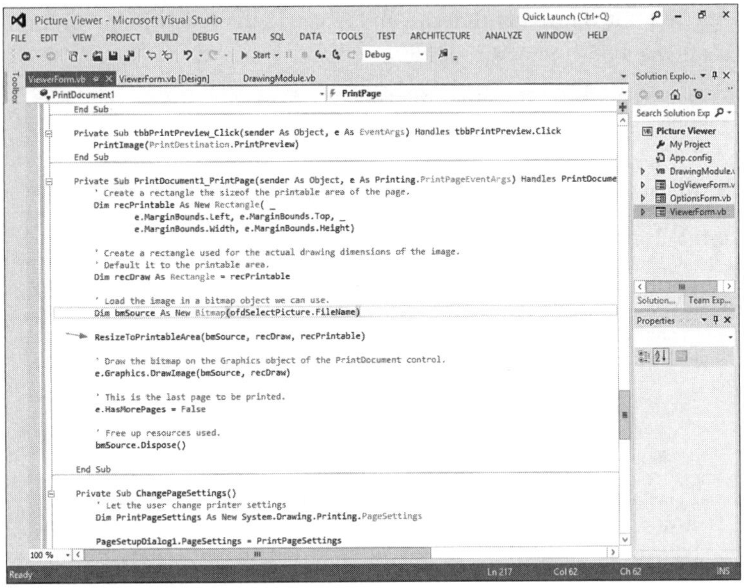

FIGURE 25.15
The ResizeTo-
PrintableArea
procedure modi-
fies the recDraw
rectangle so that
the image is ren-
dered in the mar-
gins without
being stretched.

Follow these steps to test your code:

1. Run the project and choose an image to display.

2. Click the Print Preview button on the toolbar to display the Page Settings dialog box.

3. Set the Top and Bottom margin properties to 4, as shown in Figure 25.16.

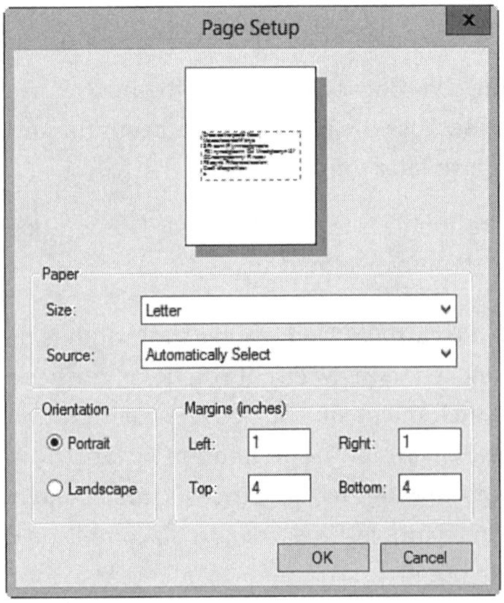

FIGURE 25.16
Notice the desig-
nated printable
region on the
page.

4. Click OK to preview the document.

5. Notice how the image is constrained within the margins, but renders without stretching (see Figure 25.17).

FIGURE 25.17
The scaling rou-
tine makes sure
that the image is
printed within
the margins, but
that it isn't
stretched.

Go ahead and stop the project now and save your work.

Summary

Printing in Visual Basic is tricky. There are multiple controls involved, and you must be intimately familiar with drawing to render a document to print. In this chapter, you learned how to use the `PrintDocument` control to print a document. You also learned how to use the `PrintPreviewDialog` to show the user a preview of what is to be printed, as well as the `PageSetupDialog` control to allow the user to change printers or page settings. Finally, you created a procedure to determine the proper rendering rectangle to use to print the image within the specified page margins, but without stretching it. As I mentioned earlier, if you have lots to print within an application, using a third-party reporting component is probably your best option. However, if you need to add printing directly to your application, you now know how.

Q&A

Q. *Can I print text files instead of graphics?*

A. Yes, but it's not a simple matter of passing the text to the `PrintDocument` object. You need to use drawing methods such as `DrawText` to render the text to a Graphics object, just as you did with the image. This can be even trickier than sending graphics to the PrintDocument object.

Q. *Can I programmatically select a printer or set page settings?*

A. Yes, because the printer and the page settings are all part of the controls you learned how to use in this chapter. You can set properties of the controls and related objects directly to do things like set page sizes and margin boundaries.

Workshop

Quiz

1. What control is used to print something to the printer?
2. In what event do you place code to generate the actual document to send to the printer?
3. What can you create to allow developers to pass one of a set of named values to a property, parameter, or variable?
4. How do you print more than one page?
5. How do you let users choose a printer and specify page settings?

Answers

1. The `PrintDocument` control
2. The `PrintPage` event
3. You can create an enumeration.
4. In the `PrintPage` event, you would set `e.HasMorePages = True` to cause the event to fire multiple times, and you would have to create the Graphics object for the page each time.
5. Use the `PrintPageSettings` control.

Exercises

1. Add Print and Print Preview items to the File menu and hook them up to your printing code.
2. Modify your code to default the page margins to 2 inches on all sides. Hint: Set the margins of the PrintPageSettings object in the procedures ChangePageSettings. Margins are in 100ths of an inch, so use a value of 200.

HOUR 26

Creating User Controls

What You'll Learn in This Hour:

▶ Creating an inherited control

▶ Enforcing numeric entry in a text box

▶ Adding balloon help to a control

▶ Creating an aggregate control

▶ Creating custom properties

▶ Creating custom methods

You've come a long way to get to this chapter, creating many forms with many controls. What you may not have realized is that you can create your own controls that can be placed on forms. Creating custom controls is my favorite development topic—I love creating custom controls! The idea of putting useful code in a reusable format and wrapping it up in a tidy little component with an optimized user interface appeals to me in many ways; any time I find myself extending the functionality of an existing control, I consider wrapping that functionality into a custom control. For example, you will often need to prevent users from typing non-numeric text into a text box. You could add the necessary code to the appropriate events for each control on each form that needs this, or you could write your own numeric text box that has this functionality built right in. After it is developed as a custom control, you need to only drop it on a form and you instantly have a text box that limits the user's input to numeric values. You build such a control in this chapter, as well as an extended version of the control that includes a calculator button that displays the Windows Calculator.

> You can purchase commercial controls from many vendors, and I do encourage you to explore commercial options when you're on a deadline; you can buy a serious amount of functionality for relatively little money. However, when you need small tweaks to existing controls, or you need something completely out of the ordinary, building your own control is the way to go.

Think of custom controls as small applications in and of themselves. You have to put thought into the user interface, as well as what functionality you want to expose by way of properties, methods, and events. You can create a number of different types of controls. Some possibilities include the following:

▶ **Invisible-at-runtime controls:** These controls, of which the Timer control is an example, don't have a physical interface, but can be used by programmers to implement specific functionality. I suggest you just create a class for such functionality, rather than create an invisible-at-runtime control.

▶ **Container controls:** Container controls allow the developer to put additional controls onto them. The standard Frame control is an example.

▶ **Inherited controls:** These controls use the object-oriented functionality of .NET to enable you to easily build new controls based on existing controls.

▶ **Aggregate controls:** Aggregate controls are like forms: You can place any controls you want on them to create a new interface.

▶ **Owner-Drawn controls:** These controls have nothing placed on them; their interface consists solely of what you draw on them, using the various drawing features of GDI+.

You are going to build two different user controls in this hour. The first uses inheritance to extend the functionality of the standard text box. You add code to limit the user's input to numeric data only, creating a numeric text box. The second control you build is an aggregate control and includes your numeric text box, along with a button that the user can click to start Windows calculator.

> Creating custom controls is an advanced topic and I can only scratch the surface of what is possible in this chapter. Creating custom controls for commercial use requires you to develop a high level of skills in almost every topic in this book. My goal is not to make you an expert on creating custom controls, but to teach you some of the possibilities of this amazing technology and to show you just how much fun it can be.

Creating an Inherited Control

In Hour 3, "Understanding Objects and Collections," you learned about objects. Forms are objects, controls are objects—everything in .NET is an object. Object-oriented programming offers some amazing capabilities. A notable one is that you can *inherit* from an existing object to create a new type of object. You are going to be astonished at how easy this is to do!

Begin by starting Visual Basic and creating a new Windows Forms Application called **Custom Controls**, rename your main form MainForm.vb, and change the form's text property to Custom Controls. Next, choose Add Class from the Project menu and create a new class called `clsNumericTextbox.vb`.

As requested, Visual Basic creates a new, empty class (see Figure 26.1). Because everything is an object, everything starts with a class. Building like objects from scratch, such as forms, would take thousands of lines of code per object if there wasn't a way to build on existing code. Inheritance enables a class to instantly take on the characteristics of some other class. When you create a form, for example, Visual Basic creates a class that inherits from Windows. This code is hidden from you by default, but you can see it by choosing to view all files in the Solution Explorer, expanding a form class, and double-clicking the designer item that appears. Doing this shows you the hidden code that actually defines the form. Figure 26.2 shows an example of what this looks like. Notice the `Inherits` statement toward the top of the class; a new form inherits from System.Windows.Forms.Form. This base class has all the logic necessary to create a form so that you just have to build on what's already been created.

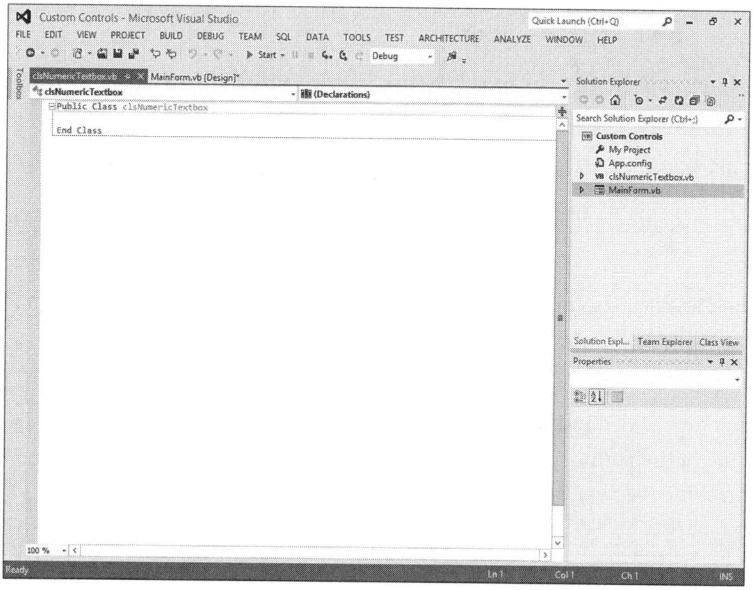

FIGURE 26.1
Everything starts with a blank class.

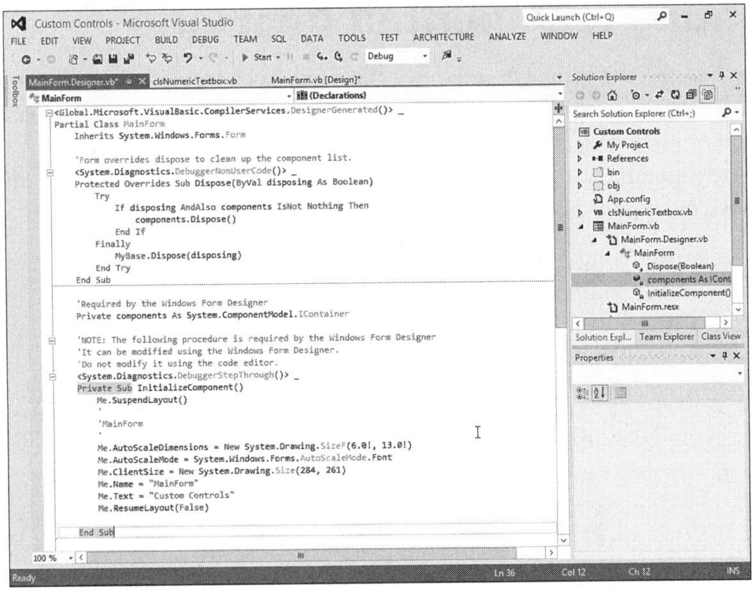

FIGURE 26.2
Classes can
take on all attrib-
utes of another
class through
the use of inheri-
tance.

You are going to make a custom control based on the standard text box, so you will
inherit from the standard text box. Add the following statement to your class, just
after the class declaration:

```
Inherits Windows.Forms.TextBox
```

You have just created a text box control! To see this, follow these steps:

1. Click Save All on the toolbar.

2. You need to build your project to use your control on a form, so choose Build
   CustomControls from the Build menu.

3. Click the MainForm.vb [Design] tab to display the default form in the project.

4. Open the toolbox and notice your custom control listed at the top (see Figure
   26.3).

5. Double-click clsNumericTextbox in the toolbox to add the control to your form.
   Set the form's Location property to **91, 95**.

Go ahead and take a moment to look at the properties for this control Short of the
classname of the control in the Properties window, you can't tell that this is not a
standard Windows text box because at this point in time, it *is* a standards Windows
text box.

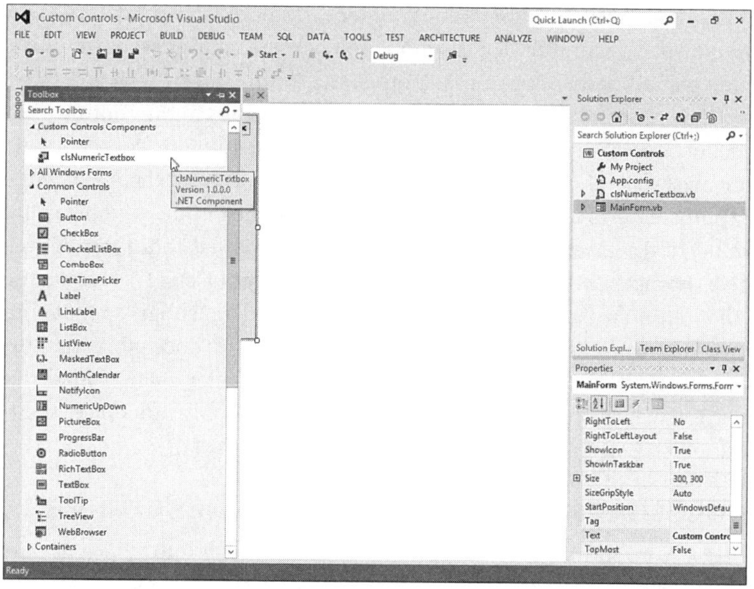

FIGURE 26.3
Custom controls
in the toolbox
appear just
like standard
controls.

Enforcing Numeric Entry in the Text Box

The next step in building your control is to modify the behavior of the base class (the bass class is the class you inherited from—the Windows text box). Follow these steps to prevent the user from entering non-numeric values into the text box:

1. Click the clsNumericTextbox.vb tab to return to the code for your custom control.

2. Open the object drop-down in the upper-left corner of the code designer and choose clsNumericTextbox Events.

3. Open the event drop-down list in the upper-right corner of the code designer and choose the KeyPress event.

4. Enter the following code into the KeyPress event:

```
If Not (IsNumeric(e.KeyChar)) Then
    Select Case Microsoft.VisualBasic.AscW(e.KeyChar)
        Case Keys.Enter, Keys.Back, Keys.Tab, Asc("$"), Asc("."), Asc(",")

    Case Else
        e.Handled = True
    End Select
End If
```

None of this code is new. What this procedure does is check the key being pressed to determine whether it's numeric or not. If the character is numeric, nothing is done and the key is accepted. If the key is not numeric, it still may be a key that you want to allow and you test for that. For example, you don't want to prevent the Tab key from being pressed or the user can't tab out of the control. Likewise, if you trap the Back key, the user can't press Backspace to delete characters in the control. The period (.) and dollar sign ($) are acceptable characters for some numeric values, so the code allows them as well. The `Select Case` construct simply looks at the ASCII value of the pressed character (every key on the keyboard has a unique numeric value called an ASCII value) and sees whether the value is one of the allowed characters. If it's not an acceptable character, `e.Handled` is set to `True`. Recall from Hour 17, "Interacting with Users," that setting `e.Handled = True` causes the key to be "eaten" so that it doesn't get processed by the text box. Choose Build CustomControls once more from the Debug menu and then press F5 to run the project. Try to enter a non-numeric value—you can't. You just created a custom text box that accepts only numeric entries!

Keeping Users from Pasting Non-Numeric Values

As you develop applications or controls, you sometimes run into problems that you didn't anticipate. There is one such problem in your custom control. To see it, follow these steps:

1. Open the Windows Start menu and launch Windows Notepad.

2. Enter the text **not a number** into Notepad.

3. Highlight the text you just entered and press Ctrl+C to copy the text.

4. Press Alt+Tab to switch back to your running program. When the cursor is in your numeric text box, right-click the numeric text box and choose Paste. You'll find that the control allows the non-numeric data!

5. Stop the running project now.

As I mentioned in Hour 17, a paste operation isn't actually a key press, so you can't control what is pasted in the text box through the use of the `KeyPress` event. However, you can prevent non-numeric values from being pasted by using the `TextChanged` event. In essence, you look at any pasted value and determine whether it is a number. If not, you set the control's `Text` property back to what it was before the paste. The `TextChanged` event doesn't have a handled parameter, so there is no intrinsic way to cancel what the user pasted. You address this by keeping the last valid value of the text box in a module variable.

Follow these steps to prevent non-numeric values from being pasted into your control:

1. Scroll to the top of the `clsNumericTextbox` class and enter this text right below the `Inherits` statement:

```
Private m_strLastValue As String
```

2. Choose (clsNumericTextbox Events) in the object drop-down list and then choose `TextChanged` from the event drop-down list.

3. Enter the following text into the `TextChanged` event:

```
If Not (IsNumeric(Me.Text)) And Me.Text.Length > 0 Then
    ' The value is not a number.
    MyBase.Text = m_strLastValue
Else
    m_strLastValue = MyBase.Text
End If
```

This code looks at the text that's been sent to the control. If the text is non-numeric and not empty, the `Text` property of the text box is set back to its previous value. Referring to `MyBase` in this case is similar to using `Me`, but it references the base class from which you inherited. Note that if the value is numeric or empty, the module variable is set to the current `Text` property, so that it becomes the new "undo value" if invalid data is passed to the control in the future.

Choose Build CustomControls from the Debug menu again and press F5 to run the project. Try pasting text into your control—you can't. You might see the text you paste for a brief moment, but then it is replaced by the last valid value of the numeric text box control.

Stop your running project now to return to the code designer and then save your work.

Adding Balloon Help to Your Control

So far, you've been able to create a useful, fully featured custom control with very little code. You can continue to expand on the base class in interesting ways. For example, the Windows text box doesn't have a `tooltip` property. You are now going to add a tooltip to your custom control that will display balloon help to your control's users.

You create balloon help by using the `tooltip` control. The `tooltip` control is an invisible-at-runtime control that can be added to a form. However, you don't have a form. This isn't a problem because you can use code to create instances of controls virtually.

Follow these steps to add a tooltip and balloon help to your control:

1. Scroll to the top of the class and add the following statement, right below the declaration of the private variable m_strLastValue. This statement creates a private, module-level variable that holds an instance of a `tooltip` control:

```
Private m_ttTooltip As New Windows.Forms.ToolTip
```

2. Open the object drop-down list and choose clsNumericTextbox and then choose New from the event drop-down list to access the New event for your control. This event fires when the control is first created on a form.

3. Enter the following code into the New event:

```
With m_ttTooltip
    .IsBalloon = True
    .ToolTipIcon = ToolTipIcon.Info
    .ToolTipTitle = "Numeric entry required"
    .InitialDelay = 0
    .ReshowDelay = 0
    .SetToolTip(Me, "Please enter a number.")
End With
```

This code simply sets a number of properties of the tooltip control, such as the icon and text to display, and then calls the SetToolTip() method, which binds the tooltip control to your custom control. I use a With structure here, so I don't have to repeat the object reference to m ttTooltip on each statement.

Test your project once again by choosing Build CustomControls from the Debug menu and then pressing F5 to run the project. Move your mouse over the numeric text box, and balloon help appears (see Figure 26.4).

Stop the running project now and save your work.

FIGURE 26.4
Balloon tips can aid users in understanding what is required of them.

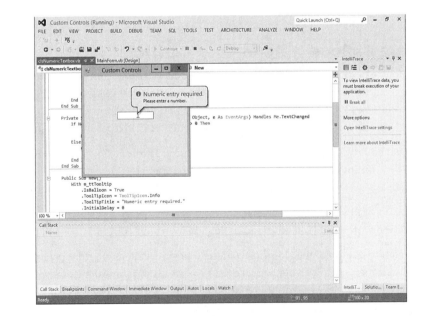

Creating an Aggregate Control

Inheriting from an existing control is very powerful, and I have only scratched the surface of the concept. Most likely, though, you won't be inheriting from existing controls but rather building your controls from scratch. Visual Basic includes a special object for this—one that is much like a form but behaves as a custom control: the UserControl.

A UserControl is a blank canvas. It has no interface and no code. What a UserControl starts with is everything it needs to be a control and to be placed on a container such as a form; when you add a new UserControl to a project, the plumbing of a standard control comes with it, but no functionality. You're going to create a UserControl that aggregates two other controls: the numeric text box you built in the previous section and a button. The user can click the button to launch the Windows Calculator. You will build a custom method, property, and event with this control.

Begin by choosing Project, Add New Item, and click User Control. Be sure not to select User Control (WFP). Set the Name of the User Control **ucNumericWithCalc.vb** and click Add. Visual Basic creates an empty UserControl object, ready for you to build the control's interface (see Figure 26.5).

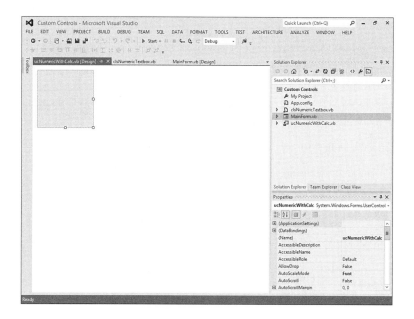

FIGURE 26.5
UserControl objects are similar to Form objects.

Adding Existing Controls to Your Custom Control Interface

A new UserControl is nothing but a blank gray square that you can place on a form. You can use drawing methods to draw an interface, or you can place existing controls on them like a form, which you're going to do in this example.

Follow these steps to build your interface:

1. Open the toolbox and double-click your custom control clsNumericTextbox to add it to your user control. Change its Name property to **numTextbox**.

2. Double-click Button to add a new button to your user control. Set the properties of the button as follows:

Property	Value
Name	btnCalc
Image	(Use the file Calculator.png supplied at my website or a 16×16 pixel image of your choice.)
Location	106, 0
Size	25, 20
Text	(Make this property empty—delete the text Button1 and do not enter any other text.)

3. Choose Build CustomControls from the Debug menu to compile the project and add the control to the toolbox.

4. Click the MainForm.vb [Design] tab to change to the form designer.

5. Open the toolbox and locate your new control (see Figure 26.6).

6. Double-click ucNumericWithCalc to add a new instance of the control to your form.

7. Set your control's Location property to **91, 41**.

There is no need to set the position of the button at design time, because you'll ensure the button is always in the proper location with code you write next.

The interface for your control is now complete.

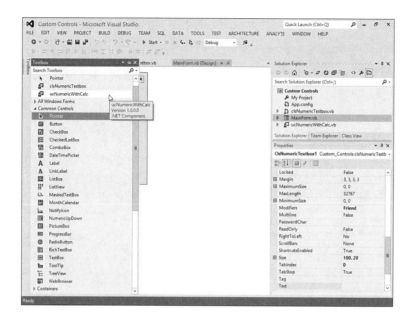

FIGURE 26.6
UserControls appear in the toolbox just as inherited controls do.

Making Your Control Display Properly When Resized

In the case of UserControls, just as with forms, what you see is what you get. After adding your custom control to the form in the previous steps, your form looks like that shown in Figure 26.7. Go ahead and drag the sizing handles—notice that the background of your custom control changes size, but the contents are static; the text box doesn't get bigger or smaller and the button doesn't move. You have to write code to be called in the Resize event of the user control to fix this.

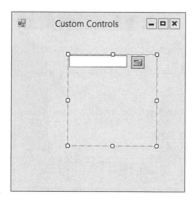

FIGURE 26.7
A new instance of a custom control has the same dimensions it had at design time.

To make your custom control properly display itself on a form, follow these steps:

1. Delete the instance of the ucNumericWithCalc control from your form.

2. Click the ucNumericWithCalc.vb [Design] tab to view the interface for your user control.

3. Double-click anywhere on the background of your control, but not on the text box or the button.

4. Notice the warning at the bottom of the screen (see Figure 26.8). This warning is there to remind you that you need to rebuild the project before you return to the form, or the form will still use the previously compiled version.

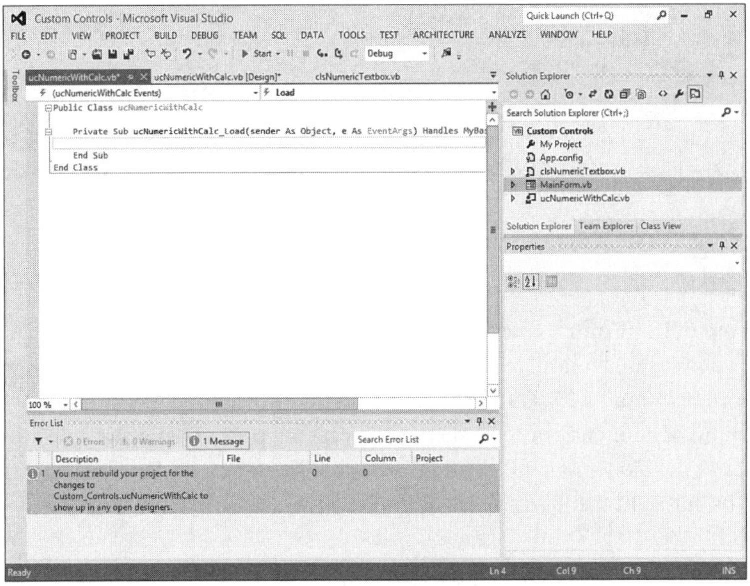

FIGURE 26.8
Whenever you make changes to your user control, you have to rebuild the project to see the changes take effect.

5. Delete the shell of the Load event that is created for you.

6. Enter the following code (note that the private variable is a module variable and not declared in the procedure):

```
Private m_blnCalcButtonVisible As Boolean = True

Private Sub DrawControl()
    ' Keep a fixed height because a textbox has a fixed
    ' height unless it is set to multi-line
    Me.Height = numTextbox.Height

    If m_blnCalcButtonVisible Then
        btnCalc.Visible = True
        ' Because the button has a fixed width, start
        ' by aligning it to the right edge of the user control
```

```
      btnCalc.Left = Me.Width - btnCalc.Width

   Else
      btnCalc.Visible = False
      ' Move the button so it is just off the right edge
      ' of the control
      btnCalc.Left = Me.Width
   End If

   numTextBox.Width = btnCalc.Left - 1
End Sub
```

The DrawControl() procedure you've just created contains comments that explain what's going on. As you know from Hour 7, "Working with Traditional Controls," a single-line text box can't have its Height property changed, so the user control (Me) is set to the height of the numeric text box. You will create a property in the next section that the user can set to determine whether the calculator button is visible or not, and the property value will be stored in the module variable m_blnCalcButtonVisible. If this variable is set to True, the calculator button is made visible and its right edge is aligned to the right edge of the user control. If the variable is False, the calculator button is hidden and its *left* edge is aligned to the right edge of the user control. It's important that the button be placed in the correct spot, whether it's visible or not, because the last statement adjusts the Width of the text box so that it butts up against the button. If the button is not visible, the text box stretches to the right edge of the user control.

You now need to ensure that the DrawControl() procedure gets called at the right times. You need to call this in the New() and Resize() events of the user control. Follow these steps to hook up the DrawControl() procedure:

1. Choose ucNumericWithCalc from the object drop-down list and then choose New from the event list to create the New() event procedure. Enter the following statement after the second comment in the procedure:

   DrawControl()

2. Choose ucNumericWithCalc Events in the object drop-down list and then choose Resize from the event drop-down list. Enter the following statement in the Resize() event:

   DrawControl()

Choose Build UserControl from the Build menu and then click the MainForm.vb [Design] tab to return to the form designer. Once again, open the toolbox and double-click the ucNumericWithCalc item to add an instance of the custom control to your form. This time, the control sizes itself properly. Go ahead and move the control and drag its sizing handles—the control always draws itself properly (see Figure 26.9).

Note: You could have used the Anchor property to handle the duties of resizing the controls on the user control. However, as you create more advanced user controls, you will at times use a combination of controls and graphics methods, and I wanted you to get the feel for what you can do with code.

Set the properties of the user control as follows:

Property	Value
Name	numInput
Location	58, 58
Size	166, 20

Click Save All on the toolbar to save your work.

Creating a Custom Property

All controls have properties and you've worked with dozens of them already. In addition, in Hour 16, "Designing Objects Using Classes," you learned how to create a custom property for a class. Creating a custom property for a user control is exactly the same as creating a custom property for a basic class—there's nothing new here. You're going to create a new property called `CalcButtonVisible` that is used to determine whether the calculator button is visible or not. You've already created the private module variable to hold the value of the property, so all you need to do is create the property procedure. Follow these steps to create and test the property procedure:

1. Click the ucNumericWithCalc.vb tab to switch to the code view for your user control.

2. Scroll down to the end of the class and enter this property procedure right before the `End Class` statement:

```
Public Property CalcButtonVisible() As Boolean
    Get
        Return m_blnCalcButtonVisible
```

```
      End Get
      Set(ByVal value As Boolean)
         m_blnCalcButtonVisible = value
         DrawControl()
      End Set
   End Property
```

3. Choose Build CustomControls from the Build menu.

4. Click MainForm.vb [Design] tab to return to the form designer.

5. Click your user control on the form to display its properties in the Properties window. Change its `CalcButtonVisible` property to `False` and the button disappears. Change it back to `True` and the button reappears.

Creating a Custom Method

Creating a method for a user control is identical to creating a method for a form or any other type of class; you create a procedure with `Sub` or `Function` and declare it as `Public`. That's it! All public procedures are automatically exposed to the programmer as methods.

Creating a Custom Event

You're going to add code to the Calculator button that displays the Windows Calculator when clicked. But what if programmers want to display their own calculator applications? You're going to create a custom event that lets them do just that.

You're going to create a custom event that fires whenever a user clicks the Calculator button. This event has a `Handled` parameter just like the `e.Handled` property in the `KeyPress` event. If developers put in their own code for displaying a calculator, they can set `Handled` to `True` and the Windows calculator isn't displayed.

Follow these steps to create your custom event:

1. Click the ucNumericWithCalc.vb tab to display the code for your user control.

2. Scroll to the top of the procedure and enter the following statement under the declaration of the variable m_blnCalcButtonvisible:

   ```
   Public Event OnCalcButtonClicked(ByRef handled As Boolean)
   ```

   An event declaration is essentially a procedure definition. Think about it for a second—when you choose an event from the event drop-down list on the code editor, what happens? Visual Basic creates a new event *procedure*. If you replaced the word `Event` with `Sub`, you would know exactly what this does.

When you declare a public event, you simply tell Visual Basic the event's name and what parameters will be created in the new event procedure.

3. You're now going to add the code that displays the Windows calculator. Open the object drop-down list and choose btnCalc, and then choose Click from the event drop-down list.

4. Enter the following code in the button's `Click()` event:

```
Dim blnHandled As Boolean = False

RaiseEvent OnCalcButtonClicked(blnHandled)

If Not blnHandled Then
    Shell("calc.exe")
End If
```

The `Shell()` command tells Windows to launch an executable, and it takes the name of the executable as its parameter. `Calc.exe` is the name of the Windows calculator, so `Shell` simply starts the Windows calculator. If you weren't going to allow a developer to potentially display a different calculator, this is the only statement that would be necessary. However, you want to allow the developer the option to display a calculator application of his or her choosing. Of course, the meat of this is handled with the `RaiseEvent` statement. RaiseEvent does exactly that—it raises an event in the client code. In this case, it raises the `OnCalcButtonClicked()` event. When you declared the event, you created a single parameter—handled. In this code, you created a Boolean variable called `blnHandled` and you are passing it to the event in the `RaiseEvent` call. Because you used `ByRef` in the declaration of the event, any changes made to the parameter by the developer come back into this `Click()` event. If the user sets `Handled` to `True`, you won't show the calculator program.

Testing Your Aggregate Control

You're now going to test the functionality of your user control. You'll first run it as it is and test the calculator button. You'll then write code in the custom event to prevent the calculator from appearing. Follow these steps to test your custom control:

1. Choose Build CustomControls from the Debug menu.

2. Click the MainForm.vb [Design] tab to return to the form designer.

3. Double-click the instance of the numInput control to access its events.

4. Open the events drop-down and locate and select the `OnCalcButtonClicked` event (see Figure 26.10).

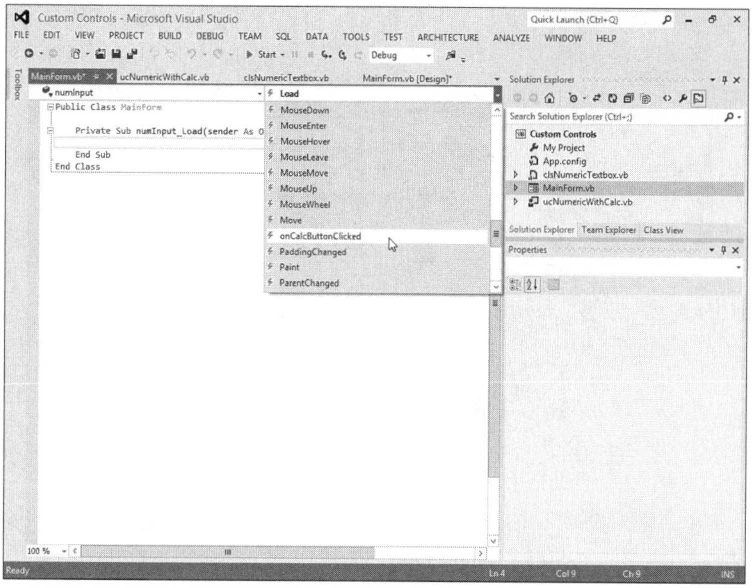

FIGURE 26.10
You can create as many custom events as you need.

5. Enter the following code into the `OnCalcButtonClicked` event:

```
If MessageBox.Show("Show the calculator?", "", _
        MessageBoxButtons.YesNo) = Windows.Forms.DialogResult.No Then
    handled = True
End If
```

6. Press F5 to run the project and then click the Calculator button.

7. Answer Yes to the prompt and the Windows calculator appears (see Figure 26.11).

8. Close the calculator and click the button once more. This time, answer No and the calculator doesn't display.

FIGURE 26.11
The functionality
of a custom con-
trol is limited
only by your
imagination!

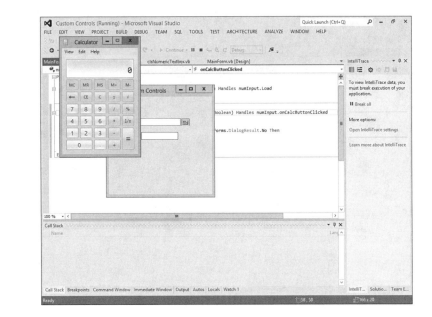

Summary

In this chapter, you have begun exploring the fascinating world of custom control development. Realize that every control in your Visual Basic toolbox started its life with the basics you learned here, from the simple label to complex dialog boxes and grids. In this hour, you learned about the different types of custom controls. You used Inheritance—a true object-oriented principle—to create a numeric text box based on the functionality of the standard text box. You also learned how to build an aggregate control that comprised both your inherited control and a standard button. You created a custom property, and a custom event, and you learned how to build and test your custom controls. These are great skills!

As you move beyond the basics, there is a lot to learn about custom control development. Custom controls take time and effort to build, and you have to balance your needs with the time and budget available. Often, purchasing a third-party custom control makes a lot of sense, but there will be times that you need to make small tweaks to existing controls, or you need something that just isn't available commercially. In these cases, building your own custom control might be the best solution.

Q&A

Q. *Can I get information about or interact with the form upon which my control is placed?*

A. Yes, you can reference the parent form upon which the control is sited by referencing `Me.Parent`.

Q. *Can I give my custom control a unique icon in the toolbox?*

A. It is possible to assign a unique toolbox icon to your controls by assigning a class attribute called `ToolboxBitmap`, but it doesn't always work. Microsoft has numerous articles on this with potential ways to solve the problems, and I suggest you research this if you want to create a unique icon for your custom control.

Workshop

Quiz

1. The process of creating one control by basing it off an existing control class is called what?

2. What type of custom control has an interface made of other controls?

3. Instead of creating an invisible-at-runtime control, what should you create?

4. What statement is used to call an event procedure in the client code?

5. What do you need to do before testing after making any changes to a custom control?

Answers

1. Inheritance

2. An aggregate control

3. A normal class

4. `RaiseEvent`

5. Build the project.

Exercises

1. Create a custom method for your user control called `ShowCalculator()`. The method should show the Windows calculator when called.

2. Add a property to your inherited control called `DisplayErrorMessage`. When set to `true`, if the value found in the `TextChanged` event is not numeric, show an error message to the user.

Index

properties (objects)

Q–R

Sams **Teach Yourself**

When you only have time
for the answers™

Whatever your need and whatever your time frame, there's a Sams **Teach Yourself** book for you. With a Sams **Teach Yourself** book as your guide, you can quickly get up to speed on just about any new product or technology—in the absolute shortest period of time possible. Guaranteed.

Learning how to do new things with your computer shouldn't be tedious or time-consuming. Sams **Teach Yourself** makes learning anything quick, easy, and even a little bit fun.

Visual C# 2012 in 24 Hours: Complete Starter Kit

Scott J. Dorman

ISBN-10: 0672336847
ISBN-13: 9780672336843

Windows Phone 7 Application Development in 24 Hours

Scott J. Dorman, Kevin Wolf Nikita Polyakov, Joe Healy

ISBN-10: 0672335395
ISBN-13: 9780672335396

Microsoft Dynamics CRM 2011 in 24 Hours

Anne Stanton

ISBN-10: 0672335379
ISBN-13: 9780672335372

SharePoint 2010 Development in 24 Hours

Sohail Sayed, Manpreet Singh, Vinu Santhakumari

ISBN-10: 0672335794
ISBN-13: 9780672335792

Windows Phone 7 Game Programming in 24 Hours

Jonathan Harbour

ISBN-10: 0672335549
ISBN-13: 9780672335549